VARIORUM COLLECTED STUDIES SERIES

Law and History in the Latin East

Peter W. Edbury

Peter W. Edbury

Law and History in the Latin East

Published in the Variorum Collected Studies Series by

Ashgate Publishing Limited
Wey Court East
Union Road
Farnham, Surrey
GU9 7PT
England

Ashgate Publishing Company
Suite 3–1
110 Cherry Street
Burlington, VT 05401–3818
USA

www.ashgate.com

ISBN 9781472441966

British Library Cataloguing in Publication Data
A catalogue record for this book is available from the British Library.

The Library of Congress has cataloged the printed edition as follows: 2014943722

VARIORUM COLLECTED STUDIES SERIES CS1048

The paper used in this publication meets the minimum requirements of the American National Standard for Information Sciences – Permanence of Paper for Printed Library Materials, ANSI Z39.48–1984. ∞ ™

MIX
Paper from
responsible sources
FSC
www.fsc.org   FSC® C013985

Printed in the United Kingdom by Henry Ling Limited, at the Dorset Press, Dorchester, DT1 1HD

CONTENTS

Preface   ix

Acknowledgements   xiv

LEGAL LITERATURE AND THE LAW IN THE LATIN EAST

I   Fiefs, vassaux et service militaire dans le royaume latin
        de Jérusalem   141–150
        Le Partage du Monde: échanges et colonisation dans la
        Méditerranée médiévale, eds M. Balard and A. Ducellier.
        Paris: Publications de la Sorbonne, 1998

II   Fiefs and vassals in the kingdom of Jerusalem: from
        the twelfth century to the thirteenth   49–62
        Crusades 1. Aldershot: Ashgate, for the Society for the Study
        of the Crusades and the Latin East, 2002

III   Philip of Novara and the *Livre de Forme de Plait*   555–569
        Praktika tou tritou diethnous kyprologikou sunedriou
        (Lefkosia, 16–20 April 1996), ed. A. Papageorgiou.
        Nicosia: Etaireia Kupriakon Spoudon, 2001, Vol. 2

IV   The *Livre des Assises* by John of Jaffa: the development
        and transmission of the text   169–179
        The Crusades and their Sources: Essays presented to
        Bernard Hamilton, eds J. France and W.G. Zajac. Aldershot:
        Ashgate, 1998

V   Women and the customs of the High Court of Jerusalem
        according to John of Ibelin   285–292
        Chemins d'outre-mer: Études d'histoire sur la Méditerranée
        médiévale offertes à Michel Balard, eds D. Coulon,
        C. Otten-Froux, P. Pagès and D. Valérian. Paris: Publications
        de la Sorbonne (Byzantina Sorbonensia 20), 2004

VI   Cultural Encounters in the Latin East. John of Jaffa
        and Philip of Novara   229–236
        Cultural Encounters during the Crusades, eds K.V. Jensen,
        K. Salonen and H. Vogt. Odense: University Press of Southern
        Denmark, 2013

VII   The *Assises d'Antioche*: law and custom in the
        principality of Antioch   241–248
        Norman Expansion: Connections, Continuities and Contrasts,
        eds K.J. Stringer and A. Jotischky. Farnham: Ashgate, 2013

THE OLD FRENCH WILLIAM OF TYRE AND ITS CONTINUATIONS

VIII   The French translation of William of Tyre's *Historia*:
        the manuscript tradition   69–105
        Crusades 6. Aldershot: Ashgate, for the Society for the Study
        of the Crusades and the Latin East, 2007

IX   The Old French William of Tyre and the origins of
        the Templars   151–164
        Knighthoods of Christ: Essays on the History of the Crusades
        and the Knights Templar, Presented to Malcolm Barber, ed.
        N. Housley. Aldershot: Ashgate, 2007

X   The Old French William of Tyre, the Templars and
        the Assassin envoy   25–37
        The Hospitallers, the Mediterranean and Europe. Festschrift
        for Anthony Luttrell, eds K. Borchardt, N. Jaspert and H.J.
        Nicholson. Aldershot: Ashgate, 2007

XI   The Lyon *Eracles* and the Old French Continuations
        of William of Tyre   139–153
        Montjoie: Studies in Crusade History in Honour of Hans
        Eberhard Mayer, eds B.Z. Kedar, J. Riley-Smith and R.
        Hiestand. Aldershot: Ashgate / Variorum, 1997

XII   New perspectives on the Old French Continuations of
        William of Tyre   107–113
        Crusades 9. Aldershot: Ashgate, for the Society for the Study
        of the Crusades and the Latin East, 2010

XIII   Gerard of Ridefort and the battle of Le Cresson
       (1 May 1187): the developing narrative tradition   45–60
       On the Margins of Crusading: The Military Orders, the
       Papacy and the Christian World, ed. H.J. Nicholson.
       Farnham: Ashgate, 2011

XIV   A new text of the *Annales de Terre Sainte*   145–161
       In Laudem Hierosolymitani: Studies in Crusades and Medieval
       Culture in Honour of Benjamin Z. Kedar , eds I. Shagrir,
       R. Ellenblum and J. Riley-Smith. Aldershot: Ashgate, 2007

CYPRUS AND LATER NARRATIVE WRITING

XV   Redating the death of King Henry I of Cyprus?   339–348
       Dei gesta per Francos: Etudes sur les croisades dédiées à
       Jean Richard, eds M. Balard, B.Z. Kedar and J. Riley-Smith.
       Aldershot: Ashgate, 2001

XVI   The De Montforts in the Latin East   1–11
       Proceedings of the Durham Conference 1999, eds M.
       Prestwich, R. Britnell and R. Frame (Thirteenth Century
       England 8). Woodbridge: Boydell, 2001

XVII   The arrest of the Templars in Cyprus   249–258
       The Debate on the Trial of the Templars (1307–1314), eds
       J. Burgtorf, P.F. Crawford and H.J. Nicholson. Aldershot:
       Ashgate, 2010

CYPRUS

XVIII Latins and Greeks on crusader Cyprus   133–142
       Medieval Frontiers: Concepts and Practices, eds D. Abulafia
       and N. Berend. Aldershot: Ashgate, 2002

XIX   The Templars in Cyprus   189–195
       The Military Orders: Fighting for the Faith and Caring for
       the Sick, ed. M. Barber. Aldershot: Ashgate / Variorum, 1994

XX   The 'Cartulaire de Manosque': a grant to the Templars
       in Latin Syria and a charter of King Hugh I of Cyprus   174–181
       Bulletin of the Institute of Historical Research 51, 1978

CRUSADING

XXI   The crusades and their critics   179–194
       Archaeology and the Crusades: Proceedings of the Round
       Table, Nicosia,1 Feburary 2005, eds P. Edbury and
       S. Kalopissi-Verti. Athens: Pierides Foundation, 2007

XXII   Looking back on the Second Crusade: some late
       twelfth-century English perspectives   163–169
       The Second Crusade and the Cistercians, ed. M. Gervers.
       New York: St Martin's Press, 1992

XXIII Preaching the crusade in Wales   221–233
       England and Germany in the High Middle Ages, eds
       A. Haverkamp and H. Vollrath. Oxford: Oxford University
       Press for the German Historical Institute, 1996

XXIV   Celestine III, the crusade and the Latin East   129–143
       Pope Celestine III (1191–1198): Diplomat and Pastor, eds
       J. Doran and D.J. Smith. Farnham: Ashgate, 2008

Addenda and Corrigenda   1–3

Index   1–15

This volume contains xiv + 332 pages

PUBLISHER'S NOTE

*The articles in this volume, as in all others in the Variorum Collected Studies
Series, have not been given a new, continuous pagination. In order to avoid
confusion, and to facilitate their use where these same studies have been
referred to elsewhere, the original pagination has been maintained wherever
possible.*

*Each article has been given a Roman number in order of appearance, as
listed in the Contents. This number is repeated on each page and is quoted in
the index entries.*

PREFACE

The theme that links most of the papers in this volume is the Old French legal and historical literature that survives from the Latin East. Whereas it would not be true to say that writing in Latin died out in the East after 1187, there is no doubt that in the thirteenth century pride of place passed to works composed in French, and not least those belonging to these two related genres, History and Law.

Arguably it is the assemblage of legal treatises composed by members of the Latin community in the East that stands out as the most impressive of all the thirteenth-century achievements. Sometimes referred to collectively – and misleadingly – as the *Assises de Jérusalem*, they tell of court procedure in both the High Court and the *Cour des Bourgeois* and how to plead as well as what laws and legal principles were applied. It was Jonathan Riley-Smith who in the late 1960s first introduced me to these writings while I was still an undergraduate, and some of my earliest publications were concerned with trying to make sense of them.[1] Much more recently I have re-edited two of the most important: the treatises on the workings of the High Court by John of Ibelin count of Jaffa and by Philip of Novara.[2] Essays I–VI reprinted here are papers that in various ways are associated with these two projects or with my 1997 monograph, *John of Ibelin and the Kingdom of Jerusalem*[3] which can be thought of as a sort of 'prequel' to the edition of John's text. Inevitably there is a degree of overlap between some of these essays, and it is only to be expected that on certain points I have over time modified my views (see the 'Corrigenda' at the end of this volume). These essays should be considered alongside two earlier papers, one of which was designed to clear up the confusion surrounding the authorship of the two treatises by Geoffrey le Tor and indicate some of the places from which he drew his material; the other established, at least to my own satisfaction, that the doctrine of *Les Letres dou Sepulcre* was a legal fiction

---

[1] 'Feudal Obligations in the Latin East' *Byzantion* 47 (1977), pp. 328–56; 'The Disputed Regency of the Kingdom of Jerusalem, 1264/6 and 1268' *Camden Miscellany* 27 (1979) (= Camden 4th series, 22), pp. 1–47. Both are reprinted in my earlier Variorum volume: *Kingdoms of the Crusaders: From Jerusalem to Cyprus* (1999).

[2] John of Ibelin, *Le Livre des Assises* (Brill, Leiden, 2003); Philip of Novara, *Le Livre de Forme de Plait* (Cyprus Research Centre, Nicosia, 2009).

[3] Boydell and Brewer, Woodbridge.

designed to defend Latin Syrian customary law from some of the attacks on it that arose in the thirteenth century.[4]

The first two papers were in part designed as a riposte to Susan Reynolds's *Fiefs and Vassals: the Medieval Evidence Reinterpreted* (O.U.P., 1994): whatever may have been true in western Europe, it seemed to me that there is sufficient contemporary evidence from before 1187 to show that feudal obligations and the customary law governing the transmission of fiefs were in place in the kingdom of Jerusalem by the end of the third quarter of the twelfth century at the latest. What is less clear is whether the holders of the great lordships thought in these terms. It has recently been brought to my attention that at around this period some of the most powerful nobles in the East were asserting that they held their lands 'by the grace of God', and that surely has to be seen as an assertion of autonomy and as a sign that they were not going to let the king treat them as vassals in the same way as they treated the run-of-the-mill knights. Two of the more notable men to adopt this style were Reynald of Châtillon for Outrejourdain and Balian of Ibelin in 1185 for his wife's dower land at Nablus. But there were others besides, and the whole question would repay a thorough investigation.[5] A second issue that these papers raise is the question of continuity across the 1187 divide. The kingdom of Jerusalem collapsed and was then partially restored. Apart from the loss of territory, what had changed? The thirteenth-century legal works, with the *Livre au Roi* leading the way, manage somehow to give the impression that in terms of the institutions of government, the law and the administration of justice the answer is 'nothing at all'. But is that right? More specifically – and this is where Susan Reynolds and I would doubtless agree in wanting to be cautious – how justified are we in projecting back our understanding of the thirteenth century into the twelfth in any attempt to see how people thought and how society operated?

Essays III and IV both date from the time that I was engaged on my editions of John of Ibelin and Philip of Novara and reflect what was then 'work in progress'. My ideas about these texts changed as the work proceeded, but the papers retain their value, not least because it is important to recall quite how bad the nineteenth-century editions on which everyone had hitherto relied actually were. V and VI, on the other hand, postdate the editions and point the way to

---

[4] 'The "Livre of Geoffrey le Tor" and the "Assises" of Jerusalem' in *Historia administrativa y ciencia de la adminstración comparada. Trabajos en homenaje a Feran Valls i Taberner*, 15 (Barcelona, 1990), pp. 4291–8; 'Law and Custom in the Latin East: *Les Letres dou Sepulcre*' in *Intercultural Contacts in the Medieval Mediterranean: Studies in Honour of David Jacoby*, ed. B. Arbel (= *Mediterranean Historical Review* 10) (Frank Cass, London, 1996), pp. 71–9. Both are reprinted in *Kingdoms of the Crusaders* (as note 1).

[5] *RRH*, nos. 454, 551 (Reynald), 640b (Balian). I thank Professor Hans Mayer for generously sharing his thoughts on this topic.

the sorts of discussion to which a close reading of these texts might lead. Essay VII, a brief look at *Assises d'Antioche*, marked a new line of enquiry. This text is little studied – not least because it only survives in a thirteenth-century Armenian translation – and I set myself the task of seeing if there were aspects of it that reflected the Norman origin of the first princes and of many of their followers.

My current project is even more ambitious than re-editing the legal treatises: in collaboration with Dr Massimiliano Gaggero, it is to produce a new critical edition of the Old French Continuations of William of Tyre and the associated text we know as *La Chronique d'Ernoul et de Bernard le Trésorier*. Here too my first confrontation with these texts dates to the late 1960s. There were two major issues: how do the various versions of the Continuations relate to one another, and what is to be made of the Old French translation of William of Tyre? My earliest excursion into investigating how the texts relate and what conclusions might be drawn appeared in a paper jointly authored with the late John G. Rowe in 1978. I now know that the premise on which that paper was based is completely wrong.[6] My next attempt, here reprinted as essay XI, has weathered better and on its publication in 1997 pointed the way to a truer understanding of the relationship of the principal versions of the Continuations and their respective dates.

Back in the 1980s John Rowe and I had been rightly rebuked by a reviewer of our 1988 study on William of Tyre for dismissing the potential value of the translation of William's Latin text,[7] and eventually, alerted to the fact that different manuscripts contain significantly different readings, I turned attention to the translation and began a systematic examination of the manuscripts. At the outset I had assumed, naïvely as it turned out, that I could create a neat stemma into which all the fifty-one medieval manuscripts could be given a place on a tidy 'family tree'. In the event I was able to identify those manuscripts which appear to be closest to the original version of the translation and do little more than sort the rest out into groups with shared characteristics. I now believe that the most of the surviving manuscripts were produced in *ateliers* either in Paris or in the East, presumably in Acre, from unbound quires in the possession of the *ateliers* and that the copyists commonly switched exemplars; that would explain the hybridisation that became apparent as a feature of many manuscripts and with it the consequent impracticability of devising a stemma.

---

[6] 'William of Tyre and the Patriarchal Election of 1180' *English Historical Review* 93 (1978), pp. 1–25. Reprinted in *Kingdoms of the Crusaders* (as note 1).

[7] P.W. Edbury and J.G. Rowe, *William of Tyre: Historian of the Latin East* (Cambridge University Press, Cambridge, 1988), p. 4. See the review by Bernard Hamilton, *TLS*, 18–24 November 1988, p. 1276.

My findings were published as essay VIII in this collection. Essays IX and X give examples of the sort of directions in which these investigations can lead and for the first time ever provide critical editions of sample chapters that utilize all the manuscripts and are based on those that stand closest to the original form of the translation. (The nineteenth-century editions are based on a seemingly random selection of manuscripts and with no indication that the editors had any understanding of how the text developed.) The whole issue of the Old French translation of William of Tyre has now been taken significantly further by my former PhD student, Dr Philip Handyside, and the publication of his monograph on this subject should see the light of day at about the same time as the appearance of this present volume.[8]

Turning to the manuscripts rather than relying on the nineteenth-century printed editions meant that an investigation of the Continuations could advance on a much securer footing. Essay XII gives a more up-to-date account of my views of the relationships between the various versions and builds on my findings in essay XI. Essay XIII is a first attempt at seeing how a textual analysis based on thorough study of the manuscripts might lead to a new interpretation of familiar historical incidents.

The acquisition of microfilms of almost all the manuscripts of the French William of Tyre led to one particular unexpected discovery: the Florence, Bibliotheca Medicea Laurenziana, MS Pluteus LXI.10 (an Acre manuscript that dates from shortly before 1291) contains a text of the *Annales de Terre Sainte* that has escaped the notice of modern scholarship. There are, it is true, a few references to it buried deep in the annotations to the nineteenth-century edition of the Continuations, but otherwise it has passed unremarked. That is all the more odd in view of the fact that it is kept in a major public collection, that extracts from the text of the Continuation that it contains were edited by Ruth Morgan in the 1980s and that its miniatures have attracted attention from art historians.[9] This version of the *Annales de Terre Sainte*, which incidentally is in a significantly earlier manuscript than those utilised by Röhricht and Raynaud for their 1884 edition, was edited for the first time as essay XIV.

The *Annales de Terre Sainte* and those writings that drew on them including the *Gestes des Chiprois* and, in its later stages, the William of Tyre Continuations provide a considerable amount of historical information. Essay XV tackles the question of whether these texts begin the year in January or March – not surprisingly there is no consistency on this point – and it takes as

---

[8]   *The Old French William of Tyre* (Brill, Leiden), forthcoming.

[9]   *La Continuation de Guillaume de Tyr (1184–1197)*, ed. M.R. Morgan (Paul Geuthner, Paris, 1982), pp. 108–98, and see p. 14; J. Folda, *Crusader Manuscript Illumination at Saint-Jean d'Acre, 1275–1291* (Princeton University Press, Princeton, NJ, 1976), pp.111–16, 192–6.

its starting point the death of Henry I of Cyprus. Much of the discussion retains its value, but the central suggestion, that Henry died on 18 January 1254 (and not 1253 as is usually stated), has been challenged by Chris Schabel. Schabel quite properly used evidence that I had overlooked and argued for Henry's death occurring on 18 October 1253. However, although I am prepared to admit to being mistaken on this point, Hans Mayer remains unconvinced by Schabel's arguments and considers my January 1254 date to be correct. It is an unusual position in which I find myself – perhaps it is best left for others to decide![10]

The remaining papers are less obviously focused on the Old French literature from the Latin East, although several of them touch on this subject at crucial points. Essay XVI draws attention to the death of Philip of Montfort's first cousin, Simon earl of Leicester, as recorded by the 'Templar of Tyre'. Simon, so it would seem, did not die in the engagement at Evesham in 1265 but was taken alive; he was then killed in cold blood and his body dumped on the field of battle so that whoever found it would assume he had died in the fighting. So far as I know there is no corroboration for this report, but all the same it is of interest as a record of a story that had somehow reached the East where it had found a sympathetic reception. Essay XVII is largely concerned with the account to be found in sixteenth-century Italian text known as the *Chronique d'Amadi* of the arrest of the Templars in Cyprus. Although this is a 'late' source, the anonymous compiler is here using a near-contemporary French-language history which does not survive in its original form. Of the others, essay XXI offers some perspectives on more modern attitudes to crusading, while XXII–XXIV in their widely differing ways nibble at the edges of a major topic on which I have long harboured an ambition to write, the Third Crusade.

PETER EDBURY

Cardiff
June 2014

---

[10] C. Schabel, 'The Greek bishops of Cyprus, 1260–1340 and the *Synodikon Kyprion*', Κυπριακαί Σπουδαί 64/65 (2000/2001), p. 220 n.10; *Die Urkunden der lateinischen Könige von Jerusalem*, ed. H.E. Mayer, 4 vols (Verlag Hahnsche Buchhandlung, Hannover, 2010), vol. 3, pp. 1396–9.

ACKNOWLEDGEMENTS

Grateful acknowledgement is made to the following institutions, publishers and individuals for their permission to reproduce the articles included in this volume: Renaud Le Goix on behalf of *Publications de la Sorbonne*, Paris (Studies I and V); Martin Lindø Westergaard on behalf of the University Press of Southern Denmark, Odense (Study VI); Boydell and Brewer, Woodbridge (Study XVI); Dr Jane Winters on behalf of *Historical Research* (formerly *Bulletin of the Institute of Historical Research*), London (Study XX); Dr Yiannis Toumazis on behalf of the Pierides Foundation, Athens (Study XXI); Professor Michael Gervers (Study XXII); and Oxford University Press (Study XXIII).

Every effort has been made to trace all the copyright holders, but if any have been inadvertently overlooked the publishers will be pleased to make the necessary arrangement at the first opportunity.

I

FIEFS, VASSAUX ET SERVICE MILITAIRE
DANS LE ROYAUME LATIN DE JÉRUSALEM

A la fin de son traité sur les travaux de la Haute Cour du royaume de Jérusalem, Jean d'Ibelin, comte de Jaffa, fournit une liste des services militaires [1]. Jean écrivait aux alentours de 1265. Comme l'a montré le professeur Jean Richard dans un article publié il y a plusieurs années, la liste elle-même date du milieu des années 1180, un an ou deux avant la défaite de Hattin, et la conquête par Saladin de Jérusalem et de la plus grande partie du royaume [2]. Le document commence par les services dus par les plus grands seigneurs avant de s'arrêter aux chevaliers des cités qui faisaient partie du domaine royal – des hommes qui n'auraient jamais reconnu aucun autre seigneur que le roi – et ensuite aux sergents qui devaient être recrutés par les plus grandes églises ou par les villes. Il ne s'agit pas d'un relevé complet des ressources militaires du royaume : on n'y fait pas mention des ordres militaires, pas plus que des Turcoples, des sergents à cheval ou des mercenaires, bien que l'on puisse rencontrer ce type d'hommes, inclus pour une raison quelconque dans le total des données recueillies. Même ainsi l'importance de ces listes est incontestable.

Sur la centaine d'individus nommés dans ce document, environ une cinquantaine sont connus par d'autres sources. Les femmes mentionnées sont

---

1. Jean d'Ibelin, *Livre*, éd. A. Beugnot (*Recueil des historiens des croisades. Lois*, 1), p. 422-427. Je travaille actuellement à la réédition de ce texte.

2. J. Richard, « Les listes de seigneuries dans *Le Livre de Jean d'Ibelin*. Recherches sur l'Assebebe et Mimars' », *Revue historique de droit français et étranger*, 4ᵉ s., 35 (1954), p. 563-577.

probablement des veuves ou des héritières, bien que dans certains cas, il puisse s'agir d'épouses dont les maris étaient alors retenus comme prisonniers de guerre. Quelques noms évoquent la région d'origine – Picquigny, Saint-Bertin, Soissons, Saint-Denis, Brie, Falaise, Mechelen, Douai – le nord de la France et les Pays-Bas. Ce que corrobore d'autres témoignages nous apprenant que beaucoup de colons dans le royaume de Jérusalem étaient, comme les princes eux-mêmes, originaires de France, ou des terres d'empire toutes proches et francophones. Rares sont les cas où nous sommes renseignés sur la durée du séjour de ces hommes avec leurs familles en Orient. Nous pouvons encore moins rechercher leurs ancêtres en Occident dans les jours qui précèdent les croisades. Quelques-uns d'entre eux purent être des descendants des participants à la première croisade ; d'autres se seraient installés plus récemment. Un certain nombre acquit leur nom de famille d'après des toponymes orientaux, et d'autres seraient le fruit d'unions mixtes comme Simon, fils de Pierre l'Ermin (= l'Arménien) [3]. Tous les chevaliers cités ne moururent pas à Hattin et quelques familles vécurent pendant des générations suffisamment longtemps pour jouer un rôle majeur en Orient, soit dans le royaume de Jérusalem au XIIIe siècle ou dans celui de Chypre. Les Picquigny, les Saint-Bertin ou les Malembec restèrent prééminents en Syrie franque, et les Babins, Mimars, Soissons et les Montgisard se trouvaient encore à Chypre au XIVe siècle.

Plutôt que d'effectuer une étude prosopographique, je souhaiterais prendre en considération la nature du document lui-même. J'aimerais plus particulièrement examiner ce qu'il nous dit sur le service militaire dans la société franque en Orient à la lumière du livre récent de l'historienne anglaise, Susan Reynolds. L'ouvrage de Susan Reynolds, *Fiefs and Vassals : The Medieval Evidence Reinterpreted*, fut publié en 1994. Comme tous les travaux de réinterprétation, il doit naturellement faire l'objet de discussions, bien que les recensions qui retinrent mon attention au moment de rédiger cet article lui soient favorables [4]. S. Reynolds conteste plusieurs hypothèses longtemps soutenues. Elle se demande si les fiefs, les vassaux et le contrat féodal entre seigneur et vassal occupaient, comme on le croit normalement, une position centrale dans la société médiévale avant le XIIIe siècle. Elle affirme cette idée reçue parce qu'un chevalier au service d'un seigneur ne devenait pas nécessairement son vassal ou ne tenait pas ses terres de lui en fief. Elle indique qu'en France, au moins avant le XIIIe siècle, peu de témoignages précisent la quantité des services dus au seigneur, en échange du fief. Et jusqu'au XIIIe siècle on ne considérait pas les propriétés des grands seigneurs comme des fiefs. Les serments de fidélité n'impliquaient pas la possession de

---

3. Jean d'Ibelin, *op. cit.*, p. 423.

4. *London Review of Books*, 23-02-1995, p. 26 ; *The Times Highter Education Supplement*, 7-04-1995, p. 24.

fiefs, et un homme décrit comme un *fidelis* n'est pas nécessairement un vassal : tous les sujets sont ou devaient être des *fideles* de leur roi ou de leur seigneur ; après tout, si vous n'êtes pas *fidelis* vous devenez forcément un *infidelis* et aucun seigneur ne saurait tolérer la déloyauté ou l'infidélité [5].

« Les historiens », écrit Susan Reynolds, « font souvent référence à la fois aux fiefs et aux vassaux quand aucun de ces mots n'est dans leurs sources » [6], et elle poursuit jusqu'à fustiger plusieurs savants distingués pour leurs suppositions malencontreuses – suppositions qu'elle attribue finalement à l'influence des juristes académiques du bas Moyen Age et à l'utilisation du traité composite de Lombardie qu'on situe entre le XIIe et le début du XIIIe siècle, et plus connu sous le nom de *Libri Feudorum*. Il est dommage qu'elle choisisse de ne pas discuter de la question des fiefs, des vassaux et du service militaire dans l'Orient latin, car je suis persuadé qu'elle nous aurait conduits à rejeter l'idée du royaume de Jérusalem comme le « parfait état féodal » considéré par des savants antérieurs tel Joshua Prawer.

Que peut nous apporter la liste conservée par Jean d'Ibelin sur le service militaire, les fiefs et les vassaux ? Jusqu'à récemment, j'ai supposé qu'elle décrivait le service féodal. Le rédacteur du document souhaitait enregistrer les maîtres des seigneuries et les chevaliers qui tenaient leurs terres sous forme de fiefs et devaient fournir au roi un quota de chevaliers en échange de leur fief. On doit remettre en question cette hypothèse à la lumière de la position soutenue par Susan Reynolds contre l'orthodoxie établie, en particulier au vu de ce qu'elle peut soutenir sur le caractère non féodal de la société du nord de la France d'où étaient originaires les colons de l'Orient latin. Le mot « fief » est utilisé une seule fois : Baudouin d'Ibelin doit quatre chevaliers eu égard à deux clans Bédouins : probablement avait-il le droit de lever sur eux un impôt (« tallage ») pour l'usage des pâtures [7]. En dehors de cela le texte évite complètement de faire référence aux fiefs et aux vassaux. Il parle plutôt des seigneuries et des services que devaient rendre les hommes. Il commence avec le comté de Jaffa et d'Ascalon et les seigneuries de Ramla-Mirabel, et d'Ibelin, qui ensemble, fournissent 100 chevaliers. Tout cela paraît très « féodal » avec une hiérarchie de seigneuries dans laquelle Ramla-Mirabel et Ibelin sont tenues du comte de Jaffa et d'Ascalon. Au milieu du XIIe siècle, Ramla, Mirabel, Ibelin avaient été enlevées du territoire du comté de Jaffa, et des documents de 1177 et de 1181 semblent encore suggérer que le comte et la comtesse de Jaffa étaient encore suzerains

---

5. S. Reynolds, *Fiefs and Vassals : The Medieval Evidence Reinterpreted*, Oxford, 1994, p. 6-7, 59, 69, 131, 146, 155, 164-168, 179, 276-288, 306-308 et *passim*.

6. S. Reynolds, *op. cit.*, p. 2.

7. Jean d'Ibelin, *op. cit.*, p. 424.

144

de Ramla et de Mirabel [8]. Ainsi l'interprétation traditionnelle peut donc être retenue. Mais je me sens mal à l'aise sur un petit détail : si le comté de Jaffa et d'Ascalon formait une unité dirigée par un comte [9] – dans les années 1180 il s'agissait du futur roi Guy de Lusignan – pourquoi les services des deux principales villes comtales Jaffa et Ascalon devaient être notés séparément ? La rubrique suivante, relative à la principauté de Galilée qui devait aussi fournir 100 chevaliers, présente la même difficulté : il y a seulement un prince et une principauté, et si le rédacteur s'intéressait seulement à la description des obligations féodales, pourquoi nécessairement distinguer le nombre de chevaliers provenant des terres à l'ouest du Jourdain de ceux venant de l'est du fleuve ?

J'aimerais pouvoir suggérer à ce stade que le document n'est peut-être pas du tout une description des obligations féodales, mais simplement une liste des services que le roi pouvait exiger en tenant compte ou pas du fait que les gens concernés n'avaient aucune obligation formelle précise résultant de la tenue de leurs fiefs. Les entrées séparées pour Jaffa et Ascalon et pour les zones géographiques principales de la principauté de Galilée pouvaient refléter la façon dont les forces militaires du royaume seraient rassemblées et donc fourniraient peut-être ainsi des indications sur l'endroit où les chevaliers tenus au service se présentaient pour se rendre aux ordres du roi en tenue de combat. Retenons cette idée en abordant la rubrique suivante : la baronnie de Sidon et de ses dépendances, Beaufort, Césarée et Bethsan. Ces places devaient fournir à elles seules plus de 100 chevaliers. Le même langage est utilisé pour Jaffa et Ascalon mais la réalité historique paraît plus problématique. Le château de Beaufort mieux connu sous le nom arabe de Qal'at al-Shaqif, était une possession des seigneurs de Sidon et ne présente pas de difficulté. Mais mis à part ce cas, il n'y a aucun témoignage stipulant que Césarée ou Bethsan sont des fiefs des seigneurs de Sidon. Sidon et Césarée avaient été tenus, il est vrai, par le même seigneur vers les années 1110 et le début des années 1120, mais Hans Mayer a démontré que Sidon a échappé aux mains de la famille Grenier alors que celle-ci reste seigneur de Césarée [10]. Pour Bethsan, il n'existe aucune raison de la relier à Sidon ou de penser que son seigneur ne reconnaissait une autre suzeraineté que celle du roi. Quel sens pourrions-nous donc dégager de cette rubrique ? Je suis bien

---

8. *Regesta Regni Hierosolymitani* (1097-1291), éd. R. Röhricht, Innsbruck, 1893-1904, n° 545-546, 603.

9. H. E. Mayer, « The Double County of Jaffa and Ascalon : One Fief or Two ? », dans P.W. Edbury (sous la direction de), *Crusade and Settlement*, Cardiff, 1985, p. 181-190. Le point de vue de Mayer est bien fait, mais sa critique de mes propres arguments dans cet article semble éloignée de la cible.

10. H.E. Mayer, « The Wheel of Fortune : Seigneurial Vicissitudes under King Fulk and Baldwin III of Jerusalem », *Speculum*, 65 (1990), p. 870-876.

obligé de proposer une hypothèse. Il semblerait que le seigneur de Bethsan, à côté de sa seigneurie, possédait des terres à l'intérieur de la seigneurie de Césarée [11]. Si c'était le cas, il semble possible qu'ait pu être accordé plus tôt au XIIe siècle au seigneur de Bethsan de servir avec son contingent de chevaliers de Bethsan avec le seigneur de Césarée plutôt qu'avec le roi. Le lien avec Sidon pourrait s'expliquer par l'héritage d'une double seigneurie donnée en jouissance par Eustache Grenier soixante ans plus tôt. D'un autre côté, de toutes les principautés du royaume de Jérusalem, Césarée était l'une des moins exposées aux attaques des musulmans puisqu'elle fut plus éloignée de n'importe quel territoire musulman. Quand l'armée était convoquée, il se pourrait que les forces de Césarée (plus celles de Bethsan) aient été habituellement envoyées pour renforcer les hommes du seigneur de Sidon, particulièrement en cas d'une attaque provenant de Damas. Cette rubrique manque de fondement si nous cherchons la présence d'une structure féodale ou d'une hiérarchie seigneuriale, mais elle peut avoir un sens si nous pensons en terme de rassemblement et de déploiement des effectifs. Si la rubrique sur Sidon donne une fausse impression de décrire une hiérarchie seigneuriale, peut-être en fut-il de même pour la rubrique sur Jaffa.

Cependant, l'idée que ce document concerne d'abord la façon dont les effectifs étaient rassemblés s'effondre avec ce que nous lisons plus loin. La rubrique suivante relative à la seigneurie du comte Joscelin (il devait 24 chevaliers), était un assemblage de domaines situés pour la plupart aux environs d'Acre, acquis par petits bouts à partir du milieu des années 1170. On aurait pu espérer que ses services seraient inclus avec ceux des chevaliers d'Acre, mais ils ne le sont pas. De même, les chevaliers des petits domaines ecclésiastiques de Lydda et de Nazareth (respectivement 10 et 6 chevaliers) auraient sûrement pu servir avec des compagnons venus d'ailleurs tandis que Toron et Maron (18 chevaliers) représentent en effet le reste d'une plus grande seigneurie tenue par les chrétiens et centrée sur Banyas, une ville perdue au profit des musulmans en 1164.

Il ne fait aucun doute qu'au milieu des années 1180 seigneurs et chevaliers avaient des obligations militaires, mais comment répondons-nous à la question que Susan Reynolds ne manquerait pas de poser : ces obligations proviennent-elles du fait de tenir des terres ou rentes en fiefs ? Il n'est pas indispensable de se référer à des sources plus tardives, car elles pourraient bien projeter sur une époque antérieure les institutions et les questions de

---

11. S. Tibble, *Monarchy and Lordships in the Latin Kingdom of Jerusalem, 1099-1291*, Oxford, p. 67. Quelque chose de similaire peut s'appliquer à la petite seigneurie de Blanchegarde (Jean d'Ibelin, *op. cit.*, p. 425). Elle est située dans le sud du royaume près d'Ascalon, mais son seigneur devait servir avec les chevaliers d'Acre. Il s'avère qu'en plus de tenir sa seigneurie, il avait également une propriété dans le voisinage d'Acre, et ceci explique pourquoi il servait si loin. Cf. S. Tibble. *op. cit.*, p. 76-77.

leur temps. Mais nous avons la chance d'avoir deux sources contemporaines bien connues et qui peuvent fournir une réponse à cette question. La première est la célèbre histoire écrite par l'archevêque Guillaume de Tyr qui termine son ouvrage vers 1184 et qui met ainsi la dernière touche à son oeuvre presqu'au même moment où ces listes étaient composées. L'autre source est la précieuse collection de chartes enregistrant le développement de la seigneurie du comte Joscelin entre 1179 et 1186. La documentation juridique enregistrant les transactions entre les laïcs est plus rare que celle qui concerne les transactions entre clercs et laïcs, mais ces chartes survivent car au XIIIᵉ siècle les terres concernées devinrent des possessions des Chevaliers teutoniques, et l'ordre préserva les vieux documents se rapportant à leur titre de propriété.

On se rend bien compte en lisant ces chartes que nous sommes dans un monde où les chevaliers tenaient des fiefs et devaient un quota de services militaires. Ainsi en 1179 Joscelin acquit des domaines dans le fief du chambellan du roi et il devait en retour le service de deux chevaliers à perpétuité ; en 1181 pour le loyer d'Acre qui appartenait à Philippe le Roulx il était obligé de fournir encore 2 autres chevaliers. Plus tard d'autres documents fournissent la même impression – qu'au moins pour les plus petites propriétés terriennes, on devait un quota précis de chevaliers au roi. Fréquemment, mais pas toujours, que ces propriétés sont décrites comme des fiefs [12] et quelques documents mentionnent spécifiquement l'hommage dû par les propriétaires [13]. Une concession de 1179 stipule que les terres concernées doivent être possédées libres de tout service, mais le comte Joscelin, l'oncle du prince était certainement capable d'acquérir des terres à des conditions avantageuses [14]. Il est clair cependant que ceux des documents de cette collection traitant longuement des seigneuries ne parlent pas des services. Ainsi, en 1161, quand la seigneurie d'Oultrejourdain fut accordée à Philippe de Naplouse, on ne mentionne pas de quota de chevaliers pour le service de l'ost royal. De même en 1186 quand la seigneurie de Toron et de Château Neuf fut donnée à Joscelin, les services ne furent pas détaillés mais devaient être les mêmes qu'au temps du propriétaire précédent [15].

Les témoignages suffisent pour conclure qu'à la fin du XIIᵉ siècle les hommes dont les noms apparaissent dans ces listes – comme devant fournir

---

12. *Tabulae OrdinisTheutonici*, éd. E. Strehlke, Berlin, 1869, n° 10, 13. Cf. n° 4, 7, 16, 22.

13. E. Strehlke, *op. cit.*, n° 3, 14.

14. E. Strehlke, *op. cit.*, n° 11.

15. E. Strehlke, *op. cit.*, n° 3, 21. D'un autre côté, en 1169 il est établi que Baudouin III promit à Joscelin Pisellus *feodum cum militum in Babilonia cum deus eam christianis dederit.* Cf. E. Strehlke, *op. cit.*, n° 5.

un petit nombre de chevaliers ou un seul chevalier devaient normalement des obligations militaires vis-à-vis de la couronne en échange des fiefs qui leur étaient accordés. On peut cependant douter que cela ait toujours été vrai, entre autre parce qu'il est peu vraisemblable que ces hommes qui conquirent la Terre sainte pendant et après la première croisade furent familiers de ce type d'organisation sociale et militaire. Des témoignages plus tardifs suggèrent qu'il n'y avait pas dans les premiers temps du royaume de limitation en matière d'héritage pour des parents lointains, ni de contrôle seigneurial sur le mariage des héritières, et ni de contrôle seigneurial sur un héritier et sur ses terres dans le cas d'une minorité. Par ailleurs, il n'existait aucun droit d'entrée (ou relief) pour les héritiers et pratiquement pas d'aides [16]. Tous ces éléments sembleraient montrer que les tenanciers possédaient ces terres librement comme alleux plutôt que comme des fiefs. Toutefois, nous devons être prudents car les sources latines concernant la Syrie ne semblent pas utiliser le mot d'« alleu ». En conséquence, je suis poussé à croire que plus tôt dans le XIIe siècle, les chevaliers servaient, non parce qu'ils avaient des fiefs qui les plaçaient sous une obligation contractuelle, mais simplement parce qu'ils étaient chevaliers, et qu'à leur statut social et militaire s'ajoutaient les besoins évidents du royaume, de sorte qu'on exigeait d'eux qu'ils servissent ainsi le roi ou le seigneur dans la mouvance dans laquelle ils vivaient. Plus tardivement, se précisèrent les services attendus, et un vocabulaire féodal né des exigences toujours plus grandes des princes et des seigneurs, changea la façon dont les hommes considéraient leurs terres et leurs obligations.

Mais si les chevaliers ordinaires devaient ces services en échange de leurs fiefs, qu'en était-il pour les grands seigneurs ? Se considéraient-ils comme des vassaux et leurs seigneuries comme des fiefs devant fournir un quota de chevaliers pour l'ost royal ? Les données recueillies dans les documents et discutées plus haut représentent-elles simplement ce que le roi pouvait normalement attendre quand les seigneurs concernés venaient avec leurs hommes se joindre à l'armée royale ? Le témoignage de Guillaume de Tyr est révélateur à cet égard. Guillaume de Tyr est limité dans son usage du vocabulaire féodal. Les vassaux (*vassali*) ne sont mentionnés qu'une seule fois, et les fiefs (*feoda*) deux fois, et ceci pour un texte dont l'édition récente avoisine les mille pages. En 1183, Guy de Lusignan désigné comme régent surtout à cause de l'incapacité de Baudouin IV « ordonna à ses fidèles et dans l'ensemble à tous les princes de devenir ses vassaux et de lui prêter fidélité

16. P.W. Edbury, « Feudal Obligations in the Latin East », *Byzantion*, 47 (1977), p. 345-347, 349-350. Les conclusions et les hypothèses de cet article doivent être revues totalement à la lumière de cette discussion.

par la main » [17]. La plus haute noblesse est constituée de vassaux – au moins en 1183. Guillaume savait parfaitement ce qu'il disait : il aurait écrit ce passage un an au plus après les événements décrits. J'ai le sentiment qu'au XIIᵉ siècle les nobles avaient toujours prêté serment de fidélité à leur gouvernants, mais peut-être était-ce seulement à ce moment qu'ils pouvaient se considérer comme vassaux. Leurs seigneuries étaient-elles tenues ainsi en fief ? Des deux références de Guillaume relatives aux fiefs l'une concerne l'Europe occidentale et paraît utiliser le mot dans le sens d'une seigneurie supérieure [18] ; l'autre concerne Raymond de Poitiers et son accord avec l'empereur Jean Comnène en 1137. Raymond devait restituer Antioche ; en échange, Jean et ses héritiers rendraient Alep, Shaizar et d'autres places à perpétuité « comme un bénéfice [*beneficium*] – ce qui est communément appelé un fief » [19]. On ne peut rien dire de plus de cette assertion, Raymond était de toute façon en position de faiblesse : le mot *feodum* était une glose personnelle de Guillaume. On doit cependant soulever le problème de savoir si Guillaume utilise ailleurs le mot *beneficium* dans le sens de « fief ». Le mot peut bien sûr se référer aux bénéfices ecclésiastiques ou simplement renvoyer à un acte de générosité sans davantage de précision. Mais il y a quelques exemples où Guillaume l'utilise pour désigner les fiefs de chevaliers ordinaires mais non de grands seigneurs [20]. Plus généralement les grandes seigneuries sont mentionnées comme l'héritage (*hereditas*) ou la possession (*possessio*) de leur propriétaire, ou sont concédées *iure hereditario*, termes que Susan Reynolds associerait avec la propriété complète [21]. On doit me convaincre que les grandes seigneuries du royaume latin de Jérusalem dans les années 1180 étaient considérées comme fiefs ou que leur tenue résultait des liens contractuels par lesquels les seigneurs entreprirent de fournir au roi un quota de chevaliers pour le prix de leur domaine.

Beaucoup de ce que j'avais à dire dans cet article reste encore dans le domaine de la recherche, et je considère mes conclusions comme provisoires. Je n'ai pas encore eu la possibilité de résoudre toutes les implications induites par les sources et de donner vraiment toute leur considération à la

---

17. Guillaume de Tyr, *Chronique*, éd. R.B.C. Huygens, Turnhout, 1986, p. 1049 : *fidelibus suis et generaliter principibus omnibus ut eius vassalli fierent et ei manualiter exhiberent fidelitatem*, lignes 22-24.

18. Guillaume de Tyr, *op. cit.*, p. 632, ligne 50. Pour l'usage du mot « fief » utilisé dans ce sens, cf. S. Reynolds, *op. cit.*, p. 271, 275.

19. Guillaume de Tyr, *op. cit.*, p. 671, ligne 43 : *in beneficio, quod feodum vulgo dicitur*. Pour une phrase similaire, cf. S. Reynolds, *op. cit.*, p. 120, 165.

20. Guillaume de Tyr, *op. cit.*, p. 653, 785.

21. Guillaume de Tyr, *op. cit.*, p. 651, 655, 828, 1019, 1055, (*hereditas*) ; p. 601, 654, 778, 779, 826, 877 (*possessio*) ; p. 464, 519, 568, 651, 657, 837, 878, 1012 (*iure hereditario*), dans S. Reynolds, *op. cit.*, p. 145, 268.

littérature secondaire. La société de l'Orient latin n'était pas figée, et comme le disait Joshua Prawer, les relations féodales n'apparurent pas complètement établies après la conquête, mais prirent le temps d'évoluer [22]. Les simples chevaliers tenaient clairement leurs terres en fiefs dans les années 1180 et devaient un quota de services en retour. Mais ils auraient été plus sensibles à la pression d'en haut que les nobles, et cela n'empêche pas les grands seigneurs de considérer leurs seigneuries comme des fiefs, comme le faisaient leurs homologues en France à la même période. On aurait beaucoup plus de choses à dire à ce sujet, mais si les seigneuries n'étaient pas tenues en fief au cours du premier royaume de Jérusalem – avant les désastres de 1187 – ceci expliquerait au moins les caractéristiques bien connues des seigneuries à ce moment. Si, par exemple les seigneurs avaient l'entière possession de leurs domaines, on expliquerait que la seigneurie dirige l'ost royal quand celui-ci mène sa campagne à l'intérieur de ses domaines [23]. On expliquerait ainsi l'étendue des pouvoirs de juridiction d'un seigneur à l'intérieur de sa seigneurie – droits connus sous les dénominations de *cour, coins et justise* – qui lui procurent une complète maîtrise de la justice, le corollaire étant que les officiers de la couronne n'y avaient aucune autorité [24].

Constater que les seigneurs auraient la pleine possession de leurs terres jetterait une lumière sur un épisode particulièrement célèbre, tout en le plaçant dans un contexte beaucoup plus crédible. En 1186, lors d'une trêve entre chrétiens et musulmans, Renaud de Châtillon, seigneur d'Oultrejourdain, attaqua une caravane musulmane et prit l'une des soeurs de Saladin en captivité. Le roi Guy de Lusignan ordonna à Renaud de restituer la caravane et la soeur au sultan : « Il respondi que il n'en rendroit point, car aussi estoit il sires de sa terre come il [i.e. Guy] de la soue... » [25]. Nous pouvons considérer l'épisode de ce tout puissant-baron comme un morceau de bravoure, comme le fait d'un seigneur exerçant son autorité sur ses propres terres et non comme celui d'un vassal tenant un fief conditionnel du roi. Dès lors l'attitude de Renaud n'était pas aussi injustifiée qu'on le dit d'habitude

Quand les croisés s'installèrent pour la première fois en Terre sainte après la première croisade, les terres furent accordées en pleine possession aux grands et aux petits. Avec le temps, les plus petits chevaliers considérèrent ces biens comme des fiefs et eux-mêmes comme des vassaux devant un

---

22. J. Prawer, *Crusader Institutions*, Oxford, 1980, p. 3-19.

23. *La Continuation de Guillaume de Tyr (1184-1197)*, éd. M. R. M organ, Paris, 1982, p. 53-54.

24. J. Riley-Smith, *The Feudal Nobility and the Kingdom of Jerusalem, 1174-1247*, Londres, 1973, p. 26.

25. *La continuation de Guillaume de Tyr, op. cit.*, p. 36. Je dois remercier mon collègue John France, pour avoir relevé la pertinence de cet événement dans mon argumentation.

quota précis de services au roi ou à leur seigneur. On aura encore à déterminer quand et comment intervient ce changement, bien que le processus ait pu s'étaler sur plusieurs décennies. Mais pour les plus grands seigneurs, l'idée qu'ils étaient aussi des vassaux et que leurs seigneuries étaient tenues en fiefs, fut lente à accepter – elle était loin d'être reconnue au milieu des années 1180. Cette conception entraîne une cassure complète à l'égard de la tradition qui considère le royaume latin de Jérusalem comme « le parfait état féodal », une cassure plus radicale que celle proposée par Joshua Prawer et par d'autres savants écrivant il y a à peu près une génération. Le problème est que la perte du royaume au profit des musulmans en 1187 et que la restauration partielle effectuée par les armées de la troisième Croisade changèrent beaucoup de choses, et ce qui a pu être valable après 1192 ne l'aurait pas été plus tôt. Il reste beaucoup d'hypothèses, mais je pense que nous pouvons abandonner l'idée de Jean d'Ibelin à la fin de son traité qui représente un guide dans un royaume où la féodalité était la règle suprême.

II

Fiefs and Vassals in the Kingdom of Jerusalem: from the Twelfth Century to the Thirteenth

Historians of the Middle Ages are used to the idea that social and institutional developments advance in a lineal fashion, even if at some periods the pace of change seems quicker than at others.[1] In the twelfth and thirteenth centuries we would expect to find practice and precedent hardening into custom; we would expect to find social, legal and administrative ideas acquiring an ever greater degree of sophistication and we would expect to find a greater reliance on written instruments rather than on orality. The Kingdom of Jerusalem, however, presents a problem in this respect. After almost ninety years of existence the Frankish kingdom collapsed to the forces of Saladin in 1187. There then followed the Third Crusade and a partial recovery of its territory; after that a further hundred years until the final loss of Acre in 1291. One question that perhaps deserves greater consideration than it has received in the past is what effect the events of 1187–92 had on society and institutions. How did Frankish society differ subsequently? What changes can we detect in the ideas and institutions that underpinned that society? How far was there continuity from the so-called "First Kingdom," and how far did the period of the Third Crusade mark a new beginning? Usually historians have simply assumed that after 1192 things were much the same as before 1187, albeit within much narrower borders. Otherwise the question has often gone unasked.

Shortly after the appearance of Susan Reynolds's *Fiefs and Vassals* in 1994, I tried to imagine how her ideas might apply to the Latin East, and a version of a paper I wrote at that time appeared in 1998.[2] It concentrated attention on the closing years of the "First Kingdom" — the generation before 1187 — and I argued that in that period, whereas knights possessed estates or incomes, which in some sources are referred to as "fiefs," in return for fixed quotas of military service, it could have been the case that the great lords did not have a formal obligation to produce a stipulated number of knights, even though the

---

[1] My thanks are due to Benjamin Z. Kedar and the members of the workshop on the governance of the Frankish kingdom of Jerusalem held at the Institute for Advanced Studies, The Hebrew University of Jerusalem, 7–12 July 1999, which considered the views of Dr Susan Reynolds, the author of *Fiefs and Vassals: The Medieval Evidence Reinterpreted* (Oxford, 1994). Particular gratitude is due to Jonathan Riley-Smith for reading an earlier draft of this paper.

[2] "Fiefs, vassaux et servise militaire dans le royaume latin de Jérusalem," in *Le Partage du Monde: échanges et colonisation dans la Méditerranée médiévale*, ed. Michel Balard and Alain Ducellier (Paris, 1998), pp. 141–50.

king knew what military resources he could expect from them when they came to serve on campaign. I also suggested that the vocabulary used of the great lords and their lordships was more in keeping with the sort of terminology for "freehold" property that Dr Reynolds finds in the West at the same period.

That paper focused on three very well known texts (or collections of texts) relating to the years just before 1187. Each has the great merit of being strictly contemporary: the lists of services and lordships preserved by John of Ibelin, count of Jaffa, at the end of his legal treatise;[3] the charters relating to the so-called "Lordship of Count Joscelin,"[4] and the celebrated history of William of Tyre who appears to have finished writing his *magnum opus* in 1184.[5] It is my belief that the list of services from John of Jaffa can be dated to 1185 and the reign of Baldwin V.[6] It provides the names of a hundred knights from the royal domain — about half of them known from other sources — owing specified quotas of service. The idea that a specific service was owed is confirmed by the Count Joscelin charters, some of which speak of particular numbers of knights owed in return for landed fiefs or fief-rents. These charters have frequently been discussed.[7] They survive because in the thirteenth century many of the estates mentioned passed into the possession of the Teutonic Knights, who then preserved this earlier material concerning their title in their archive. For our purposes they are particularly precious since they form by far the most substantial assemblage of charters recording grants to laymen to have survived from the Kingdom of Jerusalem. As mentioned, several relate to "fiefs" owing a fixed service, but in the grants of major lordships — Outrejourdain (1161) and Toron and Château Neuf (1186) — the lordship is not termed a "fief" and the service is not specified.[8] Interestingly, the 1161 Outrejourdain document uses the word *feodum* several times of other, lesser properties. If indeed there was a distinction at that time between lay land-holders of moderate standing holding their property as fiefs and owing one or more knights to their lord, and the lords of the great lordships holding their property in outright ownership and with no specified *servitium debitum*, it is a point that is worth emphasizing. There is, however, a danger here of arguing *ex nihilo*: absence of evidence that lordships were regarded as fiefs, albeit on a grand scale, and that even the greatest lords were contractually bound to produce a fixed number of knights when summoned by the king is not evidence that such features did not exist. In another document preserved in the

---

[3] Now re-edited in Peter W. Edbury, *John of Ibelin and the Kingdom of Jerusalem* (Woodbridge, 1997), pp. 118–24.

[4] *Tabulae Ordinis Theutonici*, ed. Ernst Strehlke (Berlin, 1869). Reprinted with a new introduction by Hans E. Mayer (Toronto, 1975). Hereafter cited as Strehlke.

[5] WT.

[6] Edbury, *John of Ibelin*, pp. 129–31.

[7] Notably Hans E. Mayer, "Die Seigneurie de Joscelin und der Deutsche Orden," *Die geistlichen Ritterorden Europas*, ed. Josef Fleckenstein and Manfred Hellmann, Vorträge und Forschungen 26 (Sigmaringen, 1980), pp. 171–216.

[8] Strehlke, nos. 3, 21.

II

Teutonic Order's archive, a charter of King Amaury dated 1169, the king announces that he has "given and conceded *feodum c[entum] militum in Babilonia* when God shall have given it to the Christians" to Joscelin Pisellus and his heirs.[9] As is well known, 1169 was a key year in Amaury's attempts to conquer Egypt, and here, in what is admittedly a provisional grant which anticipated a military success that in the event failed to materialize, we have the creation of *feodum centum militum*. Clearly this was a grant that would have catapulted the recipient into the highest rank of the kingdom's aristocracy. In John of Jaffa's list only the principality of Galilee is credited by itself with a hundred knights.[10] But what did this phrase *feodum centum militum* mean? Is it that Joscelin Pisellus will henceforth be obliged to produce a hundred knights to serve in the royal host as the *quid pro quo* of his tenure? Or is it that the grant will be large enough for him to provide revenues for a hundred knights, men who would be needed to control the territory with its huge population that King Amaury hoped to conquer?

William of Tyre is sparing in his use of "feudal" vocabulary. Vassals (*vassalli*) are referred to just once, and fiefs (*feoda*) twice, and this in a text that in its modern edition runs to over a thousand pages. In 1183 Guy of Lusignan became regent for the incapacitated Baldwin IV, and the king sought to secure Guy's position, *precipiens fidelibus suis et generaliter principibus omnibus ut eius vassalli fierent et ei manualiter exhiberent fidelitatem.*[11] The precise nuance conveyed by the word *generaliter* is open to some doubt, but I think we have to construe this sentence to mean that in 1183 the princes — and by this William means the higher nobility — were vassals and that they took a ritual oath *manualiter*, placing their hands in those of their lord as they repeated the formulae. It is important to remember that William was writing not more than about a year after these events took place, and so, even though he seems not to have been present on that occasion,[12] it is likely that he had precise information as to what actually happened. As for the two references to *feoda*, one relates to western Europe and appears to relate to superior lordship,[13] and the other to the prince of Antioch, Raymond of Poitiers, and his agreement with Emperor John Komnenos in 1137: Raymond was to surrender Antioch and in return he and his heirs were to hold Aleppo, Shaizar and other places in perpetuity *in beneficio, quod feodum vulgo dicitur.*[14] Not too much should be read into this statement: Raymond was in a weak position; William was being disparaging about what was on offer. In any case his testimony was scarcely

---

[9] Strehlke, no. 5.
[10] Edbury, *John of Ibelin*, p. 118. The other units with a hundred knights: Jaffa, Ascalon, Ramla, Mirabel and Ibelin; and Sidon, Caesarea and Bethsan were both made up of several lordships.
[11] WT 22.26.22–24, p. 1049.
[12] As indicated by William's use of the verb *perhibetur* immediately after the passage quoted (p. 1049, line 25).
[13] WT 14.1.50, p. 632; cf. Reynolds, *Fiefs and Vassals*, pp. 271, 275.
[14] WT 14.30.43, p. 671; cf. Reynolds, *Fiefs and Vassals*, pp. 120, 165.

II

52

contemporary. William's equation of *feodum* and *beneficium* does, however, prompt us into considering his use of that term as well. The word *beneficium* can of course bear several meanings, but William does seem to use it a couple of times to denote fiefs — the property of ordinary knights, not great lords.[15] More normally the greater lordships are referred to as the inheritance (*hereditas*) or the possession (*possessio*) of their owners, or were granted *iure hereditario* — terms which Susan Reynolds would associate with outright ownership, although whether William himself would have intended that they should carry this connotation is far from clear.[16]

There are problems in using William of Tyre. William clearly saw himself as a Latin stylist. On the whole he tries to avoid neologisms — we have seen already how he apologises for using *feodum*: "in beneficio, quod feodum vulgo dicitur." A further indication that he was selective in his use of vocabulary is revealed by an analysis of how he employs the word "baro." Professor Huygens's concordance points us to a number of instances of its use, but on closer examination it turns out that a clear majority are not in William's own writing but occur in the documents he inserted into his text — notably the *Pactum Warmundi* of 1123. Left to himself William preferred to use *princeps* or *nobilis*. The paucity of references to "fiefs" or "vassals" may therefore be explained by an unwillingness on stylistic grounds to use what may have been current terminology rather than by assuming that fief-holding and vassalage were little known in the East. Another problem in deconstructing William is that as an educated ecclesiastic and a lawyer he is exactly the sort of person who will want to make things look tidier and more schematized than perhaps they were. To take an example highlighted by John Gillingham: William recorded that in 1180 the king gave (*tradit*) his sister Sibylla as wife to Guy of Lusignan.[17] This statement is no doubt true in the sense that William, the trained lawyer, is describing the legal formalities — after all, for a king to give away his sister in marriage was what was supposed to happen — but, as Gillingham points out, that was certainly not the whole story, and other evidence suggests that it was Sibylla who took initiative or, at very least, that Sibylla and Guy chose each other.[18] So William tells the truth, but is it the whole truth? As Umberto Eco makes one of his characters say when referring to popular hostile perceptions of the Templars, "... it was William of Tyre's fault, treacherous historiographer that he was."[19]

Frankish society in the twelfth century was not tidy; nor was it schematized.

---

[15] WT 14.16.41, 17.17.85, pp. 653, 785.

[16] For references, Edbury, "Fiefs, vassaux et servise militaire," p. 148 n. 21.

[17] WT 21.1, p. 1007 rubric, cf. lines 16–18.

[18] John Gillingham, "Love, Marriage and Politics in the Twelfth Century," *Forum for Modern Language Studies*, 25 (1989), 293–95. Reprinted in John Gillingham, *Richard Coeur de Lion: Kingship, Chivalry and War in the Twelfth Century* (London and Rio Grande, 1994), pp. 244–48.

[19] Umberto Eco, *Foucault's Pendulum* (London, 1989), p. 88.

The settlers from the West would have brought with them a whole range of experiences and assumptions about relations between lords and men, rulers and ruled, families and neighbours. They arrived at different times during the century and from different parts of Europe. In the early twelfth century military obligation and patterns of inheritance cannot have been systematized, and the high mortality and the uncertain commitment to remaining in the East ensured that social custom and aristocratic structures would remain fluid. As Joshua Prawer proved many years ago, the Frankish conquest of the Holy Land at the start of the twelfth century did not entail the importation of a fully-fledged "feudal system" from the West.[20] It was only gradually with the consolidation of royal and seigneurial authority and the establishment of custom and precedent that a recognizable and orderly system of land tenure and military obligation of a sort that historians delight in uncovering began to emerge. If by the 1180s ordinary knights held their lands as fiefs and owed a quota of service in return, it does not follow that such arrangements had been in place a generation earlier. By its very nature the evolution of custom in the twelfth century is difficult to trace in the sources. Doubtless landed men of moderate wealth would have been more susceptible to pressure from above and so more likely to accept closely defined obligations than would the nobles. It does not follow because a man holding one village or a rent worth a few hundred bezants annually accepted that he owed the service of one knight, that the great lords would have regarded their lordships in the same way, any more than their counterparts in France would have done at the same period. Quite how lords would have viewed their lordships was probably ill-defined, but if we think of the lordships in the "First Kingdom" being in practice more akin to outright property rather than treated as fiefs, that would help explain the rule which said that the lord led the vanguard of the royal host when it was campaigning within his own lordship. It might also explain the piece of bombast from the lord of Outrejourdain, Reynald of Châtillon, who is supposed to have told Guy of Lusignan when upbraided for breaking the truce with the Muslims that he would not return his booty and captives "for he was lord of his land just as he (Guy) was lord of his."[21] Maybe, in the years before 1187, there was pressure to get nobles to accept that their lordships should be put on the same footing as the fiefs of the lesser knights. If so, that might help explain the context of Baldwin of Ibelin's refusal to do homage to Guy of Lusignan in 1186.[22] It could even be that one reason for the resentment against Guy of Lusignan as regent in 1183 was that the nobles, in William of Tyre's words, had been obliged to "become his vassals" (*eius vassalli fierent*) and that besides signalling their duty to obey Guy as the king's surrogate it presaged a diminution of their own autonomy.

So far I have been trying to build up a picture of how the sources allow us

---

[20] Joshua Prawer, *Crusader Institutions* (Oxford, 1980), pp. 3–45 *passim*.
[21] *La Continuation de Guillaume de Tyr (1184–1197)*, ed. M. Ruth Morgan (Paris, 1982), pp. 36, 53–54.
[22] *La Continuation de Guillaume de Tyr*, p. 35.

to perceive fiefs and vassals in the Kingdom of Jerusalem on the eve of Hattin. I now come back to my original question and ask what changed once the dust had settled on the events of 1187–92. What happened after 1192 has not attracted anything like the same degree of attention from historians as the generation before 1187. There are good reasons why this should be — the 1180s are, after all, extremely interesting — but it is also true that our sources for the later period are not so helpful, and it is inevitable that historians tend to follow where their materials lead. The comparative poverty of our sources is especially true of the narrative material. The Old French Continuations of William of Tyre and the associated text known as the *Chronique d'Ernoul et de Bernard le Trésorier* are patchy in their coverage and anecdotal, and only reached the form in which they have been preserved during the second quarter of the thirteenth century.[23] They certainly fall far behind William of Tyre, who, despite my earlier strictures, was a very fine historian. It is true that we have one of the most informative of medieval travellers — Wilbrand of Oldenburg — but he was in the East twenty years after the end of the Third Crusade. The sparsity of the narrative materials is only partially offset by the presence of the earliest of the legal treatises, the *Livre au Roi* (*c*.1200), as well as the surviving charters and papal letters.

There is no doubt that the years 1187–92 had a devastating effect on Frankish society in the East. For example, as Bernard Hamilton has pointed out, by 1192 only two of the bishops of the kingdom who were in office in 1187 — Joscius archbishop of Tyre and Monachus archbishop of Caesarea — were still alive.[24] The effect on the nobility must have been of a similar order, with the carnage at Hattin and the deaths, many of them from disease, at the siege of Acre taking a heavy toll. But some members of the higher nobility who had taken part in the events leading up to Hattin survived the end of the Third Crusade: besides Guy of Lusignan (d. 1194) and Queen Isabella (d. 1205), mention might be made of Aimery of Lusignan (d. 1205), Maria Comnena (d. after 1207), Reynald of Sidon (d. *c*.1201), Balian of Ibelin (d. 1193), Ralph of Tiberias (d. *c*.1220), his brother Hugh of Tiberias (d. after 1204), and Humphrey of Toron (d. 1197).[25] Doubtless there were others.[26] But it is also noteworthy how readily newcomers to the East after 1192 could gain access to the highest positions. Among the new names that appear as frequent witnesses to the charters of

[23] Peter W. Edbury, "The Lyon *Eracles* and the Old French Continuations of William of Tyre," in *Montjoie*, pp. 140–44.

[24] Bernard Hamilton, *The Latin Church in the Crusader States: the Secular Church* (London, 1980), p. 243. Hamilton repeats the frequent error in calling Monachus "Aimery."

[25] For Reynald, Balian, Ralph and Hugh, see Edbury, *John of Ibelin*, pp. 23, 25, 26, 30. For a notice of Humphrey's death, Roger of Howden, *Chronica*, ed. William Stubbs, RS 51 (London, 1868–71), 4:78.

[26] For example, of those listed as knights in the list preserved by John of Jaffa, Reynald of Soissons, Walter Le Bel and Milo of Colovardino. Edbury, *John of Ibelin*, pp. 148, 152.

Henry of Champagne and Aimery of Lusignan were Thierry of Dendermonde, Milo *Brebenz*, Thierry of *Orca* and Villein of *Alneto*.[27] Count Berthold of Katzenellenbogen had arrived by 1200, and he was soon to be joined by two other western nobles who had dissociated themselves from the army of the Fourth Crusade: Guy of Montfort, the brother of Simon the Elder, and Walter of Montbéliard.[28] The fact that in the wake of the destruction and the territorial losses these and other western nobles could still make careers in the East and, as in the cases of both Guy and Walter, marry into the local Frankish nobility is itself suggestive. Despite the catastrophic losses, there must have been sufficient military and political stability in the Latin East after 1192 and sufficient economic resources to attract them to stay. Their presence would also seem to suggest that in the 1190s and early 1200s the older Frankish noble families were either unable or unwilling to monopolize power for themselves by excluding such newcomers from their ranks. By 1200 the survivors from the "First Kingdom" would have formed only a small minority of the men in attendance on the king, and these westerners together with the new generation of the surviving nobility would have had to come to terms with the fact that the restoration of the Kingdom of Jerusalem to its former glory could not readily be achieved.

So what was the Latin East like after 1192? We know that much of the kingdom's territory remained in Muslim control and that there had been widespread devastation. The sources tell us little about the process of reconstruction, and so, for example, we know nothing about the investment needed to restore the gardens and vineyards around Acre which must have been destroyed in the course of the two-year siege of 1189–91. It is quite likely that much of the land notionally in Christian hands after 1192 remained derelict or exposed to petty brigandage. It was only at the time of the Fifth Crusade that Caesarea and 'Atlit were fortified, and we have to wait until the late 1220s for the refortification of Sidon (held for much of the intervening period in some form of condominium with the Muslims) and Jaffa (which changed hands in 1197 and again in 1204 and was noted as being desolate in 1217)[29] and the building of the castle of Montfort. The charters issued in the aftermath of the Third Crusade show rulers regularizing the position of the Italian mercantile communities whose presence was still much needed in the East but whose privileges, granted at times of military crisis and political turmoil between 1187 and 1192, needed to be curtailed.[30] Other charters survive in favour of the Hospitallers and the Teutonic Knights which show them being given sections

---

[27] *RRH*, nos. 707, 709–10, 713, 716–17, 720–22, 724, 735, 743–44, 746, 773–74, 776, 812.

[28] Jonathan Riley-Smith, *The Feudal Nobility and the Kingdom of Jerusalem, 1174–1277* (London and Basingstoke, 1973), p. 23; Edbury, *John of Ibelin*, pp. 25, 27.

[29] Thietmar, *Mag. Thietmari Peregrinatio*, ed. J.C.M. Laurent (Hamburg, 1857), p. 24. The same author (pp. 23–24) also notes desolation at Arsur and Ramla.

[30] *RRH*, nos. 707, 713, 721, 724.

of the town walls at Acre or Jaffa — presumably to be repaired and then defended — together with other properties, perhaps intended as *douceurs* to persuade them to bear this added responsibility.[31] Early in 1192, even before the crusade was over, Guy of Lusignan gave the Hospitallers substantial property within Acre.[32] Charter evidence only survives when the recipients were in a position to preserve it, and so what does remain is extremely fragmentary and by its very nature gives a distorted picture. Even so, this material points to trends clearly discernible in the thirteenth century: the increasing political and military role of the military Orders, and the greater economic power of the Italians. Historians have frequently commented on these developments. But the corollary of enhanced power for the Orders and the Italians is also significant: in terms of the total sum of power and wealth in the Latin East, the secular nobility was correspondingly diminished.

The *Livre au Roi*, which dates to the reign of King Aimery of Lusignan (1197–1205), provides a commentary on the status and assumptions of the nobility at that time. We are in a world in which the king or the queen can give fiefs comprising land, vines or villages, with or without service, can create liege men and can remit their service. Title to land is enshrined in sealed charters.[33] The *chevalier houme lige*, which in the modern edition is translated "vassal," is clearly important. Service is demanded; fiefs can be confiscated for various reasons; there are rules about rights of inheritance and the wardship of minor heirs; widows need their lord's permission to remarry, and so on. The details may vary, but we are in the classic thirteenth-century feudal world in which the rights of the king and the *chevaliers houmes liges* are held in balance. Even so — curiously in view of its treatment by later writers in the thirteenth century — there is no reference to King Amaury's *Assise sur la ligesse* which was to prove such a fertile starting point for considering the status of the vassals of the nobility and, more particularly, the rights to the vassals to limit the power the monarch.[34]

Whereas the *Livre au Roi* can be read simply as a description of legal custom as it existed at the time of writing, the author would certainly have had a propagandist intent. He had much to say about the royal power and the institutions of monarchy in the Kingdom of Jerusalem.[35] Some of the most interesting sections are those dealing with the royal succession, and it is here that the internal evidence for the dating, with its allusion to the situation at the time of Aimery of Lusignan's reign, is to be found.[36] The modern editor, Myriam Greilsammer, is undoubtedly right to conclude that the book was connected with Aimery's programme of re-establishing strong monarchy in the

---

[31] *RRH*, nos. 701, 709, 710, 716, 717, 744, 746.
[32] *RRH*, no. 698.
[33] *Le Livre au Roi*, ed. Myriam Greilsammer (Paris, 1995), chap. 3.
[34] Riley-Smith, *Feudal Nobility*, pp. 145–84 *passim*.
[35] See Greilsammer's analysis. *Livre au Roi*, pp. 71–76.
[36] *Livre au Roi*, chaps. 5, 6. cf. pp. 83–86.

kingdom. The title by which it is known, *Le Livre au Roi*, finds only tenuous support in the surviving manuscripts,[37] but it ought perhaps to be regarded as the dedication: "The Book dedicated to the King." Most likely it was the work of a member of Aimery's entourage. There is no doubt that the *Livre au Roi* is an attempt to describe royal rights as tempered by the rights of the liege men and other inhabitants of the kingdom: the question is how tendentious is it.

Later in the thirteenth century Aimery of Lusignan was remembered as an accomplished lawyer in his own right. Philip of Novara, and, drawing on his writings, a later thirteenth-century redactor of John of Ibelin's treatise, credited Aimery with wanting to reconstruct the pre–1187 laws only to be frustrated by Ralph of Tiberias who declined to co-operate.[38] Maybe Aimery did invite Ralph to work on just such a codification, but, even if he did, it was never written. Philip's tale belongs with his story of the *Letres dou Sepulcre*, which, as I have tried to demonstrate elsewhere, is a later legal fiction designed to explain away the inadequacies of Jerusalemite customary law as exposed by the exponents of French or Roman law.[39] No doubt the exercise of royal authority and the administration of justice needed reasserting in the aftermath of the Third Crusade, and no doubt lawyers with experience of the working of the courts from before 1187 would have been in demand. But even if we reject the story of the *Letres dou Sepulcre* and place a question mark against Aimery, Ralph of Tiberias and the codification of the laws, the very fact that the *Livre au Roi* was written when it was should be seen as a contribution to the process of reconstruction and consolidation after 1192.

One particular passage in the *Livre au Roi* is clearly connected to the losses in 1187. From chapter 36 we learn that if fiefs in territory currently in Muslim hands are recovered by the Christians they must pass immediately to the closest heir of the last in seisin.[40] John of Ibelin was later to use the phrase *force de Turs ne tolt seisin* — forcible occupation by Turks does not affect seisin — in this context.[41] Clearly it was a sensitive issue. As the Third Crusade had shown, crusaders from the West were often reluctant to respect the rights of the former owners. Indeed the French Continuation of William of Tyre tells of the burgesses of Acre complaining loudly after the surrender of Acre in July 1191 that they had been prevented from regaining their former homes and properties.[42] Thirteenth-century evidence confirms that ownership of recovered

---

[37] *Livre au Roi*, pp. 30, 97, 135.

[38] Philip of Novara, "Livre de forme de plait," *RHC Lois* 1:522–23; John of Ibelin, "Livre," *RHC Lois* 1:429–30.

[39] Peter W. Edbury, "Law and Custom in the Latin East: *Les Letres dou Sepulcre*," in *Intercultural Contacts in the Medieval Mediterranean: Studies in Honour of David Jacoby*, ed. Benjamin Arbel (London, 1996), pp. 71–79. Reprinted in Peter W. Edbury, *Kingdoms of the Crusaders: From Jerusalem to Cyprus* (Aldershot, 1999), IX.

[40] *Livre au Roi*, pp. 239–40.

[41] John of Ibelin, pp. 107–9.

[42] *La Continuation de Guillaume de Tyr*, pp. 125, 127. See Raymond C. Smail, "The International Status of the Latin Kingdom of Jerusalem, 1150–1192," in *The Eastern

lands was a contentious matter, and it is not surprising that the Syrian Franks were insistent on their rights. Each new crusade held out the prospect of recovering territory, and it was probably in anticipation of the crusade of the Emperor Henry VI that in February 1196 the canons of the Holy Sepulchre had Pope Celestine III confirm their properties in the East, most of which were then in Muslim hands.[43] It is not known whether they approached the secular rulers in the East for a similar confirmations — if they did they have not survived — but it may be that the canons reckoned that a papal confirmation would be more effective in vindicating their claims to recovered properties against the crusaders than a charter from Henry of Champagne or Aimery of Lusignan.

The principle *force de Turs ne tolt seisin* was clearly an attempt by the Latin Syrian Franks to protect their own interests. It also enshrined the hope that one day the clock would be turned back and the rest of the kingdom would once more be in Christian hands. John of Ibelin decided to include the list of services as they had been "before the land was lost."[44] By the time he was writing — the mid–1260s — hopes of a restoration must have faded, and we are in the world of antiquarianism, hankering after the memory of a long-lost golden age, but earlier, and for much of the first half of the thirteenth century, it is my belief that people really did believe that the whole of the kingdom would one day be restored to its rightful owners. Successive crusading expeditions from the West coupled with the Ayyubids' concessions in 1229 and 1240–41 would have fuelled such hopes. Even as late as the mid–1250s it was believed in the Muslim world that the sultan of Damascus was ceding the Christians everything west of the Jordan.[45]

It is against this background that we should see Aimery of Lusignan's 1198 coronation oath as preserved in the cartulary of the Holy Sepulchre, and in particular the provision that the king would maintain laws and customs as they related to both the Church and the whole people of the land, "just as King Amaury and King Baldwin his son had ... and I shall abolish novelties chiefly introduced since the destruction of the land ... ."[46] The oath was presumably drafted by members of the clergy — perhaps by Patriarch Monachus himself — and it could well be that in writing of the customs to be maintained and the novelties to be abolished they were thinking primarily in terms of ecclesiastical issues, not least the protracted and acrimonious circumstances of Monachus's

---

Mediterranean Lands in the Period of Crusades, ed. Peter M. Holt (Warminster, 1977), pp. 23–43. The translator of William of Tyre into Old French who was at work sometime in the early decades of the thirteenth century appears to have believed that the principle *force des Turs ne tolt seisin* was applied at the time of the Christian recovery of Banyas in 1140. John Pryor, "The *Eracles* and William of Tyre: an Interim Report," *Horns*, p. 285.

[43] *Cart St Sép*, no. 170.

[44] Edbury, *John of Ibelin*, p. 117 line 65 (= John of Ibelin, p. 421 cf. p. 24).

[45] Edbury, *John of Ibelin*, p. 90.

[46] *Cart St Sép*, no. 172.

own election as patriarch in the time of Henry of Champagne.[47] The reference to Amaury and Baldwin IV is repeated in the coronation oath as recorded by John of Jaffa about seventy years later,[48] and so it presumably became an accepted part of the oath as used subsequently. There seem to me to be two ways of reading this text. One is to see it as an attempt to expunge the years between the death of Baldwin IV in 1185 and the accession of Aimery in 1198 from the legal memory. The minority of Baldwin V, the catastrophic reign of Guy of Lusignan, the problematic authority wielded by Conrad of Montferrat, and then the rule of the uncrowned Henry of Champagne who had been in conflict with the Church over the election of the patriarch who was to administer the oath in 1198 could all be set aside. The other approach is to see the 1198 oath as looking back to the last kings of the "First Kingdom" as major legislators and upholders of good custom — and indeed that is how the reference to these kings in the version of the oath to be found in John of Jaffa's treatise should be understood. But however we approach it, the coronation oath can be placed alongside the principle *force de Turs ne tolt seisin* in pointing to the conclusion that people in the East were consciously trying to minimize the legal consequences of the events of 1187–1192.

Many years ago, in 1977, I published a paper with the title "Feudal Obligations in the Latin East."[49] In it I relied appreciably, though by no means exclusively, on the works of the mid thirteenth-century legal writers, chiefly Philip of Novara and John of Jaffa. I argued that military service in the East owed from fiefs was heavy and, after the loss of Latin Syria in 1291, it continued to be exacted in Cyprus late into the fourteenth century. I still believe this to be true, and accordingly I would maintain that Susan Reynolds's remark that "Outside England the obligation to military service ... was generally nominal"[50] needs at very least to be modified by making an exception for Jerusalem. More problematic are other aspects of my paper. Expanding a point made by Jonathan Riley-Smith in his *Feudal Nobility* which had appeared a few years earlier,[51] I reviewed the evidence indicating that the assortment of rights that historians of medieval England refer to collectively as "feudal incidents" were almost non-existent. In the East lords could not charge heirs relief or entry fines; they had no right to *primer seisin*; they did not exercise the wardship of the lands of minor heirs (unless there was no kin); they had limited control over the marriage of heiresses and only minimal rights to demand aids. What was more, in the East there was no institutionalised system of commuting military service to a money payment — nothing equivalent to the English *scutage*. In

---

[47] Peter W. Edbury and John G. Rowe, "William of Tyre and the Patriarchal Election of 1180," *English Historical Review* 93 (1978), 14–17 (reprinted Edbury, *Kingdoms of the Crusaders*, II); Hamilton, *The Latin Church*, pp. 244–45.

[48] John of Ibelin, p. 30.

[49] *Byzantion* 47 (1977), 328–56. Reprinted in Edbury, *Kingdoms of the Crusaders*, III.

[50] Reynolds, *Fiefs and Vassals*, p. 69.

[51] Riley-Smith, *Feudal Nobility*, pp. 38–39.

other words military service was exacted, but the fiscal potential of feudal tenure familiar to all English-trained medievalists from Magna Carta of 1215 was not available to kings and lords in the East. I used to think this absence of "feudal incidents" in the East was rather odd — I am now prepared to believe that it was England that was odd — and I sought to explain this phenomenon by putting forward the thesis that the pattern I have described — heavy military service exacted but next to no incidents — dated from early in the kingdom's history and had come into being at a time of acute manpower shortage. Kings and lords were desperate for knights to serve them; any knight worth employing could demand a permanent, heritable fief; the last thing a lord would want to do was to deter the heir from taking over his ancestor's land by demanding a relief or claiming the right to assume charge during a minority and so on. As a hypothesis this view has an internal consistency, but it begs some important questions. Projecting thirteenth-century evidence back into the twelfth century in trying to describe tenure and its associated duties and other implications is perilous. In consequence I assumed that feudal institutions were fixed far earlier than now would seem to be the case. But the problem I sought to address is still there. The thirteenth-century evidence presents us with an orderly, schematised picture of tenurial relations in which fief holding is the norm and in which detailed custom is established. There is no reason to doubt that the tenurial customs described by the mid thirteenth-century lawyers were applied in the thirteenth century. However, the question remains: when and how did they come into being?

It is well nigh impossible to trace the evolution of custom, not least because contemporaries tended to assume that what was then customary had remained unchanged since earliest times. From what it tells of the rights of the closest heirs of the last in seisin to inherit land recovered from the Muslims and from other evidence, the *Livre au Roi* indicates that inheritance custom was well-established and essentially immutable by around 1200. From thirteenth-century evidence we learn that property could be held on the basis of a grant to a man and all his heirs or a grant to a man and his heirs descended from his espoused wife only, thus disqualifying collateral members of the family from inheriting. Whereas grants to the recipient and all heirs had been normal in the beginning, this more limited form of grant was known to the author of the *Livre au Roi* and was employed exclusively in Lusignan Cyprus, settled in the 1190s.[52] The implication appears to be that by the start of the thirteenth century this type of grant was normal in Jerusalem as well. But was it? And if it was, when did this change come about? Joshua Prawer found an instance of a grant with this limitation dating from 1152, and two more, issued by King Amaury, from 1169 and 1174.[53] In 1178 Prince Bohemond III of

---

[52] *Livre au Roi*, p. 282; Philip of Novara, p. 504; John of Ibelin, p. 235.
[53] Prawer, *Crusader Institutions*, p. 35 and note 56. *Cart Hosp*, 2:903, no. XI; Strehlke, nos. 5, 7.

Antioch made a grant to Count Joscelin III, again with this limitation,[54] but not one of the charters issued in Joscelin's favour in the Kingdom of Jerusalem between 1179 and 1186 which speak of Joscelin's heirs as the eventual beneficiaries specify that these heirs have to be those descended from Joscelin and his wife.[55] The clear implication is that these grants were intended to be inherited by any heir. We might reasonably conclude from this that there was a lengthy period of overlap when donors sometimes gave grants to the recipient and any heir and sometimes to the recipient and his heirs by his espoused wife only, but it is also possible that Joscelin, a powerful man who was closely related to the king, could well have been receiving these grants on more advantageous terms than was normal at the time.

Occasionally we are more fortunate. For example, in the thirteenth century it was believed that the rule that heiresses divide inheritances instead of the eldest acquiring the entire property was established by a precedent apparently dating from 1171 following the death of a prominent nobleman named Henry Le Bufle.[56] But more commonly enquiries only raise more questions. Thus Philip of Novara tells us about seigneurial control of the marriage of heiresses: originally heiresses married whoever they wished; Philip then says that as this was a far from satisfactory state of affairs the lords intervened to take full control; this in turn displeased the kinsmen of the heiresses, and the current arrangement whereby the king or the lord nominated three candidates and the heiress (or her family) selected one came into being as a compromise.[57] It is an extremely interesting story and has obvious importance for questions such as the status of women in the East and the development of seigneurial control. The problem is that there is no indication as to when these changes took place, and, given the importance of heiresses in the East, it is striking that outside the thirteenth-century legal treatises there is no evidence whatever for lords preparing short-lists of three candidates from which the heiress or her kin would chose. Indeed, what little evidence there is for the disposal of heiresses, suggests that at least by the mid-thirteenth century the woman's family made a financial proffer to the king or the lord who then agreed to let her marry the man of their choice.[58]

I want to end by saying something about the mediatization of public justice. According to John of Jaffa lords of significant lordships all enjoyed the rights known as *cour et coins et justise* and controlled the *cour des bourgeois* within their lordships. What these rights added up to was complete juridical autonomy within each lordship, with the consequence that, while the lord could control the courts and the patronage that that control afforded and help himself to the

---

[54] Strehlke, no. 9.
[55] Strehlke, nos. 11, 14, 16, 17, 18, 21, 22.
[56] For references, Edbury, *John of Ibelin*, p. 9.
[57] Philip of Novara, pp. 558–59. Also John of Ibelin, pp. 359–65.
[58] Edbury, "Feudal Obligations," p. 347.

profits of justice, the royal law officers had no jurisdiction there.[59] This sort of judicial franchise is common enough in the West. What is striking about the situation in the East is the implication that the devolution of public juridical authority had been made systematically. John of Jaffa says that a chief purpose in writing his treatise is to try to educate his fellow owners of these legal franchises into applying the same procedures and principles as in the High Court.[60] John's evidence would indicate that these franchises operated before Hattin, and presumably dated from the foundation of Latin rule. Whatever the origins of this situation, we might assume that the king, inspired perhaps by the example of a Henry II of England or a Philip Augustus of France, would want to curb the juridical authority of his nobility and centralise the administration of justice in his own hands. The events of 1187–92 and the need to reconstruct the kingdom almost from scratch provided the ideal opportunity to do just that. It was an opportunity that was allowed to pass by.

---

[59] Edbury, *John of Ibelin*, pp. 115–17, 155–62.
[60] John of Ibelin, p. 27.

III

PHILIP OF NOVARA AND THE *LIVRE DE FORME DE PLAIT*

Philip of Novara came from Novara in northern Italy but lived most of his life in Cyprus, and although we have neither the date of his birth nor that of his death, it is generally agreed that he survived to a ripe old age and died around the year 1270. He was a knight who by his own account played a full and vigorous role in the struggle against the emperor Frederick II, but he is chiefly remembered today as the author of three major literary works written in the French vernacular of the time: a history of the conflict between the Ibelins and the Hohenstaufen from the mid–1220s to 1242,[1] a treatise on knightly manners known as the *Les quatre âges de l'homme*,[2] and the treatise on the law and customs of the High Court which goes under the name of *Le Livre de forme de plait* or *Le Livre à un sien ami*.[3] Philip was well equipped to write about the legal practices of the royal court. In 1264 or just after, Hugh of Brienne, a cousin of the then king of Cyprus, went on record as saying that Philip was considered the best pleader in the East, and the fact that a decade earlier he had been nominated as one of King Henry I of Cyprus's executors can also be seen as evidence for his standing as a legal expert.[4]

Philip was a vassal of successive lords of Beirut and held fiefs in both Cyprus and the Latin kingdom of Jerusalem. But there is no doubt at all that his legal treatise was written primarily with the High Court of Cyprus specifically in mind, and as such it is one of the most important and most interesting literary compositions by a member of the Frankish ruling class on the island at any time during the entire Lusignan period. One of the clearest indications that Philip was writing from a Cypriot perspective is to be found in chapter nine. If in a dispute over money one party wishes to chal-

---

1. The most recent edition which for the first time has utilized the unique 14th–century ms is edited by Silvio Melani as Filippo da Novara, *Guerra di Federico II in Oriente (1223–1242)* (Naples 1994). This edition has a full bibliography of earlier work on Philip and his writings.

2. Ed. Marcel de Fréville (Paris 1888).

3. Ed. Auguste Beugnot, *Recueil des historiens des croisades* (henceforth: *RHC*) Lois, vol. 1 (Paris 1841).

4. Peter W. Edbury, 'The Disputed Regency of the Kingdom of Jerusalem 1264/6 and 1268', *Camdem Miscellany*, 27 (= Camdem Fourth Series vol. 22: 1979), p. 25; Louis de Mas Latrie, *Histoire de l'île de Chypre sous le règne des princes de la maison de Lusignan* (Paris 1852–61), vol. 3, p. 652.

556

lenge one of the guarantors nominated by the other party and the guarantor is not present in court, there can be a delay of fifteen days for him to be produced; but forty days is allowed if he is in Syria and it is summer, or three months if it is winter; and a year and a day is allowed if he is *outre mer* (i.e. in the West).[5] Clearly a voyage by sea is envisaged before the individual concerned can arrive. In addition Philip cites a number of examples of legal disputes or precedents from Cyprus, and in a hitherto unpublished passage which is found only in a manuscript now in Munich we are specifically told that the customs described there relate to the kingdom of Cyprus.[6] Other indications that Philip was writing about Cyprus and not about the kingdom of Jerusalem include the manner in which he discussed the question of whether precedents from Jerusalem can be cited in the High Court.[7]

In his prologue Philip speaks of writing his treatise for his 'lord and friend',[8] and historians generally assume that the dedicatee was in fact John II, lord of Beirut. John's father, Balian of Ibelin, had been lord of Beirut from 1236 until 1247 and had been Philip's feudal lord and companion in arms. John in his turn was lord of Beirut from 1247 until his death in 1264. Besides Beirut, which was one of the most important lordships in the kingdom of Jerusalem, John would have inherited the lands in Cyprus that had belonged to his father and before that to his grandfather, John I of Beirut, the man who had led the opposition to Frederick II and who had triumphed in the civil wars of 1229–33. We know little about the Cypriot lands of this branch of the Ibelin family. Early in the fourteenth century John II's daughter and eventual heiress was lady of Lapithos, and it is possible that this estate had previously belonged to her father and his forebears.[9]

The idea that John II of Beirut was the 'lord and friend' addressed in the prologue is supported by such indications as the text provides as to the date of composition. Philip has occasion to refer to a count of Jaffa who is clearly John of Ibelin, who was a cousin of the lords of Beirut and who died in 1266. John is famous as the author of a treatise on the law and customs of the High Court of the kingdom of Jerusalem. In an early version of his own treatise he plagiarized the chapter containing a reference to 'the count of Jaffa' from Philip and changed the phrase in question so as to speak

---

5. Beugnot, p. 482.

6. Beugnot, pp. 515–16, 536, 540, 544, 545–6. Munich, Bayer. Staatsbibliothek: Ms. cod. gall. 771, fol. 162ʳ. See appendix A.

7. Beugnot, p. 524. Other pointers to a Cypiot location for Philip's treatise include his discussion of the customs govering the inheritance of fiefs and the absence of references to lords holding franchisal rights known as 'cour, coins et justise'.

8. Beugnot, p. 475.

9. For John I's Cypriot properties, 'Les Gestes des Chiprois', *RHC Documents arméniens*, vol. 2, p. 666. Balian's lands included a *casal* named as *Magaza*. Oliver Berggötz, *Der Bericht des Marsilio Zorzi. Codex Querini–Stampalia IV 3 (1064)* (Frankfurt am Main 1990), p. 191, cf. p. 189. For Lapithos, 'Chronique d'Amadi', ed. René de Mas Latrie, *Chroniques d'Amadi et de Strambaldi* (Paris 1891–3), vol. 1, p. 295, cf p. 267.

of himself in the first person.[10] John only acquired Jaffa in 1246 or 1247, and so for Philip to have referred to him as the count means that he must have been at work after that date. On the other hand, we know that John of Jaffa was writing his own *magnum opus* in the years immediately before his death in 1266,[11] and, as he evidently knew Philip's work, it must already have been in existence by then. Presumably therefore Philip was composing his treatise in the 1250s or early 1260s.

There are three surviving manuscripts of Philip's *Livre* dating from before the middle of the seventeenth century, each of which preserves a markedly different version of his treatise. Together they leave the impression that Philip may have been at work over an extended period and that his treatise passed through several stages of composition. In a study of fundamental importance published in 1926, Maurice Grandclaude discussed the manuscripts in some detail.[12] He argued, rightly in my view, that the 17th–century Munich manuscript (Bayerische Staatsbibliothek: Codex Gallus 771) gives the closest available approximation to Philip's final version. In that sense it is to be preferred to the fourteenth–century manuscripts now in Venice (Biblioteca Nazionale Marciana: Ms. fr. app. 20 (=265)) and Paris (Bibliothèque nationale: Ms. fr. 19026). Unfortunately Count Beugnot, the 19th–century editor of what is still the standard edition of Philip's text, was unaware of the existence of the Munich manuscript. As Grandclaude demonstrated, the text in the Venice manuscript, an 18th–century copy of which formed the basis for Beugnot's edition (ms A), contains a number of loose ends which taken together would indicate that it represents an uncompleted revision. For example, the Venice manuscript has ten chapters tacked on after Philip's conclusion. The Munich manuscript, however, places seven of them in the main body of the text, but lacks the other three. The Munich manuscript also preserves one chapter not found elsewhere. The sequence in which the chapters appear in these two manuscripts differs considerably, but on the whole their order in the Munich manuscript seems to me to be more successful.[13]

The Paris manuscript (Beugnot's ms B) is different again. It consists of 53 chapters, whereas the Munich and Venice manuscripts have 84 and 89 respectively, and so

10. Beugnot, p. 544, cf. p. 540. The passage concerned is not in the printed text of John's treatise (ed. Beugnot, *RHC Lois*, vol. 1), but is to be found in the oldest extant ms (ca. 1280): Paris, Bibliothèque nationale: Ms. fr. 19025, fol. 105ᵛ. John has adapted Philip's 'moult s'en entremist le conte de Jaffe' to read 'je meismes m'en entremis moult'. For this manuscript, Peter W. Edbury and Jaroslav Folda, 'Two Thirteenth–century Manuscripts of Crusader Legal Texts from Saint–Jean d'Acre', *Journal of the Warburg and Courtauld Institutes*, 57 (1994), pp. 243, 250, 253–4 and plate 32.

11. Maurice Grandclaude, *Étude critique sur les Livres des Assises de Jérusalem* (Paris 1923), p. 88.

12. 'Classement sommaire des manucrits des principaux livres des Assises de Jérusalem', *Revue historique de droit français et étranger*, series 4, vol. 5 (1926), pp. 426–40.

13. Chapters 63, 66, 78 of Beugnot's edition are missing from the Munich ms. Beugnot realised that the ten additional chapters ought to have been incorporated into the body of the text and so made his own attempt to do so in his edition. See the table in appendix B where the additional chapters in the Venice ms (=A) are numbered 80–89 inclusive.

contains little more than half the total text. Allowing for instances in which chapters are divided or run together, the first 48 chapters in the Paris manuscript are more or less the same, albeit in a slightly different order, as the first 53 chapters in the Venice manuscript.[14] From this we can conclude that the Paris text was derived from a version more akin to that in the Venice manuscript than to that in the Munich manuscript, albeit one that was truncated.[15] We might note in passing that the Paris manuscript also contains a version of the text known as the *Livre au Roi*, and here too substantial sections are missing.[16] At the end of the Paris manuscript of Philip of Novara there are five chapters not found in either of the others. As I have demonstrated elsewhere, two of these were either adapted from the work of another mid thirteenth–century writer on legal practice, Geoffrey Le Tor, or were derived from the same lost original as Geoffrey's.[17] A third chapter comes from the *Livre au Roi*,[18] while another of these additional chapters alludes to King Hugh III's settlement with Julian lord of Sidon, which presumably took place after Hugh became king of Jerusalem in 1269.[19] The absence of passages elsewhere in Philip's treatise lifted from other identifiable sources coupled with the evident lateness of the section relating to Julian of Sidon strongly suggest that these chapters were added subsequently. The Paris manuscript also shows signs of later editing. One instance in particular is instructive. In chapter nine of Beugnot's edition which sets out the rules for challenging the guarantors in disputes over money and to which I have already referred, where the Venice manuscript gives the time limit for bringing a guarantor from Syria, the Paris manuscript speaks of Armenia instead.[20] The last strongholds in the kingdom of Jerusalem and the other Latin possessions in Syria fell to the Muslims in 1291, but the kingdom of Cilician Armenia remained under Christian rule until late in the fourteenth century. Clearly someone working after the fall of Latin Syria had been bringing Philip's work up to date.

We are left with the anomaly that the one manuscript which gives what appears to be a full version the final form of Philip's text is also by far the latest. The Munich

14. The Paris ms lacks two chapters found in the Venice ms before the end of chapter 53, namely chapters 47 and 48 (= Beugnot chapters 47 and 49). See appendix B.

15. But the similarities may not have been close. For example, whereas the Venice ms places the passage that constitutes the last six lines of Beugnot's chapter 13 (p. 486) at the end of chapter 13, the Munich and Paris mss agree in placing it at the end of chapter 28 (p. 502).

16. *Le Livre au Roi*, ed. Myriam Greilsammer (Paris 1995), pp. 31–2, 65–6.

17. Beugnot, chapters 54–5, pp. 529–30; Geoffrey Le Tor, 'Livre', *RHC Lois*, vol. 1, chapters 6–7, pp. 436–7. Peter W. Edbury, 'The "Livre" of Geoffrey Le Tor and the "Assises" of Jerusalem', in Manuel J. Peláez (ed.), *Historia administrativa y ciencia de la administración comparada* (= *Trabajos en jomenaje a Ferran Valls i Taberner*, vol. 15: Barcelona 1990), pp. 4292–3.

18. Beugnot, chapter 58, p. 531; *Le Livre au Roi*, p. 214.

19. Beugnot, chapter 57, pp. 530–1; Jean Richard, *The Latin Kingdom of Jerusalem*, trans. Janet Shirley (Amsterdam 1979), p. 409.

20. Beugnot, p. 482 and note 6.

manuscript dates to the early 17th century and is a copy of another manuscript which postdated the accession of Queen Charlotte of Cyprus in 1458 and which in turn incorporated material including Philip of Novara's treatise from a copy made by a certain Pol Castressio who completed work on 4 August 1344.[21] Inevitably successive scribes will have modernized the orthography, and this in itself raises the difficult question of the extent to which characteristic Cypriot word–forms and spellings may have survived. Inevitably the copyists will have introduced their own blunders. For example, in the passage referred to above, where the Venice manuscript has 'en la Surie' and the Paris manuscript has 'en Hermenie', the Munich manuscript has 'enseignit' which makes no sense in this context. Elsewhere, where the Venice manuscript makes its only reference to *archontes* ('arcondes'), the Munich manuscript has the meaningless 'orandes'.[22] On the other hand, the Munich manuscript does allow us to fill the *lacunae* in Beugnot's chapter 71 which relates to the partition of fiefs among co–heiresses.[23]

But if the antecedents of the Munich manuscript can be traced back in 1344, the internal evidence provided by the text itself brings us far closer to Philip's own day. A feature of the surviving texts of John of Jaffa's treatise is that they contain chapters copied from Philip's. John's treatise went through several recensions, and with each new revision more material from Philip was added.[24] One chapter (no. 29 of Beugnot's edition) appears in a considerably modified form in all the manuscripts of John's work, and so must either have been part of his treatise from the outset or was incorporated into it at a very early point in the text's history, almost certainly by John himself.[25] The oldest manuscript containing John's work had been dated to *ca.* 1280 and also provides what would appear to be its most primitive extant text. This manuscript uniquely contains the chapter from Philip's work mentioned above in which Philip had referred to John and in which someone, presumably John himself, had

21. Grandclaude, 'Classement sommaire', pp. 467, 468.
22. Beugnot, p. 536. Ms. cod. gall. 771, fols 59ᵛ, 78ᵛ. Cf Venice, Bibl. Marciana: Ms. fr. app. 20 (=265), fol. cclviiiʳ (the ms reads 'artondes' for 'arcondes').
23. Beugnot, p. 542. Ms. cod. gall. 771, fol. 153ʳ. In the Venice ms (fol. ccxxxviiᵛ) the copyist has deliberately left gaps in the text which would indicate that his exemplar was damaged or illegible. With the missing phrases supplied from the Munich ms (in italics) the text reads as follows: 'Apres avint que Dieu fist son coumandement dou riche home quii avoit a nom messire Henri le Buffle. *Celuy avoit trois filles* et estoit seignor de saint Jorge de Labana et de tout *le plus la montaine d'Acre.* Et quant celui fu mort, le conte *Estienne de Blois dist que les trois seurs doivent* partir par connoile, cest a dire que...' Stephen (Estienne) was count of Sancerre (1152–90) and the younger brother of Thibaut V count of Blois (1152–91). Cf Edbury, 'Disputed Regency', pp. 14, 31, 34.
24. Grandclaude, 'Classement sommaire', pp. 441, 445–7. For a fuller discussion, Peter W. Edbury, 'The *Livre des Assises* by John of Jaffa: the Development and Transmission of the Text', in John France and William G. Zajac (eds), *The Crusades and their Sources: Essays Presented to Bernard Hamilton* (Aldershot 1998), pp. 169–79.
25. Beugnot, pp. 232–5, 503–6. Note also that all versions of the text of John of Jaffa chapter 71 and the opening passage of Philip of Novara chapter 28 have distinct textual relationship. Beugnot, pp. 114, 501. See Appendix C.

altered the relevant phrase to introduce the first person. An examination of the manuscripts concerned shows that the John of Jaffa text has followed the chapter divisions of Philip's work as preserved in the Munich manuscript, whereas the Venice manuscript has run two chapters together at this point. In other words, in this instance at least, John of Jaffa was using a text closer to the Munich version than to the Venice version.[26]

The same would seem to be true of the next stage in the development of John's treatise. The manuscript that contains the Venice text of Philip's work also contains John of Jaffa's *magnum opus*. But although the two texts are bound within the one volume, it is clear from paleographical and other internal evidence that they were copied at widely different periods. Jaroslav Folda and I have argued that while the section of the manuscript containing Philip's text dates to the mid fourteenth century, that containing John's writings was copied in Acre in about 1290.[27] The version of John's treatise as contained in the Venice manuscript includes several more chapters 'borrowed' from Philip. One in particular is of interest. Chapter 69 is taken from Philip of Novara chapter 18. But whereas the printed text of Philip's chapter 18, which here follows both the Venice and the Paris manuscripts, stops about half way through the chapter as it appears in John's treatise, the Munich manuscript has the chapter in its entirety. So, the redactor of the Venice text of John's treatise – quite possibly John himself – also had in front of him a version of Philip's work that would seem to have been nearer to that preserved in Munich than to those in the other manuscripts.[28] Two other instances point to the same conclusion. Whereas the Venice and Paris manuscripts of Philip's treatise both present the chapter edited by Beugnot as chapter 11 as a single entity, it is divided in two in the Munich manuscript and the division is preserved in John of Jaffa's treatise at chapters 39 and 40.[29] The Venice manuscript treats the material edited by Beugnot as chapter 51 of Philip's treatise as a single chapter, but the Munich and Paris manuscripts divide it into three shorter chapters; in chapter 199 of the Venice text of John of Jaffa's treatise the redactor has started his interpolation at the point at which the second of these three chapters begins.[30]

So in the late thirteenth century and probably as early as the mid 1260s, a version of Philip of Novara's legal treatise was in existence in which at least some of the chapter divisions were more like those in the Munich manuscript than in the two surviving manuscripts that date from the fourteenth century. But that is not to say that John of Jaffa or whoever was responsible for inserting the sections from Philip's work in-

26. Ms. fr. 19025, fols 105^r–106^r; Ms. cod. gall. 771, fols 133^v–135^v. (The chapter is missing from the Paris ms of Philip of Novara). Cf above, note 10.

27. Edbury and Folda, 'Two Thirteenth–century Manuscripts', pp. 244–9, 250–3.

28. Beugnot, pp. 112–13, 492–3. Ms. cod. gall. 771, fols 83^v–84^v. Cf Paris, Bibliothèque nationale: Ms. fr. 19026, fol. 241^v; Ms. fr. app. 20 (=265), fols ccxiii^v–ccxiv^r.

29. Ms. cod. gall. 771, fols 79^v–81^r; Beugnot, pp. 63–5, 484–5.

30. Ms. cod. gall. 771, fols 121^r–122^v; Ms. fr. 19026, fols 261^v–262^v; Beugnot, pp. 319–20, 526–7.

to the Venice text of his work had a version that was identical in form to the Munich version. In the Venice John of Jaffa we find two instances in which chapters drawn from Philip's work follow directly one after another. Chapters 209 and 210 contains the chapters printed by Beugnot as chapters 37 and 39 of Philip's work. In both the Munich and the Venice manuscripts these chapters are separated by the chapter that Beugnot numbered 38, but in the Paris manuscript these two chapters follow one another directly as in the John of Jaffa text.[31] Similarly chapters 238 and 239 of the Venice John of Jaffa come from chapters 35 and 38 Beugnot's edition of Philip. Again, it is in the Paris manuscript, but not in the other two where they are separated by other discussion, that this material is contiguous, forming part of a much longer chapter which also includes most of the text given by Beugnot as chapters 32–4.[32] These points of similarity between the ordering of the material in the Paris manuscript of Philip's *Livre* and the Venice John of Jaffa must surely be more than just coincidence. However, the Venice text of John of Jaffa contains material from Philip of Novara that is absent from the Paris manuscript,[33] and in other respects, as shown in the discussion in the previous paragraph, the evidence from the interpolations in the John of Jaffa texts indicates that the redactor had a text of Philip of Novara that was unlike that preserved in the Paris manuscript. Further work needs to be done on how the chapters added to John of Jaffa's treatise might allow us to understand the shape and form of Philip's treatise that was available in the thirteenth century. In particular we need to investigate whether the readings in the interpolated passages in the John of Jaffa texts reveal a closer affinity with any one Philip of Novara text than with the others. Such an investigation will require a line–by–line analysis of the text, something which cannot readily be done at present given the inadequacies of Beugnot's edition.

So while a strong case can be made for the text of Philip of Novara that was utilized by John of Jaffa or his redactor in the thirteenth century being more like the Munich version than either the Paris or the Venice versions, it would probably not have been completely identical. But the fact that people who were interested in the law and procedures of the High Court should want to re–cycle Philip's material provides an indication of the importance and influence of his work. Indeed, we find other sections from Philip's *Livre* in later John of Jaffa texts that are preserved in manuscripts in Oxford, Paris, and Rome.[34] What seems to have happened is that John's treatise, which even without the interpolations is considerably longer than Philip's, acquired a greater reputation with the result that in the late thirteenth century and

---

31. Ms. fr. 19026, fols 253ʳ–254ʳ; Beugnot, pp. 334–5, 514, 516.
32. Ms. fr. 19026, fols 249ᵛ–252ᵛ; Beugnot, pp. 382–4, 509–13, 515–16.
33. John of Jaffa chapter 247 is drawn from Philip of Novara chapter 62. Beugnot, pp. 394–5, 532–4. Parts of John of Jaffa chapters 4 and 273 contain material from Philip of Novara chapters 47 and 94. Beugnot, pp. 25–6, 429–30, 521–2, 569–70.
34. See Appendix C.

early fourteenth people were improving it by quarrying sections from Philip of Novara and other writers to fill some of the gaps that John had left in his discussion. In the end, in 1369, it was John's treatise, by now incorporating a sixth if not more of Philip's book, that became an official work of reference in the Cypriot High Court. Some of the chapters from Philip's writings that found their way into the various recensions of John's work are of no particular interest, but it is noteworthy that the doctrine of the *Letres dou sepulcre* only appears in John's treatise because the passage concerned had been adapted from Philip's,[35] and that a theme of several of the chapters inserted into John's treatise is the problem of disputes that arise because the lord has behaved wrongly towards his vassal.[36]

Philip's influence is also to be seen in the writings of his contemporary, Geoffrey Le Tor, with the final eleven chapters of the 'A' text of Geoffrey's work being adapted from Philip's treatise.[37] What is more, his work was still being copied a century or so after it was written. Both the Venice and Paris texts are in compendiums of legal treatises copied in the fourteenth century almost certainly on Cyprus, and, as mentioned already, the Munich text also was derived at one remove from a manuscript copied in 1344.[38] In the early seventeenth century, whoever arranged for the Munich manuscript to be prepared can only have had an antiquarian interest in Philip's *Livre*, but in the fourteenth century it would still have been of practical value to those members of Frankish society in Cyprus who had access to the High Court.

It is, as Grandclaude argued, difficult to reconstruct the text of Philip's treatise as Philip would have wanted it from the surviving manuscripts, although his pessimism on this point may be somewhat overstated.[39] However, it could well be that Philip was never fully satisfied with his work and continued revising it, leaving it incomplete when he died. But even in the unsatisfactory state in which it appears in Beugnot's edition, it stands out as being of considerable interest. How to plead and what the law was are the twin subjects of the book, but on the way there are many insights into the mentalities of the age and the nature of the Lusignan regime. Medieval society in Cyprus was hierarchic, with class, race and religion all having a bearing on legal status and privilege. At the top of the scale were the Frankish vassal–knights, and, so Philip informs us, a knight could not be appealed in a case which could end in trial by battle by a sergeant or burgess or indeed anyone who was not a knight.[40] So while the vassals were not above the law, it would be hard for anyone else to gain redress from

---

35. Peter W. Edbury, 'Law and Custom in the Latin East: *Les Letres dou Sepulcre*', *Mediterranean Historical Review* 10 (1995), pp. 71–9. The essential passages are Beugnot, pp. 25–6, 521–2.

36. Beugnot, pp. 492–3 (cf. pp. 112–13), 507 (cf. p. 238), 508–12 (cf. chapter 240 of John of Jaffa in Ms. Fr. 19026, fols 190ʳ–192ʳ), 514–16 (cf. pp. 334–5, 383–4), 526–7 (cf. pp. 319–20).

37. Edbury, 'The "Livre" of Geoffrey Le Tor', pp. 4293–4.

38. Grandclaude, 'Classement sommaire', pp. 459–62, 467.

39. Grandclaude, 'Classement sommaire', pp. 439–40.

40. Beugnot, p. 486.

one of their number in the courts. This advantageous legal position was reinforced by a rule that said that no one could testify as a bearer of warranty against a Frank in the High Court (and so be liable to fight a judicial battle) if he were not a Catholic ('of the law of Rome'). That immediately ruled out most of the population, but, if that were not enough, no one similarly could bear warranty against a Frank if his testimony was suspect on the grounds that he had lost a lawsuit, or was a perjurer or was guilty of breach of faith. Also barred were defeated champions or men who had served the Muslims in arms against the Christians for more than a year and a day. Philip adds that he is uncertain whether men who had served the Greeks – presumably he means the Byzantines – in arms against the Latins fall under the same exclusion. He then lists bastards, serfs of whatever religion and clergy who had renounced their orders as also disqualified from bearing warranty.[41] But if lawsuits brought by people of other confessions was weighted heavily in the Franks' favour, there was of course plenty of scope for litigation between the members of the ruling elite, and it is with how disputes among the feudatories were to be conducted that Philip's work is primarily concerned. The Cypriot vassals formed a close-knit caste, and their exclusivity is underlined by Philip in the passage that follows the one I have just described:

If the lord has given a fief[42] to a serf or someone disqualified for one of the reasons mentioned above and wants to have him sit in his court saying that he his liege man, and if the court or one of the parties to a dispute wants to bar him, he may well say to the lord, 'Sire, you have the right to enfranchise him since that is your wish, and if he is your vassal you will keep faith with him as you ought, but you are not keeping faith with us. With due respect, neither can you nor should you enfranchise him, nor can you make him our peer.'[43]

It comes as no surprise therefore in a treatise dealing with the business of the High Court that references to non-nobles are sparse. Philip makes it clear that lower down the social scale there was a legal pecking-order determined by religion. If a party to a legal dispute had an *essoin* – a legitimate excuse for non-attendance at court on a particular day – he should report the matter to the court using a Latin Christian as his messenger whenever possible. But if that were not possible, he could use a non-Latin Christian and, failing that, a Muslim.[44] In cases of assault, compensation of 100

41. Beugnot, pp. 501–2, cf. p. 114. For Franks serving in Muslim and Byzantine armies, Jean Richard, 'An Account of the Battle of Hattin referring to the Frankish Mercenaires in Oriental Muslim States', *Speculum* 27 (1952), pp. 171–5.

42. Following the reading of both the Ms. fr. 19026, fol. 245ᵛ and the Ms. cod. gall. 771, fol. 76ʳ ('fié'). This makes better sense than 'feme' as given in the printed text on the basis of the Bibl. Marciana: Ms. fr. app. 20 (=265). Beugnot p. 502 and note 9.

43. Beugnot, p. 502.

44. Beugnot, p. 499. In describing the same topic John of Jaffa (Beugnot, pp. 98–9) puts Jews on the same level as Muslims.

bezants was due to the victim if he were a Frank and another 100 bezants to his lord, but if he were a Syrian, a Greek or a serf, the compensation was a mere 50 *sous* to the victim though 50 bezants were still payable to the lord.[45] The fullest expression of this social stratification comes in Philip's chapter describing the procedure for establishing property boundaries in cases where it would be necessary to rely on local knowledge taken on oath. If possible the group to whom the enquiry had been delegated would take evidence from a Latin Christian. If no one could be found who could testify, they could take evidence from a Syrian; failing that from a Greek, then a Christian of another eastern confession and finally a Muslim. The reference to Syrians – Arabic – speaking Christians – is noteworthy. It probably means that Philip is describing a procedure that had come to Cyprus from the mainland of Latin Syria, and indeed he says as much at the beginning of the chapter. However, there would have been communities of Syrian Christians in the towns on the island at the time he was writing, and, if indeed this passage means that in Cyprus the testimony of a Syrian was to be preferred to that of a Greek, then it can serve as a forceful illustration of the low esteem in which the ruling class viewed the overwhelming majority of the indigenous population.[46] Not that Philip had a particularly high opinion of Syrians either. Elsewhere in his treatise he lambasts them for being more credulous than any other people when it came to believing in astrology.[47]

The Greeks of Cyprus are all but invisible in Philip's treatise. Apart from the instances to which I have just alluded, there are a few scattered references to 'vilains'. It is clear that Philip uses this word to denote the unfree rural population, the *paroikoi* of the Byzantine texts. They were regarded as a type of chattel. 'Vilains on the land or other things that pertain to a fief' can be the subject of litigation, and the lord may demand from his vassal 'land, vilains, a sum of money or anything else that the vassal holds'.[48] 'Vilains' who abscond from the land should be returned, although they too can give rise to disputes between land owners, and the 'vilain' who strikes a knight will loose his right hand.[49] If a 'vilain' dies without heirs, the lord will take two thirds of his effects, leaving the remainder for his widow If she is unable to continue to pay the levies on the land the lord will take her plough and her donkey.[50]

45. Beugnot, p. 546.
46. Beugnot, pp. 532–3. This chapter is included in some mss of John of Jaffa. Beugnot, pp. 394–5.
47. Beugnot, p. 567.
48. Beugnot, pp. 496, 519 (following the reading of the Ms. fr. 19026, fol. 260ᵛ).
49. Beugnot, pp. 535–6, 547.
50. Thus the hitherto unpublished chapter from the Munich ms. See appendix A. On agrarian conditions generally, Jean Richard, 'Agriculture in the Kingdom of Cyprus', in Kenneth M. Setton (ed.), *A History of the Crusades* (Philadelphia/Madison 1955–89), vol. 5, pp. 267–84. Also Peter W. Edbury, 'La classe des propriétaires terriens franco–chypriotes et l'exploration des ressources rurales de l'île de Chypre', in Michel Balard (ed.), *État et colonisation au Moyen Age* (Lyon 1989), pp. 145–52; *idem*, 'Le régime des Lusignan en Chypre et la population locale', in Michel Balard and Alain Ducellier (eds.), *Coloniser au Moyen Age* (Paris 1995), pp. 354–58, 364–5.

So Philip does provide a few glimpses of Cypriot society beyond the circle of the king and his vassals, but what little he does tell us suggests that the regime pressed heavily on the indigenous population. Whether the mass of the peasantry was any worse off under the Franks than they had been under the Byzantines is difficult to know. I suspect that for the individual *paroikos* the change of masters had made little difference. But for those higher up the social ladder the change may have been harsh. Speaking of those vassals whose fiefs consisted of scattered parcels of land, Philip lets slip the information that some of them at least had been endowed with the sequestered lands of churches or abbeys or with the holdings of former Greek *archontes*, a class that seems largely to have disappeared from the Cypriot countryside in the thirteenth century.[51]

51. Beugnot, p. 536, and see above, note 22. Cf. Edbury, 'Le régime des Lusignan en Chypre', p. 355–7; G. Grivaud, 'Les Lusignan et leurs archontes chypriotes (1192–1359)', in *Les Lusignans et l'Outre Mer* (Poitiers 1994), pp. 150–8. Grivaud proves the existence of Greeks in responsible positions in the administration and the civil–service, but evidence for Greek laymen as the holders of significant rural property is lacking.

APPENDIX A

The Bayerische Staatsbibliothek: Codex Gallus 771 contains a single chapter that was unknown Beugnot and so has remained unpublished. Its existence was, however, noted by Grandclaude.[52] The first sentence appears in the manuscript as the concluding lines of the previous chapter (chapter 62 of Beugnot's edition). I have modernized the punctuation and changed 'u' to 'v' where appropriate. Otherwise I have retained the orthography, notably the doubling of the 's' and the running together as a single word of 'desson' for 'de son', 'lesseignour' for 'le seignour' etc.

[fol. 162ʳ] Apres vous devizerai aucune choze de par l'uzage des villains s.ᵃˢ(*sic*) du roiaume de Chippre.

[fol. 162ᵛ] **Sy orés l'uzage des hoirs des villains**

Se il avient que aucun vilain meurt sans hoirs et n'en ay devize faite par le coumandement desson seignour, canque le dit villain a doit estre desson seignour sauve le tiers de tous ses biens que sa feme doit avoir et thenir toute sa vie. Et ce il avient choze que le dessus dit villain deust dete asson seignour ou autre, la dete doit estre paiée. Et c'il avenist que la feme morust sans hoirs, le baron doit avoir le cart de tous ses biens coume de meuble. Et ce elle a heritages de terre ou d'autre chozes, le baron s'ajoiete du cart toute sa vie, et coument que le villain meurt la feme doit faire ce que la charue doit. Et ce ele ne voloit paier les droitures de la charue, lesseignour [fol. 163ʳ] doit avoir la charue garnie et l'ahne.[53] Et c'il avenist que la feme morust et elle lait hoirs apres luy et l'oir meurt aussy, le pere doit avoir et thenir tous les biens et joir s'en toute sa vie. Et tout ausy est il de l'oume coume de la feme.

52. Grandclaude, 'Classement sommaire', p. 432.
53. Cf. Richard, 'Agriculture in the Kingdom of Cyprus', p. 271 and note 82.

APPENDIX B

The table below sets out the sequence of chapters as they appear in the various manuscripts and the printed edition. The Paris manuscript (= B) is the only one in which the copyist provided chapter numbers.

Key:

M: Munich: Bayerische Staatsbibliothek: Codex Gallus 771, fols 52^r–183^r

A: Venice: Biblioteca Nazionale Marciana: Ms. fr. app. 20 (= 265), fols ccv^r–cclx^v

B: Paris: Bibliothèque nationale: Ms. fr. 19026, fols 235^v–264^v

RHC: *Recueil des historiens des croisades. Lois*, ed. Auguste Beugnot, vol. 1, pp. 469–571.

Pro = Prologue. Numbers with 'a', 'b' etc mean first or second part of the chapter.

M	A	B	RHC
Pro	Pro	Pro	Pro
1	1	1	1
2	2	2	2
3	3	3	3
4	4–6	4	4–6
5	7	5	7
6	8	6	8
7	9	7	9
8	10	8	10
9	12	10	12
10	13	11a	13
11–12	14	11b	14
13	15b	22	15b
14	16	23	16
15	15a	21	15a
16	86	–	76
17	82	–	77
18	65	–	75
19	28	26	28
20	83	–	89
21	85	–	90
22	84	–	65
23–4	11	9	11
25	24	18	24
26	25	19	25
27	18	13	18
28	17	12	17
29	19b	14b	19b
30	19a	14a	19a
31	20	15	20
32	21	16	21
33	22	33	22
34	29	34	29
35	31	36	31
36	30	35	30
37	87	–	64
38	23	17	23
39	32a	27	32a
40	32b–34	28a	32b–34
41	35	28b	35
42	36	29	36
43	37	30	37
44	38	28c	38
45	39	31	39
46	40	32	40
47	41	37	41
48	42	38	42

M	A	B	RHC
49	47–9	–,41c	47,49–50
50	50a	42	51a
51	50b	43	51b
52	50c	44	51c
53	51	45–7	52
54	52–3	48	53, 59
55	43	39	43
56	45	41a	45
57	46	41b	46
58	70a	–	83a
59	70b	–	83b
60	26	20	26
61	63a	–	73a
62	63b	–	73b
63	64	–	74
64	69	–	82
65	44	40	44
66	71	–	84
67	72	–	85
68	27	24–5	27
69	68	–	81
70	57–8	–	67–8
71	59	–	69
72	60	–	70
73	61–2	–	71–2
74	73	–	86
75	81	–	48
76	56	–	62
77	–	–	–
78	66	–	79
79	67	–	80
80	74–5	–	87–8
81	76	–	91
82	77	–	92
83	78	–	93
84	79	–	94
–	54	–	60
–	55	–	61
–	80	–	63
–	88	–	78
–	89	–	66
–	–	49	54
–	–	50	55
–	–	51	56
–	–	52	57
–	–	53	58

III

APPENDIX C

Not all the extraneous material incorporated into the various recensions of John of Jaffa's treatise can be identified as originating in other extant works. What follows is a provisional list of those chapters from Philip's treatise that have been inserted or adapted, wholly or in part, into the manuscript copies of John's treatise. The chapter numbers refer to Beugnot's edition except where stated.

1. All the manuscripts of John of Jaffa contain one chapter (155) adapted from Philip of Novara chapter 29.

2. Paris: Bibliothèque nationale: Ms. fr. 19025 (Beugnot's ms C) contains most of Philip of Novara chapter 73 (above note 25).

3. Oxford: Bodleian, Selden Supra 69 (unknown to Beugnot) contains Philip of Novara chapter 48.

4. Venice: Biblioteca Nazionale Marciana: Ms. fr. app. 20 (= 265) (the ancestor of Beugnot's ms A), Paris: Bibliothèque nationale: Ms. fr. 19026 (Beugnot's ms B), and Rome: Vatican, Codex Vaticanus Latinus 4789 (the ancestor of Beugnot's mss D and E) have a number of chapters from Philip of Novara in common: Philip of Novara chapters 11 (= John chapters 38–40); 20–2 (= John chapter 170); 30 (= John chapter 158); 37 (= John chapter 209); 38 (= John chapter 239); 39 (= John chapter 210), 51 (= John chapter 199); 62 (= John chapter 247). In addition, parts of Philip of Novara chapters 47 and 94 have been incorporated into John of Jaffa chapters 4 and 273.

5. In addition the Venice and Vatican mss both have Philip of Novara 18 (= John chapter 69), and the Venice ms and the Paris Ms. fr. 19026 both have Philip of Novara 35 (= John chapter 238).

6. The Paris Ms. fr. 19026 has a fuller version of chapters 20–2 than the Venice ms (See John chapter 170). It also contains Philip of Novara 32 beginning of 35 (chapter 240 of ms) and 92 (chapter 258 of ms) neither of which are in Beugnot's edition of John of Jaffa.

7. The Codex Vat. Lat. 4789 is derived from the official version of John's treatise as established in Cyprus in 1369. Chapter 266 of this ms is a greatly expanded version of Philip of Novara chapter 30 which also appears earlier in more or less its original form. Like the Paris Ms. fr. 19026 it also contains Philip of Novara 32–beginning of 35 (chapters 254–5 of ms) and 92 (chapter 274 of ms) neither of which are in Beugnot's edition.

The *Livre des Assises* by John of Jaffa: The Development and Transmission of the Text

John of Ibelin, count of Jaffa, was one of the greatest noblemen in the Latin East in the mid-thirteenth century. Indeed, during the two decades which preceded his death in 1266 he was part of the small coterie of closely related aristocrats that dominated the truncated kingdom of Jerusalem. John's father, Philip of Ibelin, had acted as regent of Cyprus for most of the 1220s, and his uncle, John of Ibelin, lord of Beirut, had led the opposition to the emperor, Frederick II, and his supporters in Cyprus and Latin Syria between 1228 and 1236. The Ibelins were closely related by marriage to the royal houses of both Cyprus and Jerusalem, and John of Jaffa, who was born c. 1215, inherited property in both kingdoms. In the years 1232-33 he was just old enough to be a participant in the closing stages of the civil war in Cyprus against the emperor's partisans, but his greatest prominence began in about 1246 when he acquired the county of Jaffa. It has been suggested that he obtained it as part of a deal which opened the way for the then king of Cyprus, Henry I, to take control in Acre – at that time by far the wealthiest city in Christian hands in the Levant. As count of Jaffa, John was responsible for the most southerly Christian-held territory in the Latin East. He himself briefly held the regency of the kingdom of Jerusalem (1254-56), and in 1258 he intervened decisively in the War of St Sabas, fought between the Genoese and the Venetians in and around Acre, by bringing the authorities there firmly over to the side of the Venetians. His marriage to an Armenian princess also involved him in the politics of Cilician Armenia, and his illicit relationship with the widowed queen of Cyprus around 1260 was sufficiently notorious to earn him a rebuke from Pope Urban IV. There is some reason to suppose that his pre-eminence faded in the last few years of his life. Jaffa itself fell to the Muslims in 1268, two years after his death.[1]

In the mid-1260s, not long before he died, John composed a treatise on the procedures of the High Court of Jerusalem and the customary law of the kingdom.[2] He wrote in French, and his treatise together with some other similar though shorter works by his contemporaries, Philip of Novara and Geoffrey Le Tor, and by his son, James of Ibelin, comprise a major source for our understanding of the social and legal fabric of the Latin East. Rather misleadingly these works are usually known collectively as the '*Assises* of Jerusalem'. John's treatise continued to be copied and modified in Cyprus after the fall of Latin Syria in 1291, and in 1369 a version of his work was adopted as an official work of reference in the Cypriot High Court. It retained its importance long after, and in 1531 the Venetian authorities in Cyprus had it translated into Italian.[3]

The text of John's treatise has been published twice. The earlier edition by G. Thaumas de la Thaumasière appeared in 1690 and was taken from a late and very corrupt manuscript copy.[4] The edition still used by modern scholars was prepared for publication by Comte A. Beugnot and appeared in 1841 in the first volume of the *Recueil des historiens des croisades: Lois*. The manuscript tradition was elucidated by Maurice Grandclaude in an article published in 1926.[5] In this article Grandclaude exposed the inadequacies of Beugnot's edition, but until now no one has taken up the challenge to examine the manuscripts further and set about preparing a critical edition.

---

[1] J. Riley-Smith, *The Feudal Nobility and the Kingdom of Jerusalem, 1174-1277* (London, 1973), chapters 7-8 passim. For a debate over particular aspects of his career, see P.W. Edbury, 'John of Ibelin's Title to the County of Jaffa and Ascalon', *English Historical Review* 98 (1983), pp. 115-22; H.E. Mayer, 'John of Jaffa, his Opponents and his Fiefs', *Proceedings of the American Philosophical Society* 128 (1984), pp. 134-63.

[2] For the date, M. Grandclaude, *Étude critique sur les livres des assises de Jérusalem* (Paris, 1923), p. 88.

[3] Grandclaude, *Étude critique*, pp. 82-3.

[4] G. Thaumas de la Thaumasière, ed., *Coustumes de Beauvoisis, par Messire Philippes de Beaumanoir Bailly de Clermont en Beauvoisis. Assises et bons usages du royaume de Jerusalem, par Messire Jean d'Ibelin Comte de Japhe et de Ascalon, S. de Rames et de Baruth* (Bourges, 1690). For the inadequacies of the text as published in 1690, see P.W. Edbury, 'The Disputed Regency of the Kingdom of Jerusalem, 1264/6 and 1268', in *Camden Miscellany* 27, *Camden Fourth Series* 22 (London, 1979), pp. 2-3.

[5] M. Grandclaude, 'Classement sommaire des manuscrits des principaux livres des assises de Jérusalem', *Revue historique de droit français et étranger*, sér. 4, 5 (1926), pp. 418-75.

Five medieval manuscripts of John's treatise survive, and these five manuscripts will form the basis for a modern edition:

(1) Paris, Bibliothèque Nationale (BN): ms. fr. 19025 (= Beugnot's manuscript C)

(2) Oxford, Bodleian: Selden Supra 69 (not used by Beugnot)

(3) Venice, Marciana: fr. app. 20 (= 265) (not used by Beugnot who used an eighteenth-century copy as his manuscript A)

(4) Paris, Bibliothèque Nationale (BN): ms. fr. 19026 (= Beugnot's manuscript B)

(5) Rome, Vatican: Codex Vaticanus latinus 4789 (not used by Beugnot who used corrupt seventeenth-century derivatives as his manuscripts D and E).

Each manuscript is unique, with no two preserving an identical text. All contain material added after John of Jaffa had laid down his pen. Beugnot's printed edition reproduces more or less the text as found in the Marciana manuscript, but, as will be seen, that manuscript contains a version of the text that stands mid-way in its development.

The oldest manuscript is the BN 19025, which was copied in Acre in the 1280s.[6] The manuscript contains solely John's treatise, and the text would seem to be the closest we can get to his original. But even this manuscript, copied perhaps no more than a decade and a half after his death, contains at least one interpolation. Sandwiched between the chapters which in Beugnot's edition are numbered 143 and 144 there is a passage lifted from Philip of Novara's treatise. It appears in no other John of Jaffa manuscript, but is of considerable interest.[7] In Philip's version of this passage there is mention of John of Jaffa himself, and in the BN 19025 the phrase is recast into the first person: it reads 'je meismes m'en entremis moult' for 'moult s'en entremist le conte de Jaffe'. This immediately raises the question of whether John himself was responsible for this insertion. It is quite likely that he was. Elsewhere there is another chapter taken from Philip of Novara which appears in a modified

---

[6] P.W. Edbury and J. Folda, 'Two Thirteenth-Century Manuscripts of Crusader Legal Texts from Saint-Jean d'Acre', *Journal of the Warburg and Courtauld Institutes* 57 (1994), pp. 250, 253-4 and plate 32.

[7] BN 19025, chapter 129/fol. 105ᵛ. This chapter consists of approximately three-quarters of Philip of Novara's chapter 73 ('Livre de forme de plait', *RHC Lois*, 1.543-4 [hereafter Philip of Novara]). One manuscript of Philip's treatise has a chapter-break where the chapter ends in John of Jaffa. Munich, Bayerische Staatsbibliothek: ms. cod. gall. 771, fols 133ᵛ-135ᵛ.

form in all the manuscripts of John of Jaffa's law book.[8] It must therefore have been inserted at a very early stage in the transmission of the text and indeed was probably part of John's original version.

The Selden manuscript in the Bodleian Library in Oxford is datable to the fourteenth century and is of Cypriot provenance. In the sixteenth century it belonged to Francesco Attar, a member of the commission set up by the Venetian authorities in Cyprus to arrange the translation of John's treatise into Italian.[9] The text is very close to that in the BN 19025; indeed, of all the medieval manuscripts, these two are by far the closest. It lacks the chapter from Philip of Novara found in the BN 19025 that refers to John of Jaffa, but instead it contains another chapter from Philip's work which is not found elsewhere in the manuscripts of John's law book.[10] Incidentally there is one other chapter common to both these first two manuscripts, but not found in any of the others. It concerns trial by battle in disputes over debt.[11]

The Marciana manuscript is really rather special. This is a large and lavishly produced codex which consists of two separate sections. The first, which starts with John of Jaffa's treatise, contains a fine miniature which is undoubtedly the work of the artist Professor Folda rather unhelpfully dubbed the 'Hospitaller Master' and who was probably at work in Acre from around 1276 until its fall in 1291.[12] This manuscript – or rather this section of the manuscript – seems to date to c. 1290, and it contains besides John's treatise, his discourse on the

---

[8] John of Ibelin, 'Livre des Assises de la Haute Cour', *RHC Lois*, 1, chapter 155/pp. 232-5 [hereafter John of Ibelin]; Philip of Novara, chapter 29/pp. 503-6.

[9] Grandclaude, 'Classement sommaire', pp. 456-8. There are various reports on population and other information about Cyprus in the sixteenth century attributed to Francesco Attar. See B. Arbel, 'Cypriot Population under Venetian Rule (1473-1571): A Demographic Study', *Meletai kai Ipomnimata* 1 (1984), pp. 194-5.

[10] Selden Supra 69, fol. 30[r-v]. It is placed between chapters 44 and 45 of Beugnot's edition of John's text, and is Philip of Novara, chapter 48/p. 523.

[11] BN 19025, fols 207[v]-209[r]; Selden Supra 69, fols 289[r]-291[v]. It is not published by Beugnot. Grandclaude ('Classement sommaire', p. 441 n. 5) errs in claiming that it is John of Ibelin, chapter 250 *bis*/pp. 401-2, although the rubric is very similar. A marginal note in the Selden ms. asserts that it is taken from Philip of Novara, but I have not found it there.

[12] Edbury and Folda, 'Two Thirteenth-Century Manuscripts', pp. 243-9, 250-3 and plate 31 which reproduces the miniature which shows Godfrey of Bouillon standing in the city of Jerusalem presenting the laws of the kingdom to the assembled notables. For the 'Hospitaller Master', see J. Folda, *Crusader Manuscript Illumination at Saint-Jean d'Acre, 1275-1291* (Princeton, 1976), chapters 3-4.

regency of Jerusalem, the 'A' text of Geoffrey Le Tor,[13] the treatise by John's son, James of Ibelin, which was written in 1276, the earlier recension of the *Lignages d'Outremer* which appears to have been compiled in the 1270s, a short treatise on trial by battle which until recently was believed to belong to the mid-fourteenth century, and the pleading between King Hugh III of Cyprus and James of Ibelin in the dispute of 1271 as to whether the knights of Cyprus owed service outside the island. The second part of the Marciana manuscript would appear to have been copied in Cyprus towards the middle of the fourteenth century and contains five other texts including Philip of Novara's law book and the so called *Abrégé du livre des assises de la cour des bourgeois*. The text of John's treatise in this manuscript contains a substantial number of interpolations scattered through it. The most obvious category of these additions comprises passages copied or adapted from Philip of Novara, including much of the material which makes up the final chapter in Beugnot's edition of John of Jaffa, a chapter which is absent from both the manuscripts discussed in the previous paragraphs. In all there are about a dozen chapters as well as shorter extracts taken from Philip of Novara. In other words, the phenomenon that we have seen already in the earlier versions is here continued on a much larger scale.[14] Two particular aspects of this material are worth noting. The sole reference in Beugnot's edition of John of Jaffa to the *Letres dou Sepulcre* is introduced at this stage from Philip of Novara's treatise with the result that the apparent unanimity of the two writers on this question proves to be a chimera. I have argued elsewhere that the *Letres dou Sepulcre* were a piece of mid-thirteenth-century legal fiction designed to protect Latin Syrian

---

[13] For Geoffrey Le Tor and his writings, see P.W. Edbury, 'The *Livre* of Geoffrey Le Tor and the *Assises* of Jerusalem', in *Historia administrativa y ciencia de la administración comparada*, ed. M.J. Pelaez, *Trabaios en homenaje a Ferran Valls i Taberner* 15 (Barcelona, 1990), pp. 4291-8.

[14] In the following list the chapters in the text of John of Jaffa's treatise either copy the chapters from Philip of Novara's treatise or employ material adapted from it. John, chapter 4 = Philip, chapter 47; John, chapters 38-40 = Philip, chapter 11; John, chapter 69 = Philip, chapter 18 (the text of Philip of Novara in the Munich, Bayerische Staatsbibliothek: ms. cod. gall. 771, fols 83ᵛ-84ᵛ gives the entire chapter as it appears in John's treatise, whereas the published edition of Philip of Novara (at pp. 492-3) has only about half); John, chapter 158 = Philip, chapter 30; John, chapter 170 = Philip, chapters 20-2; John, chapter 199 = Philip, chapter 51; John, chapter 209 = Philip, chapter 37; John, chapter 210 = Philip, chapter 39; John, chapter 238 = Philip, chapter 35; John, chapter 239 = Philip, chapter 38; John, chapter 247 = Philip, chapter 62; John, chapter 273 = Philip, chapter 94.

practice from being overridden by arguments from French customary law.[15] Secondly, in one of these passages where Philip refers to John of Ibelin, the Old Lord of Beirut (died 1236), the John of Jaffa text refers to him in the way John normally does – as 'my uncle, the Old Lord of Beirut' – and the author alludes to himself in the first person.[16] This raises various questions: was John of Jaffa himself responsible for including this passage in this version of his treatise? If so, had he revised his work so as to include all the other passages and extracts that are in the Marciana manuscript but not in the BN 19025 or the Selden Supra 69? Alternatively, has a later redactor inserted these passages and been rather clever in adapting the allusion to John of Beirut to bring it into line with the other instances in which he appears in the treatise? If John himself revised the work to include this new material, he must have done so very soon after the completion of the first version as represented by the BN 19025 and the Selden Supra 69. The Marciana manuscript, though copied c. 1290, would thus contain a text that had been in existence since the mid-1260s. On the other hand, if the new material was added by someone else, then there are two and half decades in which this could have happened. As has been noted, several of the other texts in this part of the manuscript date from the 1270s. Maybe these revisions date from that period too, in which case we might wonder whether John's son, James of Ibelin, had some part in them.

But there are other additions in the Marciana version of John of Jaffa's treatise that are not from Philip of Novara and which I have not been able to identify. Chapter 130 deals with debt; chapters 193-4 deal with oaths due to the king or regent; chapter 228 discusses aspects of *servise de mariage* – the lord's rights to oblige heiresses to marry; and chapters 251-5 consider the subject of serfs. Clearly there was an awareness that, long though it was, John's original treatise had not discussed everything, and so someone – perhaps John himself, perhaps his son James, perhaps another person altogether – felt free to add texts culled from elsewhere, in particular from the treatise by Philip of Novara, or to include new material. Perhaps these interpolations warrant special attention as concerning matters that people may have considered important. But in connection with Philip of Novara, there is another point that is worth making. The BN 19025 and the Marciana manuscript both date from the closing decades of the thirteenth century; they are thus

---

[15] P.W. Edbury, 'Law and Custom in the Latin East: *Les Letres dou Sepulcre*', *Mediterranean Historical Review* 10 (1995), pp. 71-9.

[16] John of Ibelin, chapter 239/pp. 383-4 left-hand column; Philip of Novara, chapter 38/pp. 515-16. For John of Beirut as the author's uncle, John of Ibelin, pp. 112, 325, 327.

appreciably older than any manuscript copy of Philip of Novara's work (two mid-fourteenth-century manuscripts and one early seventeenth-century manuscript),[17] and so the interpolations drawn from there would be of the utmost importance in the preparation of any new edition of Philip's treatise – itself a subject that is both strewn with difficulties and at the same time a major desideratum.

Like the Marciana manuscript, the BN 19026 contains several works: part of the *Livre des assises de la cour des bourgeois*, the *Lignages d'Outremer*, James of Ibelin, the 'B' text of Geoffrey Le Tor, Philip of Novara and the *Livre au Roi*. It appears to date from the mid-fourteenth century and is probably from Cyprus.[18] The text it gives of John of Jaffa's treatise is best thought of as a development from the text found in the Marciana manuscript. It has grown even longer, with eleven more chapters, of which six were not printed by Beugnot in his edition of John of Jaffa.[19] Some are lifted from other extant writings: Philip of Novara yet again, Geoffrey Le Tor and the *Assises de la cour de bourgeois*.[20] Others I am unable to identify. Maybe they were composed by the redactor of the version preserved in this manuscript. Perhaps the most interesting are two chapters outlining the moral qualities that are expected of a ruler with references to Aristotle and Cicero.[21] But despite their intrinsic interest, these chapters seem far removed from the twin subjects of John's treatise: the law and procedures of the High Court.

Finally we come to the text preserved in the Vatican manuscript. This is a fifteenth-century codex containing John's law book together with an early fourteenth-century version of the *Lignages d'Outremer* and some other, later accretions. It starts with a prologue explaining how John's treatise was revised

---

[17] Grandclaude, 'Classement sommaire', pp. 459-60, 467-71; Edbury and Folda, 'Two Thirteenth-Century Manuscripts', p. 244.

[18] Grandclaude, 'Classement sommaire', pp. 459-60.

[19] Published by Beugnot: John of Ibelin, chapters 176 *bis*, 226 *bis* (where 'manuscrit C' is an error for 'manuscrit B'), 234 *bis*, 250 *bis*, 250 *ter*/pp. 277-9, 358-9, 372, 401-3. Not published by Beugnot: BN 19026, chapters 9, 240, 254, 257, 265, 266.

[20] BN 19026, chapter 9 = 'Livre des assises de la cour des bourgeois', *RHC Lois*, 2, chapter 2/p. 20; BN 19026, chapter 240 = Philip of Novara, chapters 32-4 and the beginning of 35/pp. 508-12; BN 19026, chapter 257 = Geoffrey Le Tor, 'Livre', *RHC Lois*, 1, chapter 16/p. 449; BN 19026, chapter 258 = Philip of Novara, chapter 92/pp. 564-7. The BN 19026 also has a fuller version of Philip of Novara, chapters 20-22 than in the printed text at chapter 170/pp. 261-2.

[21] BN 19026, chapters 125-6/fols 206^r-207^r. These chapters were printed by G. Thaumas de la Thaumasière (above note 4) from a manuscript derived from the Vaticanus latinus 4789 at pp. 187-8.

and established as a work of reference in the High Court of Cyprus following the murder of King Peter I in January 1369. The clear implication is that this is a copy of that revision. It contains embedded within it the text of the *bailliage* pleading from the 1260s and the formal claim for the throne advanced by King Hugh IV of Cyprus in 1324.[22] The *Lignages d'Outremer* is similarly treated as an integral part of the text. Comparing the text with that of the Marciana and BN 19026 manuscripts we find that, while it is broadly similar, there are some new additions, several of which can be identified as coming from Philip of Novara, James of Ibelin, Geoffrey Le Tor or the *Livre au Roi*.[23] Three of the eleven chapters found in the BN 19026 but not in the Marciana manuscript are omitted.[24] How many of these additional chapters were introduced in 1369 and how many were already in the text or texts that were being employed at that time is unknowable. Of the unidentified additions, there is one that is of especial interest in the light of an earlier aspect of this discussion: a chapter that is unique to this version of John of Jaffa's treatise again refers to John of Ibelin, lord of Beirut, as 'my uncle'.[25] It is impossible to know what to make of this addition or when it first appeared in a text of the treatise: there is no particular reason to believe that it was new in 1369. The genealogical information in the *Lignages* stops dead in the first decade of the fourteenth century, and it may be wondered whether some of the other additions or modifications belong rather to that period than to 1369. How the text as preserved in the Vaticanus latinus 4789 fared as an official work of reference is not at all clear: when, in 1531, the Venetians decided that they wanted an Italian translation prepared they appear to have been unaware of this version and relied instead on the manuscript now in Venice.

Perhaps the most obvious point to be made by way of conclusion is that in its original form John of Jaffa's law book was not nearly as similar in content

---

[22] The 1260s *bailliage* pleading has been re-edited from the Vaticanus latinus 4789 in Edbury, 'Disputed Regency' (see note 4). For Hugh IV's accession, see *RHC Lois*, 2.419-22. The Vaticanus latinus 4789 also includes the texts published as 'Bans et Ordonnances des rois de Chypre', *RHC Lois*, 2, nos. 25, 31, 33/pp. 368-70, 373-7, 378-9 [hereafter 'Bans et Ordonnances']. No. 33 should be dated 16 January 1368 (i.e. 1369 n.s.).

[23] Vaticanus latinus 4789, chapter 265 is adapted from James of Ibelin, 'Livre', *RHC Lois*, 1, chapter 62/p. 467; the opening of chapter 266 comes from Philip of Novara, chapter 30/p. 507; chapter 273 = 'Livre au Roi', *RHC Lois*, 1, chapter 21/p. 620; chapters 283-4 = James of Ibelin, chapter 1/pp. 453-4.

[24] BN 19026, chapters 9, 177 (= John of Ibelin, chapter 176 *bis*/pp. 277-9), 237 (= John of Ibelin, chapter 234 *bis*/p. 372).

[25] John of Ibelin, chapter 63 *bis*/p. 103.

and style to Philip of Novara's as is usually assumed. It should also be realized that John of Jaffa wrote appreciably less than might be imagined from using the standard edition of his work. The text as given in the Vaticanus latinus is around 25-30% longer than in the earliest manuscript, the BN 19025. After the original version had been composed, the work was modified, largely by inter-polations from other works. Where there is new material which cannot be identified, it could be that we are seeing fragments of a lost treatise or treatises, or it may be that the redactor has written something new. The additions, and also the changes in chapter divisions – not a subject which is necessary to discuss here – and the chapters which only appear in one or perhaps two manuscripts and are then lost to view suggest that the five manuscripts that survive from the middle ages represent only a tiny proportion of the whole and a plethora of different texts had once existed. Were another manuscript to come to light, it might well have a version that is different again. Identifying the provenance of the interpolations is all very well, but there is another, as yet unexplored, dimension to the problem: how far do the modifications to the text represent changes in the law or the customary procedures? As with modern law text-books that go through numerous editions, so changes to the text may, in certain instances, reflect changes to the law. Law is not static, and, in the absence of other evidence, a line-by-line, chapter-by-chapter analysis may produce indications of legislation and changes to legal custom in the century between the mid-1260s and the death of Peter I of Cyprus in 1369. This is a matter for future study. If the book was to be of practical use to lawyers, then we might expect to find it brought up to date by subsequent generations. But was it? The decision to make it an official work of reference in Cyprus in 1369, and the decision to have it translated into Italian in 1531 suggest that the answer is yes. On the other hand, the manu-scripts do not have the sort of marginal annotations we might expect to find if practitioners in the courts were utilizing them in preparing their pleas. Moreover, some of the accretions seem to betray an interest in constitutional and genealogical rather than legal matters and so add an antiquarian flavour to the work. Antiquaries in France in the seventeenth century such as Peiresc sought out copies of the work; maybe even earlier it was valued more for its intellectual stimulus and historical information than for its utility in the courts – but that is another topic for another occasion.

Appendix

This discussion has highlighted the need for a new edition of John of Jaffa's treatise, but until such time as one is forthcoming historians will have to continue using Beugnot's text in the *Recueil des historiens des croisades: Lois*. These notes are designed to help readers find their way round that edition in the light of what has been said.

There are some variations in the order the chapters appear in the manuscripts, and in some instances chapters have been divided or run together. I shall not attempt to list these variants, and in any case they are probably of little significance.

1) Beugnot used a copy made from the Marciana manuscript as his base (ms. A). This means that his edition, excluding the chapters that he numbered *bis* or *ter* (e.g. 63 *bis*, 250 *ter*), gives a close representation of the Marciana text.

2) The earlier form of John's treatise is represented by the BN 19025 and the Selden manuscripts. These two manuscripts give an almost identical text except for the two single additions from Philip of Novara described above (notes 7 and 10). Neither of these chapters is included in Beugnot's edition of John's treatise. Beugnot used the BN 19025 as his ms. C, and the chapters that were added subsequently are usually indicated by the words 'manque dans C' in the apparatus. They are Beugnot's chapters 38-40, 69, 130, 158, 165, 170, 193-4, 199, 209-10, 228, 238-9, 247, 251-5, 273 together with all the chapters numbered *bis* or *ter*. For an example of a shorter omitted passage (dealing with the *Letres dou Sepulcre*), see John of Ibelin, p. 25 n. 42. There is one chapter in these two manuscripts that is not published by Beugnot and is not found in the other manuscripts (above note 11).

3) The version in the BN 19026 (Beugnot's ms. B) marks a development of the Marciana text though lacks Beugnot's chapter 69. It does however contain chapter 2 of the *Assises de la cour des bourgeois* sandwiched between Beugnot's chapters 8 and 9; chapters 32-4 and the beginning of chapter 35 of Philip of Novara (between chapters 236 and 237); chapter 16 of the 'B' text of Geoffrey Le Tor and chapter 92 of Philip of Novara (immediately before chapter 251). In addition it contains the chapters numbered by Beugnot as 176 *bis*, 226 *bis*, 234 *bis*, 250 *bis* and 250 *ter*. Two chapters which appear immediately before Beugnot's chapter 256 are not printed by

Beugnot, but are to be found in la Thaumasière's edition (see above note 21).

4) Beugnot did not use the Vaticanus latinus 4789, but he did have two manuscripts (D and E) as well as la Thaumasière's edition (T) which were derived from it. Those texts are seriously defective, with substantial omissions; in consequence, the words in Beugnot's apparatus, 'manque dans DET', are of no help in establishing what the Vaticanus latinus 4789 contains or does not contain. The Vaticanus latinus 4789 lacks Beugnot's chapters 130, 176 *bis*, 193, 234 *bis*, as well as the chapter from the *Assises de la cour des bourgeois* found in the BN 19026. Otherwise it contains all the material in the BN 19026. It alone of the medieval manuscripts contains the following chapters: 63 *bis*, 127 *bis*, 170 *bis*, 172 *bis*. There is also a short chapter printed by Beugnot in his apparatus (John of Ibelin, p. 128). Sandwiched between Beugnot's chapters 225 and 226 there is an unpublished chapter on the subject of summonses to court. Between Beugnot's chapters 247 and 248 there is a chapter taken from James of Ibelin (chapter 62) and a much expanded version of Philip of Novara (chapter 30). After Beugnot's chapter 249 there is a chapter from the *Livre au Roi* (chapter 21). Immediately before Beugnot's chapter 194 (itself re-positioned later in the text) there are two chapters derived from the first chapter of James of Ibelin's treatise. There is a substantial body of material inserted between Beugnot's chapters 259 (the office of the chamberlain) and 260 (the start of the account of the ecclesiastical hierarchy in Jerusalem). This consists of: (i) the texts from the 1260s edited by Beugnot as 'Documents relatifs à la successibilité au trône et à la régence', *RHC Lois*, 2, chapters 3-17/pp. 401-19 and for which a modern edition exists (see above note 22); (ii) an ordinance of 1311 (1310 o.s.) from Cyprus published as 'Bans et Ordonnances', no. 25/pp. 368-70; (iii) Hugh IV's claim to the throne of Cyprus, 1324: 'Documents relatifs à la successibilité', chapter 18/pp. 419-22; (iv) ordinances of 1355 and 1369, also from Cyprus: 'Bans et Ordonnances', nos. 31, 33/pp. 373-7, 378-9. At the end of the text the recension of the *Lignages d'Outremer* dating from the 1300s follows without a break and with continuous chapter numbers (chapters 331-61).

V

Women and the customs of the High Court of Jerusalem according to John of Ibelin

John of Ibelin completed his *Livre des assises et des usages et des plais de la haute cort dou reiaume de Jerusalem* in the mid 1260s. It is a long work – 160,000 words – and additions made by John himself after his first version was completed and then by later redactors made it longer still.[1] It falls into two main parts: a description of the laws and procedures of the High Court of Jerusalem, and, secondly, a description of the feudal customs of the kingdom. Frankish society in the Latin East was, as elsewhere in the middle ages, male dominated, and that was certainly true of the courts. However, the right of women to legal protection through the courts was never in question, and John was careful to give their position and concerns due weight in his discussion. He made numerous references to women in his text, many of them in the context of such gender-specific topics as the rights of heiresses, marriage, widowhood and dower. At first sight it would appear that he gave much less attention to the rights and attributes of the woman litigant, although, as will be seen, he did include some revealing material on this topic as well.

The right of a woman to inherit property was never in doubt. John explains that on the death of a fief-holder, the fief would pass by inheritance to the closest eligible relative of the deceased. A male heir would always inherit in preference to a female heir in the same degree of relationship, but, as is clear from John's treatment of the subject, a female had precedence over a more distantly related male.[2] If the deceased had had just one fief, it would pass in its entirety to the eldest male heir and any younger brothers would get nothing, but if there was no male heir, then all the female heirs in the same degree of relationship to the deceased – most commonly these would be his daughters – would divide the fief among themselves. However, if the deceased had held several fiefs and there were several male heirs in the same relationship to the deceased, they would be entitled to inherit one fief each and would chose them in order of seniority. If this happened, and there were more fiefs than there were male heirs, then, after the men had made their choices, any female relatives in the same relationship could have a part in the inheritance too. But whereas the male heirs would each take a complete fief – the principle being that, if there were more heirs than fiefs, the younger heirs would get nothing – the women would split the fiefs so that every relative in the same relationship to the deceased would get a share. Indeed, John was careful to specify

1. For a new edition, carefully distinguishing the original material from later additions, JOHN OF IBELIN, *Le Livre des Assises*, ed. P. W. EDBURY, Leiden 2003 (The medieval Mediterranean 50). This supersedes the nineteenth-century edition in *RHC Lois*, I.
2. JOHN OF IBELIN, p. 331, 391.

that the only circumstance in which a fief owing a single knight to the lord could be divided was when there were several co-heiresses, and he described at some length the details of precisely how, in the absence of a male heir, the fief was to be divided among sisters.[3]

Behind these inheritance customs lay the lord's need to preserve military services. Lords did not want a single individual acquiring more than one fief for which personal *servise de cors* was owed, as in these circumstances the holder would need to find someone to deputise for him in all the fiefs but the first: hence the rule that the accumulated holdings should be divided among his heirs rather than pass intact to the eldest. But, on the other hand, there was the obvious danger that if a fief was split into units owing less than a knight to the lord's host, the lord might be unable to extract the service of a knight when he needed it. But that does not explain why heiresses could divide a fief and its attendant services into fractions, and John made no attempt to justify this feature of inheritance law. His slightly older contemporary, Philip of Novara, stated in his treatise that originally the eldest heiress would have inherited a fief in its entirety in the absence of a male heir, and the principle that she would have to divide it with her younger sisters was only established as a legal precedent following the death of a nobleman named Henry Le Bufle. Henry's death can be dated to between 1165 and 1171, and the decision to divide his holdings was said to have been taken on the advice of Count Stephen of Sancerre who was then in the East. Henry's fief had owed ten knights to the king, and by the terms of the settlement each of Henry's three sons-in-law became liable to the service of three and one third knights. It would seem that Stephen was advising the court to follow a practice that was widespread in the West, but it is difficult to avoid the suspicion that the decision came about because the husbands of Henry's younger daughters – the principal beneficiaries of his advice – had the necessary influence.[4]

A woman could marry at the age of twelve. At that age an heiress to a fief owing *servise de cors* could be required by her feudal lord to take a husband, and, until such time as she married, whoever had held the wardship (or *bailliage*) of her inheritance during her childhood would continue to hold it. Similarly, the feudal property of an unmarried heiress who was over twelve when she inherited it would be administered by whoever would have been entitled to the wardship had she been under age, and this state of affairs would continue until she married. Then again, an unmarried woman over the age of twelve who acquired rights of wardship over the property of a relative owing *servise de cors* would herself now be liable to marry at the behest of the lord of the fief.[5]

The right of the lord to summon the heiress to a fief owing *servise de cors* to take a husband was never in question, the rationale being that the husband could thereupon be called upon to perform the service owed.[6] The heiress could therefore be said to 'owe the lord marriage' although it might be noted that John is sparing in his use of the phrase 'servise de mariage' that modern writers frequently employ

3. *Ibid.*, p. 321-326.
4. PHILIP OF NOVARA, Livre de Philippe de Navarre, *RHC Lois*, I, p. 542-543. (The *lacunae* in the text can be filled from the readings in a manuscript not used by the editor. See P. W. EDBURY, Philip of Novara and the *Livre de forme de plait*, Πρακτικά του Τρίτου Διεθνούς Κυπρολογικού Συνεδρίου, 2, ed. A. PAPAGEORGIOU, Nicosia 2001, p. 559 n. 23); JOHN OF IBELIN, p. 763, 766.
5. *Ibid.*, p. 379-380, 383.
6. *Ibid.*, p. 379, 394, 398, 483.

V

to denote this obligation.[7] Failure to answer summons, or, when summoned, to chose a husband was punishable by the loss of the fief for a year and a day, and at the end of this period the fief would be returned and the lord would summon the heiress afresh.[8] Should the heiress hold fiefs from more than one lord, she was to respond to the summons from the lord to whom *servise de cors* was owed, and, as an heiress could only marry one husband, the other lords would accept that they had no say in the matter.[9] If on the other hand she married without waiting for the lord's summons, all the lords could confiscate her fiefs and hold them for as long as the marriage lasted.[10] John, however, does not say whether the other lords could seize the heiress's fiefs for a year and day if she failed to respond to the original summons. The vassal who married the heiress to a fief held from his own lord without that lord's permission was in breach of faith and was therefore liable to be challenged to a judicial duel if he took *seisin* of his wife's fief, but if he did not – the implication being that *seisin* of the fief passed to the lord – the lord had no claim against him.[11]

When an heiress was summoned to take a husband, she was confronted by the requirement to chose one of three candidates of comparable social standing selected by the lord.[12] Philip of Novara, in his discussion of this topic, explained that this practice had taken time to evolve and that it represented a compromise between the demands of the lord and the interests of the woman's kin.[13] (The other members of her family would have had a vested in who she married and in all likelihood would have determined the choice.) John, however, made no comment on the rationale for this system, nor did he consider the question of what would happen if the woman or her kin wanted to challenge the choice of a candidate on the grounds that he was not the woman's peer and so would disparage her. How this system worked out in reality is problematic. It is unfortunate for the historian that no anecdotal evidence survives that records an instance of an heiress making her choice from a panel of three candidates. One may suspect that the woman or her relatives would have sought to ensure that the lord nominated the man of their choice as one of the candidates, but if that did happen we may question whether the lord then bothered to find two other men to make up the number. On the other hand, the lord might use the marriage as a form of patronage to assist the fortunes of one of his own men or of someone else he wished to advance. Whatever happened, the lord probably did well out of it financially, thanks to a proffer either from the heiress or her kin or from prospective suitors, but, as such considerations fell outside the legal aspects of the marriage, John did not deal with them in his treatise.[14] It might be noted in passing, however, that the financial value to the lord of his right to supervise the marriage of heiresses is clearly implied in the arrangement made in Cyprus in 1306 at the time King Henry II was suspended from office.[15]

7. For an example of his use of this phrase, *ibid.*, p. 324.
8. *Ibid.*, p. 379, 398, 510-511.
9. *Ibid.*, p. 512-513.
10. *Ibid.*, p. 514-515.
11. *Ibid.*, p. 516-521.
12. *Ibid.*, p. 381, 508-509.
13. PHILIP OF NOVARA, p. 558-559.
14. But note John's use of phrase 'de finer de lui de son mariage' (p. 383).
15. Texte officiel de l'allocution adressée par les barons de Chypre au roi Henri II pour lui notifier sa déchéance, ed. L. DE MAS LATRIE, *Revue des questions historiques* 43, 1888, p. 539.

V

288

Financial advantage or the exercise of patronage could also come to a lord by not allowing an heiress to marry. John described the situation in which a lord chose to delay a marriage indefinitely so that the holder of the wardship could continue to enjoy the revenues of the fief. The woman or her kin could seek to persuade the lord to put an end to this situation, if necessary by making a financial proffer to get the lord to summon the heiress to take a husband, and, if that failed, they could take the more risky path of instituting court proceedings to compel him to issue the summons.[16]

But whereas lords could control the marriage of heiresses, they had no such control over widows who were not heiresses but who held dower. Nevertheless, the widow still owed homage to the lord of the fief and the lord had to signify his consent if she wished to remarry. Dower was fixed at half of whatever her husband had held at the time of his death, although John specified that this provision did not hold good for the queen and the wives of the four barons of the realm.[17] There is good evidence to support the idea that the widow was entitled to half her husband's holding,[18] but why the queen and the wives of the barons were excluded from the rule is not explained. Presumably the idea was that, as so much of the revenue from these major political units was already committed for purposes of defence, to endow the widow so generously was out of the question. But that would also have been true of the other major lordships that were not designated baronies.[19] As in the case of the marriage of heiresses, John was concerned with the strictly legal aspects of dower, not with the everyday practicalities of how dower was arranged. So for example, how an heir was supposed to manage if, as must often have happened, both his mother and his grandmother were still alive is not mentioned. Presumably he would have been heavily dependant on their generosity to support himself and his feudal obligations.

Widows and orphans were recognised as being vulnerable and needing special protection.[20] Even so the widow who was herself the legitimate daughter of a knight and his lady, besides having rights to her dower, had certain other privileges. She could, for example, purchase a knight's fief put up for sale in accordance with *assise de vente*, although if it was burdened with *servise de cors* she would then be liable for *servise de mariage*.[21] It often happened that a widow, besides acquiring half her husband's holding as her dower, also had custody of the other half by virtue of the wardship (or *bailliage*) to which she was entitled because his heir, the child of their marriage, was under age. In these circumstances she would be subject to *servise de mariage*, but she could avoid this obligation by relinquishing the wardship and the half of her husband's property that went with it to the lord who would then hold them himself until the heir came of age.[22]

16. JOHN OF IBELIN, p. 379-382.
17. *Ibid.*, p. 394-398, 514.
18. *The Cartulary of the Cathedral of Holy Wisdom of Nicosia*, ed. N. COUREAS, C. SCHABEL, Nicosia 1997, no. 87 (at p. 227).
19. For further discussion, see P. W. EDBURY, *John of Ibelin and the Kingdom of Jerusalem*, Woodbridge 1997, p. 167-168.
20. JOHN OF IBELIN, p. 73, 571.
21. *Ibid.*, p. 421-424.
22. *Ibid.*, p. 397-398.

The heiress who was widowed was still liable for *servise de mariage*. There was, however, an upper age limit of sixty. John did not mention this feature of the legal custom in the East, but there is extended treatment of it in one of the chapters that was inserted into a later recension of his text at some date before 1291.[23] (This chapter may have been written on the island of Cyprus as the author speaks of 'uz... ou reiaume de Jerusalem ou en cestui de Chipre', although several lines further on he turns the phrase round and writes 'en cestui reiaume de Jerusalem ne en celui de Chipre'.) The principal argument takes the line that it would be inappropriate to make women over 60 years of age remarry since men over sixty were no longer required to perform *servise de cors*. It is only then, and much more briefly, that the author added that it was also inappropriate because at that age a woman is long past child-bearing. (Nowhere does John mention that men over sixty were no longer liable for *servise de cors*, although that point too was introduced into the treatise after his death. The nearest he comes to referring to it is his statement that men over sixty can employ a champion if appealed by wager of battle.[24])

The secular law of the High Court, though it encompassed the rights of the lord to demand *servise de mariage*, did not have cognizance of matrimonial disputes. Matters such as the legality of a marriage and the related issues of divorce, adultery and illegitimacy belonged to the Church Courts. Accordingly John had little to say on such topics, although he did include bastards and adulterers in his list of people who could not bear testimony in the High Court.[25] The unmarried sexual partner – John uses the word 'soignant' and the phrase 'tenue... en soignantage' – is only given legal recognition in the context of categories of people for whose murder someone can bring accusations.[26] Seducing the wife or daughter of one's lord, or turning a blind eye to someone else doing so, is included in John's list of things that constitute a breach of homage. So too is seducing the lord's sister 'tant con ele est damoisele en son hostel'.[27] Similarly the vassal who abducts the wife, daughter, mother or sister of the lord by force is guilty of treason towards his lord, 'quar tos sont si prochains dou seignor qui son ausi come sa char et lui meimes'.[28]

It is with the subject of rape that we come to the problems surrounding the status of the woman litigant. John lists the accusation of rape – 'ce est de feme esforcee' – among the charges that must be answered immediately. In other words, the accused cannot simply ask for an adjournment without entering a plea. John, however, does not give the subject any separate treatment, but simply lumps it together with other acts of violence. If the victim is married she can get her husband to offer proof in a judicial duel, but if he is not prepared to risk wager of battle on her behalf, she can only employ someone else as her champion with his agreement. Without her husband's agreement she cannot bring charges and, if nobody else will, the culprit cannot be dealt with in the court. In this situation the unmarried woman is in a stronger position, since she at least has autonomy in

23. *Ibid.*, p. 656-659. It is present in MS A which dates to ca. 1290 as well as the later MSS B and V. See J. FOLDA, P. W. EDBURY, Two Thirteenth-Century Manuscripts of Crusader Legal Texts from Saint-Jean d'Acre, *Journal of the Warburg and Coutauld Institutes* 57, 1994, p. 244-249.
24. JOHN OF IBELIN, p. 250, 695-696.
25. *Ibid.*, p. 167.
26. *Ibid.*, p. 188.
27. *Ibid.*, p. 440, 461. See the discussion in the introduction, p. 20-21.
28. *Ibid.*, p. 228.

initiating the case.[29] It would seem that what normally happened was that when a married woman wished to initiate litigation, her husband would start the process on her behalf by requesting that the court assign her a member of the court as her counsel. Alternatively the husband could, without having been given counsel, plead on his wife's behalf. [30]

Subject to her husband's approval, a woman was able to initiate accusations of rape, assault, highway robbery and other capital offences as well as engage in litigation over land or other property. Court procedure required that the apellant (*apeleor*) should produce two witnesses to testify to the truth of the accusation. They, or rather their *avantparlier*, an experienced member of the court assigned to them for this purpose, recited their testimony, and then the witnesses were required to take an oath on the gospel book that this was a true statement. It was at the moment of taking the oath that the defendant, unless he was going to allow his case to collapse, would have to challenge one of the witnesses as a perjurer. Then, unless composition was agreed, the defendant and the witness would fight a judicial duel. If the witness lost, he would be hanged and the woman burnt at the stake. If the witness was entitled to employ a champion to fight on his behalf and the champion lost, all three – woman, witness and champion – would be executed. If on the other hand the defendant lost, he would be hanged. That at least is the procedure as John described it.[31] He made it clear that the lord who presided at the court had limited power to exercise clemency,[32] but the high body-count raises the question of how often these procedures were followed through. John was describing the process before the court, and so was not concerned with out-of-court settlements. He did indicate the possibility that 'pais en seroit faite' right up to the last moment before the battle,[33] but he made no comment on how a settlement might be achieved and gave no indication of the frequency with which such settlements were made. The fact that the Cypriot chronicler recorded that an appeal of murder in 1314 ended in a duel may suggest that such events, at least at that period, were something of a rarity.[34]

John alluded on a number of occasions to women defendants, and it would appear from comments scattered through his treatise that their position was no different from that of their male counterparts.[35] It should be noted, however, that a woman convicted of a capital offence would be burnt and not hanged.[36] Similarly when it came to litigation over land and the rights, duties and privileges of fief-holders, the lady of a fief was on the same footing as a man, and John gives numerous instances to illustrate this point.[37] There was, however, one particular area where the law gave the woman no redress. If a woman was the victim of domestic violence and sustained visible bruising at the hands of her husband, she,

---

29. *Ibid.*, p. 184, 188, 246, 248, 250.
30. *Ibid.*, p. 66, 79, 81.
31. *Ibid.*, p. 246-247. For the judicial duel, p. 240-245.
32. *Ibid.*, p. 567.
33. *Ibid.*, p. 241.
34. Chronique d'Amadi, ed. R. DE MAS LATRIE, *Chroniques d'Amadi et de Strambaldi*, Paris 1891-1893, 1, p. 396.
35. For example, JOHN OF IBELIN, p. 84, 90, 91, 183, 264, 462-463, 470-471.
36. *Ibid.*, p. 247, 248.
37. For example, *ibid.*, p. 81, 309, 313, 323, 327, 328-330, 335, 341, 344, 348, 363, 384, 391, 408, 419, 435, 439-440, 484, 527, 543, 554.

in common with their children and serfs, was not entitled to claim compensation using the procedure known as 'cop aparant par l'assise dou roy Bauduin'. John also noted that the husband similarly could not claim compensation if assaulted by his wife.[38]

Even if we are right to suspect that very few cases were pursued to their logical conclusion in a judicial duel, legal procedure was predicated on the assumption that they might be. The role of the witness (or *garans*) therefore acquires considerable significance, since it would be the witness and not the appellant who would fight the defendant on the field. It would seem that the court would not normally allow witnesses to employ champions to fight on their behalf. That being so, John devoted a chapter to listing categories of people who could not bear witness in the High Court: people whose previous behaviour had rendered their oaths untrustworthy, non-Latins, and people – clergy, children, serfs, and women – who would not bear arms. So whereas a woman could initiate proceedings and could employ a champion in appeals of murder where by definition there were no witnesses and so the appellants themselves had to bear the responsibility of proof, and whereas the woman who was a defendant could employ a champion,[39] a woman was barred from giving testimony on the grounds that she was unable to fight the duel in person. The only exceptions to this rule arose when it was necessary to testify simply as to the age or parentage of a particular individual. Disputes over property would frequently have turned on claims of descent, and from time to time it would be necessary to establish whether a claimant had reached his or her majority. There was a well-established procedural principle that there could be no judicial duel over testimony proving age or descent, and that meant that there could be no objection to a woman bearing such testimony if she were the appropriate person to do so. John was bothered by this rule, since, without the threat of divine retribution that could be brought to bear through recourse to wager of battle, he feared that people would be more likely to perjure themselves, but, although he discussed this point at some length, it would seem he had to accept the legal procedures for what they were.[40]

Despite the extensive coverage that John gave to the legal position of women in the High Court of Jerusalem, there are many questions that historians might want to ask to which he does not provide answers. For example, could a woman who was a fief-holder in her own right but who had no husband to perform her *servise de cors* on her behalf participate in the deliberations of the court? Or could a woman who was involved in litigation dispense with the services of her counsel and conduct her own case in person? We might assume that the answers to both question is 'no', and maybe the idea that such things could happen was so unthinkable that it never occurred to John to comment, but are we right? Then again, could the lady who had inherited a lordship with *cour, coins et justise* and who had no husband preside over her seigneurial court in person, or did she have to appoint a man as her deputy? This is one aspect of the wider issue of the extent to which a noblewoman might have a visible role in public affairs, but, for all the emphasis on the early deaths of husbands in the Latin East, it is a question that has yet to be

38. *Ibid.*, p. 262-265 at p. 265.
39. *Ibid.*, p. 250.
40. *Ibid.*, p. 165, 167, 354-355, 356-362, 377.

examined fully. Even the position of the women included in the list of those obliged to provide knights to the royal host which dates from the mid-1180s and which John added at the end of his treatise is unclear. About fifteen women are mentioned out of a total of about a hundred named individuals. Most are described as the wife (*feme*) of so and so, but are they heiresses whose husbands are alive; widows who have dower and wardship of their children's inheritance, or even the wives of knights who were currently prisoners of war? Presumably when the host was summoned, the summons was addressed to these women, but there is no indication as to their precise status.

From time to time John departed from his normal practice of using male pronouns to refer to the parties to a lawsuit and employed inclusive language, as for example in the phrases, 'tos ceaus et toutes celes', 'celui ou cele' or 'ne d'aucun ne d'aucune de son lignage'.[41] Why he should do this in some places and not in others is a mystery, but it could be that behind these rather bland expressions is a memory that a woman had been a party in the specific case John had in mind as he wrote. This can certainly be demonstrated in one instance where John himself subsequently revised his account. A contentious issue in the East in the thirteenth century were the rights of heirs to lands conquered by the Muslims and then much later recovered and the rules governing inheritance when one or more generations had been unable to take *seisin*. The lawyers insisted on the principle that *Force de Turs ne tot saisine* ('forcible occupation by the Turks did not affect rights to *seisin*'), and John revised his discussion to include the story of how his aunt, Margaret of Ibelin, had successfully asserted her rights to the lordship of Ibelin, lost in 1187 and recovered in the early 1240s. What is of interest here is that in the sentences immediately before his insertion of this new material John deliberately altered the wording by including phrases such as 'et la fille' to prepare the reader for the idea that the successful claimant in such cases could be a woman.[42]

What is clear from this discussion is that John's treatise contains a wealth of information about the status and activities of women in the High Court of Jerusalem, but that what he says gives rise to further questions which cannot easily be resolved. While it is clear that women had certain disabilities at law just as they had a limited role in public life, it is also clear that they had well-defined rights and that the legal system was able to guarantee them. John never allowed himself to make pejorative remarks about women, but it was nevertheless true that the courts were primarily a place where men made the decisions and determined the outcome, and, although he never specifically said so, John would not have wanted things otherwise.

---

41. For example, *ibid.*, p. 59, 66, 198, 321, 334, 374.
42. *Ibid.*, p. 617-619, cf p. 11-12, 159-161.

Cultural Encounters
in the Latin East.
John of Jaffa and Philip of Novara

The Franks ... have neither precedence
nor high rank except that of the knights,
and have no men worthy of the name
except the knights – it is they who
are the masters of legal reasoning,
judgement and sentencing.

Usama Ibn Munqidh[1]

The treatises by John of Ibelin and Philip of Novara describe the workings of the High Courts of Jerusalem and Cyprus, where the legal business of the Frankish elite was conducted. They contain, however, a small number of references to the indigenous population, and, although they give only a limited insight into their status and relations with the Franks, what they do tell us is revealing.

At first sight, the legal treatises by Philip of Novara and his slightly younger contemporary, John of Ibelin, Count of Jaffa and Ascalon, would seem unlikely places to find evidence for relations between the Franks of Latin Syria and Cyprus and the indigenous communities over which they ruled. Both writers set out to describe the judicial procedures employed in the High Court. Philip of Novara, who would appear to have been writing in the early 1250s, seems to have been primarily concerned with the kingdom of Cyprus, although from time to time he included references to legal practices employed in the kingdom of Jerusalem.[2] John of Jaffa, whose work was heavily influenced by Philip's and who was writing in the mid 1260s, was interested in the kingdom of Jerusalem and also in the seigneurial courts there that were supposed to follow the procedures and customs of the High Court.[3] The procedures these authors described were cumbersome and, by the mid-thirteenth century, al-

---

1   Usama (2008), p. 76.
2   Novara (2009), pp. 20–22.
3   Ibelin (2003), pp. 55, 58.

most certainly considered anachronistic.[4] Unless the rights and wrongs of a particular case were so clear-cut that one of the parties had no choice but to admit defeat, it would seem to have been normal for a dispute to have ended in an out-of-court settlement.[5] If a case were allowed to run its course, in many instances the procedures would have dictated that the outcome would be decided by means of a judicial duel – what our authors refer to as a "wager of battle" – in which God's judgement was invoked to determine whether or not a witness or one of the parties to the dispute had perjured himself or herself by swearing falsely. Such duels, however, were probably uncommon.[6]

Business in the High Court

The High Courts of both Cyprus and Jerusalem dealt with the kings' legal business. They provided the public forums for grants of fiefs to royal vassals, and it was there that the kings took their vassals' homage and enacted other routine business contingent on the holding of fiefs. It was also there that the kings transferred property or other rights to churches and religious corporations and promulgated legislative ordinances. As tribunals, the High Courts were primarily the preserve of the vassals – the men and women bound to the king by homage and who held fiefs that were normally, but not invariably, burdened with military service. In other words, only a minority of the Frankish population had access: everyone else – those Franks who were not vassals, and the members of the various indigenous communities – would seek legal redress or face trial in the *Cour des bourgeois* or, if the dispute only concerned members of one of the indigenous communities and could be settled internally, in their own tribunals.[7]

John of Jaffa was one of the most powerful noblemen of his age; Philip of Novara, an Italian who appears to have been a first generation settler in the East, but who claimed to have come from a knightly family, had worked his way up to become a royal counsellor and a vassal of some substance, the sort of figure that he himself would have called a "vavassor".[8] Both men wrote treatises that testify to their ideas of noble exclusiveness and privilege, ideas underpinned by a strong sense of group identity that had been honed by their successful resistance to the political ambitions of the Emperor Frederick II in the East in the course of the second quarter of the thirteenth century.

---

4   Novara (2009), pp. 22–33, 26; Ibelin (2003), pp. 43–44.
5   For an example, see Novara (1994), p. 76.
6   For instances of duels noted in the sources, see Novara (1994), pp. 78–82; Novara (2009), pp. 188, 312; 'Amadi' (1891), p. 396.
7   For the court of the Syrians (Melkites), see Ibelin (2003), pp. 54–55. For the rabbinical court in Acre, see Prawer (1972), pp. 240–241.
8   Novara (2009), p. 18.

Testimony

An essential feature of the High Court was that the witnesses produced by the litigants to testify to the facts of the case had to be Catholic Christians, or, to use the current terminology, "men of the law of Rome".[9] As Philip of Novara explained:

> The people who cannot bear witness in our court against Franks are all those who are not of the 'law of Rome', all convicts, all perjurers, all those who are faith breakers, all defeated champions, all those who have renounced God and gone to another 'law', and all those who have served the Saracens and other unbelieving peoples against Christians in arms for more than a year and a day.[10]

In other words, non-Franks could not testify against Franks in the High Court; with them were bracketed people who were deemed to be untrustworthy and so had lost their voice in court: convicted felons, perjurers, traitors, those defeated in a judicial duel[11] and apostates as well as those quasi-apostates who had fought alongside Muslims against Christians.[12] Philip then added bastards, serfs and clergy to his list. In a parallel passage, John of Jaffa glossed the phrase "of the law of Rome" as "obedient to Rome" and specified that those excluded included Greeks, Syrians, Armenians and Jacobites. He also stated that minors could not testify in the High Court.[13] Both authors agreed, however, that Eastern Christians could testify against people of their own 'law'.

In one respect, however, John of Jaffa differed. According to John, any baptised Christian was permitted to testify in the High Court in matters to do with age and lineage. To be more specific, any Christian could testify that he or she *believed* that a particular individual had reached the age of majority or that he or she *believed* a particular individual was related to someone in a particular way. Such testimony might well prove vital in inheritance disputes, and, provided that witnesses testified to their own beliefs and not to some external 'fact', there could be no challenge by "wager of battle".[14] It was here that the rationale may lie. This one exception apart, litigation between Franks could not be determined on the basis of the testimony of a non-Frank. When the testimony of a Frankish witness was challenged, that witness would fight a judicial duel with the defendant. Clearly, the idea of a "wager

---

9 Novara (2009), pp. 41–22, 63, 188, 193, 212–213, 225, 312, 316; Ibelin (2003), pp. 100, 146, 157, 173, 177, 211, 217, 220, 246, 251, 276, 278–279, 286, 305, 353, 375, 492, 566, 687, 704, 706.

10 "Les gens qui ne pevent porter garentie en nostre court encontre Frans si sont toutes les gens qui ne sont de la ley de Rome, et tous forjugiés, et tous parjurés, et tous ceaus qui sont fei mentie, et tous chanpions vencus, et tous ceaus qui ont Dieu reneié et devindrent d'autre lei, et tous ceaus qui ont servi sarasins et autres gens mescreans contre crestiens a armes plus d'un an et .i. jour". Novara (2009), pp. 80, 236–237.

11 Note that 'champion' in this context means those who have gone on to the field – the 'champ' – to engage in a judicial duel. Litigants could only employ a 'champion' in the sense of a surrogate warrior if they were aged over sixty, disabled or a woman. Novara (2009), pp. 50, 218.

12 Philip expressed doubts as to whether this bar extended to those who had fought for Greeks against Latins.

13 Ibelin (2003), p. 167.

14 Ibelin (2003), p. 165, cf. pp. 167, 215, 354.

Frankish boundary marker from Kibbutz Somrat with the legend 'IANUA', presumably denoting the boundary of Genoese-owned property. See Frankel (1986).

of battle" between a Frank and someone of a different religious affiliation (or 'law') was unthinkable.

Philip concluded his chapter dealing with the categories of people who did not testify against Franks with an expression of the vassals' class consciousness: a lord could, if he wished, enfranchise a serf and give him a fief, but, his legal status notwithstanding, the other vassals would not accept him as their peer.[15] Elsewhere, Philip recorded an anecdote that further illustrated noble self-esteem: Ralph of Tiberias, one of Philip's heroes, was reported to have refused King Aimery's invitation to produce a written account of the laws of Jerusalem – this would have been around 1197 – on the grounds that he would not work alongside "Raymond Antiaume or any other subtle burgess or low born lettered man".[16]

Legal Privilege

The legal privileges of the vassals went further. In the Latin East, it was normal for the victim of a crime to bring charges against the perpetrator. However, as Philip made clear, there was provision for the king or lord to act against culprits in what might loosely be termed "public prosecution". The lord's duty to do so stemmed from his general responsibility to uphold justice. That meant, for example, that he could dismiss charges brought before him in his court if he believed them to be groundless, and, in the interests of seeing justice done, he might provide arms and equipment for poor people who found themselves having to fight a judicial duel and who could not otherwise afford them.[17] It also meant that the lord could institute proceedings for a breach of his peace rather than wait for the victim to bring charges:

> With respect to *force* or assault committed at the exchange or in a covered street or in a place where a general market takes place, I have seen enquiry made on the general advice of the court and justice done as a result, because it is said that these places are the lord's *chambre*.[18]

What this meant was, that in law, these public places were seen as an extension of the lord's private residence. But vassals were exempt from such public prosecutions. Because the lord had taken their homage, he could not impose summary justice but had to allow cases in which a vassal was accused of *force* (which could include assault, rape or theft) to follow the traditional procedures which might end in a judicial duel.

Accusations of assault seem to have been common. Philip of Novara and John of Jaffa both described the procedure instituted by an enactment known as "The *Assise* of King Baldwin of *Cop aparant*". Reduced to its essentials, this *assise* made provision

---

15 Novara (2009), pp. 81, 238.
16 Novara (2009), pp. 119–120, 260; cf Ibelin (2003), p. 685.
17 Novara (2009), pp. 57, 59–60, 222, 224.
18 "Et de force faite ou de cop au change, ou en la rue couverte, ou en leu la l'on se fait marché general, j'ai veu faire enquestion par conseil general de court et faire ent justice, por ce que l'on dit que ces leus sont chambre dou seignor". Novara (2009), pp. 185–186 (at p. 186), 309–310, cf. pp. 149, 280.

for the accused to clear himself on oath rather than have witnesses give testimony under oath and thus render themselves liable to a challenge to a "wager of battle". What is of interest here are the penalties: the man guilty of an assault on a Frank had to pay a fine of 100 bezants to the lord and 100 sous to the victim by way of compensation. So, the lord's fine amounted to twenty times the compensation. But if the victim was a Syrian, a Greek or a serf, the sums were 50 bezants and 50 sous respectively – half that of a Frank. (In cases of assault in which a sharpened weapon or iron mace was used, there was no monetary penalty: the guilty party would lose his right hand.) Even more striking, however, were the penalties for assaulting a Frankish knight: Here the perpetrator had to pay 1,000 bezants to the lord

> … and give the harness of a knight to the person he had struck and such arms as would be given to someone when he is made a knight. For he who struck him does not appear to take him for a knight, and, because he has un-made him, it is indeed right that he re-makes him.[19]

This is further testimony to knightly self-perception. Someone who struck a knight with his fist would have to compensate his victim with the equivalent of the cost of a knight's arms and armour, such was the dishonour he had inflicted. So, Philip and John were describing a society which, in the eyes of the law, was graded: vassal knights; other Franks; everyone else.

The role of the subaltern classes

Despite their privileged status before the law, the vassals nevertheless had from time to time to make use of non-vassals in their legal affairs. Our authors described two circumstances in which this could occur, and in both instances they provided invaluable insights into how the ruling elite regarded the various indigenous communities. The first concerned the situation of a Frank who was engaged in litigation: the case has been adjourned, and then, while on his way to the court, he fell ill and had to notify the court of his *essoin*, thereby asking for a further adjournment. If he had a companion who is a Catholic – someone "of the law of Rome" – that man could come to the court and testify on his behalf that he was unable to attend. But if there was no Catholic with him who could do this, he could send a Christian of another 'law', in other words a Melkite or a member of one of the other eastern churches, and, if no eastern Christian was available, he could employ a Muslim. These men would swear an oath to the court using whatever form of oath was appropriate to their own religious affiliation. Philip of Novara seems to have been hesitant about whether a Muslim could perform this task: "… if there is no Christian, *it is said* that

---

19 "… et douner herneis de chevalier au batu et teiles armeures coume l'on deit doner a celui qui l'on fait chevalier. Car cil qui le bat ne semble pas que il le tinge por chevalier; et, por ce que il le desfait, est bien raizon qu'il le reface". Novara (2009), pp. 148–149 (at p. 148), 278–280; Ibelin (2003), p. 265.

a Saracen can do it".[20] In a parallel passage, however, John of Jaffa shows no such hesitancy and also specifies that this function could be performed by a Jew.[21] (This, incidentally, is the only occasion on which John mentions Jews in his treatise; Philip has no references to them at all.)

The other case involved the need to get local people to give evidence about the line (or the *devise*) of property boundaries. Here, Philip of Novara was undoubtedly writing with the conditions in the kingdom of Jerusalem in mind, and he evoked a depopulated landscape with abandoned settlements and fields. The likely context was the return of lands lost in 1187 to Christian control, either at the time of the emperor Frederick II's crusade in 1229 or the so-called 'Barons Crusade' of 1240–1241. What was happening was that the heirs of the last Christian landowners were claiming for themselves what they saw as their inheritances, and it was inevitable that there should be doubts and disputes over boundaries, especially if the territory concerned had hitherto formed part of a no man's land between the Christian and Muslim-controlled areas. The procedure involved the court appointing a four-man commission to go to the location in question and get the local people to swear on oath where they believed the boundaries to be. As in the case of *essoins*, the commission should look first to Franks – men of 'the law of Rome' – whom they considered trustworthy, and establish the boundaries on their testimony. Philip continues:

> If they do not find a Frank of the "law of Rome", and they find a Syrian whom they consider worthy of faith, they should follow him. If they do not find a Syrian and they find a Greek, similarly. If they do not find a Greek and they find some other Christian of what ever denomination he may be, similarly. If they do not find a Christian and they find a Saracen who swears according to his law and they consider him worthy of faith, as is said above, they should follow him and organize the *devise* and set boundaries.[22]

If the commissioners can find no one with the information they require, whom they can trust, they are to use their own judgement, taking into account the geographical features of the area.

By "Syrians" Philip meant Melkite Christians, and so we see here a pecking order of confessions. At the top are Catholics, men of "the Law of Rome": their oaths are to be preferred. Then follow Syrian Melkites, Greek Orthodox, the various non-Chalcedonian Christian denominations and finally Muslims.

---

20 "...se il n'a crestien, l'on dit que par sarasin le peut faire". Novara (2009), pp. 75–76 (at p. 75), 233.
21 Ibelin (2003), pp. 149–150.
22 "Et s'il ne treuvent Franc de la lei de Rome, et il treuvent Surien a qui il doingnent fei, si come il est dit dessus, il le deivent sivre. Et s'il ne treuvent Surien et il treuvent Grec aussi. Et se il ne treuvent Grec et il treuvent aucun autre crestien de queilque generation q'il seit, ainsement. Et se il ne treuvent crestien et il treuvent sarasin qui jure selon sa lei et il li doingent fei, si com il est dit dessus, sivre le deivent et pourchaucher et bonner la devise". Novara (2009), pp. 131–133 (at p. 132), 265–268. This chapter was interpolated into some manuscripts of John's treatise. See Ibelin (2003), pp. 669–673, cf. pp. 626–627.

Final comments

What John and Philip described was a legal system that privileged Franks over all other sectors of society. However, they did not indulge in pejorative remarks about non-Franks, although Philip did note, with evident distaste, that the Syrians were especially prone to belief in astrology.[23] In his description of the coronation rituals, John of Jaffa mentioned that the king swore to maintain all the Christian peoples in his kingdom and uphold their rights.[24] This legal system would have meant that it would have been extremely difficult for a non-Frank to gain legal redress against a vassal knight in the High Court, but it should be stressed that the picture the writers give is far from complete. Those people who were not vassals would have had recourse to the *Cour des Bourgeois* in the first instance, and vassals, if indicted there, still had to answer the charges. As a legal tribunal, the High Court existed primarily to settle those disputes that arose within the ranks of the fief holders. The rules were geared to preserve the privilege and status of the ruling elite, and the apparent discrimination against other groups within society should not obscure the fact that this elite nevertheless needed their labour and co-operation if they were to perpetuate their regime in the face of Muslim attack.

Bibliography
Sources

'Chronique d'Amadi', ed. René de Mas Latrie, in *Chroniques d'Amadi et de Strambaldi*, 2 vols. (Paris, 1891, 1893), vol. 1.
John of Ibelin, *Le Livre des Assises*, ed. Peter W. Edbury (Leiden, 2003).
Philip of Novara (Filippo da Novara), *Guerra di Federico II in Oriente (1223–1242)*, ed. and trans. Silvio Melani (Naples, 1994).
Philip of Novara, *Le Livre de Forme de Plait*, ed. and trans. Peter W. Edbury (Nicosia, 2009).
Usama Ibn Munqidh, *The Book of Contemplation: Islam and the Crusades*, trans. Paul M. Cobb (London, 2008).

Literature

Frankel, Rafael, 'I cippi confinari genovesi del Kibbutz Somrat', in *I comuni italiani nel regno crociato di Gerusaleme,* ed. Gabriella Airaldi and Benjamin Z. Kedar, Collana Storica di Fonti e Studi, 48 (Genoa, 1986), pp. 691–695 and plates opposite p. 337.
Prawer, Joshua, *The Latin Kingdom of Jerusalem: European Colonialism in the Middle Ages* (London, 1972).

---

23 Novara (2009), pp. 175–176, 301.
24 Ibelin (2003), p. 571.

VII

The *Assises d'Antioche*: Law and Custom in the Principality of Antioch

The *Assises d'Antioche* is a treatise on the law of the principality composed at some point between the end of the twelfth century and the year 1219. That makes it roughly contemporary with the Norman *Très Ancien Coutumier* (*c*.1200) and with the earliest of the treatises from the kingdom of Jerusalem, the *Livre au Roi*, which on internal evidence belongs to the years 1198–1205.[1] The *Assises* has never attracted much attention, probably for the simple reason that it survives only in a translation from the original French into Armenian, and most scholars, the present author included, have to rely on a translation into modern French that appeared as long ago as 1876.[2]

Antioch itself had been conquered by the armies of the First Crusade in 1098 and, as is well known, it was Bohemond, the son of Robert Guiscard duke of Apulia, who acquired control. Bohemond was followed as prince of Antioch by his nephew Tancred, then by a cousin named Roger of Salerno, and eventually by his own son Bohemond II. With Bohemond II's death in 1130, rule by the male descendants of Tancred de Hauteville, the progenitor of the Norman rulers of southern Italy and Sicily, came to an end.[3] Later in the 1130s the principality passed into the hands of Bohemond II's son-in-law, Raymond of Poitiers.

---

[1]   *Très Ancien Coutumier de Normandie*, in *Coutumiers de Normandie, textes critiques, avec notes et éclaircissements*, ed. E.-J. Tardif (Société de l'histoire de Normandie, 1881–1903); *Le Livre au Roi*, ed. M. Greilsammer (Paris, 1995).

[2]   *Assises d'Antioche reproduites en français*, ed. and trans. La Société Mekhithariste de Saint-Lazare (Venice, 1876); also available at http://rbedrosian.com/Downloads/Assises_d_Antioche.pdf [accessed 11 December 2012]. This edition of the Armenian text with a facing page French translation was the work of Father Léonce Alishan, although his name nowhere appears in the printed edition. There is also a Russian translation taken from a different manuscript: A.A. Papovian, 'Armianskii Perevod "Antiokhiiskikh Assiz"', *Vestnik Matenadarana*, 4 (Erevan, 1958), pp. 331–75. My thanks are due to Dr A. Bozoian for this reference and for providing me with a photocopy.

[3]   For the early history of the principality, see T.S. Asbridge, *The Creation of the Principality of Antioch, 1098–1130* (Woodbridge, 2000).

Raymond was a younger son of William IX, duke of Aquitaine, and thereafter it was his direct descendants in the male line who were to rule until Antioch fell to the Muslims in 1268. A significant proportion of the early Frankish settlers were, like the first princes, from southern Italy or else, in some cases, perhaps from Normandy itself, and they dominated a population in which Syrian and Armenian Christians were prominent.

The heyday of the principality lay in the earlier part of the twelfth century. It was at this period that it enjoyed its greatest territorial extent, although it was also a period when no fewer than three successive princes died fighting the Muslims. The plain of Cilicia was lost in the 1130s, and then at some point in the mid-twelfth century, possibly as early as the late 1130s, the Templars acquired control of a huge swathe of territory to the north of Antioch centred on the castle of Baghras in the Amanus Mountains.[4] In February 1187 the Hospitallers bought the castle and lordship of al-Marqab (Margat) from its lord, Bertrand le Mazoir, and thereby acquired a major responsibility for the defence of the south of the principality.[5] These acquisitions by the Military Orders meant that the prince of Antioch and his vassals retained little more than the city of Antioch itself and its lands around the lower Orontes. This development was thrown into sharper focus by the conquests of Saladin, who invaded the principality in 1188. A number of strongholds were lost at that time, including the celebrated castle of Sahyūn (re-named in recent years as Qal'at Salāh al-Dīn: 'the Castle of Saladin'). The Christians were able to hang on in Antioch and at al-Marqab, but to the north Baghras and much else besides were seized by the Muslims.

In view of these territorial losses, it will come as no surprise to find that, as we move into the second half of the twelfth century, Antiochene political and military affairs leave less of a mark on the surviving narratives: there were no local historians writing in Latin to continue the work of Walter the Chancellor, and William of Tyre – from the perspective of the kingdom of Jerusalem – gave far less attention to Antioch in the period between 1150 and 1184, which is where he ends, than he had earlier. Alongside the Muslim encroachments, the latter part of the twelfth century also witnessed the rise of a new Christian power in the region, the principality (and later kingdom) of Cilician Armenia. So, when in the course of the Third Crusade the Muslims abandoned Baghras and the other strongholds they had seized, these were occupied not by their former owners, the Templars, but by the Armenians who, from their bases in

---

[4] M. Barber, *The New Knighthood: A History of the Order of the Temple* (Cambridge, 1994), pp. 77–9.

[5] J. Riley-Smith, *The Knights of St John in Jerusalem and Cyprus, c.1050–1310* (London, 1967), p. 68.

the mountains ringing the plain of Cilicia and under the leadership of Leo the Roupenid, were keen to expand their rule.

Conflict between the Armenians and successive princes of Antioch dominates the story from the 1190s until the 1220s. Largely it was simply a matter of Armenian ambition, fuelled in part by a continuing dispute over control of Baghras, but ostensibly it centred on a succession dispute.[6] In 1195 Prince Bohemond III of Antioch, in an attempt to patch up relations with the Armenians, had agreed among other things to the marriage of Raymond, his eldest son, to Leo the Roupenid's niece. But in 1198 Raymond died, leaving his wife pregnant with a child known to historians as Raymond-Roupen. Then, in 1201, it was the turn of Bohemond to die, whereupon control of Antioch passed to his second son and namesake, Bohemond IV. The new prince already possessed the county of Tripoli, which had come his way on the death without heirs of Count Raymond III in 1187. His Armenian in-laws, however, took the view that Bohemond III's infant grandson, Raymond-Roupen, was the rightful prince.

There are, of course, echoes here of the succession dispute in the Anglo-Norman realm between King John and Arthur of Brittany at precisely the same period. Bohemond IV appears to have enjoyed considerable support in Antioch, and the idea of an Armenian-dominated regime was distasteful to both the Franks and the Orthodox community. But the Armenians had certain advantages. For a start, in 1198 Leo had acquired a crown from the German emperor, the price of which was the union of the Armenian Church with Rome. This *rapprochement* seems to have been more theoretical than real – certainly, the Armenian Church showed little sign of reforming itself to bring it into line with Western practices – but it did mean that Bohemond IV could not rely on the support of Pope Innocent III. Secondly, the Armenians were powerful, and the effective annexation of Antioch to their realm might arguably have been in the interests of the Christians in the East in the face of the likelihood of future Muslim aggression. The Armenians had support from the Hospitallers and from the new Military Order in the East, the Teutonic Knights – both were significant landholders within their realm – and in 1210 or thereabouts there was a further boost to their diplomatic support with the marriage of the youthful Raymond-Roupen to a sister of King Hugh I of Cyprus. The 'war of succession' was protracted, with repeated Armenian campaigns to take Antioch, and we find, for example, that some of those knights who chose to abandon the army of the Fourth Crusade rather than go to Constantinople were drawn into the conflict in support of the Armenians, while others were planning to take

---

[6]   For a summary account, see M.N. Hardwicke, 'The crusader states, 1192–1243', in K.M. Setton (general editor), *A History of the Crusades* (Philadelphia and Madison, Wisconsin, 1955–89), ii, pp. 532–41.

service with their opponents.[7] In 1216, with Bohemond IV conveniently out of the way in Tripoli, a group of pro-Armenian plotters managed to hand Antioch to Raymond-Roupen, but in 1219 a counter-coup reinstated Bohemond, whose position was now helped by an internecine struggle in Armenia following Leo the Roupenid's death in the same year.

The principles informing the succession conflict deserve some attention. Like King John, Bohemond IV had to contend with the claims of the child of his deceased elder brother. But there was a difference. In England, notwithstanding the precedent set by John's accession in 1199, the normal rule of inheritance that eventually came to be accepted was that the grandson, the representative heir, inherited in preference to the younger son, despite the fact that a younger son was a closer relative of the last in seisin than a grandson, and despite the fact that a younger son would be likely to have had the advantage of being of age, whereas a grandson quite likely would not. Thus, in 1377 it was Richard II who inherited the throne from his grandfather, Edward III, and not Edward's eldest surviving son, John of Gaunt. In the Latin East, however, successoral representation was not the rule. The Latin Syrian legists are clear that the younger son – or indeed the eldest daughter if there were no more sons – inherited in preference to the grandson, and so, to take another fourteenth-century example, Peter I became king of Cyprus in 1359 on the death of Hugh IV rather than Peter's nephew, the son of his long-dead elder brother. The accession of Bohemond IV on the death of his father was therefore fully in line with the practice that developed in the Latin East. Moreover, it seems noteworthy that it conformed to succession practices that were accepted in the thirteenth century in some areas of France beyond Normandy.[8]

This, then, was the background against which the *Assises d'Antioche* was composed. The preface tells us that it was compiled by Pierre de Ravendel, Thomas the Marshal and other wise men.[9] Both these named individuals were prominent vassals in the principality, with careers spanning the 1190s and the first two decades of the thirteenth century. Thomas the Marshal was a member of the Tirel family, which had made that office hereditary since the middle of the twelfth century; he was among those who engineered Raymond-Roupen's seizure of Antioch in 1216; and he evidently lived in exile after Bohemond IV's restoration three years later. As far as is known, Pierre de Ravendel, on the other

---

[7]   *Chronique d'Ernoul et de Bernard le Trésorier*, ed. L. de Mas Latrie (Paris, 1871), pp. 341, 353; *L'Estoire de Eracles empereur et la conqueste de la Terre d'Outremer*, in *Recueil des historiens des croisades. Historiens occidentaux* (Paris, 1844–95), ii, pp. 247–9, 257.

[8]   D. Power, *The Norman Frontier in the Twelfth and Early Thirteenth Centuries* (Cambridge, 2004), pp. 184–6.

[9]   *Assises d'Antioche*, p. 2.

hand, was loyal to Bohemond throughout, and so, if indeed Thomas and Pierre went their separate ways in 1219, that would suggest that the *Assises* had been composed before that date. It is possible, as Claude Cahen speculated, that it was written for Raymond-Roupen who, having been brought up in Cilicia, would have been unfamiliar with Antiochene law, but Cahen, wisely, did not insist on this idea.[10]

The preface also explains how Simon, the constable of Antioch, had passed a copy of the text, which he had had from his father who in his turn had been given it by the authors, to Sempad (Smbat), constable of Armenia and brother of the Armenian king, Hetum I (1226–69). It was Sempad, who was the author of a history of Armenia and who died in 1276, who translated the *Assises* into Armenian. Quite when the translation was made is not clear, although, as the preface indicates, it was evidently before the Mamluk conquest and destruction of Antioch in 1268. But perhaps not long before that date: Simon the constable was in office by 1262, and remained in post until the conquest.[11] We might note in passing that John of Ibelin, count of Jaffa (d. 1266), the celebrated Latin Syrian legal writer, was married to Sempad's sister and that, as John himself mentioned, on at least one occasion Sempad had consulted him about a point of law.[12]

The full title of the *Assises* was apparently 'The Usages and *Assises* of the Barony of the City of Antioch',[13] thus reflecting an idea found in the kingdom of Jerusalem that the law comprised an assemblage of both customary law and enacted law. However, the legists made no attempt to distinguish these two elements.[14] The treatise is divided into two roughly equal parts, the first dealing with the law as it affected the vassals, and the second concerned with burgess law. It is worth reminding ourselves here that the essential legal division was not, as is often assumed, between Franks – people of Western extraction – and the indigenous population comprising Christians of various hues, Muslims and Jews, but between the feudatories and the rest. Indeed, there is reason to believe that in Antioch, as elsewhere in the East, the Frankish rulers allowed the indigenous communities to settle their own internal disputes in their own

---

[10] C. Cahen, *La Syrie du Nord à l'époque des croisades et la principauté franque d'Antioche* (Paris, 1940), pp. 28–31.

[11] *Cartulaire général de l'Ordre des Hospitaliers*, ed. J. Delaville le Roulx (Paris, 1894–1906), iii, no. 3053; Cahen, *Syrie du Nord*, pp. 453, 716.

[12] John of Ibelin, *Le Livre des Assises*, ed. P.W. Edbury (Leiden, 2003), pp. 315–16.

[13] *Assises d'Antioche*, p. 2.

[14] See Philip of Novara, *Le Livre de Forme de Plait*, ed. P.W. Edbury (Nicosia, 2009), pp. 118–20.

way and according to their own customs, provided of course that no one outside their communities was affected.[15]

The text is quite short – at a rough estimate the nineteenth-century French translation runs to around 10,000 words. By comparison, Philip of Novara's treatise on the 'feudal' law of Jerusalem, written in Cyprus in about 1250, is just over 40,000 words, while the original version of John of Ibelin's *Livre des Assises*, written in the kingdom of Jerusalem in the mid-1260s, runs to over 160,000 words.[16] Despite its relative brevity, the Antiochene *Assises* does contain a large amount of information. Some elements were clearly in line with what we know of Jerusalemite custom – and, at the end of the twelfth century, the custom of Jerusalem was sufficiently solidified to be exported to the new Lusignan kingdom of Cyprus – but other elements were not. A few examples will suffice. The treatise begins with the mutual obligations of lord and man contingent on the oath of fealty, and moves rapidly to the vassal's obligation to answer summons for military service. The issue of whether or not the man had in fact been summoned properly in accord with the established procedures is dealt with in identical terms to the practice further south in Jerusalem, as is the penalty of loss of fief for a year and a day in the event of a failure to answer summons.[17] The text then moves on to the provision for a vassal to 'commend' (or surrender) his fief to his lord should he wish to avoid service. Here again, the arrangements reflect what was current in the kingdoms of Jerusalem and Cyprus. If a vassal wished to avoid performing service, he could surrender his fief for a year and a day, and then receive it back at the end of that period.[18] What none of the Latin Syrian legists suggests is that there was an institutionalised system of commuting military obligations to a money payment – in other words, there was no scutage. The vassal either served in person or, unless the lord permitted him to send a substitute, had to commend – or relinquish – his fief to his lord. We also find in the *Assises* that the widow's dower was, as elsewhere in the East, set at half her husband's fief and half his movables – and not at a third as in England.[19] It is a pity that none of the evidence allows us to see how this would have worked in practice: how, for example, would an heir cope with his obligations if both his widowed mother and his widowed

---

[15]   Cf. J. Prawer, *The History of the Jews in the Latin Kingdom of Jerusalem* (Oxford, 1988), pp. 96–8.

[16]   Philip of Novara, p. 1; John of Ibelin, p. 2.

[17]   *Assises d'Antioche*, pp. 8–10. Cf. Philip of Novara, pp. 116–18, 157; John of Ibelin, pp. 196, 431–2, 479–502, passim.

[18]   *Assises d'Antioche*, pp. 10–12. Cf. Philip of Novara, pp. 116, 159; John of Ibelin, pp. 399–400.

[19]   *Assises d'Antioche*, p. 18. Cf. John of Ibelin, pp. 394–5.

grandmother were still living and both women had re-married, with the result
that their dowers were in effect controlled by an unsympathetic step-father and
an equally unsympathetic step-grandfather?

It is where the *Assises d'Antioche* diverges from the custom of Jerusalem and
Cyprus that perhaps provides the greater interest. I shall limit myself to two
examples. When, as frequently would have happened, an Antiochene vassal
died leaving a minor heir (or heiress), control of the heir and the patrimony
would pass to the surviving parent, normally the child's mother. But if there
was no mother, or if the mother had died before the heir's majority, the lord
would take control of the inheritance, making provision from it for the heir's
support.[20] Compare this with the situation elsewhere. In England the lord
took control of the fief for the duration of the minority and, although the
mother would have her widow's dower, that was all. As in Antioch, the lord
was supposed to make provision for the heir's upbringing but, as is well known,
the English system of seigneurial wardship was open to abuse, most notoriously
during the reign of King John.[21] Yet in Jerusalem and Cyprus the situation was
totally different. There the mother would hold the inheritance and bring up
the heir, and if she too had died, the wardship of the fief would pass to the
nearest adult heir who wanted it – probably an uncle or a cousin – while the
heir would be cared for by relatives on the other side of the family.[22] This, of
course, was a device to protect the heir from that well-known character, 'the
wicked uncle'. It was only when there was no surviving parent and no suitable
potential heir that the lord could intervene. So, in this instance, the *Assises*
describes a convention which stands midway between English custom on the
one hand and Jerusalemite custom on the other.

There is at least one clear example where Antiochene practice was directly
in line with a distinctively English custom. In chapter 14 of the first part of
the *Assises*, we learn that the knight who marries a woman who has property
of her own can retain his wife's property until his own death if she predeceases
him, provided that there has been a child born to them. The chapter is careful
to specify that, if the child has died, the father continues to hold the fief, and
it is only on his death that it passes to his wife's heirs.[23] Medieval English

---

[20]   *Assises d'Antioche*, p. 16.
[21]   See, for example, J.C. Holt, *Magna Carta*, 2nd edn (Cambridge, 1992), especially
pp. 307–8, 311–14.
[22]   Philip of Novara, pp. 66–7, 69; John of Ibelin, pp. 377, 396 (cf. pp. 639–43, 741).
[23]   *Assises d'Antioche*, p. 36 (cf. p. 46). Thanks are due to Dr Gideon Brough for arranging
through Armenian friends of his for the accuracy of the French translation of this chapter to
be verified.

lawyers knew this custom as 'the curtesy of England'.[24] It was a custom that was wholly unknown to Philip of Novara, John of Ibelin and the other legal writers in the kingdom of Jerusalem and in Cyprus. In all likelihood, this is a feature that the Norman element in Antiochene society introduced, perhaps early in the principality's history at a time when the customs associated with fief-holding were still fluid. The chapter goes on to explain that if the woman has an adult male son by a previous marriage, then this son acquires the patrimony immediately and the widower is excluded, but if there are daughters by the first marriage and a son by the second marriage, then the son is her heir and his father holds the property for the duration of his life; if, however, there are daughters by both marriages and no sons, then the court will make provision for sharing her patrimony equally among the half-sisters, with the surviving father retaining his own daughters' portions during his lifetime. The detail covering these various contingencies suggests that the whole issue had been the subject of lively debate and, no doubt, litigation

Overall, however, there is no question but that in many respects the twelfth- and thirteenth-century customs relating to 'feudal' tenure, military obligation and inheritance in the Latin East, including Antioch, reflect practices found not in the Anglo-Norman *regnum* but in parts of France outside Normandy.[25] So, to mention just a few points that feature prominently in Magna Carta, relief, primer seisin and scutage were all unknown in the East. Indeed, it would appear that the customary law of the kingdom of Jerusalem was angled quite deliberately to ensure the preservation of personal military service, while the fiscal potential of fiefs to the lord was of little account, and for Western parallels we need to look elsewhere than England and Normandy.[26] A more systematic comparison of these Eastern customs with practices in other parts of the 'Norman world' and elsewhere in Western Europe would undoubtedly be worth undertaking. Certainly, the principality of Antioch and the text we know as the *Assises d'Antioche* deserve a more thorough consideration.

---

[24] The classic exposition of this doctrine is in F. Pollock and F.W. Maitland, *The History of English Law*, 2nd edn, with a new Introduction by S.F.C. Milsom (Cambridge, 1968), ii, pp. 414–20.

[25] For Normandy and its neighbours, see in particular Power, *Norman Frontier*, chapter 4.

[26] See P.W. Edbury, 'Feudal obligations in the Latin East', *Byzantion*, 47 (1977), pp. 328–56, at pp. 342–8; reprinted in my *Kingdoms of the Crusaders: From Jerusalem to Cyprus* (Aldershot and Brookfield, Vermont, 1999), chapter III.

VIII

The French Translation of William of Tyre's *Historia*: the Manuscript Tradition[1]

Archbishop William of Tyre wrote his history of the crusades and the Latin East between the late 1160s and 1184, and Robert Huygens' definitive edition of William's Latin text, based on a critical analysis of seven manuscripts (plus one fragment), appeared in 1986.[2] At some point between the end of the Third Crusade and the early 1230s someone translated the work into French,[3] and 51 manuscripts of the translation dating from before 1500 survive in public collections. These are listed below in Appendix 1.[4] The French version, usually referred to as *L'estoire de Eracles* or, more simply, *Eracles* (thanks to the mention of the seventh-century Byzantine emperor Heraklios in the first sentence), was published in 1844 in the *Recueil des historiens des croisades: historiens occidentaux*, volume 1, where the text occupies the lower half of the same page as William's Latin text, and again, in 1879–80, by Paulin Paris.[5] All modern scholars who have had occasion to refer to the translation have used one or other of these editions. Most of the *Eracles* manuscripts have continuations which take the narrative well into the thirteenth century, and these continuations were published in 1859 in *Recueil des historiens des croisades: historiens occidentaux*, volume 2. The only sections from the continuations to have been re-edited since then are those covering the years 1184–97 from the Lyon, Bibliothèque de la Ville, ms. 828 (F72)[6] and 1191–97 from the Florence, Biblioteca Medicea-Laurenziana, ms. Plu. LXI.10 (F70) which Ruth Morgan published in 1982.[7]

---

[1] Research for this paper has been facilitated by a grant from the British Academy. I thank Professor Jaroslav Folda for reading and commenting on an earlier draft.
[2] *Willelmi Tyrensis Archiepiscopi Chronicon*, ed. Robert B. C. Huygens, 2 vols., CCCM 63 (Turnhout, 1986). (Henceforth: WT)
[3] John H. Pryor, "The *Eracles* and William of Tyre: an Interim Report", in *Horns*, pp. 270–93 at pp. 288–89 (arguing for a date after 1204 and before 1234).
[4] I have seen all except the fire-damaged Turin Biblioteca Nazionale, ms. L. II. 17 .
[5] *L'estoire de Eracles empereur et la conqueste de la terre d'Outremer*, RHC Oc., 1 (1844); *Guillaume de Tyr et ses continuateurs: text français du XIIIe siècle*, ed. Paulin Paris, 2 vols. (Paris, 1879–80).
[6] To simplify referring to the manuscripts I have followed the numbering in Jaroslav Folda, "Manuscripts of the *History of Outremer* by William of Tyre: a Handlist", *Scriptorium* 27 (1973), 90–95. "F72" is thus Folda no. 72. Book and chapter numbers are given thus: 15.12.
[7] *La continuation de Guillaume de Tyr (1184–1197)*, ed. Margaret Ruth Morgan, Documents relatifs à l'histoire des croisades 14 (Paris, 1982).

70

Historical enquiry into the French William of Tyre has tended to concentrate on two distinct areas: the manuscript illuminations and the continuations. Between them Hugo Buchthal and Jaroslav Folda established that some of the most notable illuminated manuscripts of *Eracles* were produced in the Latin East in the second half of the thirteenth century, and their discoveries have shed considerable light on the artistic *milieu* there in the decades before the fall of Acre in 1291.[8] The French continuations are a major source for our knowledge of the history of the Latin East after 1184 – there was no historian there writing in Latin of the stature of William of Tyre to describe later events – and so, with the late Ruth Morgan leading the way, it is not surprising that they should have come under critical scrutiny.[9] The text of the translation itself, however, has received less attention, even though historians have been aware of significant differences between it and the original Latin version. A group of scholars met at the Institute for Advanced Studies of the Hebrew University of Jerusalem in 1987 to investigate the relationship between the *Eracles* text and William's Latin chronicle, and their report, composed by John Pryor, began by explaining that they realized from the outset that "the attainment of [their] objectives would, at the very least, be severely hampered by the unsatisfactory nature of the current edition of the *Eracles*."[10] The discussions on that occasion were fruitful, but, as the participants would doubtless be the first to admit, many problems remain. More recently, Bernard Hamilton, a member of the 1987 group, has published a detailed analysis comparing the Latin and French texts of books 21–23 which cover the reign of Baldwin IV from 1174 until the point early in 1184 at which William ceased writing.[11] This is an important article with many pertinent comments, designed to show how, and to what extent, the translator modified what was before him. However, Hamilton's analysis does require a confidence in the printed text of the translation – in this instance the Paulin Paris edition – which, sadly, is not entirely warranted. Even so, it is much to be hoped that other scholars will repeat this exercise for different periods in William's narrative.

The present paper aims to lay the groundwork for establishing a stemma of the extant manuscripts. Such an exercise has to be seen as a pre-requisite for a critical

---

[8] Hugo Buchthal, *Miniature Painting in the Latin Kingdom of Jerusalem* (Oxford, 1957); Jaroslav Folda, *Crusader Manuscript Illumination at Saint-Jean d'Acre, 1275–1291* (Princeton, 1976). For recent work, see for example Bianca Kühnel, "The Perception of History in Thirteenth-Century Crusader Art," in *France and the Holy Land: Frankish Culture at the End of the Crusades*, ed. Daniel H. Weiss and Lisa Mahoney (Baltimore, 2004), pp. 161–86, at pp. 173–78; Jaroslav Folda, *Crusader Art in the Holy Land, From the Third Crusade to the Fall of Acre, 1187–1291* (Cambridge, 2005), pp. 217–18, 235–36, 345–50, 401–8, 424–27, 495–97, 525–26.

[9] Margaret Ruth Morgan, *The Chronicle of Ernoul and the Continuations of William of Tyre* (Oxford, 1973); eadem, "The Rothelin Continuation of William of Tyre," in *Outremer*, pp. 244–57; Peter W. Edbury, "The Lyon *Eracles* and the Old French Continuations of William of Tyre," in *Montjoie*, pp. 139–53 (critical of Morgan's 1973 monograph).

[10] Pryor, "The *Eracles* and William of Tyre," p. 270.

[11] Bernard Hamilton, "The Old French translation of William of Tyre as an historical source," in *EC*, 2, pp. 93–112.

edition. By consulting those manuscripts identified as most closely preserving the text of the original translation, the sort of exercise that Hamilton embarked upon would be made more secure. In addition, an enquiry into the way in which the text developed should shed light on where and how it circulated and also on the practices followed in individual workshops. It might also be of interest to know if, and to what extent, textual affiliations run parallel to artistic linkages.

One major problem with vernacular texts from this period is that copyists did not regard the exemplars they were using as sacrosanct. That meant they would modify the text by improving or modernizing the word-order and the vocabulary. They might also change the structure of the text by dividing or amalgamating chapters, by interpolating fresh material, or by making omissions. Deliberate changes are one thing; inadvertent mistakes quite another, but both would be transmitted to posterity by a copyist utilizing a particular manuscript as his exemplar. Textual variations and changes to the structure of the books and chapters along with the presence or otherwise of rubrics provide the raw material for investigating the relationships between the manuscripts.

The procedure adopted for the analysis that follows in this paper has been to take a microfilm or microfiche of each manuscript in turn and note the first six and the last six words of each chapter; the information thus gathered provides a sample of variant readings and allows for the identification of merged, split and missing chapters. It must be stressed, however, that this analysis is not comprehensive; the conclusions are therefore not final but should be regarded as the fruits of "work in progress". In particular, it has not proved possible to construct a tidy "family tree" on which each manuscript can be assigned a place that would denote its relationship to all the other manuscripts; rather in most instances the best that can be done is to establish which manuscripts have textual affinities with which others. Part of the difficulty is that anomalies abound, and it is demonstrable that some copyists used more than one exemplar in preparing a new codex, with the result that we have hybrid texts that cannot be fitted neatly into a stemma. The thinking behind this approach perhaps needs a little more explanation. If a manuscript has a particular variant reading, or divides a chapter at a particular place, or merges two chapters and does not share this feature with any other manuscript, all that can be said for certain is that no other manuscript has been derived directly from it; indeed the feature could well have been introduced by the copyist of the manuscript in question. On the other hand, when several manuscripts share the same reading, division or amalgamation, that could indicate a common ancestor, and the textual affinity would be confirmed if the same group of manuscripts have several other similar features in common. It has, however, to be remembered that such features might arise independently: after all, if a scribe wanted to split a chapter into two there are only so many possible places he could do so sensibly. As will become clear later, one of the problems faced in undertaking this project results from the lack of consistency within each manuscript which means that particular copies may have features in common for a limited section of the text, only to lose this common ground thereafter.

72

Neither of the nineteenth-century editions is satisfactory. The *Recueil* edition was based on readings supplied by a selection of manuscripts chosen primarily, so it would seem, because they happened to be in Paris. Apparently the editors used the fifteenth-century Paris, BN, ms. fr. 2627 (F02) as their base manuscript which they compared with three other Paris manuscripts: BN, ms. fr. 2825 (F58), BN, ms. fr. 2827 (F48), and BN, ms. fr. 9082 (F77).[12] They seem to have been rather arbitrary in deciding which readings to prefer. They also adopted a policy of altering the structure of the French translation to bring the chapter divisions into conformity with the divisions in the Latin text. This approach meant that some chapters were made to begin and end where the Latin begins and ends and not where they do in the manuscripts. It also led to a number of chapters in the French version being split in two and those in the rest of the book in question being renumbered accordingly. (For details see below, Appendix 2.) The *Recueil* edition comes with a complete set of rubrics, pieced together from those contained in F58 and F77 – F02, the Paris, BN, ms. fr. 2627, lacks rubrics. Paulin Paris chose a manuscript datable to ca. 1300 – and so by no means the earliest – as his base: it is now the Baltimore, Walters Art Gallery, ms. 142 (F52). Had he simply transcribed this manuscript and modernized the punctuation, we should, as will become clear presently, possess an edition that would be reasonably dependable. What he did was to create a pastiche by introducing readings from the *Recueil* edition into his text, and he also appears to have made some use of the manuscript that is now the Baltimore, Walters Art Gallery, ms. 137 (F31); moreover, he followed the *Recueil* by imposing many of the same unwarranted chapter divisions, and he added the rubrics from the *Recueil*, although here again there were none in his base manuscript.

In the nineteenth century, Louis de Mas Latrie and Paul Riant listed the manuscripts then known, sorting them into groups depending on whether they contained a version of the continuation to William's text, and, if so, where they ended.[13] In 1973, Folda published a handlist, essentially an up-dated version of Riant's work, in which he noted new discoveries and current shelf marks, and it is on this guide to the manuscripts that I have relied.[14] Following his nineteenth-century models, Folda divided the *Eracles* manuscripts into four groups:

- Those with no continuation (F01–F06)
- Those with a continuation that is virtually identical to the text known as the *Chronique d'Ernoul et de Bernard le Trésorier* for the period beginning in

---

[12] *RHC Oc.*, 1, p. xxvi. For the modern shelf marks, see Paul Riant, "Inventaire sommaire des manuscrits de l'*Eracles*," *AOL*, 1 (1881), 247–52 at pp. 248 (nos. 1, 3), 250 (no. 32), 251 (no. 67). The editors claimed that what is now the ms. fr. 2627 is a thirteenth-century manuscript when in reality it dates to the fifteenth.

[13] Louis de Mas Latrie, "Essai de classification des continuations de l'historie des croisades de Guillaume de Tyr," in *Chronique d'Ernoul et de Bernard le Trésorier* (Paris, 1871), pp. 473–565 at pp. 480–88; Riant, "Inventaire sommaire," pp. 247–52, cf. pp. 716–17.

[14] Folda, see above note 6.

the mid-1180s and ending with events in Latin Greece datable to 1232 (F30–F51)[15]
* Those with the further continuation for the period 1232–61 known as the "Rothelin Continuation" (F52–F66)[16]
* Those with a completely different continuation for the period 1232 onwards, in several instances going on to the 1260s or 1270s, and which is known as either the "Acre Continuation" or the "Noailles Continuation" (F67–F78).[17]

For scholars more interested in the continuations than the text of the translation itself, this categorization was sensible, but it is of limited value in an analysis of the translation. A number of manuscripts lack their concluding folios, usually breaking off in mid-sentence at the end of a page, and so we can never know for certain where they originally finished. Thus three of the six manuscripts of the first group (F01, F03 and F04) are truncated, while the same is true of eight out of the 22 manuscripts in the second group (F30, F32, F34, F35, F41, F43, F49, F51). On the other hand, some manuscripts had continuations added later. A good case in point is the Walters Art Gallery, ms. 142 (F52) which provided Paulin Paris with his base. Here the text originally finished at fol. 263r where the Latin text ends with the events of 1184; fol. 263v is blank, and then the continuations, which conclude with the Rothelin text, follow in a different hand starting at fol. 264r. Folda has suggested that the text of the translation was copied ca. 1300 and the continuations added ca. 1340.[18] There is therefore a good case for considering this manuscript in conjunction with the other manuscripts with no continuation rather than with the Rothelin group. Similarly the Brussels, Bibliothèque Royale, ms. 9492–3 (F54) originally ended in 1232 at fol. 380r, and the Rothelin continuation, beginning at fol. 381r, was clearly added subsequently. Arguably it belongs with the other 1232 manuscripts, and features of the text of the translation in this manuscript support that view.

The Original Translation

William's Latin text broke off with the events of early 1184 and the appointment of Count Raymond III of Tripoli as regent of the kingdom of Jerusalem. Three of the *Eracles* manuscripts (Paris, BN, ms. fr. 2627 (F02), Paris, BN, ms. fr. 9081 (F05), and Rome, Biblioteca Apostolica Vaticana, ms. Pal. lat. 1963 (F06)) plus a fourth, the Baltimore, Walters Art Gallery, ms. 142 (F52) where the continuation was added subsequently, end at the same place as the Latin text. The existence of this group is sufficient to show that the French translation was in circulation before someone decided to bring the narrative closer to the present – in fact to 1232 – by adapting

---

[15] *Chronique d'Ernoul et de Bernard le Trésorier*, ed. Louis de Mas Latrie (Paris, 1871).
[16] *RHC Oc.*, 2: 483–639.
[17] *RHC Oc.*, 2: 380–481.
[18] Folda, *Crusader Manuscript Illumination*, p. 212. See also the catalogue description at pp. 212–13.

the so-called *Chronique d'Ernoul et de Bernard Le Trésorier* and pasting it on at the end. The Paris, BN, ms. fr. 9081 (F05) is the earliest *Eracles* manuscript with illustrations; it was executed in Paris in the years 1245–48, in other words on the eve of Louis IX's crusade.[19] Folda has argued that the Biblioteca Apostolica Vaticana, ms. Pal. lat. 1963 (F06) originated in Antioch, and he has recently proposed that it is to be dated to between ca. 1260 and the city's destruction in 1268.[20] Although the Paris, BN, ms. fr. 2627 (F02) was made in the fifteenth century, it is clear from an analysis of the variant readings that it was a faithful copy of an early version of the text, and so the editors of the *Recueil* had justification for choosing it as their base manuscript. The Baltimore, Walters Art Gallery, ms. 142 (F52), which dates from ca. 1300 and which was used by Paris for his edition, would also seem to provide a text that comes close to the original form of the translation.

Whilst the original translation did not follow William's text slavishly, it did at least follow his chapter divisions to a considerable extent. So when we are faced with a manuscript that contains a number of examples of William's chapters having been divided or amalgamated, we can conclude that such a feature indicates a move away from the original structure of the translation. In other words, the fewer examples there are of divisions or amalgamations, the closer we might appear to be to the original. Of the four manuscripts mentioned as ending in 1184, F02 has just one example of a chapter split into two, and one example of two chapters run together; for F05 the totals are again one and one; F06 by contrast has four chapters split into two, one split into three and 15 examples of chapters run together, while F52 lacks 8.23 but has no examples of divided chapters and only one instance, at 13.24–25, of an amalgamation.[21] F05, which dates from the mid-1240s, is among the earliest surviving manuscripts, but three other manuscripts, which have been dated to about the same period or slightly later, show no clear pattern. The mid-thirteenth-century London, BL, Henry Yates Thompson ms. 12 (F38), perhaps the oldest extant manuscript to have a continuation, contains just one split chapter and one example of two chapters run together in the text of the translation. Similarly the Paris, BN, ms. fr. 2826 (F04), which, so it is claimed, dates to the first half of the thirteenth century, has no split chapters and 11 amalgamations, yet another early manuscript, the Paris, BN, ms. fr. 2632 (F03), has 149 split chapters but just one amalgamation. The rather later Paris, BN, ms. fr. 67 (F41), another manuscript with the 1232 continuation, has just two amalgamated chapters and no examples of

---

[19] Ibid., p. 31 and n. 27; *Crusader Art in the Holy Land*, pp. 217, 235–36 and n. 44 (p. 614).

[20] Jaroslav Folda, "A Crusader Manuscript from Antioch," *Atti della Pontificia Accademia Romana di Archeologia*, Ser. 3, *Rendiconti*, 42 (1969–70), 283–98; *Crusader Art in the Holy Land*, pp. 218 n. 614 (p. 611), 347–50 and n. 877 (pp. 641–42).

[21] It is possible that this apparent amalgamation in fact preserves an original feature of the translation as there is no chapter division in the Latin text at this point. Four other manuscripts, F36, F43, F44, F73, none of which is particularly close to the original, also run 13.24–25 together, but all the other seemingly "primitive" versions of the text have a division here.

VIII

chapters that have been divided. Apart from F03, these figures are very low, as the table listing these divisions and amalgamations in Appendix 4 makes clear. Anyone wishing to find manuscripts with a text of the translation that most closely reflects the original version might well begin with an examination of F02, F04, F05, F38, F41 and F52, all of which come near to preserving the chapter divisions found in William's Latin text.[22]

Unfortunately things are by no means so simple. By far the most frequently occurring amalgamation is at 22.24–25. Of the 50 manuscripts under consideration, 38 run these chapters together, while 11 retain the division as found in the Latin text, and one (F01) lacks this section of the narrative. But of those 11 manuscripts, only one (F52) is among those identified at the end of the last paragraph as preserving an early version of the text. F06, the manuscript attributed to Antioch that ends where William's Latin does, is another, but the remaining 9 are problematic. Two, F03 and F46, have numerous divided chapters, and it could be that a copyist, who was evidently prone to split chapters had, perhaps without knowing, restored the division at the original point in what had now become a rather lengthy chapter. However, such a coincidence seems less likely in respect of F70 or F74 or the closely interrelated group of manuscripts with the Rothelin continuation, F60, F61, F62, F63 and F65. These manuscripts have somehow managed to preserve a feature that could well have been present in the original version of the translation even though, in other respects, they are further removed from that original than several others in which these two chapters are merged.

Two Distinct Manuscript Traditions

At an early stage in my investigation it became clear that a major bifurcation exists in the manuscript tradition. A significant group of manuscripts all have the same features in common: 1.2 follows 1.1 without a break, and then 1.2 itself is divided into three; moving on we find that the following chapters are merged: 3.24–25, 5.4–5, 8.21–22, 12.24–25, 19.9–10, 21.17–18, 21.20–21 and 22.25–26. It is a pattern that is shared by 24 manuscripts:[23]

F06 Rome, Biblioteca Apostolica Vaticana, ms. Pal. lat. 1963 (Antioch: 1260s)
F30 Arras, Bibliothèque Municipale, ms. 651 (N. France: early 14th century)
F32 Bern, Bürgerbibliothek, ms. 112 (N. France: ca. 1270)
F33 Bern, Bürgerbibliothek, ms. 163 (N. France: 3rd quarter of 13th century)
F37 London, BL, Royal ms. 15. E. I (Flanders: late 15th century)

[22] The translator evidently used a Latin manuscript which lacked William's autobiographical chapter (19.12) and which probably resembled most closely those in Huygens's β group (though without the reference to Pontigny at 12.7). See the introduction to the Latin edition, pp. 3–19.
[23] Allowing for the fact that F54, F55 and F65 are damaged and in each case lack the first element.

F39   Paris, Bibliothèque de l'Arsenal, ms. 5220 (N. France: 3rd quarter of 13th century)

F40   Paris, Bibliothèque du Ministère des Affaires Etrangères, Mémoires et Documents 230*bis* (S. France: 3rd quarter of 13th century)

F42   Paris, BN, ms. fr. 68 (Flanders: ca. 1450)

F43   Paris, BN, ms. fr. 779 (N. France: ca. 1275)

F44   Paris, BN, ms. fr. 2629 (Flanders: ca. 1460)

F45   Paris, BN, ms. fr. 2630 (N. France: 3rd quarter of 13th century)

F47   Paris, BN, ms. fr. 2824 (N. France: ca. 1300)

F48   Paris, BN, ms. fr. 2827 (N. France: 3rd quarter of 13th century)

F51   Paris, BN, ms. fr. 24208 (N. France: 3rd quarter of 13th century)

F53   Brussels, Bibliothèque Royale, ms. 9045 (Flanders: ca. 1460)

F54   Brussels, Bibliothèque Royale, ms. 9492–3 (Paris: ca. 1291–95)

F55   Lyon, Bibliothèque de la Ville, ms. Palais des Arts 29 (Paris: ca. 1295–96)

F58   Paris, BN, ms. fr. 2825 (Paris: early 14th century)

F60   Paris, BN, ms. fr. 9083 (Ile de France: 2nd quarter of 14th century)

F61   Paris, BN, ms. fr. 22495 (Paris: 1337)

F62   Paris, BN, ms. fr. 22496–7 (Paris: ca. 1350)

F63   Paris, BN, ms. fr. 24209 (Ile de France: 3rd quarter of 14th century)

F64   Rome, Biblioteca Apostolica Vaticana, ms. Reg. Suec. lat. 737 (Paris: early 14th century)

F65   Turin, Biblioteca Nazionale, ms. L I. 5 (France: 15th century)

Three further manuscripts should be associated with this group. The Besançon, Bibliothèque Municipale, ms. 856 (F34 – N. France: ca. 1300) has all the listed features bar two (no amalgamation at 8.21–22, and 12.24–25), and the Geneva, Bibliothèque Publique et Universitaire, ms. 85 (F36 – Artois: 3rd quarter of the 15th century) has the last five amalgamations but not the others. In both cases it may be wondered whether there had been a change of exemplars at some previous point in the transmission of the text.[24] The Paris, BN, ms. fr. 2754 (F46 – N. France: ca. 1300), which only begins at 16.1, has two out of the four amalgamated chapters in the extant portion of the text, and should perhaps therefore be considered as belonging with this group.[25] Variant readings confirm this division in the manuscript tradition. A clear example is provided by the concluding phrase of 13.7 where none of the manuscripts included in the list given above (including F34 and F36) contains the word "onques" in the phrase "onques fait devant," whereas all the others do.[26]

---

[24] The idea that the central section of F34 may be derived from a manuscript from a different tradition is perhaps confirmed by the fact that in four instances chapters are divided in the same place as the β manuscripts, F31 and F35: 7.25, 7.19, 9.13, 16.21.

[25] A feature of F46 is the large number of divided chapters, and it is possible that the copyist responsible for most of these divisions reintroduced divisions at 21.17–18 and 22.25–26.

[26] The only exceptions are F45 and F46 (and also F77) where the folios with this passage are missing.

It is highly significant that the Antioch manuscript, F06, falls into this category, as it is sufficient to prove that manuscripts with these diagnostic features – nine amalgamated chapters and one chapter split into three – were already in circulation before it became normal to attach a continuation to the text. F06 is also the only manuscript out of the total of 28 that has been attributed to the Latin East. None of the manuscripts from Acre (F49, F50, F69–F73, F78) and none of the manuscripts with the so-called "Acre" or "Noailles" continuation (F67–78) appears in this group. What is striking is that, with the exception of F06 and also F40 (which, it is suggested, was copied in southern France),[27] all the manuscripts datable to the latter part of the thirteenth century or the very beginning of the fourteenth – F30, F32, F33, F34, F39, F43, F45, F47, F48, F51, F54, F55, F58 – are from northern France. This list includes a distinctive group of seven manuscripts – F32, F33, F39, F43, F45, F48, F51 – which, as Jaroslav Folda has kindly informed me, contain related cycles of miniatures.[28] Of the manuscripts with the fewest merged or divided chapters, and hence *prima facie* those closest to the original, mention should be made of the Paris, Bibliothèque de l'Arsenal, ms. 5220 (F39) with, apart from the merged and divided chapters that identify this group, no divided chapters and seven amalgamated chapters; the Paris, BN, ms. fr. 2825 (F58) with four and five; the Rome, Biblioteca Apostolica Vaticana, ms. Pal. lat. 1963 (F06) with four and six; the Paris, Bibliothèque du Ministère des Affaires Etrangères, Mémoires et Documents 230*bis* (F40) with three and nine; the Rome, Biblioteca Apostolica Vaticana, ms. Reg. Suec. lat. 737 (F64) with five and seven; and the mutilated Lyon, Bibliothèque de la Ville, ms. Palais des Arts 29 (F55) with three and five.

Henceforth I shall refer to the manuscripts which do not share the characteristics of the group discussed here as the "alpha (α) group", and the manuscripts listed above as the "beta (β) group."

The α group

Having already listed the manuscripts which together make up the β group, it will be helpful now to provide a similar list of those 23 manuscripts which comprise the α group:

F01   Cambridge, Sidney Sussex College, ms. 93 (England: late 13th century)
F02   Paris, BN, ms. fr. 2627 (N. France: 15th century)
F03   Paris, BN, ms. fr. 2632 (Latin East or France: 1st half of 13th century)
F04   Paris, BN, ms. fr. 2826 (Latin East or France: 1st half of 13th century)
F05   Paris, BN, ms. fr. 9081 (Paris: ca. 1245–48)
F31   Baltimore, Walters Art Gallery, ms. 137 (Paris: ca. 1295–1300)

---

[27] Folda, 'Manuscripts', p. 94; cf *Crusader Manuscript Illumination*, p. 146 n. 129.
[28] Private communication.

VIII

78

F35 Epinal, Bibliothèque Municipale, ms. 45 (Paris: ca. 1295–1300)
F38 London, BL, Henry Yates Thompson ms. 12 (England: mid-13th century)
F41 Paris, BN, ms. fr. 67 (N. France: 2nd half of 13th century)
F49 Paris, BN, ms. fr. 9085 (Acre: ca. 1277–80)
F50 Paris, BN, ms. fr. 9086 (Acre: ca. 1255–60)
F52 Baltimore, Walters Art Gallery, ms. 142 (Paris: ca. 1300 and ca. 1340)
F57 Paris, BN, ms. fr. 2634 (Ile de France: 1st quarter of 14th century)
F67 Amiens, Bibliothèque Municipale, ms. 483 (Flanders: mid-15th century)
F68 Bern, Bürgerbibliothek, ms. 25 (N. France: 1st half of 15th century)
F69 Boulogne-sur-Mer, Bibliothèque Municipale, ms. 142 (Acre: ca. 1287)
F70 Florence, Biblioteca Medicea-Laurenziana, ms. Plu. LXI. 10 (Acre: ca. 1290, and Italy: 1st half of 14th century)
F71 St Petersburg, National Library of Russia / Российская Национальная Библиотека, ms. fr. f° v. IV.5 (Acre: ca. 1280)
F72 Lyon, Bibliothèque de la Ville, ms. 828 (Acre: ca. 1280)
F73 Paris, BN, ms. fr. 2628 (Acre: late 1250s/early 1260s and late 1270s)
F74 Paris, BN, ms. fr. 2631 (Lombardy: ca. 1291–95)
F77 Paris, BN, ms. fr. 9082 (Rome: 1295)
F78 Paris, BN, ms. fr. 9084 (Acre: ca. 1286)

Taken together, the features that distinguish the β group are unmistakable, but it is nonetheless true that a few of the α manuscripts share some of them. Thus four – F04, F70, F72 and F77 – all begin with 1.2 following 1.1 without a break and then dividing 1.2 into three;[29] F04, F70 and F72 and also F73 then merge 3.24–25, and F04 and F72 also merge 5.4–5. Several others – F67, F68, F69, F74 and F78 – merge 8.21–22. When we turn to examine the variant readings, we find instances of F04, F70 and F72 sharing characteristic readings with the β group, as for example in the final phrase in 4.18, and, in the case of F70 and F72, at the end of 4.20.[30] It would therefore appear either that somewhere in their ancestry, a copyist had begun by copying a manuscript from the β group before switching to one from the α group, or that some of the characteristic features in the β group appeared in the manuscript tradition before others, and that these manuscripts preserve part of this transitional stage. But apart from this handful of exceptions, the α manuscripts have none of the other group's distinctive merged chapters in common.

The manuscripts which earlier were identified as preserving the most primitive form of the translation – F02, F04, F05, F38, F41 and F52 – require further consideration. In F02, F04, F05, F41 and F52 the chapters are numbered, a feature not shared by most of the manuscripts in either the α group or the β group. It seems clear that numbering chapters was characteristic of earliest versions, and that this

---

[29] It is not entirely clear whether F04 has the two chapter divisions in 1.2, as the folio is largely illegible.
[30] 4.18: "bobans" or "bouban" for "feste;" 4.21: "ou que .iiii." for "ou que .iii. ."

practice was jettisoned as the manuscript tradition developed. In F04 and also in F03 the chapters are provided with numbers, but not where a chapter has been divided with the result that the numbers assigned to chapters later in the same book remain unchanged. An echo of the practice of numbering chapters is preserved in some of the later α manuscripts which were either copied in Acre or which are derived from those that were. At the end of 19.23 we are told that Muslim losses amounted to 1,500 men,[31] and this figure is repeated in almost all the manuscripts. However, F49, F70, F72, F77 give the figure as 1,524. It is apparent that what has happened is that the copyist of the ancestor of this group, working from a manuscript in which the chapters were numbered, conflated the figure in the text with the chapter number that followed in his exemplar.

The British Library, Henry Yates Thompson ms. 12 (F38) is of particular interest. As mentioned already, it may well be the oldest surviving manuscript to contain the continuation to 1232 adapted from the *Chronique d'Ernoul et de Bernard le Trésorier*. The text of the translation appears to be very close to F05 except in one important respect: there are three places – at 19.21, 19.30 and 22.29 – where other passages from the *Chronique d'Ernoul* have been interpolated.[32] This is the only manuscript with these interpolations, and so it stands alone in the manuscript tradition. What they show is that an editor, evidently working at some point between 1232, which is when the continuation concludes, and around 1250 when the manuscript was produced, was not content simply to attach the portion of the *Chronique d'Ernoul* relating to the period 1184–1232 to the end of the translation, but attempted to integrate the two texts. As Folda has pointed out, the illustrations too represent a unique, independent cycle. One, at the beginning of book 21, showing schoolboys pinching the future leper king Baldwin IV, and William of Tyre himself examining the royal prince, is particularly striking. (It was this incident as recorded by William in the first chapter of book 21 that provided the first inkling that the young Baldwin was afflicted with leprosy.)[33]

The rather later Paris, BN, ms. fr. 67 (F41) similarly has a text that is close to F05 and F38, although in this case there are no miniatures. This manuscript too has a unique feature in that it alone of all the *Eracles* manuscripts is prefaced by an annal in French, covering the period from the time of Julius Caesar to 1095, which fills the first 81 folios. According to the catalogue in the reading room of the Bibliothèque Nationale, this annal is from the world history by Guillaume de Nangis. I have not yet been able to investigate this text further, but its presence here is suggestive. In Acre in the second half of the thirteenth century a substantial number of French William of Tyre manuscripts were produced – eight survive, and no doubt many

---

[31] Cf WT, p. 901.

[32] Respectively *Chronique d'Ernoul*, pp. 25–31, 35–41, 114.

[33] Folda, *Crusader Manuscript Illumination*, p. 32 n. 33. The miniature is reproduced in Bernard Hamilton, *The Leper King and his Heirs: Baldwin IV and the Crusader Kingdom of Jerusalem* (Cambridge, 2000), p. 251.

VIII

80

more have not. At the same period the other principal historical text that was being copied in Acre was the compendium of biblical and classical knowledge known as the *Histoire Universelle*. This work ends with the rule of Julius Caesar, and so it may be wondered whether someone sought to fill the gap between the two works by introducing this extended annal. F41 was not copied in the Latin East, but it could well be that whoever commissioned its production was attuned to the intellectual world which accorded prominence to these two texts, the French William of Tyre and the French *Histoire Universelle*.

The Paris, BN, ms. fr. 2632 (F03) is a manuscript which is thought to date from the first half of the thirteenth century, but unlike the other earliest manuscripts it has many examples of chapters that have been split into two or more parts. In common with the other early copies, the chapters are numbered, but, as mentioned previously, the new chapters formed from dividing the longer chapters are not normally assigned numbers of their own. There are no miniatures, although at fol. 16r there is a rather splendid mermaid in the margin and later, at fol. 37r, more marginalia with a cross of Jerusalem and what may well be intended as a Lusignan lion. The importance of this manuscript lies in the clear affinity its text has with that to be found in two others of an appreciably later date – the Baltimore, Walters Art Gallery, ms. 137 (F31) and the Epinal, Bibliothèque Municipale, ms. 45 (F35), both of which are believed to be of Parisian provenance from the very end of the thirteenth century. Folda has discussed the evident relationship between the miniatures in F31 and F35 and the extent to which they were influenced by those executed in Acre.[34] Textually F31 and F35 are very close. They have a large number of chapter divisions in common, many of which, at least until 16.18, they share with F03; thereafter the distinguishing characteristics do not cease entirely but become appreciably less frequent. Clearly they are derived from a text that in many respects resembled F03. An important feature of F31 and F35 (but not F03) is that they contain as an interpolation a prose version of the text known as the *Ordene de la Chevalrie*, which is inserted after 21.27. At the end of 21.27 (21.28 in the Latin text) William recorded the capture of Hugh of Tiberias in 1179. The *Ordene* then follows with its fictional account of how Saladin persuaded Hugh to instruct him in the ways of western chivalry and dub him knight.[35]

Two other manuscripts that have recognizable affinity are the Baltimore, Walters Art Gallery, ms. 142 (F52) copied in Paris ca. 1300 (with the continuations from 1184–1261 added ca. 1340) and the Cambridge, Sidney Sussex College, ms. 93 (F01) which would seem to be of late thirteenth-century English provenance. The Cambridge manuscript ends part-way through 16.15, and several of the earlier folios are missing. Unlike F52, which seems to have preserved the chapter-structure of

---

[34] Folda, *Crusader Manuscript Illumination*, pp. 146–51. See also the catalogue descriptions at pp. 205–11.
[35] WT, p. 1002. In F35 the latter part of the interpolation is lost due to a missing folio.

the original, F01 has several examples of chapters that have been split in two, or, in one instance (1.5), into three. What seems to have happened is that there were two distinct elements in its make-up. At the beginning and at least until 2.19 it shares a number of features in common with a group of Acre or Acre-related manuscripts: F50, F73 (and the associated F57), F69 (and the associated F67 and F68), F74 and F78. There are ten examples between the start of the manuscript and 2.19 where F01 has chapter divisions found in all or most of these others. It might be added that, although F01 was not illustrated, the decorated capitals at the start of each book appear to be rather basic adaptations of characteristic Acre initials. After book 2, however, this textual affinity with the Acre manuscripts ceases, and the similarities with F52 come to the fore. The most obvious point in common is that both F01 and F52, alone of all the *Eracles* manuscripts, lack 8.23. I have also noted several instances in which F01 and F52 share readings which set them apart from those found in the other manuscripts with "primitive" versions of the text: F02, F05, F38, and F41. Thus, for example, at the start of 4.24, F01 and F52 read "autres grans princes des mescreanz" whilst the others (and also F03, F04, F31 and F35) have "autres mescreans princes." William's Latin reads "ceteros infidelium principes,"[36] and so here at least the readings in F01 and F52 would seem preferable. Another example is provided at the end of 12.24 where F01 and F52 read "… l'en asserroit icele cite [Tyre] sanz demeure" while all the others lack the final two words. Here again, F01 and F52 would seem to be preferable, preserving a rendering of William's phrase "sine questione."[37] At the end of 5.21 (5.22 in the Latin text), speaking of the dead bodies lying in the streets of Antioch, the other manuscripts, but not F01 and F52, include the words "tuit nu" in the phrase "gisoient tuit nu parmi les rues." There is no warrant for "tuit nu" in William's Latin. Here the other manuscripts divide over whether to read "rues" (F02, F03, F31, F35 plus F01 and F52) or "voies" (F04, F05, F38, F41). On the other hand, at the start of 12.1 the French translation, although not the Latin text, made mention of the ancient Persian ruler Xerxes, but here these manuscripts divide quite differently: F02, F03, F05, F38 and F41 call him "Xerses," while F04, F31, F35 plus F01 and F52 call him "Perses;" F01 alone of the manuscripts under discussion here introduces the word "mult" into the phrase "Perses fu .i. mult puissanz rois."[38]

The other α manuscripts were all either products of the Acre scriptorium from the second half of the thirteenth century (F49, F50, F69–F73, F78) or in some way derived from them. Two fifteenth-century manuscripts with a version of the so-called "Acre continuation" ending in 1275 (the Amiens, Bibliothèque Municipale, ms. 483 (F67) and the Bern, Bürgerbibliothek, ms. 25 (F68)) have as their direct ancestor the Boulogne-sur-Mer, Bibliothèque Municipale, ms. 142 (F69) which was

---

[36] WT, p. 267.
[37] Ibid., p. 577 at line 49. The chapter divisions in the Latin and French versions do not coincide here.
[38] F01 shares this reading with F78 and F36.

produced in Acre ca. 1287.[39] This can be shown not just from the fact that F67 and F68 replicate the chapter divisions and amalgamations found in F69, but also because they lack a passage that is missing from F69 as the result of a lost bifolium from the middle of the signature.[40] The missing section extends from part-way through 22.19 to part-way through 22.22, and the copyists of F67 and F68 simply wrote down what was in front of them, seemingly ignoring the evident disjuncture in the text.

The Paris, BN, ms. fr. 2628 (F73), which was produced in Acre in the late 1250s or early 1260s and was completed there in the late 1270s, and the Paris, BN, ms. fr. 2634 (F57), an early fourteenth-century manuscript from the Ile de France, are the only two manuscripts to preserve the so-called Colbert-Fontainebleau text of the continuation for the period 1184–1232.[41] Not surprisingly, these two manuscripts also have many features in common in their text of the translation. Indeed, until the beginning of book 15 they share almost every merged or divided chapter; after that point their unanimity wavers somewhat, and the differences are sufficient to indicate that F57 was not derived from F73 itself but from a manuscript containing a similar, if not totally identical, version.[42]

Eight manuscripts dating to the second half of the thirteenth century survive from Acre. Following the work of Folda, who has made a special study of them, we can divide them on the basis of date and artistic considerations into three groups:

1   The Paris, BN, ms. fr. 9086 (ca. 1255–60) (F50 = *RHC Oc.*, ms "C") is a high-quality manuscript but has no miniatures.[43] Unlike the others it concludes with the events of 1232. Of approximately the same date is the Paris, BN, ms. fr. 2628 (F73 = *RHC Oc.*, ms "B") which does have a series of miniatures, and which, as mentioned in the previous paragraph, contains the "Colbert-Fontainebleau" continuation.[44]

2   Two manuscripts from the late 1270s or early 1280s have miniatures that are the work of the same artist: the St. Petersburg, National Library of Russia, ms. fr. f° v. IV.5 (F71) and the Lyon, Bibliothèque de la Ville, ms. 828 (F72 = *RHC Oc.*, ms "D"). Folda has argued that F71 slightly pre-dates F72.[45] From the same

---

[39]   F68 and F69 end with the events of 1275. F67 seems to have lost the last folio or folios and breaks off in 1274.

[40]   Between fol. 276v and fol. 277r. This loss explains the aberrant six-folio signature (no. 35) noted by Folda in his catalogue description of this manuscript. See Folda, *Crusader Manuscript Illumination*, p. 185.

[41]   This version of the continuation is published as the principal version of the continuation in *RHC Oc.* 2, pp. 1–379 with the text adapted from the *Chronique d'Ernoul* noted as variants or provided in small print at the foot of the page. It would appear to have been a product of the 1230s or 1240s.

[42]   For the unique nature of the continuation in F57 (= ms. A), see Morgan, "The Rothelin Continuation," pp. 245, 252–53.

[43]   Catalogue description in Folda, *Crusader Manuscript Illumination*, p. 175.

[44]   Description in Folda, *Crusader Art in the Holy Land*, pp. 639–40.

[45]   Catalogue description in Folda, *Crusader Manuscript Illumination*, pp. 176–78.

workshop and approximate date is the Paris, BN, ms. fr. 9085 (F49).[46] This manuscript is been extensively mutilated and all the miniatures it once possessed cut out. The text ends in the middle of the description of the events of 1187; whether it originally ended in 1232 or, like the others, included the "Acre" continuation cannot be known.

3   The final three manuscripts were produced in the last few years of Christian rule in Acre and contain miniatures that are the work of the "Paris-Acre Master."[47] In order of production, they are the Paris, BN, ms. fr. 9084 dated to ca. 1286 (F78),[48] the Boulogne-sur-Mer, Bibliothèque Municipale, ms. 142 of ca. 1287 (F69),[49] and the Florence, Biblioteca Medicea-Laurenziana, ms. Plu. LXI. 10 of ca. 1290 (F70).[50]

Associated with these Acre manuscripts are two of Italian provenance dating from shortly after the end of Christian rule in the Levant: the Paris, BN, ms. fr. 2631 (F74) which has been ascribed to Lombardy ca. 1291–95,[51] and the Paris, BN, ms. fr. 9082 (F77 = *RHC Oc.*, ms "G") which, as its colophon informs us, was produced in Rome in 1295.[52] It would seem likely that these manuscripts were copied from manuscripts from the Acre scriptorium.

When we turn from an art-historical analysis to a textual analysis, we find that the Acre manuscripts no longer slot neatly into these same three groups. Indeed, taken together they lack common defining textual characteristics and show a surprising absence of consistency. For example, F70 and F72 frequently share features that set them apart from the others, but equally, on occasion, they have distinctive readings in common with some of them. Table 1 shows the chapters that are run together without a break. What this illustrates is that no two manuscripts keep in step throughout, although, like F70 and F72, F50 and F73 usually do. The Paris-Acre Master manuscripts, F78 and F69, frequently merge the same chapters, but they have few examples in common with F70, the third manuscript he illustrated. F49, F50, F71, F73, and the Italian F77 have three proximate instances in common – 6.10–11, 6.20–21 and 7.12–13 – but none elsewhere. Similarly, F50, F73, F74 and F77 share the same five examples in book 8, but again this pattern is not repeated in other parts of the work.

This lack of a consistent pattern is, at first sight, bewildering. On reflection, however, it does suggest an important possibility about the way in which the workshops in Acre operated. If a client wanted to commission a copy of the French

---

[46]   Ibid., pp. 175–76; *Crusader Art in the Holy Land*, p. 407 and note 370 (p. 657).
[47]   Otherwise known as the "Hospitaller Master." He is known to have accepted a commission from the Hospitaller Guillielmo di S. Stephano.
[48]   Catalogue description in Folda, *Crusader Manuscript Illumination*, pp. 182–84.
[49]   Ibid., pp. 184–87.
[50]   Description in Folda, *Crusader Art in the Holy Land*, pp. 663–64.
[51]   Catalogue description in Folda, *Crusader Manuscript Illumination*, pp. 199–200.
[52]   Ibid., pp. 200–204.

84

Table 1:   Amalgamated chapters in the Acre and related manuscripts[a]

	50	73	70	72	49	71	78	69	74	77
1.1–2			X	X	–	–				X
1.12–13			X	X	–	–				
3.24–25		X	X	X						
5.11–12	X	X			X					
5.20–21	X	X	X		X					
6.10–11	X	X			X	X				X
6.20–21	X	X			X	X				X
6.22–23					–	X				X
7.12–13	X	X			X	X				X
7.18–19	X	X			–					X
7.20–21	X	X			–					X
8.1–2	X	X			–	–	X	X	X	X
8.4–5	X	X			–				X	X
8.6–7	X	X			–				X	X
8.13–14	X	X			–				X	X
8.15–16	X	X			–				X	
8.19–20	X	X	X	X	–				X	X
8.21–22					–		X	X	X	
9.14–15	X	X	X	X						X
9.19–20		X	X							
10.8–9	X	X	X	X						X
10.17–18							X			X
11.20–21								X	X	
12.5–6		X	X	X						X
12.11–12	X	X		X			X	X	X	
12.19–20	X	X	X							
13.2–3	X	X								–
13.7–8			X	X						–
15.19–20			X	X						
16.1–2					–	X	X	X	X	
16.18–19			X	X	X	–				
17.11–12	X	X								X
18.6–7					–		X	X		
18.25–26			X	X	X					
19.12–13			X				X			
20.27–28		X							X	X
21.2–3		X	X	X	X	X	X	X		
21.14–15		X	X	X	X	X	X	X	X	
21.26–27		X	X							
22.2–3		X	X							
22.11–12							X		X	
22.24–25	X	X		X	X	X	X	X		X

   [a] This table only gives instances where two or more manuscripts amalgamate the same chapter. A dash indicates that the chapters are missing from the manuscript.

William of Tyre, he did not borrow a manuscript from an acquaintance and tell the staff to copy it. If that were so, then each manuscript would preserve the same amalgamations as its exemplar, perhaps adding some more depending on the copyist's whim, and it would be fairly easy to prepare a stemma on the basis of data of this sort. Certainly the information tabulated above would show a clearer lineal development. What instead seems to have happened was that when a client commissioned a manuscript, the scribes would use their own workshop copies, often switching between those manuscripts they had to hand. For practical reasons it would have been easier for scribes to work from texts kept in unbound signatures rather than from fully bound codices, and, if that surmise is correct, then swapping between versions would almost certainly have occurred. If this theory is right, that at least could explain the feature mentioned at the end of the previous paragraph: that it is possible to identify patterns common to several manuscripts which only continue for a limited extent. Perhaps we can go further. If we imagine a situation in which the atelier owned several copies, and hence several versions, of a popular text, then it could well be that manuscripts were being produced commercially for sale to the public "off the shelf," and not just in response to a client's order. Thus a wealthy collector, visiting Acre from western Europe, could purchase a ready-made manuscript rather than have to wait for one to be copied, illuminated and bound – a process which might well take far longer than his proposed stay in the East. Folda has drawn attention to evidence which shows that one of the Acre manuscripts was not taken to the West as soon as it was made, but remained in the East for several years before being completed.[53] But it may be that that was an exception. The very fact that these manuscripts as well as manuscripts of other works from the Acre scriptorium survive at all stems from their having been removed from Latin Syria within a few years of their production.

The hypothesis that these manuscripts were derived from several different exemplars can be tested by broadening the enquiry to look at some examples of variant readings and at those chapters that were divided into two or more parts. It is clear from Table 1 that the two earliest Acre manuscripts, F50 and F73, have many merged chapters in common. When we add in those instances of merged chapters that are unique to individual Acre manuscripts and so do not appear on the table, we find that in total F73 has seven examples not in F50, and F50 has just three examples not in F73. It may be that most of these represent the vagaries of the individual scribes responsible for the execution of the actual manuscripts, rather than merged chapters that had already found their way into the manuscript tradition. But it is striking that there is a cluster of examples from near the beginning: F73 but not F50 has merged chapters at 2.3–4, 2.17–18, 3.17–18, and 3.24–25, while F50 but not F73 has merged chapters at 4.15. When we turn to the examples of chapters split into two or more parts, we find a similar picture. Before the end of book 4 there are six

---

[53] Folda, *Crusader Art in the Holy Land*, p. 403.

examples of F50 and F73 sharing the same divisions, but F73 has six instances of divided chapters not shared with F50, and F50 has four examples not shared with F73. After book 4 there are just two examples of F50 having divided chapters not in F73, none at all of F73 with split chapters absent from F50, and fourteen that are common to both manuscripts. All this points to the conclusion that these two manuscripts or their antecedents had different exemplars for the early books, but for the later portions of the text depend on a common source. This conclusion is amply confirmed by an examination of a sample of variant readings. F73 has, it will be recalled, an associated fourteenth-century manuscript, F57 (= *RHC Oc.*, ms "A"). At 2.22 and at 4.21 the name of the Greek commander ("Tatinus" in the Latin text) is given uniquely in F73 and F57 as "Stacins" or "Statins," while F50 and most of the other manuscripts read "Tatins" or "Tantins." At the end of 4.18, F50 uniquely adds the phrase "por ceste merveilleuse chose;" at the end of 4.20, F57 and F73 alone read "eschapa mie .ii. ." But after the start of book 5, F50 and F73 come into harmony. So for example, at the start of 12.23, F50, F73 and F57 alone of all the manuscripts begin with the words, "En la noise …," and the same three, once again uniquely, begin 12.25 with the words, "Tuit li baron et li prelat …"

These last two examples help locate another *Eracles* text. In addition to the manuscripts under discussion in this paper, there is a substantial fragment of the French William of Tyre copied into the version of the report from the mid-1240s by the Venetian *bailo* Marsilio Zorzi preserved in the Venice Biblioteca Querini-Stampalia Cod. IV.3 (1064). This fragment comprises 12.22–3.14 and describes the siege and capture of Tyre in 1124.[54] The copy employed by Marsilio was closely related to F50 and F73. His version of the text shares the distinctive readings at 12.23 and 12.25 mentioned at the end of the last paragraph, as well as the phrase "quil eussent la vile prise" which ends 13.11 in F50, F57 and F73, and is not found in any other manuscript. In common with these three manuscripts, the Marsilio text also merges 13.2–3 and divides 13.7.[55] What this means is that Marsilio, who was in Acre in the mid-1240s, had access to an *Eracles* text that would seem to have closely resembled these two manuscripts of Acre provenance which date from around 1260.

Moving on, we turn to F72 and F70. Probably about ten years separate the production of these two manuscripts. F70 could well be the last surviving illustrated manuscript to have been produced in the Acre scriptorium before the destruction of the city in 1291; alone of the Acre manuscripts, it has a complete (and unique) set of rubrics, and, alone of all the *Eracles* manuscripts, it is prefaced by a version of the *Annales de Terre Sainte*. F72 (the so-called "Lyons *Eracles*") has a unique continuation for the period 1184–97, and F70 has a related version of this continuation for the period 1191–97.[56] These two manuscripts share fifteen

---

[54] *Der Bericht des Marsilio Zorzi: Codex Querini-Stampalia IV3 (1064)*, ed. Oliver Berggötz (Frankfurt am Main, 1991), pp. 102–8, 116–34.

[55] *Der Bericht des Marsilio Zorzi*, pp. 103, 107, 119 note u, 125, 133.

[56] Edited by Ruth Morgan. See above note 7.

examples of merged chapters; in addition, F72 has five not in F70, and F70 has twelve not in F72. There are only three instances of F70 and F72 sharing merged chapters with F50 and F73; it is perhaps significant that these come fairly close together – 8.19–20, 9.14–15, 10.8–9 – and that in each case they share this feature with F77, one of the manuscripts of Italian provenance. The statistics for split chapters are not too dissimilar: F72 and F70 have twelve in common; F72 has six more not in F70, and F70 has seventeen not in F72. In only two instances do F72 and F70 share a divided chapter with F50 and F73 – at 10.5 and 15.1 – and there is just one instance in which F70 but not F72 shares one with F50 and F73. The divisions at 10.5 and 15.1 are also shared with F77 as well as with F03 and F31.[57] F72 and F70 also have readings in common that set them apart from the other Acre manuscripts. Two examples will suffice: at the start of 5.11 they (and the Italian F77) have "bone cite" instead of "saint cite," and at the end of 11.14 they alone of the all the *Eracles* manuscripts wrongly give the date as 12 May instead of 19 December.

Before considering the implications of this data, we need to examine two other related manuscripts, F78 and F69, both of which were illustrated by the Paris-Acre master and date to ca. 1286–87. As they come from the same scriptorium and were produced in quick succession, we might assume that their texts would be closely related. F78 and F69 have eight merged chapters in common; F78 has four more not in F69, and F69 three not in F78. They share two of the merged chapters they have in common with F72 and F70 and three others with F50 and F73. Far more impressive are the figures for divided chapters. Here I have counted 34 instances of chapters divided in both manuscripts in the same place against just two instances of a division in F78 not found in F69 and four in F69 not in F78. With one exception these extra divisions are unique to these manuscripts, and so we can perhaps assume that they were probably introduced by the copyists and were not transmitted as part of the manuscript tradition. Table 2 shows which other manuscripts share the divided chapters found in both F78 and F69. Early on F01 and F73 feature strongly. As argued already, it would appear that both these manuscripts switched to different exemplars thereafter, respectively akin to F52 and F50. While this table shows that F78 and F69 have noticeably little similarity with F72 and F70 or, after the first two books, with F50 and F73, there is a clear connection between F78 and F69 and, on the one hand, the earlier, defective F71 and, on the other, the later Italian F74.[58]

F71 is the manuscript illustrated by the same artist as F72, but textually they have few distinctive features in common. It is much closer to F49, another defective manuscript from the same workshop and of about the same date. But an analysis of their relationship to the other manuscripts shows two quite distinct patterns. As mentioned earlier (and as shown in Table 1), F49 and F71 merge chapters 6.10–11, 6.20–21 and 7.12–13 in common with F50, F73 and F77; and perhaps associated

---

[57]   F35, the other manuscript associated with F03 and F31 shares the division at 10.5 but not 15.1.
[58]   For example, F74 is the only manuscript to omit the first sentence in 2.1 in common with F69 (plus the derivative F67 and F68) and F78.

Table 2: Split chapters common to F78 and F69 that are also to be found in other Acre and related manuscripts.[a]

	69/78	01	03/31/35	50	73	49	71	72	70	74	77
1.2	X	X		X	X	–	–			X	
1.5	X	X		X	X	–	–			X	
1.5	X	X			X	–	–			X	
1.6	X		X			–	–				
1.7	X	X		X	X	–	–		X	X	
1.9	X		X			–	–				
1.9	X	X		X	X	–	–			X	
1.10	X					–	–				
1.14	X	X			X	–	–			X	
1.15	X	X			X	–	–			X	X
1.20	X	X			X	–	–			X	
2.2	X	X	X		X	–	X			X	X
2.2	X		X			–	X			X	
2.7	X		X			–	X			X	
2.19	X	X	X	X		–	X			X	
3.6	X		X			–	X			X	
4.2	X		X			–	X				X
4.11	X		X								X
4.21	X		X			X	X			X	X
7.13	X									X	
7.21	X		X				–			X	
8.3	X		X				–			X	
9.22	X	–					–	–			
10.15	X		X				X			X	
12.12	X[b]		X				X			X	
13.27	X	–	X	X	X		X			X	
14.5	X		X			–	X			X	
15.7	X		X				X	X	X	X	
15.12	X		X				X			X	X
15.13	X		X				X			X	
15.23	X					X	X			X	
16.16	X	–	X				X			X	
20.18	X	–	X				X	X	X		
20.24	X	–	X			X	X				
21.9	X	–								X	

[a] A dash indicates that the chapter is missing from the manuscript.
[b] In F69 only.

with this cluster are 5.11–12, merged in F49, F50 and F73, and 5.20–21, merged in F49, F50, F70 and F77. But when F49 reappears later, its affinity is clearly with F72 and F70. F49, F72 and F70 are the only manuscripts to merge 16.18–19 and 18.25–26, and then these same three manuscripts, along with F71, F78, and F69, merge 21.2–3 and 21.14–15.[59] These combinations also appear when we turn to the divided chapters. F49, F50, F71, F73 and F77 all divide chapters 6.11 and 6.21. F49, F50 and F73 also share a division at 5.12, at 8.16 (together with F74) and at 8.18 (with F74 and F77). But towards the end of work, we find that F49 shares a division in common with F72 and F70 at 16.12, and then at 20.18 the same manuscripts that merge 21.2–3 and 21.14–15 (F49, F72, F70, F71, F78 and F69) also split 20.18.[60] Similarly, as noted in a different part of this discussion, F49, F72, F70 and also F77 share the error at the end of 19.23 which, by adding on a chapter number, changed the number of Muslim casualties from 1,500 to 1,524. So if F71 has much in common with F78 and F69 throughout, F49 seems to move from having an affinity with F50 and F73 in the early books to an affinity with F72 and F70 later on. There is just one instance – interestingly poised in the middle of the text at 10.5 – where F49 divides a chapter in the same place as both F50 and F73 *and* F72 and F70, and also F77.

What this rather laborious discussion has shown is that it is possible to identify clusters of instances where particular groups of manuscripts seem to run in parallel before diverging. All the Acre manuscripts plus the two Italian manuscripts from the 1290s have enough in common to show that they belong in the same tradition, but within that tradition there are various re-alignments which would seem to confirm the hypothesis that copyists had more than one exemplar from which to work. I have noted one instance in which a copyist has apparently conflated readings from different versions. It was observed above that at the end of 5.21 some of the early *Eracles* manuscripts read "parmi les rues" while others have "parmi les voies;" F72, F70 and F77 read "parmi les rues et par les voies" – perhaps evidence that the scribe of the common ancestor of these manuscripts had two copies to hand from which he was working. Indeed, such is the nature of the textual affinity between the Acre manuscripts, that, for the second half of the thirteenth century, we can be reasonably confident in speaking of "scriptorium" in the singular rather than "scriptoria."

The question remains of how the texts in these manuscripts relate to the early versions of the text as preserved in F02, F03 (and the associated F31 and F35), F04, F05, F38, F41 and F52. With the exception of F03, F31 and F35, these manuscripts have few merged or divided chapters, and those that they do have shed no light on possible connections with the Acre group. F03, F31 and F35 share a large number of divided chapters – far more than in any of the Acre group manuscripts – but on a number of occasions where a chapter division is common to several of the Acre-group manuscripts, these three manuscripts have it as well. A sample of

---

[59] 21.14–15 is also merged in F74.
[60] Similarly F49, F71, F78 and F69 all split 20.24.

variant readings points in differing directions. To start with the examples identified previously in which F52 and F01 differ from the others: at the start of 4.24, F50, F69, F71, F73, F74 and F77 all follow the lead given by F52 and F01, while only F70 and F72 follow F02, F03, F04, F38 and F41; at 12.24 all the Acre manuscripts follow F51 and F01 in preference to the readings found in the others;[61] at 5.21 the Acre manuscripts all follow F52 and F01 in preference to the readings found in the others except for F70, F72 and F77 – which, as mentioned in the previous paragraph, have their own distinctive variant. At the start of 5.20 the Acre group follow F52 and F01, except for F70, F72 and F77 which follow the readings found in the other early versions. At the end of 11.14 where the date in the Latin text is given as 19 December,[62] we find the following alignment: all the early versions and F49, F71, and F78 have 19 December; the two later manuscripts associated with F03, F31 and F35, and most of the rest of the Acre manuscripts have 10 December; F72 and F70 go their own way with 12 May. At the start of 12.1, F02, F03, F05, F38, F41, F50, F70, F71, F72, F73, F77 all give the ancient Persian ruler as "Xerses" or "Xerces," while F01, F04, F31, F35, F52, F69, F74 and F78 have "Perses" or "Perces."

It is all rather confusing, but some points do seem to emerge. Clearly the Acre group and F52 (and the associated F01) have antecedents in common, but so too do they have common antecedents with F03 (and the associated F31 and F35). Some of the Acre manuscripts share the β-group features found in F04. While none of the Acre group have the interpolations found in F38, there are common readings with F05, F41 or the late F02. In other words, the distinctive features of F38 apart, there is nothing in the early group of manuscripts which cannot be found in those from the Acre scriptorium.

The β Group

Their defining characteristics aside, the β group show only a limited degree of homogeneity. A few manuscripts have large numbers of chapters that are split or merged. Thus the fifteenth-century Geneva, Bibliothèque Publique et Universitaire, ms. 85 (F36) has 97 divided chapters and 101 instances of chapters that are merged, while another fifteenth-century manuscript, the Paris, BN, ms. fr. 2629 (F44), has a staggering 214 instances where two chapters have been run together. Two earlier manuscripts, the Brussels, Bibliothèque Royale, ms. 9492–3 (F54), which has been attributed to a Parisian workshop from ca. 1291–95, and another northern French manuscript, the Paris, BN, ms. fr. 2754 (F46), which is apparently slightly later, have striking numbers of divided chapters. In the case of F54, a change of hand at fol. 144r (= 11.24) signals a major change: up to this point just two chapters have

---

[61] F49 and F77 lack the folios containing this chapter. The same pattern is discernible at the end of 13.28 where all the Acre manuscripts plus F01 and F52 lack the word "clers" in the final phrase.

[62] WT, p. 519.

been split;[63] subsequently there are no less than 363 instances of divisions. F46 only comprises books 16 to the end, but even in these surviving seven books we find 64 instances of divided chapters. These are extreme examples, but what is even more striking are the comparatively few instances where particular chapter divisions are shared by two or more manuscripts. F54 has 43, or, in other words, 322 instances of divided chapters which are unique among β group manuscripts. F46 has 24 split chapters shared with one or more other manuscripts in the β group and 40 that are unique. So the fact that F54 and F46 have 18 divided chapters in common can scarcely be used as an argument for any particular textual affinity between them. The high incidence of unique divisions is not simply a feature of the manuscripts with an abnormally large number of split chapters. At one extreme F33 has 30 unique divisions out of a total of 32, while several others – F06, F30, F32, F40 and F47 – have around two-thirds of their divided chapters all to themselves. On the other hand, every instance of a divided chapter in F55 and F65 is to be found elsewhere. Turning to the merged chapters, we discover that here the proportion of instances that are unique to a single β manuscript is on the whole lower, usually totalling between a third and a half. F44 has 125 cases of merged chapters not found elsewhere out of a total of 214, and F06 with 11 unique examples of merged chapters out of 15, F48 with 10 out of 14, F55 with 6 out of 9, and F58 with 9 out of 14 are others with a high proportion.

With these features in mind, identifying discrete groups of manuscripts with enough merged or divided chapters in common to indicate a clear textual affinity requires the establishment of a clear recurrent pattern and needs to be approached in conjunction with a search for distinctive variant readings. The most obviously related group of manuscripts, all of which contain the Rothelin continuation, are F60, F61, F62, F63 and F65. All date to the fourteenth century – F61 bears the date 1337 – or, in the case of F65, to the fifteenth. F65 is a fire-damaged manuscript in Turin; the others all have the same additional materials prefaced to the *Eracles* text, but whether F65 also once had these additional texts is not clear. These manuscripts have 27 instances of merged chapters and 3 examples of divided chapters in common. There are several more instances in which two of more share merged or divided chapters. They also have similar rubrics and lack a section of the text at 12.15–12.17. Not surprisingly they share some variant readings, as for example at the end of 11.13 giving the date wrongly as 8 April.[64] Two other Rothelin manuscripts, F58 and F64, both of which contain the French text of the *De Excidio Urbis Acconis*, also have features in common with each other: 5 merged chapters and 4 divided chapters, and the same distinctive readings at the end of 15.27, 19.23

---

[63] These figures ignore the two divisions in 1.2 which are a defining characteristic of the β group.

[64] The only other manuscripts to share this reading (*recte* 27 April) are the α group F31 and F35. Morgan ("The Rothelin Continuation," p. 246) identified four of these five manuscripts as having a closely related text of the Rothelin continuation, and her research showed that the Rothelin text appended to F52 also belongs with this group. The exception is F62.

92

and 19.24. Another pair of late manuscripts, the fifteenth-century London, BL, Royal ms. 15. E. I (F37) and the Paris, BN, ms. fr. 68 (F42), similarly have 10 divided chapters and 10 merged chapters in common and share a number of distinctive readings; for example, in the final phrases of 4.18, 4.20, 13.18 and 21.8. F43, F45 and F51 have 3 divided chapters and 18 merged chapters in common; in several instances these features are shared with F47 and F53; all five assert that the Templars had nineteen brothers at the time of the council of Troyes in 1129, whereas all the other manuscripts put the figure at nine.

The only β group manuscript attributed to the Latin East is the Rome, Biblioteca Apostolica Vaticana, ms. Pal. lat. 1963 (F06). Alone of all the β group manuscripts it has no continuation but ends where William's Latin finished, and Folda has argued that it is from Antioch and dates to the 1260s. Its importance is therefore beyond doubt, but when compared with the other manuscripts in this group, or indeed with the α group manuscripts, what is striking is its unique quality. It shares divided chapters with F37 and 42 at 15.23 and with F36, F44, F51 and F53 at 19.10, but otherwise has none in common with other β manuscripts. It is therefore to be assumed that these divisions are coincidental and not attributable to any common original. An analysis of the merged chapters reveals a similar lack of any discernable pattern: at 5.15–16 it has merged chapters in common with F30, F36 and F44; at 18.1–2 with F43, F45 and F54; and at 22.23–24 with F33, F34, F36, F40, F43, F44, F45 and F51. Moreover, F06 has a number of unique variant readings. At the start of 4.21 it alone reads "Tandis com cil desleaux Grex ...," while most of the other manuscripts have (with a wide variety of spellings) "Tatins cil desloiaus Griex ...;" at the end of 7.19, alone of all the *Eracles* manuscripts, it gives the date as the "sisieme jor davrill;" at the end of 10.8 it alone speaks of "li roiaume de Jerusalem" instead of "le roiaumes de Surie;" at the end of 11.14 it alone has the date as 17 December instead of 19 December. Most of these variants should probably be regarded as the result of careless copying, but at the beginning of 12.16, where the manuscripts that are closest to the original form of the translation and most of the β group read "Un voisin avoit li rois d'outremer ...," and F06 has "rois de Surie," it is clear that a scribe has made a deliberate alteration. The "rois d'outremer" in this context is Baldwin II of Jerusalem, but because for someone working in the East Jerusalem is "deca mer,"[65] it is understandable why such a change should have been introduced.[66]

If F06 preserves a number of unique features that isolate it from the rest of the β manuscripts, it is also true that the western manuscripts in this group that can be dated to the thirteenth century or the early years of the fourteenth century – F30, F32, F33, F34, F39, F40, F43, F45, F46, F47, F48, F51, F54, F55, F58 – show little consistency in dividing or amalgamating chapters, although, as noted above, F43,

---

[65] For the use of "deca mer," there contrasted with "la terre de crestiens," see 12.7.

[66] The Acre group of α manuscripts also suppress the word "outremer," though without using the phrase employed in F06.

F45 and F51, and to a lesser extent F47 and the fifteenth-century F53, have a number of divisions and amalgamations in common. On the other hand, none of these fifteen manuscripts has distinctive readings that set it apart to the extent that F06 does. The conclusion has to be that F43, F45, F47, F51 and F53 have a common ancestor which itself was closely derived from the β group archetype, and that all the others listed above were either derived directly from that archetype, or, if they were derived from it indirectly, that no other manuscript with the same immediate ancestor has survived. So, whereas the Acre manuscripts and the others associated with that group seem to have had at least three source-texts and reveal some hybridization, these manuscripts come from a single source which gave the copyists no clear lead as to which chapters they should merge or divide. On the other hand, the copyists do seem to have kept reasonably close to the text. What may have happened is that all or most of the manuscripts mentioned in this paragraph were produced at the same workshop in Paris over the course of some thirty to forty years from exemplars kept in that workshop. That conclusion would also be consistent with the fact that several of these manuscripts have a related cycle of illustrations.

Although it has not yet been possible to construct a stemma, it is now possible to sort the manuscripts into groups based on an analysis of the text of the translation rather than on the contents of the continuations.

- Those manuscripts with texts closest to the original translation are F02, F04, F05, F38, F41 and F52. Although it has many more divided chapters, F03 also seems to preserve a primitive version of the text itself and so should be included with these others. Associated with F03 are F31 and F35, and associated with F52 is F01.
- The eight manuscripts copied in Acre in the second half of the thirteenth century (F49, F50, F69, F70, F71, F72, F73, F78) have, despite their differences, features that link them into a definite group, and to this group should be added two manuscripts from Italy, F74 and F77. Associated with F73 is F57; associated with F50 and F73 is the fragment preserved by Marsilio Zorzi; derived from F69 are F67 and F68.
- The manuscript attributed to Antioch, F06, shares the characteristics of the β group but otherwise stands alone.
- A large group of β manuscripts that were produced in France in the latter part of the thirteenth century or the very beginning of the fourteenth (F30, F32, F33, F34, F39, F40, F43, F45, F46, F47, F48, F51, F54, F55, F58) all seem to derive directly or indirectly from the same exemplar. F43, F45, F47 and F51, together with the fifteenth-century F53, comprise a recognizable sub-group; as do F58 and F64.
- Of the later β manuscripts, F60, F61, F62, F63, and F65 share a common source, as do F37 and F42.

This just leaves two other fifteenth-century β group manuscripts: F36 (the Geneva, Bibliothèque Publique et Universitaire, ms. 85) and F44 (the Paris, BN, ms. fr. 2629), both of which extensively rephrase and, in places, abbreviate the text.

Along the way there have been a number of important discoveries, but this analysis cannot be seen as either complete or final; there are unanswered questions, both about the precise relationship between the surviving manuscripts, and about the process of production and circulation. It would seem that in Acre, and probably in Paris too in the later years of the thirteenth century, copies were being produced commercially and not only in response to specific commissions. An examination of the manuscripts may reveal more about their owners, although few seem to give any clues from before the seventeenth century. There is, for example, no conclusive evidence that any were owned by members of the Latin Syrian or Cypriot royal family or nobility. As for the stemma, a closer examination of variant readings than has been attempted here is needed to test and refine my findings: one way forward will be to collate all the manuscripts, and so produce a critical edition, of one or more sample chapters.[67]

One final question that should be addressed is when and where the major developments in the text took place. It is assumed that the translation was made in the West for a Western audience by a cleric who had at some point visited the East,[68] and this would seem to be supported, for example, by the readings of the earliest manuscripts at the beginning of 12.16 which speak of Baldwin II as the "rois d'outremer." This opening phrase does not find a counterpart in the Latin text.[69] But if the translation was made in the West, all the continuations appear to have been written in the East, and so where and how they were added also needs more thought. The fact that the earliest surviving manuscripts with the *Chronique d'Ernoul* continuation to 1232 were produced in the West does not necessarily mean that adding this continuation began there. The Rothelin continuation is only found in manuscripts copied in the West; it too appears to have been composed in the East, but, unlike the *Chronique d'Ernoul*, so far as is known it seems not to have circulated as an independent work. With the Acre continuation we are on safer ground. Composed in the East and found primarily in manuscripts copied in the East, there is no doubting its provenance. But this work too, and the related versions of the *Annales de Terre Sainte* and associated texts, would repay further enquiry.

---

[67] Since completing the present paper I have edited two sample chapters (12:7 and 20:30): "The Old French William of Tyre and the Origins of the Templars," in *Knighthoods of Christ: Essays on the History of the Crusades and the Knights Templar presented to Malcolm Barber*, ed. Norman Housley (Aldershot, 2007), pp. 151–64; "The Old French William of Tyre, the Templars and the Assassin Envoy," in *The Hospitallers, the Mediterranean and Europe from the Crusades to the Ottomans*, ed. Karl Borchardt, Nikolas Jaspert and Helen Nicholson (Aldershot, 2007), pp. 25–37.

[68] Pryor, "The *Eracles* and William of Tyre," pp. 276–77, 284, 288, 293 *et passim*; Hamilton, "The Old French translation of William of Tyre," pp. 93–94.

[69] WT, p. 565.

Appendix 1: The Manuscripts

This list is based on the guide published by Jaroslav Folda in *Scriptorium* 27 (1973),[1] which in turn followed the pattern established in the nineteenth century by Louis de Mas Latrie and Paul Riant.[2] These scholars sorted the manuscripts into groups depending on whether they contained a version of the continuation to William's text, and, if so, where they ended. F7–15 comprise manuscript fragments from the French William of Tyre, and these have not been analysed in this discussion. F16–29 (Section II) are not manuscripts of William of Tyre at all but of the *Chronique d'Ernoul et de Bernard le Trésorier* or of the text known as the *Estoires d'Outremer et de la naissance Saladin*. Four other items in Folda's list have also been disregarded: F56 is an abbreviated version of the French William of Tyre; F59 is an eighteenth-century copy of F60; F75 is an eighteenth-century copy of F77; and F76 is an eighteenth-century copy of the continuation as published by the Maurists in 1729.[3]

Section I: No Continuation

F01   Cambridge, Sidney Sussex College, ms. 93 (England:[4] late 13th century)
F02   Paris, BN, ms. fr. 2627 (N. France: 15th century)
F03   Paris, BN, ms. fr 2632 (Latin East or France: 1st half of 13th century)
F04   Paris, BN, ms. fr. 2826 (Latin East or France: 1st half of 13th century)
F05   Paris, BN, ms. fr. 9081 (Paris: ca. 1245–48)[5]
F06   Rome, Biblioteca Apostolica Vaticana, ms. Pal. lat. 1963 (Antioch: ca. 1260–68)[6]

Section III: Continuations to 1232

F30   Arras, Bibliothèque Municipale, ms. 651 (N. France: early 14th century)
F31   Baltimore, Walters Art Gallery, ms. 137 (Paris: ca. 1295–1300)[7]
F32   Bern, Bürgerbibliothek, ms. 112 (N. France: ca. 1270)[8]
F33   Bern, Bürgerbibliothek, ms. 163 (N. France: 3rd quarter of 13th century)

---

[1]   Folda, "Manuscripts", pp. 90–95.
[2]   Mas Latrie, "Essai de classification", pp. 480–88; Riant, "Inventaire sommaire", pp. 247–52, 716–17.
[3]   *Veterum Scriptorum et Monumentorum ... Amplissima Collectio*, ed. Edmond Martène and Ursin Durand, 5 (Paris, 1729), 581–752.
[4]   Folda says southern France, but the writing is clearly an example of English Court or Business Hand of the period.
[5]   For the date, see Folda, *Crusader Art in the Holy Land*, pp. 217, 235–36.
[6]   For the date, ibid., pp. 218, 347–50.
[7]   For the place of production and the date, see Folda, *Crusader Manuscript Illumination*, p. 208.
[8]   For the date, see ibid., p. 33 n. 38.

96

F34 Besançon, Bibliothèque Municipale, ms. 856 (N. France: ca. 1300)
F35 Epinal, Bibliothèque Municipale, ms. 45 (Paris: ca. 1295–1300)[9]
F36 Geneva, Bibliothèque Publique et Universitaire, ms. 85 (Artois: 3rd quarter of 15th century)
F37 London, BL, Royal ms. 15. E. I (Flanders: late 15th century)[10]
F38 London, BL, Henry Yates Thompson ms. 12 (England: mid-13th century)
F39 Paris, Bibliothèque de l'Arsenal, ms. 5220 (N. France: 3rd quarter of 13th century)
F40 Paris, Bibliothèque du Ministère des Affaires Etrangères, Memoires et Documents 230*bis* (S. France: 3rd quarter of 13th century)
F41 Paris, BN, ms. fr. 67 (N. France: 2nd half of 13th century)
F42 Paris, BN, ms. fr. 68 (Flanders: ca. 1450)
F43 Paris, BN, ms. fr. 779 (N. France: ca. 1275)
F44 Paris, BN, ms. fr. 2629 (Flanders: ca. 1460)
F45 Paris, BN, ms. fr. 2630 (N. France: ca. 1250–75)[11]
F46 Paris, BN, ms. fr. 2754 (N. France: ca. 1300)
F47 Paris, BN, ms. fr. 2824 (N. France: ca. 1300)
F48 Paris, BN, ms. fr. 2827 (N. France: ca. 1250–75)[12]
F49 Paris, BN, ms. fr. 9085 (Acre: ca. 1277–80)[13]
F50 Paris, BN, ms. fr. 9086 (Acre: ca. 1255–60)[14] (= *RHC Oc.*, 2, ms. C)
F51 Paris, BN, ms. fr. 24208 (N. France: ca. 1250–75)[15]

Section IV: The "Rothelin" Continuation to 1261

F52 Baltimore, Walters Art Gallery, ms. 142 (Paris: ca. 1300 and ca. 1340)[16]
F53 Brussels, Bibliothèque Royale, ms. 9045 (Flanders, ca. 1460)
F54 Brussels, Bibliothèque Royale, ms. 9492–3 (Paris: ca. 1291 95)[17]
F55 Lyon, Bibliothèque de la Ville, ms. Palais des Arts 29 (Paris: ca. 1295–96)[18] (= *RHC Oc.*, 2, ms. E)
F57 Paris, BN, ms. fr. 2634 (Ile de France: 1st quarter of 14th century) (= *RHC Oc.*, 2, ms. A)
F58 Paris, BN, ms. fr. 2825 (Paris: early 14th century)[19] (= *RHC Oc.*, 2, ms. F)

---

[9] For the place of production and the date, see ibid., p. 205.
[10] Folda says ca. 1475, but the Tudor rose incorporated into the design of fol. 1r might suggest a post-1485 date.
[11] For the date, see Folda, *Crusader Manuscript Illumination*, p. 33 n.36.
[12] Ibid.
[13] For the date, ibid., p. 175.
[14] Ibid.
[15] For the date, ibid., p. 33 n.36.
[16] For the place of production and the date, ibid., p. 212.
[17] Ibid., p. 198.
[18] Ibid., p. 204.
[19] Ibid., p. 213.

F60   Paris, BN, ms. fr. 9083 (Ile de France: 2nd quarter of 14th century) (= *RHC Oc.*, 2, ms. H)

F61   Paris, BN, ms. fr. 22495 (Paris: 1337) (= *RHC Oc.*, 2, ms. I)

F62   Paris, BN, ms. fr. 22496–7 (Paris: ca. 1350)

F63   Paris, BN, ms. fr. 24209 (Ile de France: 3rd quarter of 14th century) (= *RHC Oc.*, 2, ms K)

F64   Rome, Biblioteca Apostolica Vaticana, ms. Reg. Suec. lat. 737 (Paris: early 14th century)[20]

F65   Turin, Biblioteca Nazionale, ms. L I. 5 (N. France: 15th century)

F66   Turin, Biblioteca Nazionale, ms. L. II. 17 (Ile de France: 1st quarter of 14th century) – not seen

Section V: The "Acre" Continuation, beyond 1232

F67   Amiens, Bibliothèque Municipale, ms. 483 (Flanders: mid-15th century)

F68   Bern, Bürgerbibliothek, ms. 25 (N. France: 1st half of 15th century)

F69   Boulogne-sur-Mer, Bibliothèque Municipale, ms. 142 (Acre: ca. 1287)[21]

F70   Florence, Biblioteca Medicea-Laurenziana, ms. Plu. LXI. 10 (Acre: ca. 1290, and Italy: 1st half of 14th century)

F71   St. Petersburg, National Library of Russia / Российская Национальная Библиотека (formerly M. E. Saltykov-Schchedrin State Public Library), ms. fr. f° v. IV.5 (Acre: ca. 1280)

F72   Lyon, Bibliothèque de la Ville, ms. 828 (Acre: ca.1280) (= *RHC Oc.*, 2, ms. D)

F73   Paris, BN, ms. fr. 2628 (Acre: late 1250s/early 1260s and late 1270s)[22] (= *RHC Oc.*, 2, ms B)

F74   Paris, BN, ms. fr. 2631 (Lombardy: ca. 1291–95)[23]

F77   Paris, BN, ms. fr. 9082 (Rome: 1295) (= *RHC Oc.*, 2, ms. G)

F78   Paris, BN, ms. fr. 9084 (Acre: ca. 1286)[24]

---

[20] Ibid.
[21] For the date, see ibid., p. 184.
[22] For the date, see Folda, *Crusader Art in the Holy Land*, pp. 218 n. 608, 403–5.
[23] For the date, see Folda, *Crusader Manuscript Illumination*, p. 199.
[24] Ibid., p. 182.

VIII

98

Appendix 2: Numbering the Books and Chapters

In its original form the French William of Tyre was divided into twenty-two books and followed the divisions in William's Latin text. The only exception relates to William's final book, book 23, which in the Latin version comprises an extended prologue and a single chapter. None of the French manuscripts has the prologue, and it is safe to assume that it was omitted by the original translator. The one chapter, however, was included in the translation and followed the last chapter of book 22. So what in the Latin text is 23.1, becomes in the French text 22.30. Otherwise most manuscripts preserve all or most of William's book divisions. Many have illuminations and/or decorated capitals to signify the start of a new book. Several, especially some of the later copies, have further illuminations elsewhere: these include F31, F35, F36, F37, F40, F42, F57 and the group of related manuscripts – F60, F61, F62, F63, F65; while others (for example, F31 and F35 at 10.1, 11.1 and 17.1, and F67, F68, F69, F74, F78 at 12.1 and 13.1) have instances where no new book is signalled where it might be expected.

It is when we turn to the question of numbering the chapters that the situation becomes much more complicated. As explained above, in both nineteenth-century editions the normal policy was to alter the structure of the French translation to make the chapter divisions coincide with the divisions in the Latin text, even though there was no warrant for this in the manuscripts themselves. Thus in a few instances chapters were made to begin and end where the Latin begins and ends and not where they do in the manuscripts.[25] It also led to a number of chapters in the French version being split in two,[26] and those in the remainder of that book being renumbered accordingly. The situation is made more complicated by the fact that Huygens' edition of the Latin text has a number of cases where the chapter divisions in the Latin and the subsequent numbering of the chapters in the book concerned differ from the *Recueil* edition.[27] There is thus considerable scope for confusion, as the same chapter could have different numbers in the French text and each of the Latin editions. The guiding principle throughout this article is to refer to the chapters by number as they appear in the earliest versions of the translation, and the following table is intended to help identify them. Books 4, 6, 8, 12, 16 and 17 present no problems – all the chapters coincide in both the Latin and the French versions. The left-hand column gives the numbers as referred to here, and then, reading from left to right, the other columns give the numbers as they appear in the Paris edition, the *Recueil* and the Huygens' editions. It has not been thought necessary to list every chapter, but simply indicate the numbering for first and last chapter in each book and where in the book the numbering ceases to be synchronized.

---

[25] In the *Recueil* edition this is true of 10.17–18, 11.28–31, 12.5–6, 12.24–25, 13.9–10, 16.7–8 and 21.9–10, and in the Paris edition of all these except 10.17–18 plus 14.11–12.

[26] 1.14, 2.9, 5.19, 7.16, 9.22, 11.27, 13.3, 15.14, 18.32, 20.9.

[27] But note that in two instances, at 3.1–2 and 10.8, Huygens' division of chapters in his Latin edition coincides with those in the French version and differs from the *Recueil*.

Eracles	Paris	*Recueil*	Huygens
1.1	1.1	1.1	1.1
1.14	1.14–15	1.14–15	1.14–15
1.15	1.16	1.16	1.16
1.29	1.30	1.30	1.30
2.1	2.1	2.1	2.1
2.9	2.9–10	2.9–10	2.9–10
2.10	2.11	2.11	2.11
2.19	2.20	2.20	2.20–21
2.20	2.21	2.21	2.22
2.22	2.23	2.23	2.24
3.1	3.1	3.1	3.1
3.2	3.2	3.1 cont.	3.2
3.3	3.3	3.2	3.3
3.26	3.26	3.25	3.26
5.1	5.1	5.1	5.1
5.19	5.19–20	5.19–20	5.19–20
5.20	5.21	5.21	5.21
5.22	5.23	5.23	5.23
7.1	7.1	7.1	7.1
7.15	7.15–16	7.15–16	7.15–16
7.16	7.17	7.17	7.17
7.24	7.25	7.25	7.25
9.1	9.1	9.1	9.1
9.22	9.22–23	9.22–23	9.22–23
10.1	10.1	10.1	10.1
10.3	10.3	10.3–4	10.3–4
10.4	10.4	10.5	10.5
10.8	10.8	10.9–10	10.9
10.9	10.9	10.11	10.10
10.28	10.28	10.30	10.29
11.1	11.1	11.1	11.1
11.27	11.27–28	11.27–28	11.27–28[28]
13.1	13.1	13.1	13.1
13.2	13.2	13.2–3	13.2–3

---

[28] For the remainder of book 11, the chapter divisions in the French and Latin texts diverge.

VIII

Eracles	Paris	Recueil	Huygens
13.3	13.3–4	13.4–5	13.4–5
13.4	13.5	13.6	13.6
13.24	13.25	13.26	13.26
13.25	13.25 cont.	13.26 cont.	13.26 cont.
13.26	13.26	13.27	13.27
13.27	13.27	13.27 cont.	13.27 cont.
13.28	13.28	13.28	13.28
14.1	14.1	14.1	14.1
14.11	14.11	14.11–12	14.11–12
14.12	14.12	14.13–15	14.13–15
14.13	14.13	14.16	14.16
14.27	14.27	14.30	14.30
15.1	15.1	15.1	15.1
15.5	15.5	15.5	15.5
15.6	15.5 cont.	15.5 cont.	15.15 cont.
15.7	15.6	15.6	15.6
15.14	15.13–14	15.13–14	15.13–14
15.15	15.15	15.15	15.15
15.27	15.27	15.27	15.27
18.1	18.1	18.1	18.1
18.32	18.32–33	18.32–33	18.32–33
18.33	18.34	18.34	18.34
19.1	19.1	19.1	19.1
19.6	19.6	19.6–7	19.6–7
19.7	19.7	19.8	19.8
19.10	19.10	19.11	19.11
–	–	19.12	19.12
19.11	19.11	19.13	19.13
19.30	19.30	19.32	19.32
20.1	20.1	20.1–2	20.1–2
20.2	20.2	20.3	20.3
20.9	20.9–10	20.10–11	20.10–11
20.10	20.11	20.12	20.12
20.20	20.21	20.22	20.22
20.21	20.22	20.22 cont.	20.22 cont.
20.22	20.23	20.23	20.23

Eracles	Paris	*Recueil*	Huygens
20.30	20.31	20.31[29]	20.31
21.1	21.1	21.1	21.1
21.2	21.2	21.2–3	21.2–3
21.3	21.3	21.4	21.4
21.7	21.7	21.8	21.8
21.8	21.8	21.9–10	21.8 cont., 21.9
21.9	21.9	21.11	21.10
21.28	21.28	21.30	21.29
22.1	22.2	22.1	22.1
22.2	22.2	22.2–3	22.2–3
22.3	22.3	22.4	22.4
22.7	22.7	22.8	22.8–9
22.8	22.8	22.9	22.10
22.29	22.29	22.30	22.31
22.30	23.1	23.1	23.1

[29] A series of misprints in *RHC Oc* (pp. 995–1000) wrongly numbers the chapters 20.29–20.31 as 20.31–20.33.

Appendix 3: Incomplete Manuscripts

A number of manuscripts – most notably F30, F49, F55 and F71 – have missing or mutilated folios. In several instances it would appear that someone has cut out pages containing illuminations. In two cases, F01 (which ends at 16.15) and F46 (which begins at 16.1), it is possible that the manuscript was once bound in two volumes, one of which has subsequently been lost. (F62 and F71 are bound in two volumes with both parts surviving.) The fire-damaged F65 is substantially complete and legible from 1.12 onwards, although the conservators did not re-assemble all the folios in the correct order. These defects in the manuscripts mean that it is not always possible to check particular features which might help establish their interrelationship.

In some cases material is missing not because a folio is lacking or damaged, but either because of haplography or because the exemplar itself was defective. Some omissions would appear to have been deliberate, as for example in F53 book 16 where the copyist of this manuscript or its direct ancestor ended a number of chapters several sentences early. Absences from the text not resulting from missing or mutilated folios are indicated by an asterisk in the following list of chapters or parts of chapters missing from the manuscripts ("3.5pt" means that part of book 3 chapter 5 is lacking).

F01   5.22–6.1pt; 8.23*; 9.21pt–10.5pt; 12.25pt–13.4pt; 13.8pt–13.27pt; 16.15pt–
      end
F03   22.30pt
F04   22.26pt–end
F05   3.25pt–4.2pt; 5.22pt–6.1pt; 15.27pt–16.3pt; 16.23pt–16.24pt; 17.30pt
F06   2.21–22
F30   1.8pt–1.10pt; 1.12.pt–1.16pt; 1.18pt–2.4pt; 2.5pt–2.6pt; 2.7pt–3.8pt; 3.9pt–
      3.10pt; 3.12pt–3.13pt; 4.8pt–4.11pt; 4.24pt–5.2; 5.16pt–5.17; 7.6pt–7.7pt;
      8.4pt–8.6pt; 9.3pt–9.7pt; 9.10pt–9.13pt; 10.14pt–10.15pt; 11.11pt–11.13pt;
      11.22–12.20pt; 12.25pt; 13.20pt–13.23pt; 13.28pt–14.1pt; 14.17pt–14.19pt;
      14.23pt–14.27pt; 16.20pt–17.7pt; 17.8pt–17.12pt; 17.28–17.29; 18.8pt;
      18.15pt–18.17pt; 18.32pt–18.33pt; 19.1pt–19.3pt; 19.16pt–19.18pt; 19.26pt;
      19.29pt; 20.1pt; 20.22pt–21.5pt; 21.9pt–21.11pt*; 22.10pt–22.12pt; 22.17pt–
      22.20pt
F31   21.10*
F32   16.25pt–17.1pt
F33   6.1–2; 10.27pt–11.1pt; 11.28pt–12.1pt; 12.23pt–13.1pt; 18.22pt–18.31pt
F35   1.1–1.3pt; 12.1pt–12.3pt; 14.26pt–15.1pt; 17.20pt–17.23pt; 18.33pt–19.2pt;
      21.10*; interpolation (pt) and 21.28–22.1pt
F36   12.15pt–12.17pt
F37   6.9*
F38   1.1pt; 1.3pt–1.4pt

VIII

F40   10.13pt–10.15pt; 11.16pt–11.19pt; 14.11pt–15.20pt
F41   12.10–12.15*; 19.6–20.24*; 22.2pt–22.8
F43   12.20pt–12.21pt
F44   4.21*; 12.1–12.2*; 16.1–16.2pt
F45   13.5pt–13.27pt
F46   1.1–15.27
F49   1.1–3.9; 3.12pt–3.17pt; 4.2pt–4.5pt; 4.22pt–4.24; 6.1–6.3pt; 6.22pt–7.1pt;
      7.24pt–8.2pt; 8.22pt–9.1pt; 9.21pt–10.1pt; 10.28pt–11.1pt; 11.22pt–11.23pt;
      11.31pt–12.2pt; 12.24pt–13.1pt; 13.28pt–15.4pt; 15.27pt–16.3pt; 16.28pt–
      17.1pt; 17.30pt–18.13pt; 18.33pt–19.2pt; 19.29pt–20.1pt; 20.30pt–21.2pt;
      21.28pt–22.1
F52   8.23*
F53   3.22*; 15.21–23*; 15.25*; 16.5pt–16.6*; 16.9pt*; 16.13pt*; 16.15pt*;
      16.16pt–16.17*; 16.19*; 16.21pt*; 16.23pt*; 16.26pt*; 16.28pt*
F54   1.1–1.2pt
F55   1.1–5.7pt; 6.23pt–7.1pt; 7.24pt–8.1pt; 8.23pt–9.1pt; 9.23pt–10.1pt; 11.1pt;
      11.31pt–12.1pt; 12.25pt–13.1pt; 13.28pt–14.6pt; 15.1pt; 15.17pt–15.21pt;
      15.27pt–16.1pt; 16.28pt–17.1pt; 17.30pt–18.1pt; 18.33pt–19.2pt; 19.30pt–
      20.1pt; 20.17pt–20.22pt; 20.25pt–20.28pt; 20.30pt–21.1pt; 21.28pt–22.1pt;
      22.21pt–22.23pt
F58   8.3*
F60   12.15pt–12.17pt*
F61   12.15pt–12.17pt*
F62   12.15pt–12.17pt*
F63   11.8*; 11.11pt*; 11.14pt*; 11.15pt; 12.15pt–12.17pt*; 20.23pt–20.30pt*
F65   12.15pt–12.17pt*
F67   22.19pt–22.22pt*
F68   1.1–1.2pt; 22.19pt–22.22pt*
F69   17.26pt–17.27pt; 22.19pt–22.22pt
F71   1.1–1.29; 7.15pt–9.1pt; 9.21pt–10.1pt; 16.5pt–16.8pt; 16.18pt–16.19pt;
      19.9pt–19.12pt; 20.28–20.30
F77   12.20pt–13.23pt; 16.23pt–16.26pt; 17.14pt–17.17pt

Appendix 4: Chapter Divisions and Amalgamations

The statistics set out in the following table give the number of instances in which chapters have been split or run together. There are many cases of chapters having been divided into three or more parts, and also a number of examples of more than two chapters being amalgamated to form just one. These figures go some way to show how far the chapter structure of the manuscript in question has moved away from the Latin original, although the figures for incomplete or badly mutilated manuscripts (marked with an asterisk) are of course too low.

	Split	Amalgamated
*F01	11	0
F02	1	1
F03	149	1
F04	0	11
F05	1	1
F06	6	15
*F30	44	40
F31	281	5
F32	8	21
F33	32	22
F34	13	17
F35	281	5
F36	97	101
F37	13	23
F38	1	1
F39	2	16
F40	5	18
F41	0	2
F42	12	21
F43	7	38
F44	24	214
F45	8	33
*F46	64	11
F47	9	19
F48	15	14
*F49	15	12
F50	25	24
F51	7	40
F52	0	1
F53	18	24

	Split	Amalgamated
F54	365	19
*F55	3	9
F57	37	26
F58	6	14
F60	11	38
F61	9	37
F62	7	39
F63	5	41
F64	7	16
*F65	6	38
F66	–	–[30]
F67	38	11
F68	53	16
F69	38	11
F70	31	27
*F71	22	10
F72	18	22
F73	26	28
F74	40	18
F77	25	22
F78	36	12

[30] Not seen.

The Old French William of Tyre and the Origins of the Templars[1]

In a well-known chapter (XII.7), William of Tyre gave an account of the origins of the Templars. William's story is of a small group of knights who in the year 1118 were given the task of protecting pilgrims coming to Jerusalem; institutionalized as a religious order at the council of Troyes nine years later, they then grew in size and wealth so that they came to hold property throughout Europe; but with wealth came pride, and the Templars shook off the jurisdiction of the patriarch of Jerusalem and came into conflict with the secular Church over tithes and other matters. William was writing about fifty years after the founding of the order, and his version of these events has come under scrutiny in recent years, not least by Malcolm Barber in the opening chapter of *The New Knighthood*.[2] We now know that the council of Troyes took place in 1129, and there is a new consensus that would re-date the origins of the Templars to around 1120. But if William's chronology is insecure, his consistent hostility to the order renders him a highly partisan witness. In particular, in his construction of these developments, his emphasis on their poverty and insignificance before 1129 serves to underline his purpose of exposing the wickedness of the Templars' subsequent self-serving pride and arrogance.

This paper is not concerned with what happened in the 1120s, but with how William's story was developed, first by his French translator, and then by later editors and copyists of that translation. Thanks to the labours of Professor Robert Huygens, since 1986 we have had a definitive edition of the Latin text of William's history.[3] There is, however, no modern edition of the French translation.[4] William

---

1   I thank Dr Helen Nicholson for reading an earlier version of this paper and for her perceptive suggestions.

2   M. Barber, *The New Knighthood: A History of the Order of the Temple* (Cambridge, 1994), pp. 6–10. See also R. Hiestand, 'Kardinalbischof Matthäus von Albano, das Konzil von Troyes und die Entstehung des Templerordens', *Zeitschrift für Kirchengeschichte* 99 (1988), pp. 295–325; A. Luttrell, 'The Earliest Templars', in *Autour de la première croisade*, ed. M. Balard (Paris, 1996), pp. 193–202; H. Nicholson, *The Knights Templar: A New History* (Stroud, 2001), pp. 23–32.

3   WT XII.7, at pp. 553–5.

4   There are two nineteenth-century editions: *L'estoire de Eracles empereur et la conqueste de la terre d'Outremer*, RHC Oc. 1 (1844); *Guillaume de Tyr et ses continuateurs: text français du XIIIe-siècle*, ed. P. Paris, 2 vols (Paris, 1879–80).

152

laid down his pen in 1184, having provided his readers with an account of the crusading movement and the Latin principalities in the east down to his own day. Almost immediately afterwards, Saladin's victories destroyed the achievements that William had chronicled. The Third Crusade then failed to regain Jerusalem, and in the decades that followed, there were to be several more crusades preached in western Europe. It was against this background of heightened awareness of Christian failure and the weakness of the Christian position in the Levant that someone translated William's text into French, thereby making it available to a lay audience. Copies of William's Latin text found their way into the libraries of some Benedictine and Cistercian monasteries in England and France, and seven manuscripts have survived, but the French text proved much more popular: 51 complete or substantially complete manuscripts dating from between the mid-thirteenth and the late fifteenth centuries currently exist in public collections. Professor Jaroslav Folda has provided a convenient and up-to-date list, and in this article I identify the manuscripts in accordance with his numbering so that, for example, Folda no. 1 is referred to as F01.[5] These are listed, together with the foliation for XII.7, in an appendix to this paper. Until now, the manuscript tradition has remained unexplored, but my own research (to be published elsewhere) has made significant progress towards establishing a stemma.[6] In part, this paper represents a continuation of that work: never before has anyone produced a critical edition of any part of the translation on the basis of an examination of all the manuscripts.

Much of the interest in the French version of William of Tyre has hitherto concentrated on the continuations, which extended William's narrative from 1184 until well into the thirteenth century, and on the illuminations, some of which have been frequently reproduced in illustrated histories of the crusades. The translation itself has received less attention, even though historians have been aware of significant differences between it and the Latin original. A group of scholars met at the Institute for Advanced Studies of the Hebrew University in 1987 to investigate the relationship between the French and Latin texts, and their report cleared up some problems while demonstrating that many still remain.[7] For example, they were unable to assign a date to the translation closer than somewhere between the end of the Fourth Crusade and the year 1234.[8] More recently, Professor Bernard Hamilton, a member of the 1987 group, has published a detailed analysis comparing the texts for the period of Baldwin IV's reign.[9] This is a valuable article which points the way

---

5   J. Folda, 'Manuscripts of the *History of Outremer* by William of Tyre: A Handlist', *Scriptorium* 27 (1973), pp. 90–95.

6   P.W. Edbury, 'The French Translation of William of Tyre's *Historia*: The Manucript Tradition', *Crusades* (forthcoming).

7   J.H. Pryor, 'The *Eracles* and William of Tyre: An Interim Report', in *The Horns of Hattin*, ed. B.Z. Kedar (Jerusalem and London, 1992), pp. 270–93.

8   Pryor, 'The *Eracles*', pp. 288–9.

9   B. Hamilton, 'The Old French Translation of William of Tyre as an Historical Source', in *The Experience of Crusading, Volume 2: Defining the Crusader Kingdom*, ed. P.W. Edbury and J. Phillips (Cambridge, 2003), pp. 93–112.

to further investigations into the rest of the work, but it does require a confidence in the printed text of the translation – in this instance, Paulin Paris's 1879–80 edition – which, sadly, is not fully warranted.

Part of the problem lies in the fact that in the Middle Ages, copyists of vernacular texts were not always scrupulous in reproducing what was in front of them; instead, they would polish the style, modernize the orthography and, from time to time, 'improve' on the information before them. They also made mistakes in copying which then passed into the manuscript tradition, and also, where the readings in their exemplar were self-evidently blundered, they might attempt to make corrections. My earlier research has identified what I believe to be those manuscripts which are closest to the original form of the translation, and so it is now possible to examine how the translator dealt with the Latin text and at the same time see how later redactors modified the text further.

So how did the translator adapt William's Latin? And to what extent did the translation then develop a life of its own? I have been able to consult all but one of the 51 manuscripts.[10] Two others, F30 and F46, are mutilated and lack the chapter in question, and so what follows is based on an examination of 48 manuscripts. I have previously identified a group of seven manuscripts as most closely preserving the text of the translation,[11] and rather than attempt to collate all 48 manuscripts and produce an apparatus that would be confusing and extremely unwieldy, this new edition of the translation of XII.7 utilizes these seven, taking as its base the Paris, BN, ms. fr. 9,081, fols 135v–136r (F05). This manuscript has been dated on art-historical grounds to 1245–48, and was produced in Paris.[12] The other six manuscripts are:

- F02   Paris, BN, ms. fr. 2,627, fol. 80r (N. France: fifteenth century)
- F03   Paris, BN, ms. fr 2,632, fols 85v–86r (Latin East or France: first half of thirteenth century)
- F04   Paris, BN, ms. fr. 2,826, fol. 60r–v (Latin East or France: first half of thirteenth century)
- F38   London, BL, Henry Yates Thompson ms. 12, fol. 69r–v (England: mid-thirteenth century)
- F41   Paris, BN, ms. fr. 67, fols 168v–169r (N. France: second half of thirteenth century)
- F52   Baltimore, Walters Art Gallery, ms. 142, fols 104v–105r (Paris: c. 1300 with additions c. 1340).

As it happens, some of these manuscripts are among the earliest to have survived: F05 is the earliest manuscript with illustrations; F38 probably the earliest to contain a version of the continuations. But although F52, and more especially F02, are significantly later, they nevertheless preserve a primitive form of the text. None provides a rubric for this chapter.

---

10   F66, the fire-damaged Turin, Biblioteca Nazionale, ms. L. II 17.

11   Edbury, 'The French Translation' (forthcoming).

12   For the date, see J. Folda, *Crusader Art in the Holy Land: From the Third Crusade to the Fall of Acre, 1187–1291* (Cambridge, 2005), pp. 217, 235–6.

154

XII.7

[1] Si come Damedex envoie ses graces la ou lui plest, chevalier preudome qui estoient en la terre d'outremer orent talent et proposement de remanoir a tozjors ou servise Nostre Seigneur et avoir comune vie si come chanoine riglé. [2] En la main au patriarche[13] voerent chastee, obedience et renoncerent a toute proprieté. [3] Cil qui plus maintindrent ceste chose et le firent endroit aus et les autres amonesterent de fere ce meismes furent dui chevalier: l'uns ot non Hues de Paiens delez Troies; li autres Geufroiz de Saint Omer. [4] Et porce qu'il n'avoient eglise ne certaine meson ou il peussent vivre par els, li rois leur otroia atant com li pleroit un habitacle es meisons del pales que il avoit delez le Temple Nostre Seignor. [5] Li chanoine del Temple leur baillierent a cens une place qu'il avoient delez ce pales por amender leur herberiage et fere les officines qui mestier ont a gent de religion. [6] Li rois[14] et li autre baron, li patriarches et li autre prelat des eglises leur donerent rentes por leur vivre et por leur vestir; l'un firent ces dons a tozjors, li autre a une piece del tens. [7] La premeraine chose que l'en leur encharja et enjoint en pardon de leur pechiez ce fu que il gardassent les chemins par ou li pelerin venoient de robeeurs et de larrons qui granz max i soloient fere. [8] Ceste penitence lor comanderent li patriarches et li autre evesque.

[9] Neuf anz demorerent einssinc en habit des siecle, que il vestoient tex robes come li chevalier et les autres bones genz leur donoient por Dieu. [10] Ou noviesme an ot assamble un concile en France dedenz la cite de Troies. [11] La furent assamble l'arcevesques de Reins[15] et l'arcevesques de Sanz[16] et tuit leur evesque; l'evesque d'Albane[17] meismes i fu qui estoit legaz l'apostoile; l'abés de Cisteaus[18] et l'abés de Clerevaus[19] i vindrent et maintes autres genz de religion.[20] [12] La fu establi li ordres et la regle que l'en leur dona por vivre come gent religieuse; leur habiz fu comandez a estre blans par l'auctorité l'apostoile Honore,[21] qui lors estoit, et par le patriarche de Jherusalem.[22] [13] Cil ordres avoit ja duré .ix. anz si come ge vos ai dit, ne il n'i avoit encores que .ix. freres qui vivoient chascun jor d'autrui aumosnes. [14] Des lors comenca acroistre li nombres des renduz, et leur dona l'en rentes et teneures. [15] Ou tens pape Eugene[23] fu comande que il coussissent en leur chapes et en leur manteax croiz de dras rouges, porce que il fussent conneu entre les autres genz; ainssinc le firent li chevalier et le meneur frere que l'en claime sergenz. [16] Des lors crurent si leur possessions com vos poez veoir que li ordres del Temple est venuz avant; car porce que il furent herbergie premierement delez le Temple, sunt il encore apele li frere de la chevalerie del Temple. [17] Apoines porroit l'en trover deca mer ne de la terre de crestiens ou cil ordres n'oit aujordui meisons et freres et granz rentes.

---

13 Gormond of Picquigny.
14 Baldwin II.
15 Reynald II.
16 Henry Sanglier.
17 Matthew, cardinal bishop of Albano.
18 Stephen Harding.
19 St Bernard.
20 The absence of any mention of the abbot of Pontigny at this point suggests that the translator was not using a Latin text that contained this reference; see WT, p. 554, apparatus.
21 Honorius II.
22 Stephen, named in the Latin text.
23 Eugenius III.

[18] Au comencement se contindrent sagement et en grant humilité selonc ce que il por Dieu avoient lessie le siecle, mes apres, quant les richeces leur vindrent, il sembla qu'il eussent oblie leur proposement et monterent en grant orgueill, si que premierement se soutraitrent au patriarche de Jherusalem et porchacerent vers l'apostoile que cil n'eust nul pooir sor els qui au comencement les avoit establiz et fondez des biens meismes des eglise. [19] As autres religions et as eglises qui maintes beles aumosnes leur avoit donees, commercerent il a tolir les dismes et les primices et autres rentes qu'il avoient tenues jusqu'a leur tens; leur voisins troblerent et pledoierent en maintes manieres, si com il font encores.

1. Si come] F03: Se
   Damedex] F02: Damedieu; F04: Demedex; F03 F38: Damledex; F41 F52: Damediex
   a tozjors ou servise Nostre Seigneur] F52: el servise Nostre Seigneur a tozjors
   riglé] F03: reguler; F38 F52: riulé; F41: reglé
2. a toute] F03: tote
3. Paiens] F03: Paainz
   Geufroiz] F02: Geufray; F03: Jofroix; F04: Giefroiz; F38: Jefroiz; F41: Jeufroiz; F52: Jeffroiz
   Omer: F38: Homer
4. atant] F02 F04: tant
5. chanoine] F05: chenoine
   baillierent] F03: donerent
   une place] F03: une leur place
   leur herberiage] F02: leur herbergage; F05: leur heritage; F52: cel herbegage
   les officines] F02: les offices; F05: leur officines
6. firent] F03: donerent
7. premeraine] F03 F52: premiere
   max] F02: maulz; F03 F38 F41 F52: maus
9. siecle] F05: sigle
   Dieu] F04 F41: De
11. Reins et] F02 F52: Reins; F03: Rainz et; F04: Rains et
   Sanz] F02 F52: Sens; F03: Cenz; F38: Senz
   meismes i fu] F52: i estoit meimes
   Cisteaus] F02: Cisteaux; F03: Citiax; F04: Cisteax; F52: Cistiax
   Clerevaus] F02: Clervaux; F03: Cleirevauz; F04: Clerevax
12. regle] F02 F03: rigle; F38: riule; F52: rieule
   por vivre] F52: a vivre
   blans] F02: plans
   l'auctorité] F04: la victoire
   Honore] F02: Honnoure; F03 F38 F41: Honoire; F04: Honorre
   qui lors] F03 qui adonc
13. ai dit] F52: dis
15. il coussissent en … de dras rouges] F52: *il croiz cousisent de dras rouges*
   chapes et en leur manteax] F03: *mantiaus et en leur chapes*
16. herbergie premierement] F04: *premierement herberjé*

156

        chevalerie] F52: fraternité
17. meisons] F38: meisnies
18. Dieu] F04 F41: De
    siecle] F05: siegle
    des eglise] F02: de l'eglize; F04: de l'eglise
19. les dismes] F52: leur dismes
    leur tens] F52 cel tens

A perusal of the apparatus will show that none of the manuscripts differs from any of the others in any major way. Most of the variants seem to reflect no more than the orthographic preferences of the particular scribes, although F52 has a blundered reading at sentence 15. Their consistency is sufficient to indicate that this text is likely to be as close as we can come to the original form of the translation.

In this chapter, as elsewhere throughout the book, the translator veered between a close rendering of the Latin text into French and a paraphrase which no doubt was intended to make it more accessible to his audience. Here, at sentence 5, he found it necessary to explain 'officines' (Latin: 'officinarum') with the phrase 'qui mestier ont a gent de religion', and at sentence 7 he added that the brigands 'granz max (or 'maus') i soloient fere'.[24] In some places, he glossed William's Latin: thus in sentence 5, the French text has the canons of the Templum Domini leasing ('baillierent a cens') property to the Templars, whilst according to William, they granted it on certain specified conditions ('certis quibusdam conditionibus concesserunt'); again at sentence 9, where William states that the donors acted 'pro remediis animarum', the translation has 'por Dieu'. In one place, the translator changed the order in which the information is presented, moving the comment in the second part of sentence 16 from its place in the Latin text after sentence 17. There are two instances of the translator adding information that might be of interest to a lay audience: at sentence 3, he rightly stated that Hugh of Paiens was from Troyes, and at sentence 9, he specified that knights were among those who had donated clothing to the members of the order in the early days of its existence. On the other hand, he left out the name of Patriarch Stephen at sentence 12. At sentence 16, he made no attempt to translate the important information: '… ut hodie trecentos plus minusve in conventu habeant equites, albis clamidibus indutos, exceptis aliis fratribus, quorum pene infinitus est numerus', and in the same vein, he failed to continue sentence 17 with a rendering of '… et regiis opulentiis pares hodie dicantur habere copias'.

It is not necessarily true that these omissions mean that the translator was deliberately playing down the Templars' wealth and power. Whilst his attitude to the order appears generally to have paralleled William's, there are nuances in his writing that indicate even greater hostility. The opening phrase of sentence 1 is the translator's, and it is clearly designed to show that he regarded the founding of the order as an act of divine grace. The translator then expands Hugh and Geoffrey's role as the men who encouraged others to join them (sentence 3). This positive enthusiasm for the order at the beginning of the chapter therefore goes beyond William's more matter-of-fact account, and so the attack on the order in the closing sentences comes as more of a surprise. The translator is more strident in his hostility. Unlike William, he links the desire to be free from patriarchal jurisdiction to the Templars' newly acquired wealth, reminding his readers in sentence 18 that the member of the order 'por Dieu avoient lessie le siecle', a statement that is not paralleled in William's text at this point. William had explained that in freeing themselves from patriarchal

---

24   Other examples are the phrase 'qui lors estoit' at sentence 12, and the phrase 'et leur dona l'en rentes et teneures' at sentence 14.

authority the Templars had turned against their original benefactor, but only the translator links other churchmen with the patriarch whose generosity is ill repaid. Similarly, it is only the translator who records at this point that the Templars turned to the pope to gain their exemptions from the patriarchal jurisdiction, and only the translator who concludes the chapter by noting that the Templars are still even now persisting in assertive and litigious behaviour.

So seemingly playing down the order's wealth and power and expressing enthusiasm for the founders of the order in the opening lines of the chapter should not mislead us. The translator shared William's general outlook, and was prepared to enlarge on his criticisms. It is unfortunate that the present state of our understanding does not allow for a clearer appreciation of when, where and under what circumstances the translation was made, but it would seem that, so far as the translator was concerned, nothing had happened in the interval that had elapsed since William's day to make him want to soften William's onslaught. As an exempt order of the Church, the Templars often found themselves at odds with the secular hierarchy; so are we to conclude on the basis of this one chapter that the lay nobility of the early thirteenth century, the presumed audience for the French translation, was similarly disenchanted with them?

Almost all the other manuscripts fall into one of two groups. On the one hand, there is a group of eight manuscripts copied in Acre in the second half of the thirteenth century (F49, F50, F69, F70, F71, F72, F73, F78), and with these should be associated three others of a rather later date which show a close textual relationship to them (F57, F74, F77); in addition, two fifteenth-century manuscripts (F67, F68) can be proved to have been derived directly or indirectly from one of the Acre manuscripts (F69). Taken together, these manuscripts can therefore be considered as representing an eastern tradition. On the other hand, there is a much larger group of manuscripts which represent a western tradition, and which, both in this chapter and elsewhere in the text, have a substantial number of diagnostic features in common.[25] These manuscripts are listed in the appendix, but it should be noted that within this group, F43, F45, F47, F51 and F53 form a recognizable sub-group, as do F60, F61, F62, F63 and F65; F58 and F64, and F37 and F42. Only F06 was produced in the Latin east – not in Acre, but apparently in Antioch. Apart from the manuscripts employed to establish as near as possible the text of the translation, there are just three others that do not fit into either of these two principal categories: F01 is related textually to F52, whilst F31 and F35 are very similar to each other and have an affinity with F03.

In seeing how these various manuscripts differ from the original translation, it has to be remembered that whereas any additional information must indicate a deliberate decision on the part of a copyist or redactor to alter what was in the text at

---

25 In XII.7, they all omit the phrases 'furent dui chevaliers' (sentence 2), 'que il avoit' (sentence 4), 'autre' in the phrase 'autre prelat' (sentence 6), 'encores' (sentence 13), 'de la chevalerie' (sentence 16) and 'as autres religions et as eglises' (sentence 19).

his disposal, and any changes to the text may do so, omissions are more likely to be the result of scribal error, and so are inherently less significant. So if a line, phrase or word has dropped out of the text, there can be no assumption that someone was trying to alter the meaning. Some changes have to be seen as copyists' mistakes: thus 'a cens' in sentence 5 becomes 'a ceus' and hence 'a ceulx' (or similar) in a number of manuscripts (F01, F06, F34, F37, F40, F42, F45, F47, F49, F51, F53, F60, F61, F62, F63, F65). 'First fruits' ('primices' – sentence 19) becomes 'promises' (or similar) throughout almost all the Acre group manuscripts and in the some of the western group, and 'provinces' in F06, F39, F43, F45, F47, F51, F54. Perhaps because this made no sense, it was dropped altogether from the manuscripts that were the ancestors of F37, F42, F60, F61, F62, F63 and F65. Other scribal errors are equally strange: thus 'l'auctorité' of Pope Honorius at sentence 12 becomes 'la victoire' in F04, F06, F32, F39, F40, F43, F54, F48, F51. Perhaps most bizarre is the alteration of a phrase in sentence 18: where the vast majority of manuscripts inform us that the Templars 'porchacerent vers' the pope so that the patriarch should have no jurisdiction over them, two, F61 and F65, assert that they 'chevauchierent vers' him.

But if these changes to the text look like the results of carelessness, other changes could well have been deliberate. For example, at sentence 16 the knighthood ('chevalerie') of the Templars becomes the 'fraternité' of the Templars in F01, F49 and F52. In sentence 2, both F31 and F35 and the unrelated F58 and F64 have the Templars renouncing not 'proprieté', but 'prosperité' – was this a scribal slip, or have copyists decided to point up the irony of the Templars' vows in the light of their subsequent wealth and financial dealings? Similarly, it is not altogether clear whether there is any significance behind the alteration of 'herberiage' in sentence 5 ('so as to improve their lodging') to 'pellerinage' ('so as to improve their pilgrimage') in F69, F71, F74 and F78. More suggestive is the statement in sentence 4 that the king gave them 'a habitation from the houses of the *hospital* alongside the Templum Domini', rather than 'from the houses of the palace' (F43, F45, F47, F51, F53). Perhaps a scribe had assumed that the Templars' vocation more closely resembled that of the Hospitallers.[26]

Some of the most interesting changes or additions are to be found in a group of manuscripts from within the Acre group: F57, F70, F72, F73 and F77. For this section of William's narrative (though not elsewhere), they are clearly derived from a common original which itself must have been in existence before c. 1260, the date of the earliest manuscript in this group (F73), and was presumably produced in the Latin east.[27] At sentence 15, where the other manuscripts, speaking of the papal injunction that the Templars should display a red cross on their cloaks, inform

---

26   For another historical tradition linking the origins of the Templars with the Hospitallers, see Luttrell, 'The Earliest Templars', pp. 196, 198.

27   Further evidence for the affinity of these manuscripts at this point in the narrative is provided by the fact that all five divide 12.9 into two parts; nowhere else in the text do they all share the same division of a chapter – a feature that is to be explained by the propensity of the copyists in the Acre scriptorium to switch exemplars as they worked.

160

us that '… le firent li chevalier et le meneur frere que l'en claime sergenz', this group states: '… ensi firent li chevalier. Et li meneur frere, que l'en claime sergenz, portassent autres manteaus que ceaz des chevaliers, si qu'il eust division entre les chevaliers et les sergenz' (following the readings of F73). So the distinction between the order's knights and sergeants is made far more explicit. At sentence 18, where the other manuscripts record that the Templars '… se soutraitrent au patriarche de Jherusalem et porchacerent vers l'apostoile que cil n'eust nul pooir sor els …', these omit the mention of lobbying the pope and say that they '… porchacerent tant qu'il furent ostes dou poeir dou patriarche de Jerusalem si que il n'ot nul poeir sus eauz'. Earlier, at sentences 4 and 5, these manuscripts omit all mention that the property given the order near the Templum Domini was a royal palace: '… li rois leur otroia atant com li pleroit un habitacle *ovec beles maisonz* (or *et une belle maison*)[28] que il avoit delez le Temple Nostre Seignor. Li chanoine del Temple leur baillierent a cens une place qu'il avoient delez *celes maizonz*'. Among other changes, they omit the phrase 'et renoncierent a toute proprieté' in sentence 2; at sentence 11, they reduce the phrase '…l'abés de Cisteaus et l'abés de Clerevaus i vindrent et maintes autres genz de religion' to 'et maint autre preudome de religion', and in sentence 12, they leave out the name of the pope. It is difficult to know what significance to attach to these alterations: the extra attention given the distinction between knights and sergeants suggests that the redactor was interested in the order, but the other changes do not seem to reflect on the Templars' standing, although they may imply a lack of interest in Church affairs.

So although particular scribes were prepared to change the wording, no one attempted to soften the criticisms of the Templars, nor for that matter to enlarge upon them. This aspect of the various versions of the chapter appears all the more striking in the light of the fact that at least a dozen of the manuscripts were copied after the suppression of the order. The chapter contains a number of contemporary references: '… they are *still* called the brothers of the knighthood of the Temple. Scarcely can one find this side of the sea nor in the lands of the Christians anywhere that this order does not *today* have houses, brothers and great incomes … they disturbed and pleaded against their neighbours in many ways, as they *still do*.' All the manuscripts written after the early years of the fourteenth century preserve these statements as if nothing had happened. That includes F44, a fifteenth-century manuscript which alone identifies the abbot of Clairvaux mentioned in sentence 11 as Bernard, and F37, another fifteenth-century manuscript, which alone notes that Troyes is in Champagne. The nearest any of the later manuscripts come to updating the situation is to be found in F37 and the closely related F42, which at sentence 17 reads (following the readings of F42): 'Apeine pourroit on trover deca la mer de la terre de crestiens …' places where the Templars do not have properties, in place of 'Apoines porroit l'en trover deca mer ne de la terre de crestiens …'; these two manuscripts thereby suppress the distinction between the long-lost Latin east and

---

28 'ovec beles maisonz' = F57, F73; 'et une belle maison' = F70, F72, F77

western Europe. But it is hardly a convincing demonstration of adapting the text to fit contemporary realities.

What then are we to conclude? Copyists in the fifteenth century were still prepared to adapt the text, but not to the extent that they would take into account the momentous events concerning the Templars' humiliation and suppression. Maybe by then memories of that episode had faded, but it is none the less interesting that not one of the post-1312 manuscripts removed the contemporary allusions or gave any hint of the order's demise. In a sense, this aspect of their treatment of the story fits into a wider pattern discernable in the literature of the later Middle Ages. As Helen Nicholson has shown, in popular perception there was often confusion between the Templars and Hospitallers despite their widely contrasting fortunes.[29] Could it be that the failure of later copyists to alter the text, far from being a matter of simple inertia, was both a cause and a product of that confusion?

Appendix: The Manuscripts

In his hand-list, Folda, following the lead of the nineteenth-century scholar Paul Riant, listed the manuscripts according to whether they had a continuation, and if so, where it ended.[30] In his list, F01–F06 have no continuation; F30–F51 end in or before 1232; F52–F66 contain the so-called 'Rothelin' continuation ending in 1261, and F67–78 the 'Acre' or 'Noailles' continuation for the period beyond 1232.[31]

I: Manuscripts Used Here to Establish the Text of 12.7

F02   Paris, BN, ms. fr. 2,627, fol. 80r (N. France: fifteenth century)
F03   Paris, BN, ms. fr 2,632, fols 85v–86r (Latin east or France: first half of thirteenth century)
F04   Paris, BN, ms. fr. 2,826, fol. 60r–v (Latin east or France: first half of thirteenth century)
F05   Paris, BN, ms. fr. 9,081, fols 135v–136r (Paris: *c.* 1245–48)
F38   London, BL, Henry Yates Thompson ms. 12, fol. 69r–v (England: mid-thirteenth century)

---

29   H.J. Nicholson, *Love, War and the Grail: Templars, Hospitallers and Teutonic Knights in Medieval Epic and Romance 1150–1500* (Leiden, 2001), pp. 230–33.

30   Folda, 'Manuscripts'; P. Riant, 'Inventaire sommaire des manuscripts de *l'Eracles'*, *Archives de l'Orient latin* 1 (1881), pp. 247–52.

31   F7–F15 are ms. fragments; F16–F29 are not mss of William of Tyre, but of the *Chronique d'Ernoul et de Bernard le Trésorier*, or of the text known as the *Estoires d'Outremer et de la naissance Saladin*. Four other items in Folda's list have been disregarded: F56 is an abbreviated version of the French William of Tyre; F59 is an eighteenth-century copy of F60; F75 is an eighteenth-century copy of F77, and F76 is an eighteenth-century copy of the continuation as published by the Maurists in 1729.

162

F41   Paris, BN, ms. fr. 67, fols 168v–169r (N. France: second half of thirteenth century)

F52   Baltimore, Walters Art Gallery, ms. 142, fols 104v–105r (Paris: *c.* 1300 and *c.* 1340)

II: Other Manuscripts Associated with Those in Section I

F01   Cambridge, Sidney Sussex College, ms. 93, no foliation (England: late thirteenth century)

F31   Baltimore, Walters Art Gallery, ms. 137, fol. 124r–v (Paris: *c.* 1295–1300)

F35   Epinal, Bibliothèque Municipale, ms. 45, fol. 96r–v (Paris: *c.* 1295–1300)

III: The Acre Manuscripts and Those Associated with Them

F49   Paris, BN, ms. fr. 9,085, fols 136r–137r (Acre: *c.* 1277–80)

F50   Paris, BN, ms. fr. 9,086, fols 156r–157r (Acre: *c.* 1255–60) (= *RHC Oc.* 2, ms. C)

F57   Paris, BN, ms. fr. 2,634, fols 132v–133r (Ile de France: first quarter of fourteenth century) (= *RHC Oc.* 2, ms. A)

F67   Amiens, Bibliothèque Municipale, ms. 483, fol. 92r (Flanders: mid-fifteenth century)

F68   Bern, Bürgerbibliothek, ms. 25, fols 179v–180r (N. France: first half of fifteenth century)

F69   Boulogne-sur-Mer, Bibliothèque Municipale, ms. 142, fols 119r–120r (Acre: *c.* 1287)

F70   Florence, Biblioteca Medicea-Laurenziana, ms. Plu. LXI. 10, fols 130v–131r (Acre: *c.* 1290, and Italy: first half of fourteenth century)

F71   St Petersburg, National Library of Russia/Российская Национальная Библиотека (formerly M.E. Saltykov-Schchedrin State Public Library), ms. fr. f° v. IV.5, fol. 93r–v (Acre: *c.* 1280)

F72   Lyon, Bibliothèque de la Ville, ms. 828, fols 125v–126r (Acre: *c.* 1280) (= *RHC Oc.* 2, ms. D)

F73   Paris, BN, ms. fr. 2,628, fols 105v–106r (Acre: late 1250s/early 1260s and late 1270s) (= *RHC Oc.* 2, ms B)

F74   Paris, BN, ms. fr. 2,631, fols 160v–161v (Lombardy: *c.* 1291–95)

F77   Paris, BN, ms. fr. 9,082, fol. 139r–v (Rome: 1295) (= *RHC Oc.* 2, ms. G)

F78   Paris, BN, ms. fr. 9,084, fols 145v–146r (Acre: *c.* 1286)

IV: The Western Tradition

F06   Rome, Biblioteca Apostolica Vaticana, ms. Pal. lat. 1,963m fols 117v–118r (Antioch: *c.* 1260–68)

F32   Bern, Bürgerbibliothek, ms. 112, fol. 88r–v (N. France: *c.* 1270)

F33 Bern, Bürgerbibliothek, ms. 163, fol. 111r–v (N. France: third quarter of thirteenth century)

F34 Besançon, Bibliothèque Municipale, ms. 856, fol. 92v (N. France: *c.* 1300)

F36 Geneva, Bibliothèque Publique et Universitaire, ms. 85 (Artois: third quarter of fifteenth century)

F37 London, BL, Royal ms. 15. E. I, fols 181v–182r (Flanders: late fifteenth century)

F39 Paris, Bibliothèque de l'Arsenal, ms. 5,220, pages 241–2 (N. France: third quarter of thirteenth century)

F40 Paris, Bibliothèque du Ministère des Affaires Etrangères, Memoires et Documents 230*bis*, fol. 82r (S. France: third quarter of thirteenth century)

F42 Paris, BN, ms. fr. 68, fols 168v–169v (Flanders: *c.* 1450)

F43 Paris, BN, ms. fr. 779, fols 106v–107r (12.7 continues from 12.6 without a break) (N. France: *c.* 1275)

F44 Paris, BN, ms. fr. 2,629 (Flanders: *c.* 1460)

F45 Paris, BN, ms. fr. 2,630, fol. 104r–v (N. France: *c.* 1250–75)

F47 Paris, BN, ms. fr. 2,824, fol. 75r–v (N. France: *c.* 1300)

F48 Paris, BN, ms. fr. 2,827, fol. 94r–v (N. France: *c.* 1250–75)

F51 Paris, BN, ms. fr. 24,208, fol. 93v (N. France: *c.* 1250–75)

F53 Brussels, Bibliothèque Royale, ms. 9,045, fol. 133r–v (Flanders: *c.* 1460)

F54 Brussels, Bibliothèque Royale, ms. 9,492–3, fol. 150r–v (splitting the chapter into two) (Paris: *c.* 1291–95)

F55 Lyon, Bibliothèque de la Ville, ms. Palais des Arts 29, fol. 83r–v (Paris: *c.* 1295–96) (= *RHC Oc.* 2, ms. E)

F58 Paris, BN, ms. fr. 2,825, fols 107v–108r (Paris: early fourteenth century) (= *RHC Oc.* 2, ms. F)

F60 Paris, BN, ms. fr. 9,083, fol. 114r–v (Ile de France: second quarter of fourteenth century) (= *RHC Oc.* 2, ms. H)

F61 Paris, BN, ms. fr. 22,495, fol. 104r–v (Paris: 1337) (= *RHC Oc.* 2, ms. I)

F62 Paris, BN, ms. fr. 22,496–7, fol. 121r–v (Paris: *c.* 1350)

F63 Paris, BN, ms. fr. 24,209, fol. 114r (Ile de France: third quarter of fourteenth century) (= *RHC Oc.* 2, ms K)

F64 Rome, Biblioteca Apostolica Vaticana, ms. Reg. Suec. lat. 737, fols 129r–130r (Paris: early fourteenth century)

F65 Turin, Biblioteca Nazionale, ms. L I. 5, fols 196r–197r (N. France: fifteenth century)

The Arras, Bibliothèque Municipale, ms. 651 (N. France: early fourteenth century) (F30) and the Paris, BN, ms. fr. 2,754, (N. France: *c.* 1300) (F46) lack 12.7. I have not seen the Turin, Biblioteca Nazionale, ms. L. II. 17 (Ile de France: first quarter of fourteenth century) (F66). All three belong with the manuscripts listed here in Section IV.

Postscript

My colleague, Dr Helen Nicholson, has kindly shown me her transcript of an unpublished translation of the French text of XII.7 and also of XVIII.3–8 (dealing with the origins of the Hospitallers) back into Latin. These two extracts are in the British Library, London, Additional ms. 5,444, fols 242v–248r, itself an eighteenth-century copy of part of the Cotton ms. Otho B III which was destroyed in the Cottonian fire. In the light of the omissions listed in note 25, it is clear that the translator did not employ a manuscript in what I have called here the 'western tradition' (Section IV). On the other hand, he does seem to have had a text which read 'a ceus' (or similar) in sentence 5 in place of 'a cens'. An analysis of the readings in XVIII.3–8 would no doubt help further in identifying the closest extant manuscripts of the French text.

The Old French William of Tyre, the Templars and the Assassin Envoy

William of Tyre is justly famous as an early and influential critic of the military orders. Scattered through the latter part of his history are several reports of events that detract from the Templars' reputation for probity in seeking the best interests of the Latin East. These range from the Templar greed which delayed the capture of Ascalon in 1153 through to the Christian defeat at Marj Ayun in 1179, for which William held the Templar master, Odo of St Amand, responsible.[1] In some instances alternative accounts of these episodes exist in sources from Western Europe, and, by comparing them with William's version, we can glimpse something of the extent to which William was prepared to denigrate the Order.[2] William's hostility is understandable. As a bishop, he would have resented the orders' privileges, which meant that he and his fellow bishops had lost jurisdiction and income, and, as chancellor of the kingdom and thus a prominent servant of the crown, he would have been fearful of their ever- increasing wealth and military might, which in time was to bring them into a position to challenge royal authority. It is likely, but not certain, that in 1179 William had participated in moves at the Third Lateran Council to curtail their privileges,[3] and perhaps his critical anecdotes were in part an attempt to justify the attack on the orders on that occasion and to discourage people in the West from making further endowments and thus facilitating their growing power.

It is in this context that historians have tried to interpret William's well-known story of the Templars and the Assassin envoy. In late 1173 or early 1174 the leader of the Syrian branch of the Assassins sent an envoy to the king offering to convert to Christianity if the king would agree to remit the annual tribute of 2,000 dinars they were paying to the Templars who controlled Tortosa and other nearby fortresses. King Amaury was delighted by this proposal and expressed his readiness to compensate the Order from his own resources, but then the Templars ambushed and killed the

---

1   Guillaume de Tyr, *Chronique*, ed. R. B. C. Huygens, Corpus Christianorum, Continuatio Medievalis, 63, 63A (Turnholt, 1986) (hereafter WT), 17:27 (pp. 798–9), 18:9 (pp. 822–3), 19.11 (p. 879); 20.29–30 (pp. 953–5), 21.28 (p. 1002).

2   H. Nicholson, 'Before William of Tyre: European Reports on the Military Orders' Deeds in the East, 1150–1185', in *The Military Orders,* vol. 2: *Welfare and Warfare,* ed. H. Nicholson (Aldershot, 1998) pp. 111–18.

3   P.W. Edbury and J.G. Rowe, *William of Tyre: Historian of the Latin East* (Cambridge, 1988), p. 128; M. Barber, *The New Knighthood: A History of the Order of the Temple* (Cambridge, 1994), p. 107.

envoy as he was returning. The king demanded satisfaction, but the master, Odo of St Amand, refused, saying that he had enjoined a penance on the chief culprit and was sending him to the pope – in other words the master was making it clear that, thanks to the papal exemptions, the king had no jurisdiction. King Amaury, however, took matters into his own hands; he had a group of armed men enter the Templar house in Sidon and arrest the man; he was then taken to Tyre and incarcerated. William concluded his account by noting that Amaury had to exculpate himself from responsibility for the murder, and that, had he lived, he would have taken the matter up with the other Christian rulers. Leaving aside the intrinsic improbability that the Assassins would have abandoned Islam in favour of Christianity, William's story is of interest as an illustration of his view of all that was wrong with the Templars: their greed and self-interest had impeded the spread of the Christian faith, jeopardized the security of the Latin possessions in the East and harmed the reputation of the king. Reluctant to risk losing their tribute – not a huge sum – they had murdered an envoy who was travelling with the king's safe-conduct and, as a result, the prospects for both a military alliance and the conversion of Muslims collapsed. Their arrogant reliance on papal privileges had, on this occasion at least, availed them nothing – maybe it was an example that other rulers should follow.[4]

There are no accounts of this episode that might reflect a Templar perspective. According to Walter Map, whose version of these events could have been written as early as the early 1180s and almost certainly before William's work had become known in the West, the Assassin envoy approached the patriarch of Jerusalem and not the king; the Templars murdered him on his journey home, apparently fearing that if peace were to prevail they would lose their *raison d'être*. Walter seems to have been more concerned with promoting the idea that the venality of the papal court prevented any action being taken against the Order and concluded by expressing his uncertainty about the truth of the story: 'What they [the Templars] do in Jerusalem, I know not; with us they live innocently enough' ('Quid agant Ierosolimis, nescio; nobiscum satis innocenter habitant'). He then goes on to criticize the Hospitallers, mentioning the attack on their privileges at the Third Lateran Council in 1179. Like William, Walter had attended this council, and it may be wondered whether his version of the story of the murdered envoy reflects a tale that was in circulation there.[5] Later writers add nothing of any real interest. James of Vitry clearly drew on William's account, but although he noted that the Assassins paid 2,000 dinars annually to the Templars, he deliberately excised any mention of the Templars' role in the killing; in his account the villain was simply 'quidam ex nostris, vir Belial et iniquus'.[6] Other writers followed William and Walter in pointing the finger of blame at the Templars, but without going into detail: thus Guy of Bazoches had a

---

4 WT, 20.29–30 (pp. 953–5).

5 Walter Map, *De Nugis Curialium: Courtiers' Trifles*, ed. and trans. M.R. James, revised by C.N.L. Brooke and R.A.B. Mynors (Oxford, 1983), pp. 67–9, cf. pp. 69–73. For Walter's presence at the Lateran Council and the date of composition, see pp. xvii, xxiv–xxx, li–liv.

6 James of Vitry, 'Historia Hierosolimitana', ed. J. Bongars, *Gesta Dei per Francos* (Hanau, 1611), 1, pp. 1047–145 at p. 1063.

brief notice which could be thought to have been derived from William's, except that he identified the king of Jerusalem as Baldwin IV,[7] and Matthew Paris similarly spoke of a King Baldwin, although, as he appended the story to an account of the Assassins' murder of Count Raymond II of Tripoli in 1152, it could be that Baldwin III was intended.[8]

William gives by far the fullest account of the story. He was well placed to know what had happened, but how he chose to construct his narrative to put across his own particular message is another matter. Clearly he had seized on the episode as a chance to cast the Templars in a poor light, but we can never know the extent to which he embellished his tale in order to achieve that purpose. What we can do, however, is see how later generations chose to modify his narrative to suit their own perspectives, and it is here that a comparison with the Old French translation of William's work comes into play. William had written his account of this incident by 1184, within ten years of its occurrence. Later, at some point between the end of the Third Crusade and the early 1230s, someone working in Western Europe translated his history into French, and it is worth considering what light the translation sheds here on the perceptions and mentality of the translator.[9] Unlike William, whose intended readership comprised literate Latin clergy, the translator's audience was likely to have been made up of members of the lay nobility, and, unlike William, the translator would have been well aware that in 1187 Jerusalem and much of the rest of the Latin East had been conquered by Saladin and, despite the best efforts of the Christian West, had remained under Muslim control. With these circumstances in mind, there are two distinct questions that can be asked: in what ways did the translator adapt William's account? and did later copyists make further changes, and, if so, how?

Although, thanks to the labours of Professor R.B.C. Huygens, we are fortunate to have an excellent edition of William's Latin text, there is no reliable modern version of the French translation.[10] A total of 51 complete or substantially complete manuscripts of the French version copied before ca. 1500 survive in public collections, and I have recently been engaged on a research project designed to lay

7   Guy of Bazoches in Alberic of Trois-Fontaines, 'Chronica a monacho novi monasterii Hoiensis interpolata', *Monumenta Germaniae Historica, Scriptores*, 23:859.

8   Matthew Paris, *Chronica Majora*, ed. H.R. Luard, RS 57 (London, 1872–83), 2, pp. 185–86. For other references, see H. Nicholson, *Templars, Hospitallers and Teutonic Knights: Images of the Military Orders, 1128–1291* (Leicester, 1993), p. 83 n. 21 (p. 160).

9   J.H. Pryor, 'The *Eracles* and William of Tyre: an Interim Report', in *The Horns of Hattin*, ed. B.Z. Kedar (Jerusalem and London, 1992), pp. 276, 288–9. See also B. Hamilton, 'The Old French translation of William of Tyre as an historical source', in *The Experience of Crusading*, vol. 2, *Defining the Crusader Kingdom*, ed. P.W. Edbury and J. Phillips (Cambridge, 2003), pp. 93–112.

10   There are two nineteenth-century editions: *L'Estoire de Eracles Empereur et la Conqueste de la Terre d'Outremer, Recueil des Historiens des Croisades, Historiens Occidentaux*, hereafter cited as *RHC Occid.*, 1 (1844); *Guillaume de Tyr et ses continuateurs: text français du XIIIe-siècle*, ed. Paulin Paris (Paris, 1879–80).

28

the groundwork for establishing a stemma.[11] One result of this work has been the identification of those manuscripts which preserve a text that is close to the original form of the translation and, on the basis of these findings, I can now present my own critical edition of the French translation of William of Tyre's book 20 chapter 30, which contains the greater part of the story of the murder. In an article published in 1973, Professor Jaroslav Folda provided the essential, up-to-date guide to the manuscripts,[12] and, for the sake of simplicity, I am following his numbering: thus for example, the fifth manuscript in his list will be referred to as F[olda]05. I should add that the preparation of this edition and the material for the discussion that follows has allowed me to test my hypotheses about the stemma and the nature of the manuscript tradition, and this paper consciously parallels another, similar paper in which I have edited and discussed the French text of William of Tyre's book 12 chapter 7, the account of the founding of the Templar Order.[13]

I have used as my base a text found in the Paris, BN, ms. fr. 9081, fols. 279r–280r (F05). This manuscript could well be the earliest extant copy with illuminations, and these have been dated to 1245–48 and ascribed to a Paris workshop.[14] To establish the text I have collated it with six other manuscripts which appear to preserve an early form of the translation. These are:

F02 Paris, BN, ms. fr. 2627 (N. France: 15th century)
F03 Paris, BN, ms. fr. 2632 (Latin East or France: 1st half of 13th century)
F04 Paris, BN, ms. fr. 2826 (Latin East or France: 1st half of 13th century)
F38 London, BL, Henry Yates Thompson ms. 12 (England: mid-13th century)
F41 Paris, BN, ms. fr. 67 (N. France: 2nd half of 13th century)
F52 Baltimore, Walters Art Gallery, ms. 142 (Paris: ca. 1300 with additions ca. 1340)

Of the other 44 manuscripts, there is one (F66) that I have not been able to consult and four others (F01, F30, F63 and F71) that are damaged and lack the chapter in question. I have not thought it helpful to publish an apparatus detailing the variants to be found in the remaining manuscripts – such an undertaking would be extremely bulky and would not add significantly to our understanding, although attention will be drawn to particular instances where later redactors have emended the text. All the manuscripts are listed in an appendix to this paper together with the foliation for this chapter.

In William's Latin text, what follows is book 20 chapter 30; in the French text, thanks to the merging of two earlier chapters in this book, it is numbered chapter 29. None of the seven manuscripts I have used to establish the text has a rubric; the

---

11   P.W. Edbury, 'The French Translation of William of Tyre's *Historia*: the manuscript tradition', *Crusades* 6 (2007), 69–105.

12   J. Folda, 'Manuscripts of the *History of Outremer* by William of Tyre: a Handlist', *Scriptorium* 27 (1973), 90–5.

13   P.W. Edbury, 'The Old French William of Tyre and the Origins of the Templars', in N. Housley (ed.), *Knighthoods of Christ: Essays on the History of the Crusades and the Knights Templar presented to Malcolm Barber* (Ashgate, 2007), pp. 151–64.

14   J. Folda, *Crusader Art in the Holy Land, From the Third Crusade to the Fall of Acre, 1187–1291* (Cambridge, 2005), pp. 217, 235–6.

rubrics printed in the nineteenth-century editions are not translated from William's Latin text, but represent accretions that belong to a later stage in the manuscript tradition.

William of Tyre 20:30 (29)

¹ Li rois ot molt grant joie quant il oi ce message parler, et, si com il estoit bons crestiens et sages hom, il respondi mout debonerement que ja si grant chose et si haute emprise ne remanroit por la rente de .ii.m. besanz; car il estoit prez que il de ses propres rentes les asseist as Templiers en tel leu dont il se devroient bien tenir apaié. 2 Apres ce retint le message une piece del tens avec lui por acomplir les couvenances qu'il demandoit; mout li fesoit bele chiere et grant heneur. 3 Apres, quant tot fu acordé entre le roi et lui, il demanda congié et s'en parti por amener le Vieill et ses genz a fere de bon cuer ce qu'il avoient promis. 4 Li rois li bailla conduit. 5 Quant il orent passé Triple et cil estoit ja pres de son pais, ne sai quant Templier saillirent d'un guet et leur coururent sus les espees tretes. 6 Ce preudome, qui ja estoit ausint comme crestiens et mout se fioit en la leauté de nostre gent et avoit le conduit le roi, ocistrent et decopperent tot.
⁷ Quant li rois oi ceste novele, si grant duel ot et si grant courouz qu'il sembloit qu'il fust hors del sen. *⁸* Tantost envoia querre ses barons et les conjura que li donassent conseill; la chose leur conta si com il l'avoit menee. *⁹* Il respondirent tuit a une voiz que ce ne devoit il mie lessier qu'il ne fust bien amendé, car trop estoit li outrages lez et vilains, et grant honte avoit l'en fete a Damedieu et a tote crestienté et nomeement au roi. *¹⁰* Par acort de toz furent envoie dui haut home: li uns avoit non Sehers de Mamedunc;¹⁵ li autres Godechauz de Torhout.¹⁶ *¹¹* Cil vindrent au mestre del Temple, qui avoit non frere Odes de Saint Amant,¹⁷ et li requistrent de part le roi et de part les barons que cele traison et ce vilain forfet que si frere avoient fet feist amender sanz delai au roi et au regne. *¹²* L'en disoit certeinement que uns Templiers qui avoit non Gautiers del Mesnil, orgueilleus et fel, jangleus et meslis, et n'avoit qu'un oeill, avoit fete cele desleauté par le consentement des autres Templiers. *¹³* Dom il avint que li mestres l'en deporta ce qu'il pot, et respondi as messages le roi que il en avoit sa penitanence enjointe au frere qui ce avoit fet et l'en envoieroit a Rome o toutes ses letres por fere le comandement l'apostole; por ce deffendoit il bien au roi et as autres de par Dieu et de part l'apostole, que ne meissent main ou frere ne en leur choses. *¹⁴* Autres paroles meismes dist il assez de qu'il n'est pas mestiers a reconter, car eles mouvoient plus d'orgueill que de religion.
¹⁵ Li rois vint por ceste besoingne meismes a Saiete et trouva iluecques le mestre del Temple et des freres assez, celui meismes maufeteur qui estoit avec els. *¹⁶* Lors se conseilla li rois a ses homes qu'il avoit menez avec lui, et par le los de toz envoia genz a armes en la meison del Temple et prist par force ce Templier qui la cruiauté avoit fete; si l'envoia tot lié a Sur et le fist metre en la chartre. *¹⁷* Chascuns se douta ou reaume de Surie que li mestres des Harsaxis ne le feist ocirre par achoison de son message qu'il avoit ainsinc

---

15 Seher de Mamedunc witnessed as a vassal of the lords of Outrejourdain in 1168 and 1177 and attested one charter of Baldwin IV in 1179. *Regesta Regni Hierosolymitani* and *Additamentum*, ed. R. Röhricht (Innsbruck, 1893–1904) (hereafter *RRH*), nos. 454, 551, 587.

16 William noted Godechauz de Torhout's death in 1179. WT, p. 999. He is not otherwise known. Although he and his fellow envoy are described by William as 'nobiles' and here as 'haut home', the paucity of other references to them suggests that this was no high-level delegation.

17 Odo of St Amand, Templar master ca. 1171–79.

30

perdu; nequedant li rois s'en escusa bien et leur fist asavoir que ce avoit esté sor son pois tant qu'il l'en crurent bien. [18] Del templier qu'il tenoit en prison ne volt plus fere, por ce qu'il ne corroçast le Temple plus qu'il avoit fet, mes l'en cuide bien se il eust plus vescu que il eust envoié letres et bons messages par tot les princes de crestienté por mostrer le grant domage que li Templier avoient fet a la foi crestiene et nomeement au reaume de Surie; si les cuidoit bien si esmouvoir contr'els que chascuns les chaçast de son pooir. [19] Quant li noviaus tens fu revenuz en cel an meismes, Raoul l'evesques de Bethleem qui estoit chanceliers le roi, vaillainz hom larges et deboneres, mourut et fu enterrez ou chapitre de s'eglise. [20] Li chenoine s'asamblerent por eslire evesque apres lui, mes ne se porent acorder; ainçois sordie entr'els uns si granz contenz qui mout dura longuement par que l'eglise fu trop domagiee.[18]

1   ce message] F03: les messages
    sages] F03: boens
    debonerement] F03: doucement
    asseist] F04: asserroit
    dont il se devroient] F03: que il se porroient
2   le message] F03: les messages
    acomplir] F03: acointier
    demandoit] F03: avoit fait
3   tot fu] F05: il fu
    et s'en parti] F52 *lacks*
    ses gens a] F03: sa gent et
    avoient] F03: avoit
5   guet] F02: aguet; F05: guiet
6   decopperent tot] F03: decouperent
7   duel ot] F04: duel en ot
    fust hors] F05: fust touz fors
8   que li] F02: qu'ilz lui; F38: qu'il li
9   ne fust bien amendé] F02: n'en preist amende
    tote crestienté] F52: toute la crestienté
10 acort de toz] F02: leur conseil
    furent] F52: i furent
    Sehers] F38 F52: Sehiers
    Mamedunc] F02: Mamedune; F03: Mamedonc
    Godechauz de Torhout] F02: Godeschaulz de Torholt; F03: Godeschauz de Torhot; F04: Godeschauz de Torholz; F38: Godeschauz de Torholt; F41 F52: Godechauz de Torholt
11 Odes] F03: Othes; F04 F38: Oedes; F52: Huedes
    si frere] F03: li frere
    amender] F41: amendez
    sanz delai au roi et au regne] F02 *lacks*; F03: sanz delai au roi
    regne] F38: reaume

---

18   Ralph, bishop of Bethlehem (1156–74) and chancellor of the kingdom (1146–74). He is last known from a royal charter of 18 April 1174: *RRH*, no. 514. Note that the translator omits the detail that the dispute was not resolved until the second year of Baldwin IV.

12 avoit non] F03: avoit a nom
Gautiers] F02 F52: Gautier
Mesnil] F38 F41: Mesnill
fel] F03 F52: faus
et meslis] F02: et mesdisans; F03 *lacks*
avoit fete cele desleauté] F52: avoit cele desloiauté fete
cele desleauté] F02: ceste desleauté
13 sa penitanence enjointe] F04: enjointe sa penitance
Rome] F02 F52: Romme
letres] F03: penitances
l'apostole] F52: l'apostoire (x2)
au roi et as autres] F03: le roi
que ne] F03 F04 F38 F52: qu'il ne
ou frere ne en leur choses] F03: aus freres ne a lor chouse
14 assez de qu'il n'est mie mestiers a reconter] F03: que riens n'en si abeut a racorder
de qu'il n'est pas] F02 F52: que il n'est pas; F04: dont il n'est pas; F05: de qu'il n'est
mie; F38: de coi il n'est pas
a reconter] F02: de racompter; F52: de reconter
15 ceste besoingne] F52: ceste reson
Saiete] F02: Saiecte; F03: Soiete; F38: Saatte
des freres] F04: des autres freres
16 qu'il avoit menez avec lui] F03 *lacks*
menez] F04 F52: amenez
a armes] F03: armees
ce Templier qui la cruiauté avoit fete si l'envoia tot lié] F03: templiers qui estoient en
Temple et celui qui ce avoit fait et l'en envoia loié
17 Harsaxis] F03: Harsazins; F04: Harsasis; F52: Harsasys
18 por ce qu'il] F02: pour ce que; F03: por ce qui
corroçast] F03: retast
eust plus vescu] F52: i eust plus vescu
que il eust] F02: l'en eust
contr'els] F03: sor auz
19 revenuz] F02: venus; F52: venuz
Raoul] F05: Raous; F38: Raouls; F52: Raols
Bethleem] F03: Bellerm
chanceliers] F03: chevalier
larges] F03: cortois
s'eglise] F02: l'eglize
20 apres lui] F03 *lacks*
par que] F02: par quoy; F03 F52: par quoi
trop] F03: molt

The previous chapter records the beginning of this story. William starts by decrying the baleful effects of the episode he is about to describe before launching into an account of the Assassins; according to William they had resolved to renounce Islam and embrace the Christian faith, and, with this in mind, an envoy came to King Amaury with the proposal that, in return for remitting the 2,000 dinar tribute they were paying the Templars, the Assassins would accept baptism. Coming now to the chapter edited here, we find that the translator made no attempt to soften the allegations made against the Templars. Indeed, the opposite is true. In the first sentence, where William described the king as 'discretissimus' the translator has 'bons crestiens et sages hom', thereby introducing a comment on Amaury's piety: the king is pious as well as wise, and that explains his enthusiasm for the envoy's proposition. (By contrast, Templars will be seen to be lacking in piety.) According to William, Amaury, 'so it is said' ('ut dicitur') was prepared to refund the Order from his own revenues; the translator, however, is categorical: the king would recompense them, and to underline the point he adds the phrase 'en tel leu dont il se devroient bien tenir apaié' – words for which there are no equivalents in the Latin. The enormity of the offence is emphasized. In sentence 5 we are told that the Templars 'sallied forth from an ambush', whereas William's original had them 'fall on them unexpectedly' – perhaps the translator wants to make sure that his readers conceive the attack as cowardly and premeditated – and while William simply reports that they killed the envoy, the translator has 'killed and completely beheaded'. Curiously, the translator omits to translate William's phrase 'lese maiestatis crimen incurrentes'. Thereafter the translation stays fairly close to the Latin text until we reach sentence 17. Here the idea that everyone feared lest the master of the Assassins would avenge himself for his envoy by staging the murder of the king is the translator's invention; William instead speaks of the event bringing 'irreparable ruin' on the kingdom. The translator's chief addition, however, comes at the end: William simply said that, had Amaury recovered from his final illness, he would have taken the matter up with 'the kings and princes of the lands of the world', but in the translation the whole of the second part of sentence 18 is new:

> por mostrer le grant domage que li Templier avoient fet a la foi crestiene et nomeement au reaume de Surie; si les cuidoit bien si esmouvoir contr'els que chascuns les chaçast de son pooir ('to expose the great damage the Templars had done to the Christian faith and especially to the kingdom of Syria; thus it was reckoned that they would be so incensed against them that each would drive them from his dominion.')

So the translator, far from sparing the blushes of the Templars, goes beyond William in seeking to blacken their reputation, and by the sound of it he would have approved of their being expelled from their considerable holdings in the West. This tendency to heighten William's hostility is also discernable in the chapter (12:7) describing the foundation of the Order.[19] Evidently the climate of opinion in at least some circles in early thirteenth-century France was sufficiently sceptical about the Templar activities for such tales to find a ready audience.

Most of the manuscripts not utilized in establishing the text edited above fall into one of two groups. On the one hand there are eight extant manuscripts copied in Acre in the second half of the thirteenth century (F49, F50, F69, F70, F71, F72, F73, F78);[20] with them should be associated three rather later manuscripts which show a close textual relationship to them (F57, F74, F77), plus two fifteenth-century manuscripts (F67, F68) that can be proved to have been derived directly or indirectly from one of the Acre manuscripts (F69). Taken together these manuscripts may be thought of as representing an Acre tradition. On the other hand there is a much

---

19   Edbury, 'The Old French William of Tyre', pp. 157–8.
20   F71 lacks WT 20.30.

larger group of manuscripts which represent a Western tradition, and which both in the chapter discussed here and elsewhere in the text have a substantial number of features in common.[21] These manuscripts are listed in the Appendix, but it should be noted that, at least so far as their version of this chapter is concerned, within this group F60, F61, F62 and F65 form a recognizable sub-group, as do F53, F58 and F64; and F37 and F42. Of this second group, only F06 was produced in the Latin East – not in Acre but apparently in Antioch.[22] There are only two manuscripts containing William of Tyre book 20 chapter 30 that do not belong in either of these two principal categories: F31 and F35 are very similar to each other and show a marked textual affinity with F03.

In seeing how the readings in these various manuscripts differ from the original translation, it is important to avoid the trap of assigning significance to what may after all be no more than copyists' mistakes. Any additional information must indicate a deliberate decision on the part of a copyist or redactor to alter what was in the text in front of him, and any other alterations to the wording of the text may do so, but omissions are quite possibly the result of scribal error. So if a line, phrase or word has dropped out of the text, there can be no assumption that someone has intended to alter the meaning. In this chapter a number of copyists were unclear about the number of envoys, with the result that they are inconsistent as to whether to the verbs in sentences 3–6 should be singular or plural. Some changes are self-evidently erroneous: F03 describes Bishop Ralph of Bethlehem as the king's 'chevalier' rather than his 'chancelier' (sentence 19); F31 and F35 have the Templars attacking from a 'gué' (ford or ditch) rather than from a 'guet' or 'agait' (ambush), and there is similarly no significance in the fact that the fifteenth-century F37 and F42 both use the word 'embuchement' here (sentence 5); F60, F61, F62, and F65 have the king calling together his barons and requiring them to give him a 'gift' ('un don') instead of 'counsel' ('conseill') (sentence 8). In sentence 12 Gautier del Mesnil, the Templar held responsible for the murder, is described, among other things, as 'jangleus' ('deceitful'), but one fifteenth-century manuscript of French provenance (F65) turns him into 'ung anglois', and we are left to ponder whether this was a simple slip or whether a scribe had his own agenda.

Other alterations introduced into the manuscript do not change the meaning significantly but may well have been introduced for a purpose. The Acre manuscripts and those associated with them at this point in the text divide into two distinct groups: F50, F57, F73, F74, F77 and F49, F67, F58, F69, F70, F72, F78.[23] The first of these groups all read 'roiaume (or a variant spelling) de Jerusalem' for 'reaume

21   For example, in 20.30 they read 'chose ne' for 'chose et' (sentence 1), 'en ot' for 'ot' (sentence 7), 'enjointe lor penitances' (or similar) (sentence 13), 'dont il' for 'de qu'il' (sentence 14), 'autres' for 'freres' (sentence 15); and omit 'leur' (sentence 8), 'meismes' (sentence 14), 'tot lié' (sentence 16), and 'trop' (sentence 20).

22   Folda, *Crusader Art*, pp. 218, 347–50.

23   There appears to have been considerable hybridization in the transmission of the Acre manuscripts with the result that the patterns of shared characteristics may last only for a short stretch. The second of these groups all merge WT 21 chapters 2 and 3. At 12:7 F57, F70, F72, F73 and F77 form a discrete group. See Edbury, 'The Old French William of Tyre' pp. 159–60.

de Surie' in sentences 17 and 18. Presumably a scribe working in the Latin East wanted to keep the correct title of the kingdom alive. The second group, on the other hand, retains 'Surie' but has the king arrest the Templar culprit at Caesarea instead of Sidon (sentence 15). It is possible that an Acre scribe would have had access to a separate tradition that associated the arrest with Caesarea, but on balance unlikely. Some of the manuscripts in this same group (F49, F67, F68, F69, F78) make another alteration which again might possibly indicate some additional knowledge. At sentence 12, where all the other manuscripts, following William's Latin text, inform us that Gautier del Mesnil had only one eye, these report instead that he 'en avoit .iii. aveuc lui qui avoit ceste deleauté faite'.[24] The manuscripts disagree as to whether the numeral should be '.iii.' (F49, F69) or '.iiii.' (F67, F68, F78), and it is only the two fifteenth-century copies (F67, F68) that, as the sense now demands, change the second 'avoit' to 'avoient'. In view of the earlier statement at sentence 5, that the author did not know how many Templars took part, this piece of information should probably be rejected, but this alteration and the others mentioned in this paragraph do illustrate the point that copyists did embellish what they found, and their changes may shed light on the intellectual climate in which they worked.

None of these manuscripts makes any attempt to tone down the hostility towards the Templars that this chapter demonstrates. It has already been observed that the translator, if anything, heightened William's denigration of the Order, and some redactors seem to have taken an even more strident line. The translator wrote that Walter and his associates killed the envoy 'par le consentement des autres Templiers', a close rendering of William's 'de conscientia tamen fratrum'.[25] Some of the manuscripts, however, change this to imply a more proactive complicity in the deed: thus for both F57 and the closely related group, F60, F61, F62 and F65, they had acted 'par le conseil' of the other Templars; while F34, F36, F43, F45, F51 have 'par le commandement' of the others. One fifteenth-century manuscript (F44) goes further: Walter acted 'par le commandement du maistre du Temple son seigneur et des autres Templiers'. Two closely related manuscripts which have been ascribed to a Parisian *atelier* and dated to the late 1290s, F31 and F35,[26] appear to make Odo of St Amand's rejoinder to the envoys even more peremptory: where most of the others say that he forbad 'au roi et as autres de par Dieu et de part l'apostoile que ne meissent main ou frere ne en leur choses' these manuscripts read: 'le roi … qu'il ne mesfait ne meist main as freres ne a lor choses' (sentence 13). These same two manuscripts also record that the royal officers arrested more Templars at Sidon than just Gautier del Mesnil (sentence 16), but what is particularly striking about them is the rubric that they alone of all the copies share. The chapter is headed: 'La grant desloiauté que li templier fisent dont Diex les doit hair et touz li siecles'.

Whereas it is impossible to know when this particular rubric was composed, its presence in two manuscripts copied in Paris some ten years before the arrest of the Templars in 1307 is suggestive. The Order had always had its detractors, but the

---

24 Following the orthography to be found in F49.
25 WT, p. 953 lines 29–30.
26 J. Folda, *Crusader Manuscript Illumination at Saint-Jean d'Acre, 1275–1291* (Princeton, 1976), pp. 205, 208, cf pp. 146–51.

hardening of the hostile attitudes that such words would seem to imply, coupled with the more general tendency in the textual tradition to heighten rather than lessen the criticism of the Templars, must have had some influence in shaping the body of opinion that was prepared to believe the charges against the Order. Of the extant manuscripts of the French translation of William of Tyre, around a third can be ascribed to northern France and dated to somewhere between the 1260s and 1307, and although there is no way of knowing how widely read these stories of Templar skulduggery would have been, the wealthy and therefore, presumably, influential owners of these manuscripts could well have had a part, directly or indirectly, in hounding the Order out of existence.

Appendix: The Manuscripts

In his handlist, Folda, following the lead of the nineeenth-century scholar Paul Riant, listed the manuscripts according to whether they had a continuation and, if so, where it ended.[27] In his list F01–F06 have no continuation; F30–F51 end in or before 1232; F52–F66 contain the so-called 'Rothelin' continuation ending in 1261; and F67–78 contain the 'Acre' or 'Noailles' continuation for the period beyond 1232.[28]

I Manuscripts Used here to Establish the Text of 20.30

F02　Paris, BN, ms. fr. 2627, fol. 152v (N. France: 15th century)
F03　Paris, BN, ms. fr. 2632, fols 168v–169r (Latin East or France: first half of 13th century)
F04　Paris, BN, ms. fr. 2826, fol. 114v (Latin East or France: first half of 13th century)
F05　Paris, BN, ms. fr. 9081 fols 279r–280r (Paris: ca. 1245–48)
F38　London, BL, Henry Yates Thompson ms. 12, fol. 152r–v (England: mid 13th century)
F41　Paris, BN, ms. fr. 67, fols 258v–259r (N. France: second half of 13th century)
F52　Baltimore, Walters Art Gallery, ms. 142, fols 209v–210r (Paris: ca. 1300 and ca. 1340)

II The Acre Manuscripts and those Associated with them

F49　Paris, BN, ms. fr. 9085, fols 278v–279v (Acre: ca. 1277–80)
F50　Paris, BN, ms. fr. 9086, fols 317v–318v (Acre: ca. 1255–60) (= RHC Occid., 2, ms. C)
F57　Paris, BN, ms. fr. 2634, fol. 274r–v (Ile de France: first quarter of 14th century)

27　Folda, 'Manuscripts of the *History of Outremer*'; P. Riant, 'Inventaire sommaire des manuscripts de *l'Eracles*', *Archives de l'Orient latin* 1 (1881), 247–52.

28　F7–F15 are manuscript fragments; F16–F29 are not manuscripts of William of Tyre but of the *Chronique d'Ernoul et de Bernard le Trésorier* or of the text known as the *Estoires d'Outremer et de la naissance Saladin*. Four other items in Folda's list have been disregarded: F56 is an abbreviated version of the French William of Tyre; F59 is an eighteenth-century copy of F60; F75 is an eighteenth-century copy of F77, and F76 is an eighteenth-century copy of the continuation as published by the Maurists in 1729.

X

36

      (= RHC Occid., 2, ms. A)

F67   Amiens, Bibliothèque Municipale, ms. 483, fol. 179v (Flanders: mid 15th century)

F68   Bern, Bürgerbibliothek, ms. 25, fols 359r–360r (N. France: first half of 15th century)

F69   Boulogne-sur-Mer, Bibliothèque Municipale, ms. 142, fols 248r–249r (Acre: ca. 1287)

F70   Florence, Biblioteca Medicea-Laurenziana, ms. Plu. LXI. 10, fol. 245r–v (Acre: ca. 1290, and Italy: first half of 14th century)

F72   Lyon, Bibliothèque de la Ville, ms. 828, fol. 253r–v (Acre: ca.1280) (= RHC Occid., 2, ms. D)

F73   Paris, BN, ms. fr. 2628, fols 217v–218v (Acre: late 1250s/early 1260s and late 1270s) (= RHC Occid., 2, ms B)

F74   Paris, BN, ms. fr. 2631, fols 323v–324r (Lombardy: ca. 1291–95)

F77   Paris, BN, ms. fr. 9082, fols 240r–241r (Rome: 1295) (= RHC Occid., 2, ms. G)

F78   Paris, BN, ms. fr. 9084, fols 289r–290r (Acre: ca. 1286)

III The Western Tradition

F06   Rome, Biblioteca Apostolica Vaticana, ms. Pal. lat. 1963m fol. 231r–v (Antioch: ca. 1260–68)

F32   Bern, Bürgerbibliothek, ms. 112, fol. 180r–v (N. France: ca. 1270)

F33   Bern, Bürgerbibliothek, ms. 163, fol. 208v–9r (N. France: third quarter of 13th century)

F34   Besançon, Bibliothèque Municipale, ms. 856, fols 187v–188r (N. France: ca. 1300)

F36   Geneva, Bibliothèque Publique et Universitaire, ms. 85, (Artois: third quarter of 15th century)

F37   London, BL, Royal ms. 15. E. I, fols 259v–260r (Flanders: late 15th century)

F39   Paris, Bibliothèque de l'Arsenal, ms. 5220, pages 495–6 (N. France: 3rd quarter of 13th century)

F40   Paris, Bibliothèque du Ministère des Affaires Etrangères, Memoires et Documents 230*bis*, fol. 156v (S. France: third quarter of 13th century)

F42   Paris, BN, ms. fr. 68, fols 338v–339r (Flanders: ca. 1450)

F43   Paris, BN, ms. fr. 779, fols 215v–216r (N. France: ca. 1275)

F44   Paris, BN, ms. fr. 2629, fol. 268r–v (Flanders: ca. 1460)

F45   Paris, BN, ms. fr. 2630, fol. 197v–198r (N. France: ca. 1250–75)

F46   Paris, BN, ms. fr. 2754, fols 114v–115v (N. France: ca. 1300)

F47   Paris, BN, ms. fr. 2824, fols 144v–145r (N. France: ca. 1300)

F48   Paris, BN, ms. fr. 2827, fol. 189r–v (N. France: ca. 1250–75)

F51   Paris, BN, ms. fr. 24208, fol. 185r–v (N. France: ca. 1250–75)

F53   Brussels, Bibliothèque Royale, ms. 9045, fols 248v–249v (Flanders, ca. 1460)

F54   Brussels, Bibliothèque Royale, ms. 9492–3, fol. 289r–v (Paris: ca. 1291–95)

F55   Lyon, Bibliothèque de la Ville, ms. Palais des Arts 29, fol. 202r–v (Paris: ca. 1295–96) (= RHC Occid., 2, ms. E)

F58   Paris, BN, ms. fr. 2825, fols 226v–227r (Paris: early 14th century) (= RHC Occid., 2, ms. F)

F60   Paris, BN, ms. fr. 9083, fols 222v–223r (Ile de France: second quarter of 14th century) (= RHC Occid., 2, ms. H)

F61   Paris, BN, ms. fr. 22495, fols 200v–201r (Paris: 1337) (= RHC Occid., 2, ms. I)

F62   Paris, BN, ms. fr. 22496–7, vol. 2, fol. 76r–v (Paris: ca. 1350)

F64   Rome, Biblioteca Apostolica Vaticana, ms. Reg. Suec. lat. 737, fol. 256r–v

(Paris: early 14th century)

F65   Turin, Biblioteca Nazionale, ms. L I. 5, fols 358r–359r (N. France: 15th century)

IV Manuscripts that Preserve a Textual Affinity with F03

F31   Baltimore, Walters Art Gallery, ms. 137, fols 250v–251r (Paris: ca. 1295–1300)
F35   Epinal, Bibliothèque Municipale, ms. 45, fols 190v–191r (Paris: ca. 1295–1300)

Four manuscripts lack 20.30: Cambridge, Sidney Sussex College, ms. 93 (England, late 13th century) (F01); Arras, Bibliothèque Municipale, ms. 651 (N. France: early 14th century) (F30); Paris, BN, ms. fr. 24209 (Ile de France: third quarter of 14th century) (= *RHC Occid.*, 2, ms K) (F63); St Petersburg, National Library of Russia / Российская Национальная Библиотека (formerly M.E. Saltykov–Schchedrin State Public Library), ms. fr. fol. v. IV.5, (Acre: ca. 1280) (F71). I have not seen the Turin, Biblioteca Nazionale, ms. L. II. 17 (Ile de France: first quarter of 14th century) (F66).

XI

The Lyon *Eracles* and
the Old French Continuations of William of Tyre

The manuscript 828 of the Bibliothèque de la Ville at Lyon contains the text of the Old French translation of William of Tyre's celebrated history with continuations taking the narrative on to 1248. It was copied in Acre around the year 1280.[1] Its importance for the historian lies in the fact that it contains a unique version of the French Continuation from the point at which William's own text breaks off to 1197. In a study published in 1973 the late Ruth Morgan argued forcibly that this version of the Continuation brings us as close as we can get to the original form of the text for the events of these years, and in 1982 she published a new edition of it.[2] The period in question is of course of considerable interest: the accession of Guy of Lusignan to the throne of the Latin Kingdom; Saladin's victory at the battle of Hattin; the loss of Jerusalem; Conrad of Montferrat's defence of Tyre; the siege of Acre; the crusading expeditions of Frederick Barbarossa, Richard the Lionheart and Philip Augustus; the death of Conrad and the rule of Henry of Champagne; the affairs of Cyprus, Armenia and Antioch; and finally the death of Henry of Champagne and the German Crusade of 1196–98. All historians who have investigated any of these topics will have had to contend with the problems presented by the different versions of the Continuation of William of Tyre — or *Eracles*, as the text in its entirety is often called after the reference in its opening sentence to the Byzantine emperor Heraclius — and the closely related text edited in the nineteenth century as *La Chronique d'Ernoul et de Bernard le Trésorier*.[3]

The standard edition of the other versions of the French Continuation of William of Tyre remains that published in 1859 by the Académie des Inscriptions et Belles-Lettres in the *Recueil des Historiens des Croisades*.[4] The vast majority of the manuscripts containing the Continuation — no less than 44 out of a total of 49 — preserve a version of the text that is closely parallelled by that given in the

---

[1] Jaroslav Folda, *Crusader Manuscript Illumination at Saint-Jean d'Acre, 1275–1291* (Princeton, 1976), pp. 36, 216, and chapter 2 passim.

[2] Margaret Ruth Morgan, *The Chronicle of Ernoul and the Continuations of William of Tyre* (Oxford, 1973); *Cont. WT*. Important work on related texts to have appeared since 1982: Margaret Ruth Morgan, 'The Rothelin Cotinuation of William of Tyre,' in *Outremer*, pp. 244–257; Margaret A. Jubb, *A Critical Edition of the Estoires d'Outremer et de la naissance Salehadin* (London, 1990); John Pryor, 'The Eracles and William of Tyre: An Interim Report,' in *The Horns of Hattin*, ed. Benjamin Z. Kedar (Jerusalem, 1992), pp. 270–293.

[3] Ed. Louis de Mas Latrie, Paris, 1871.

[4] *Eracles*, RHC Occ 2.

140

Chronique d'Ernoul. This is the text represented by manuscript *g* in the *Recueil* edition. MS *c* in the *Recueil* is similar to *g* though with peculiarities of its own, and Morgan designated the texts found in *g*, *c* and the *Chronique d'Ernoul* under a collective short-hand term as the *abrégé*. Of the other manuscripts employed by the nineteenth-century editors, MSS *a* and *b* (containing what is sometimes known as the Colbert-Fontainebleau Continuation) provide the principal text as printed in the *Recueil*, while MS *d* is the Lyon manuscript. Where the Lyon *Eracles* differs substantially from the Colbert-Fontainebleau text, the editors published it in small print at the bottom of the page. They themselves were dependent on their correspondents in Lyon for their knowledge of this manuscript, and, as a comparison of their text with Morgan's edition amply illustrates, the *Recueil* edition of the Lyon Eracles is seriously inadequate.[5] The other manuscript that needs to be taken into account is in the Biblioteca Medicea-Laurenziana at Florence (MS Pluteus 61.10). It was not used by the *Recueil* editors for the 1184–97 section, but for the period from late 1190 through to 1197 it contains a text that is itself unique though similar to the Lyon text. Morgan published this section of it in her edition in parallel to the Lyon *Eracles*.[6]

The relationship between the various versions of the Continuation for the years 1184–97 is complex. Every version contains information that is not found in any of the others; all versions are broadly similar in tone and content. For most of this period the Lyon *Eracles* is closer to the Colbert-Fontainebleau version than to the *abrégé*, but from the 1197 onwards the relationship changes dramatically with the Lyon Eracles following the *abrégé* text. Morgan argued that the Lyon *Eracles* came closest to the original version of the text for the 1184–97 section, that the Colbert-Fontainebleau text was rather more distant from it and that the *abrégé* even further removed.[7] There can be little doubt that all these versions of the Continuation were composed in the East, and an analysis to the provenance of the manuscripts supports such a view. Of the 49 extant manuscripts of the Old French William of Tyre with continuations, 42 were copied in the West and seven in the East. Of the 42 western manuscripts, 41 preserve the *g* text and just one the Colbert-Fontainebleau text. Of the seven eastern manuscripts, three preserve the *g* text, and the others are *b*, *c*, the Lyon *Eracles* (*d*) and the Florence *Eracles* (*Fl*).[8]

* * *

The first question to be asked about the Lyon *Eracles* is when was it written. In the form that has come down to us, the text dates to some time in the 1240s. It

---

[5] For the manuscripts and sigla, *Cont. WT*, pp. 7–8. Cf. Morgan, *Chronicle*, pp. ix, 4–7. For the inadequacies of the *Recueil* edition of *d*, ibid., p. 192. Cf. *Eracles*, pp. xv–xvi.

[6] For the Laurenziana MS, Folda, *Crusader Manuscript Illumination*, pp. 111–116, 192–196. The *Recueil* editors used this manuscript to supply the continuation for the years 1275–77. *Eracles*, pp. xxi, 473–481.

[7] Morgan, *Chronicle*, pp. 82–97, with *stemma* at p. 96.

[8] *Cont. WT*, pp. 12–13.

contains a specific reference to the crusade of the king of Navarre, Count Thibault IV of Champagne, which took place in 1239–40. On the other hand, Frederick II is still emperor and the heirs of al-'Adil Sayf al-Din (died 1218) are still ruling in Egypt, and these indicators would both suggest a *terminus ad quem* of 1250. [9] But how much more of the text belongs to this late period? The Lyon *Eracles* contains other datable allusions that bring us firmly into the thirteenth century: Balian of Sidon and the treaty of Jaffa of 1229; the Cypriot nobleman Aimery Barlais prominent at around the same period; Patriarch Gerold's tower at Jaffa also built in 1229. There are also references to events in the first two decades of the century,[10] while other allusions to more recent times are less specific but could well date to as late as the 1240s:

> Et en celui tens nen i aveit bacinet ne espaulieres ne coifes pointes ne estrumelieres, ne heaumes a visieres ne porteient nului gaires, se il n'estoit roi ou conte or grant seignor. Ains estoient legierement armé. Car se le chevalier ou le serjant perdeit son cheval par aucune aventure, il se poeit aidier a pié, Deu merci. A cest tens d'ores s'arment si estreit et si pesantment que se le chevalier chiet de son cheval il ne se puet mais aidier.

Or again:

> Il avint que en cel tens les Pisans estoient de plus grant poeir en Surie que les Geneveis nen estoient. Enssi que il nen i avoit parole en celui tens fors que de Pisanz, tout aussi come il est ores en cel tens que il n'i a parole fors des Geneveis.[11]

All the references to thirteenth-century affairs mentioned so far are found only in the Lyon *Eracles* and, in some cases, in the parallel passage in the Florence *Eracles*. It is clear that the Colbert-Fontainebleau version of the Continuation (*a–b*) also reached its present form, if not as late as the 1240s, at least no earlier than the 1220s. Both *a–b* and the Lyon *Eracles* mention the Templar recovery of Baghras (1216), the Damietta campaign at the time of the Fifth Crusade (1218–21) which they link with the continuing litigation between the Teutonic Order and the Hospitallers ('Et encores est la querele entr'eaus'), and Blanche of Castile, the queen of France.[12] In addition *a–b* has what appears to be an allusion that is not in the Lyon *Eracles* to the claims of Henry of Champagne's daughters on their father's patrimony, an affair that rumbled on until the mid-1230s.[13] The shared reference to the Damietta crusade, which incidentally is presented in such

---

[9] *Cont. WT*, pp. 81, 177, 179.

[10] *Cont. WT*, pp. 81–82, 191, 193. Other allusions include the disinheritance of the lords of Nephin (1206) (p. 74); Baldwin of Flanders as emperor of Constantinople (1204–05) (p. 139); Raymond-Rupen as prince of Antioch (1216–19) (p. 169); Hugh I (1205–18) as king of Cyprus (p. 177).

[11] *Cont. WT*, pp. 149, 159.

[12] *Eracles*, pp. 137, 142, 143; *Cont. WT*, pp. 96, 99–100. For the disputes between the two military Orders which lasted well into the middle of the thirteenth century, Jonathan Riley-Smith, *The Knights of Saint John in Jerusalem and Cyprus c.1050–1310* (London, 1967), pp. 397–398.

[13] *Eracles*, pp. 195–196. See Jean Richard, *Saint Louis, Crusader King of France*, trans. Jean Birrell (Cambridge, 1992), pp. 42–46.

a way that it would seem to have occurred well before the time of writing, has to be regarded as an indication that the precursor of both versions was itself composed after the early 1220s.

By comparison, the *abrégé* texts of the French Continuation of William of Tyre on the whole lack references to later events. The one exception that I have noted concerns the marriage of Joan, Richard the Lionheart's sister, to Count Raymond VI of Toulouse. In 1190, when Richard found Joan in Sicily, he persuaded her to contribute the proceeds from the sale of her dower to his war chest in return for a promise that he would pay her back on his return to England and would marry her 'hautement et richement.' The *abrégé* then says:

> Puis la maria au conte de Saint Gile, dont ele ot .i. filz, qui cuens fu de Saint Gile quant on fist pes de la terre d'Aubijois.[14]

Joan and Raymond's son, Raymond VII, became count in 1222 and the peace of Paris which brought the Albigensian crusade to an end was concluded in 1229. Although their account of the 1190 transaction is generally similar, neither the Colbert-Fontainebleau nor the Lyon *Eracles* contains this sentence. On the other hand the Florence *Eracles* does.[15] This reference to events in the 1220s does, however, serve as a reminder that the accounts of the Third Crusade in the *abrégé* texts also reached their present form long after the events described had occurred.

So far the emphasis in this discussion has been on the comparative lateness of the texts under discussion. What seems to have happened is that material — perhaps substantial quantities of material — has at various times been introduced into earlier, and now lost, recensions of the narrative. So to what extent is it possible to identify the original common stock and assign a date to it? For the oldest identifiable material we need to look at those passages that are identical in all the versions. The Colbert-Fontainebleau texts, the Lyon *Eracles* and the *abrégé* have several sections in common, but, taking the period 1184–97 as a whole, not that many. Ignoring minor variants, the most substantial passage to be found in all the manuscripts comes almost at the beginning of the Continuation and is represented by §§4–28 in Morgan's edition of the Lyon *Eracles*. These paragraphs tell of the events from the regency arrangements made before the death of King Baldwin IV through to the reconciliation of King Guy and Raymond of Tripoli after the battle of Cresson and the beginnings of the preparations for the Hattin campaign.[16] But even here we find what appears to be an allusion to the Fourth Crusade, an allusion that is also present in the *Chronique d'Ernoul*.[17] In

---

[14] *Eracles*, pp. 160–161 variants; *Ernoul*, p. 269. Cf. *Eracles*, p. 155; *Cont. WT*, p. 109.

[15] *Cont. WT*, p. 108.

[16] *Eracles*, pp. 6–47; *Cont. WT*, pp. 20–43. There are other common passages, most of them quite short, scattered through §§49–75, i.e. from the late summer of 1187, immediately before the surrender of Ascalon, to Saladin's northern campaign of 1188. But it is a feature of this section that the Lyon *Eracles* frequently includes material not found elsewhere. *Eracles*, pp. 77–122. The passages common to all versions can be identified from the critical apparatus. Cf. *Cont. WT*, pp. 61–87.

[17] *Eracles*, p. 24; *Ernoul*, p. 96; *Cont. WT*, p. 30.

other words, all the extant versions of the Continuation stem from a recension which itself postdated 1204. But that is not to say that the original text was first composed after 1204. Indeed, in a famous passage, a group of four manuscripts of the *Chronique d'Ernoul* informs us apropos the battle of Cresson fought on 1 May 1187 that a squire of Balian of Ibelin named 'Ernous' or 'Ernoul' had first put this story into writing,[18] and the implication would seem to be that Ernoul's account was written nearer to the events. But how much ground Ernoul's narrative covered is unknown and is not a question that can be addressed here.[19]

This post-1204 source — for the sake of convenience I shall refer to it as '*O*' — which lies behind all the extant versions contained a narrative that continued at least as far as 1197. In telling of Conrad's successful defence of Tyre in the closing weeks of 1187, all the texts report that just two of the Muslim galleys escaped and went to Beirut where they 'firent puis grant damage as Crestiens, si com vos orrez de ci en avant' or 'si com vos orés en aucun tens dire.'[20] This cross-reference, which must have been present in *O*, is not picked up until very much later, in the account of the recovery of Beirut in 1197.[21] There are two important points to be made. First, *O* covered at the very minimum the period 1184–97 and perhaps substantially more. Secondly, *O* did not stop at the point where the Lyon *Eracles* loses its distinctive character but went on for at least several pages. Morgan attached considerable significance to the point at which the Lyon text ceases to be unique, seeing it as the end of 'la chronique primitive d'Ernoul',[22] but if, as I have attempted to demonstrate, the text from which the Lyon *Eracles* and all the other extant versions were ultimately derived can be shown to have continued without a break at this point, then her arguments fall down. There is no doubting the change of recension in the Lyon text, but that in itself proves nothing about the structure of its precursors. There are other possible explanations for this change: perhaps the compiler of the Lyon *Eracles* stopped writing at this point; perhaps somewhere in the transmission a copyist switched exemplars.[23]

To sum up the discussion so far: the Lyon *Eracles* and the Colbert-Fontainebleau texts were both partly derived from a source that cannot have been earlier than the 1220s, and indeed the Lyon *Eracles* would appear to belong to the 1240s; in turn, both that source and the *abrégé* drew on a common original (*O*) that extended to at least as far as the recovery of Beirut in 1197 and which itself

---

[18] *Ernoul*, p. 149. Cf. Morgan, *Chronicle*, p. 41.

[19] It has been plausibly suggested that Ernoul's account extended no further than 1187. John Gillingham, 'Roger of Howden on Crusade,' in *Medieval Historical Writing in the Christian and Islamic Worlds*, ed. David O. Morgan (London, 1982), pp. 72–73.

[20] *Eracles*, p. 109; *Ernoul*, p. 242; *Cont. WT*, p. 78.

[21] *Eracles*, p. 226 and pp. 227–228 variants; *Ernoul*, pp. 315–316.

[22] Morgan, *Chronicle*, pp. 114–116.

[23] Such a switch would have preceded the manuscript utilized by the compiler of the Florence *Eracles*.

took shape after 1204; behind *O* lurks at least one other non-extant narrative, the history written by Ernoul.

* * *

So what light do the other versions shed on the Lyon *Eracles*? To take the closest text, the Florence *Eracles* (*Fl*), first. What has undoubtedly happened at some earlier point in the transmission of this text is that a copyist changed from one exemplar to another. Up to the point where §107 of Morgan's edition of the Lyon text begins, the scribe had been following the *abrégé* recension; he then began using a text closely related to the Lyon *Eracles*. The parallel section begins with the kings of England and France wintering in Sicily. The manuscript comes from the Acre scriptorium and would appear to date from the eve of the city's fall to the Muslims in 1291.[24] A comparison of the two texts shows clearly that *Fl* tends to be more concise and that a compiler has reworked the material in a generally intelligent and successful manner. A few passages towards the end have been omitted altogether, and in a handful of places the order in which material appears has been changed. A detailed comparison shows that the compiler had at his disposal a copy of the Lyon *Eracles* that in a number of places contained better readings than the extant manuscript.[25] Certainly the Lyon manuscript was not the only copy of that version to have existed. In a few places *Fl* has information not found in the Lyon *Eracles*, and here it would seem that the compiler had drawn on material to be found in the *abrégé*. The remark about Count Raymond VII of Toulouse and the end of the Albigensian crusade is an example that has been referred to already. Another occurs in the account of the death of Henry of Champagne where *Fl*, in common with the *abrégé* and employing almost the same form of words, noted that Henry had several times ordered the railing on the window to be repaired and that he was buried in Acre in the church of the Holy Cross. The Lyon *Eracles* has none of this.[26] However, there has been no attempt to introduce original information: all the compiler of *Fl* has done is to take a few odd and ends from another version of the text.

The Colbert-Fontainebleau Continuation (*a–b*) and the Lyon *Eracles* have considerable sections in common: to use the paragraph numbers from the Morgan edition, these are §1 — beginning of §40; quite a bit of §§49–75 although the texts here frequently separate for short passages; §82- mid way through §116; and §120 — beginning of §131. In the early paragraphs the Lyon *Eracles* frequently shares readings with the *abrégé* in opposition to *a–b*, but in its general structure it follows the latter where it and the *abrégé* diverge. The first major split between the Lyon *Eracles* and *a–b* begins early in the narrative of the battle of Hattin (§40)

---

[24] Folda, *Crusader Manuscript Illumination*, pp. 111, 116.

[25] *Cont. WT*, pp. 9–12.

[26] *Cont. WT*, p. 192. Cf. p. 193; *Eracles*, p. 221 variants. Another example may be in the passage describing Richard's departure for the West in 1192. *Cont. WT*, p. 154 (first paragraph). Cf. p. 155; *Eracles*, p. 200.

and even after they rejoin (at §49 just after Conrad's arrival in Tyre), the Lyon *Eracles* frequently has information of its own, while *a–b* and the *abrégé* generally stay together. All this changes at the beginning of §82 (the story has now reached the point at which King Guy, having been refused entry at Tyre, embarks on the siege of Acre). At this point *a–b* and the *abrégé* part company and thereafter only occasionally and not until much later do they come together again.[27] On the other hand, from §82 through to §131, with one noteworthy exception (§§116–119), *a–b* and the Lyon *Eracles* stay close to each other, eventually going their separate ways as King Richard sets out on his march that will lead to the battle of Arsur and his campaigns in southern Palestine. Thereafter they give different accounts until the point at which the Lyon *Eracles* loses its distinctive character. None of the places where *a–b* and the Lyon *Eracles* diverge or converge (§§40, 75, 82, 131) can be considered natural stopping points in the narrative. It is therefore not possible to argue that these changes in the relationship between the texts indicate points at which an earlier writer had begun or finished; rather they should be regarded as places where the compilers had started or ended their revisions.

It seems to me that the beginning of §82, where *a–b* and the *abrégé* part, is an important crux. For some time *a–b* and the Lyon *Eracles* have only been together spasmodically; now they embark on a lengthy section in which they remain close. What is more, there are two pieces of evidence that strongly suggest a disjuncture in *a–b* at this point. Shortly before, at §77, the Lyon *Eracles* had recorded Saladin's slaughter of the Templars; an elderly Muslim named Caracois upbraided the sultan:

> ... Et cuidiés vos aveir finee vostre guerre? Je vos fas assavoir que les Templiers naistront o toutes lor barbes. Encore vos di ge plus, que lor amis et lor parens ne lairont mie aler lor mort a nonchaleir, ains la vodront chierement vengier et comparer.

At §84, with the arrival of the Christian fleet bearing James of Avesnes, this prophecy is taken up in a further exchange between Saladin and Caracois. Caracois is supposed to have said:

> ... ce est le secors qui vient as Frans. Je vos di bien quant vos comandastes a ocire les Templiers que il naistroient encores o toutes lor barbes.[28]

In return for these words of wisdom Saladin presented Caracois with the dubious privilege of commanding the Muslim garrison in Acre. Only the second conversation is in *a–b*, and so the reference back to the earlier exchange ('Je vos di bien quant...') is left dangling.

The second indicator is on an altogether different scale and concerns the crusade of Frederick Barbarossa. The *abrégé* and also *a–b* give a brief and totally inadequate account of his expedition and death, suggesting for example that the

---

[27] *Eracles*, p. 126. For later convergences of *a-b* and the *abrégé*, ibid., pp. 143, 170, 194–196, 198–210, 212, 217–218.
[28] *Eracles*, p. 128; *Cont. WT*, pp. 88, 90.

XI

Byzantine emperor gave full and willing assistance throughout. At the equivalent place (§74) the Lyon *Eracles* mentions that the German emperor was the first ruler to set off and announces that it will leave telling what happened until later (§§88–98). The *abrégé* has nothing more on Frederick's crusade. But *a–b*, having already given this unsatisfactory summary of events, then gives the much fuller and very different story of the emperor's crusade and death that is also to be found in the Lyon *Eracles*.[29]

These two anachronisms in the *a–b* text, both of them straddling the point at which it parts company with the *abrégé*, would seem to show that there is here a break in the recension. Any attempt to analyse of the relationship between the various versions of the Continuation should treat what comes after Lyon *Eracles* §82 separately from what has come before. Thus to return the question of internal evidence for dating: before this point there is no allusion in the *a–b* text to anything later than the Fourth Crusade; it is only afterwards that we find the references to the Fifth Crusade and the other thirteenth-century matters that *a–b* shares with the Lyon *Eracles*.[30] Before this break *a–b* is close to the *abrégé*, though not entirely the same, while the Lyon *Eracles* contains a lot of distinctive material including the reference to Thibault of Champagne's crusade of 1239–40. After it the *abrégé* is appreciably briefer than the other texts which, as mentioned, now embark on a lengthy section in which they speak with one voice. If I am right and there is a disjuncture in *a–b* at the beginning of §82, it may be that there has been a change of exemplars further back in the transmission of the *a–b* text — a change from using an exemplar similar to the *abrégé* to one more akin to the Lyon *Eracles*.

By comparing the Lyon *Eracles* and *a–b* we can see something of how the Lyon *Eracles* compiler worked. In the pre-§82 section, he seems to have been utilizing a text that resembled the *a–b* version in its essentials and was interpolating new material from time to time. A good illustration that shows him doing this is provided by the very first paragraph in Morgan's edition. Morgan, following the example of the editors of the *Recueil*, starts with what is in fact the French translation of the last chapter of William of Tyre. The Lyon text is in tune with the other versions until near the end. Guy of Lusignan had raided a Bedouin encampment near Daron. The others all read: 'La novele en vint au roi, qui en fu tout desves,' — itself a slight expansion of William's Latin.[31] The Lyon *Eracles*, however, substitutes the following:

> En la retornee que li rois fist d'Acre en Jerusalem il vint la novele coment le conte Guy de Japhe avoit coru en la terre dou Daron sur les Bedoyns qui estoient en sa fiance, dont il en fu tout desvés et apres resut la maladie dont il morut.[32]

[29] *Eracles*, pp. 116–118, 131–142; *Cont. WT*, pp. 84, 93–100.
[30] Above p. 141 and n. 12.
[31] *Eracles*, p. 3. Cf. WT 23.1, p. 1064.
[32] *Cont. WT*, p. 18.

The wording of the Latin text is sufficient to rule out any possibility that this version preserves an original, complete form of words and the others contain merely a précis. What has happened is that the Lyon compiler has used his imagination and indulged in a piece of *post hoc ergo propter hoc* reconstruction of the past. (The king heard the news; the king died; therefore the news precipitated his death). The text had just told him that King Baldwin IV had been in Acre; he also knew that he died soon after in Jerusalem (below at §5). Guy's behaviour hastened the king's demise.

Beside such small insertions which contribute little or nothing to our information, there are longer passages in the pre-§82 section where the Lyon *Eracles* provides a different text to that given by *a–b* and the *abrégé*. Sometimes the Lyon *Eracles* introduces information which appears to add to our knowledge of events. For example, it alone records the celebrated couplet said to have been sung by Guy of Lusignan's Poitevin followers to taunt the *poulains*:

Maugré li Polein
Avrons nous roi poitevin.[33]

Again, the Lyon *Eracles* alone has the detailed account of Joscelin of Edessa's failure to defend Acre directly after Hattin and its surrender by the burgess, Peter Brice. According to all the other versions, Joscelin had been among the captives at Hattin.[34] The fact that they should contradict the Lyon *Eracles* on this point is further evidence that it is the Lyon *Eracles* that has fresh material rather than that the other texts are dependent on it but have chosen to omit this particular episode. Another example of the Lyon *Eracles* containing additional information comes in the account of Conrad's exchange with his father when Saladin tried to bargain the surrender of Tyre in return for his liberty. At the end of this section the Lyon text adds:

Et l'on l'amena devant la cité. Le marquis cria et dist: 'Conrat, biau fis, gardés bien la cité!' Et il mist main a une arbaleste et traist a son pere. Quant Salahadin oï que cil avoit trait a son pere si dist: 'Cist est mescreans, et est mout cruel.'

Up to a point the compiler has been inventive since he is unlikely to have known Saladin's actual words.[35] But what is significant here is that in the sentence that immediately precedes this quotation the other texts (in common with the Lyon *Eracles*) all say that Conrad threatened to shoot at his father. Only the Lyon text says that he actually did so, a claim corroborated by an independent source, the *Itinerarium peregrinorum*.[36] Had the other narratives been abridging the text as

---

[33] *Cont. WT*, p. 53.
[34] *Cont. WT*, pp. 56–57. See *Eracles*, p. 66 and p. 68 variant.
[35] *Cont. WT*, p. 62. Cf. *Eracles*, p. 78. For another example of presumably invented direct speech, *Cont. WT*, p. 67 (last 5 lines of §53). Cf. *Eracles*, p. 87.
[36] Hans E. Mayer (ed.), *Das Itinerarium peregrinorum*, Schriften der MGH 18 (Stuttgart, 1962), pp. 266–267. I thank Dr Helen Nicholson for drawing my attention to this reference.

found in the Lyon *Eracles* they would surely have recorded that Conrad shot at his father and not stopped where they do.

Two features of the additions in the Lyon *Eracles* are worthy of note. The compiler seems to have been interested in Islam, being the only person to mention hadjis (*hages*) and fakirs (*faquirs*) and inform the reader that, '... les Sarazins dient que porc ne home qui manjue porc ne doit entrer en celui Temple que Salahadin dedia a Dieu.' Much later he refers to the sultan's ceremonial saddle cloth, the *ghashiya*.[37] Secondly, the compiler displays an ecclesiastical interest which could indicate that he was a cleric. Ruth Morgan noted a clumsily interpolated lament for the loss of Jerusalem which looks like the work of an ecclesiastic; there is also an interest in papal history not found elsewhere, and, when speaking of Saladin's cleansing of the Dome of the Rock, we are told, ' ... firent il laver le Temple en la maniere que les prelaz reconcilient les yglises qui ont esté violees.'[38] On the other hand, the Lyon *Eracles* omits the story found in both *a–b* and the *abrégé* of Balian of Ibelin and the patriarch stripping the silver from the edicule of the Holy Sepulchre to pay such troops as they had to defend Jerusalem against Saladin. Maybe the compiler was too appalled by this act of desecration to want to repeat it.[39] This strand of ecclesiastical interest also turns up later, in particular in the account of the conquest of Cyprus where the fact that the island was thereby brought into the sphere of Latin Christendom is emphasized and in the account of the election of the Patriarch Monachus of Jerusalem in the time of Henry of Champagne where the compiler introduces a discussion of a decretal of Pope Celestine III and a summary of twelfth-century relations between the papacy and the empire. The *a–b* version of the Continuation and the *abrégé* have none of this.[40]

Taking the section before §82 as a whole, it has to be said that where the Lyon *Eracles* differs from *a–b* and the *abrégé*, it often does not make convincing reading. For example, according to all the versions Saladin moved north after Hattin, taking control of Sidon, Beirut and Jubail. The Lyon *Eracles*, however, then has him continue northwards to Antioch where he occupied a number of castles including Sahyun and Baghras and laid siege to La Roche Guillaume; he was particularly anxious to take this fortress because in it was a knight named John Gale who had kidnapped his nephew and sold him to the Templars; he was then distracted from the siege by the prospect of the surrender of Tyre only to find his hopes dashed by the arrival there of Conrad of Montferrat in the meantime. This narrative simply will not do. Quite apart from the doubts surrounding of the historicity of the John Gale episode, there can be no possibility that in the late summer of 1187 Saladin went any further north than Jubail. His campaign in the principality of Antioch belongs in 1188, and indeed it is in the context

---

[37] *Cont. WT*, pp. 66, 72, 75, 173.
[38] *Cont. WT*, pp. 54–55, 73, 75, 83, 84, 88; Morgan, *Chronicle*, pp. 108, 110–111.
[39] *Eracles*, pp. 70–71, pp. 68, 71 variants.
[40] *Cont. WT*, pp. 119, 121, 161, 163. Cf. Morgan, *Chronicle*, pp. 109–110.

of the campaign of that year that *a–b* and the *abrégé* introduce the John Gale story. In other words, in this instance their chronology is more credible.[41] To a lesser extent the same can be said for the surrender of the two great castles of Oultrejourdain, Kerak and Montreal. According to the Lyon *Eracles*, Saladin was besieging Tortosa — this siege lasted for about a fortnight in July 1188 — when he was reminded that he had to release King Guy; he thereupon took Humphrey of Toron to Kerak and Montreal and had him induce the garrisons to surrender in return for his own freedom; he then went back to resume the siege at Tortosa. The chronology is clearly impossible, and the idea that Humphrey bargained his freedom for the surrender of these castles is unwarranted: in fact they were starved into surrender in November 1188 and April or May 1189 respectively. The other versions omit the role played by Humphrey and made no connection with the siege of Tortosa. Instead they claim that Kerak fell two years after the loss of the kingdom in 1187.[42] A third instance of the Lyon *Eracles*'s chronology being poor is provided by its account of the fall of Beaufort. This fortress surrendered to Saladin in 1190 after a siege lasting a year, but the Lyon *Eracles* has this episode follow immediately after Conrad of Montferrat's successful defence of Tyre at the end of 1187. On the other hand *a–b* includes its account with the events of 1192! All versions of the siege of Beaufort have much material in common, but it is here that the Lyon *Eracles* works in its allusion to the crusade of Count Thibault of Champagne in 1239–40.[43]

One final example of material unique to the Lyon *Eracles* that lacks persuasiveness is provided by an incident that supposedly occurred during the siege of Jerusalem. Saladin is said to have agreed to take the sons of Baldwin of Ibelin and Raymond of Jubail to safety; the two children were handed over to him and were well looked after; Saladin sat them on his knees and then began to weep; when asked why he was weeping he replied that, whereas now he was depriving these children of their inheritance, after his death his brother would deprive his children of theirs; this duly came to pass. It is a touching story and is of interest for the light it sheds on Saladin's later reputation and on contemporary attitudes to children, but, as a vehicle for Saladin's prophecy, there can be little doubt as to its essentially fictive nature.[44]

What then is to be made of the relationship between the Lyon *Eracles* on the one hand and the Colbert-Fontainebleau texts and the *abrégé* on the other in that

---

[41] *Eracles*, pp. 71 (and n. 30), 122–123; *Cont. WT*, pp. 57–59. The *a-b* text and the *abrégé* then spoil things by asserting that Saladin was still at the siege of La Roche Guillaume when he heard that Guy of Lusignan had begun to besiege Acre. *Eracles*, pp. 125–126. For John Gale, see Helen Nicholson, *Templars, Hospitallers and Teutonic Knights: Images of the Military Orders, 1128–1291* (Leicester, 1993), pp. 83–84. By introducing the John Gale story where he does, the compiler of the Lyon *Eracles* has managed to squeeze out the account of the death of Raymond of Tripoli. Cf. *Eracles*, pp. 71–72.

[42] *Eracles*, pp. 81–82, cf. p. 188; *Cont. WT*, pp. 86–87.

[43] *Eracles*, pp. 187–188; *Cont. WT*, pp. 79–82.

[44] *Cont. WT*, p. 65.

part of the Continuation before §82 of Morgan's edition? Some of the material in the Lyon *Eracles* that is found nowhere else is of ecclesiastical interest and could have been adapted from Latin sources. Otherwise we have anecdotes that are either inspired by material to be found elsewhere in the text or that are often self-evidently questionable and could be the product of later invention or distant reminiscence. Where the sequence of events differs, the Lyon *Eracles* offers a chronology that is less plausible. It is difficult to sustain the idea that the Lyon *Eracles* contains information that could be thought superior to that of the other versions, and it is not at all beyond the bounds of possibility that whenever the Lyon *Eracles* goes its own way we are being confronted with passages that were composed and inserted as late as the 1240s, the date at which the text reached its present form.

The relationship between the Lyon *Eracles* and the *a–b* version after §82 can be dealt with more briefly. The Lyon *Eracles* has no passages in common with the *abrégé* until 1197 and the point at which Morgan's edition ends. But, as mentioned earlier, from §82 until §131 it is very close to the *a–b* text with the exception of §§116–119. These paragraphs describe Richard's conquest of Cyprus in 1191, and the accounts diverge just as the crusaders are making their initial landing at Limassol. It has to be said that the *a–b* version is altogether more convincing.[45] The Lyon *Eracles* offers a stylized account of the campaigning and emphasizes the point that the conquest had the effect of bringing Cyprus into the realm of Latin Christendom, while the *a–b* text seems more in keeping with the secular tenor of the narrative and has a more persuasive account of the events, with several circumstantial details that add an air of plausibility. The *a–b* text is appreciably longer and, though differing in important respects, is also generally closer to the more nearly contemporary English accounts. Whether the compiler of the Lyon *Eracles* substituted his version for the *a–b* account of this episode is not entirely clear, but that conclusion would seem more likely than that the *a–b* compiler had jettisoned the Lyon text in favour of the version that we find in the Colbert-Fontainebleau manuscripts.

From §131 and the start of Richard's campaign to southern Palestine in 1191 the Lyon *Eracles* and *a–b* diverge until they come to the events of 1197.[46] But the way in the which the material is arranged suggests that the two accounts are not totally unrelated, and indeed some episodes are very similar: for example, the duke of Burgundy's decision to withdraw from Richard's campaign, the discussion of Richard's culpability for the Conrad's murder, and Richard's capture in Germany.[47] Significantly, it is those passages that bear the greatest resemblance to each other that are also parallelled in the *abrégé*.[48] Both texts contain much information not to be found in the other. The Lyon *Eracles* is about twice as long,

---

[45] *Eracles*, pp. 163–169; *Cont. WT*, pp. 119, 121.
[46] *Eracles*, pp. 182–221; *Cont. WT*, pp. 133–199.
[47] *Eracles*, pp. 185–186, 194, 201–203; *Cont. WT*, pp. 133, 135, 141, 143, 155.
[48] See *Eracles*, pp. 178–180 variants, pp. 194, 201–203; *Ernoul*, pp. 278–280, 290, 296–298.

and among the topics it deals with more fully are Richard's use of Muslim troops and spies and his capture of the Muslim caravan, Henry of Champagne's relations with the Pisans and Aimery of Lusignan, the circumstances of the election of Patriarch Monachus, affairs in the Muslim world after the death of Saladin, and the Germans' siege of Toron at the end of 1197.[49] On the other hand, *a–b* has details on the death of James of Avesnes, names the official in Tyre whose arrest of the Assassin ship led to the murder of Conrad, and gives information on the war of succession in Sicily which led to Henry VI's acquisition of power there.[50] Each text consists of a series of anecdotes rather than an annal, and the Lyon *Eracles* in particular seems to be unconcerned about arranging the material into a strict chronological sequence.

Although in this section covering the period 1191–97 the Lyon *Eracles* is longer and more informative, it is difficult to describe either text as being 'better' than the other in any qualitative sense. It is difficult to detect any clear signs that might reflect the views of the authors and the context in which they wrote, although, by comparison with *a–b*, the Lyon *Eracles* does seem to be hostile to the regime in Cyprus. We have seen already that it gives a less detailed and less convincing account of Richard's conquest of the island. It is the Lyon *Eracles* alone that has Guy consulting Saladin as to what policy to adopt in the island, and, though both texts show him recruiting settlers, it is the Lyon *Eracles* that alleges that the knights of Cyprus were descended from 'shoemakers, masons and Arabic scribes.' Again, it is the Lyon *Eracles* that claims that Richard thought better of letting Guy have Cyprus and intended transferring it to Henry of Champagne and that Guy had to resort to devious stratagems to avoid being forced to relinquish the island. This text is the only one to tell of the humiliating episode in which Aimery's wife and children were carried off by a pirate. It also emphasizes that after Guy's death his brother Aimery only came to rule in Cyprus because Geoffrey, his other brother, did not want the island.[51] The *a–b* text casts none of these aspersions; on the other hand, it contains an account of Renier of Jubail's mission to Emperor Henry VI to obtain a crown for Aimery and of Aimery's subsequent coronation at the hands of the imperial chancellor.[52] But although a bias against the regime of Guy and Aimery of Lusignan in Cyprus can be detected, it is not so easy to provide a convincing explanation of why that should be.

* * *

---

[49] *Cont. WT*, pp. 147, 149, 151, 159, 161, 163, 173, 175, 177, 195, 197.

[50] *Eracles*, pp. 184–185, 192, 205–207. Bernard of the Temple, the man named here as Conrad's *bailli* in Tyre, appears as viscount of Tyre in documents of 1187, 1188 and 1191. RRH nos. 665, 667, 674–675, 705. Cf. nos. 640, 707, 710 (where he is named as viscount of Acre), 713, 717.

[51] *Cont. WT*, pp. 139, 143, 151, 153, 161, 163, 165, 173. Cf. *Eracles*, pp. 191–192 (settlement of Cyprus and Geoffrey of Lusignan).

[52] *Eracles*, pp. 209, 212. For the suggestion that *a–b* gives a more accurate account of the terms under which Guy acquired Cyprus, see Peter W. Edbury, 'The Templars in Cyprus,' in *The Military Orders: Fighting for the Faith and Caring for the Sick*, ed. Malcolm Barber (Aldershot, 1994), pp.189–190.

It will be apparent by now that I cannot accept Ruth Morgan's thesis that the Lyon *Eracles* represents the closest we can get to the original version or versions of the Continuations for the period 1184–97. It is not just that the internal evidence shows that the text is late — almost certainly later than either *a–b* or the *abrégé* — but that when the contrasting passages are examined, the Lyon *Eracles* does not prove itself to be superior. It is much the longest version, but this in itself means nothing. Morgan seemed to have assumed that to a greater or lesser extent the various versions are epitomes of an original. The very use of the term *abrégé* implies this concept, and in her discussion of the differing accounts of the death of Henry of Champagne she gave voice to this assumption.[53] My own analysis makes the opposite point: the material that is unique to the Lyon *Eracles* is to be explained as insertions by its compiler rather than as omissions on the part of all the other versions. I see no reason why all this material should not have been added in the 1240s.

Until we reach §131 the text into which the compiler was making his insertions would seem to have been similar but not identical to *a–b*. Before §82 the relationship between the Lyon *Eracles*, *a–b* and the *abrégé* is complicated, with the Lyon text frequently having readings in common with the *abrégé* while *a–b* stands apart. Morgan made the point that the manuscripts of *a–b* are 'not good manuscripts of the text they give,' and maybe that goes some way towards explaining why the readings they give differs.[54] But the anomalies in *a–b* immediately before and after §82 suggest that the relationship cannot be understood so simply. After §131 it is clear that the compiler of the Lyon *Eracles* was no longer using a text resembling *a–b*, and the fact that where his account is similar to *a–b* it is also often similar to the *abrégé* suggests that maybe what he was now doing was re-writing and greatly expanding a text akin to the *abrégé*. With these thoughts in mind, I return to the question of the nature of the text that lies behind all the extant versions and which I earlier dubbed *O*. It seems to me that until §82 of Morgan's edition *O* would have been very similar to the *abrégé* and *a–b* texts. After §82 it resembled the *abrégé* while *a–b*, like the Lyon *Eracles*, comprises an expanded version of it. But between *O* and both *a–b* and the Lyon *Eracles* there was evidently at least one intermediate stage which among other things included a reference to the Fifth Crusade and probably included the common material stretching from §82 to §131. But no text ever consisted solely of an account of the events of 1184–97. The *Chronique d'Ernoul* extended back to the early days of the Latin Kingdom, and the Continuations were stuck on to the end of the translation of William of Tyre. This is no place to embark on an enquiry into how these works relate, but I should like to suggest some basic ideas. The original version, from which all the texts for 1184–97 are ultimately derived was basically similar to the *Chronique d'Ernoul*. With the appearance of

---

[53] Morgan, *Chronicle*, pp. 86–88. 'We can easily suppose that the three versions chose three different details...from a much longer and more elaborate source offering all three' (p. 87).

[54] Morgan, *Chronicle*, p. 35.

the French translation of William, the *Chronique* was trimmed and adapted and pasted on to the end. This resultant compilation was to all intents and purposes the *abrégé* version of the Continuation and served as the basis for the text which in turn was the base for both *a–b* and the Lyon *Eracles*. Investigations into the translation have concluded with commendable caution that it was undertaken between 1204 and 1234.[55] Within these broad margins belong also the various versions of the *Chronique d'Ernoul* and, I would suggest, the earliest version of the Continuation.

Fortune's Wheel turns: the anonymous *Chronique d'Ernoul et de Bernard le Trésorier* and the inappropriately named *abrégé* texts of the Continuation are raised aloft as the texts that take us nearest to the events themselves; the Lyon *Eracles* plunges into the abyss. Well not quite, for where the Lyon text has unique material it deserves consideration despite its uneven quality. Nevertheless, I would hope that henceforth no one will make the mistake of assuming — as in the past I myself have done — that where the versions differ the Lyon *Eracles* should automatically be preferred.

---

[55] Pryor, 'The Eracles and William of Tyre,' p. 289.

XII

New Perspectives on the Old French Continuations of William of Tyre

As is well known, it was during the 1170s and early 1180s that Archbishop William of Tyre was at work on his history of the crusades and the Frankish states in the East which covers the period from the First Crusade to 1184. Then, at some point in the first decades of the thirteenth century, his work was translated from the original Latin into French. Most of the manuscripts of the translation include additions that were composed in French and which take the story down to nearer the date they were produced. Although historians examining the period before 1184 will turn in the first instance to William's original Latin text rather than to the French translation, everyone who has studied the history of the Latin East between 1184 and 1277 has had to make use of the additional material which is usually referred to as *The Old French Continuations of William of Tyre* or *Eracles*. Closely associated with the *Continuations* is the text known by its nineteenth-century title as *La Chronique d'Ernoul et de Bernard le Trésorier*. The significance of these narratives is considerable. Together they constitute the fullest continuous account of events in the Frankish territories in the Levant between 1184 and 1277. Their interest lies partly in the historical information they contain, but also in their capacity to mirror the political and cultural preoccupations of their authors and their original audience. The large number of surviving manuscripts is a pointer to the importance of these texts in the Middle Ages: no less than fifty-one manuscripts of the French translation of William of Tyre dating from before 1500, forty-five of which contain continuations, have found their way into public collections in Europe and the United States, while the text of *Ernoul-Bernard* is preserved in eight medieval manuscripts.[1]

In an earlier paper in this journal I made a start on investigating the manuscript tradition of the French translation of William of Tyre.[2] I turn now to the *Continuations* and *Ernoul-Bernard* and offer some provisional conclusions concerning the

---

An earlier version of this paper was given at the SSCLE conference held at Avignon in August 2008.

[1] Jaroslav Folda, "Manuscripts of the History of Outremer by William of Tyre: A Handlist," *Scriptorium* 27 (1973), pp. 90–95. I follow Folda's ennumeration: thus for example "F38" denotes item 38 in Folda's catalogue.

[2] Peter W. Edbury, "The French Translation of William of Tyre's *Historia*: The Manuscript Tradition," *Crusades* 6 (2007), pp. 69–105. See also idem, "The Old French William of Tyre and the Origins of the Templars," in *Knighthoods of Christ: Essays on the History of the Crusades and the Knights Templar Presented to Malcolm Barber*, ed. Norman Housley (Aldershot, 2007), pp. 151–64; "The Old French William of Tyre, the Templars and the Assassin Envoy," in *The Hospitallers, the*

development and transmission of the material they contain. Although our present state of knowledge does not provide a precise date for the translation, the fact that a few of the manuscripts that contain what is clearly an early form of the French version of William's history end in the same place as his Latin text is a convincing indication that the translation originally circulated without any additional material.[3] What then happened – and this development would seem to belong to the 1230s – is that someone extended William's narrative by grafting a version of the *Ernoul-Bernard* text on at the end. It was a simple matter of jettisoning the material from before 1184 to be found in *Ernoul-Bernard*, and using what was left to take the story on to 1231. Fourteen of the forty-five manuscripts with the *Continuations* end in the same place as *Ernoul-Bernard*, and several more – perhaps as many as eight – which are mutilated at the end and so lack their concluding folios probably did. Of the rest, thirteen contain the *Ernoul-Bernard* continuation plus a further continuation covering the period 1231–61 which is known as the *Rothelin Continuation*, and six (all of them either copied in Acre or apparently derived from Acre manuscripts), contain the *Ernoul-Bernard* continuation and then, for the period from 1231 onwards, a version of a totally different continuation which is sometimes known as the *Acre Continuation*. That leaves four others belonging to the Acre group of manuscripts to which I shall return later. Particular attention, however, should be drawn to one Western manuscript, the British Library, Henry Yates Thompson ms. 12 (F38). This manuscript may be of English provenance and can be dated to the middle years of the thirteenth century; it could well be the earliest surviving manuscript with a continuation – but what makes it remarkable is the fact that, besides containing the *Ernoul-Bernard* continuation, it also, uniquely, has earlier passages from *Ernoul-Bernard* interpolated into the text of the translation of William's work at appropriate places.

The eight medieval manuscripts of *Ernoul-Bernard* divide into two groups: five for Ernoul, which end either in 1227, with the excommunication of the Emperor Frederick II of Hohenstaufen by Pope Gregory IX, or in 1229 with Frederick II's return to Italy from the Holy Land; and three – two of which bear the name of Bernard, treasurer of the abbey of Corbie – which end in 1231 with John of Brienne's assumption of authority in Constantinople. It is clear that the textual tradition of this work was developing rapidly in the late 1220s and early 1230s. What would appear to be the earliest version of the Ernoul text (as represented by the Bern Burgerbibliothek mss 41 (F16) and 115 (F17) and the St. Omer Bibliothèque municipale ms. 722 (F20)) lacks several important passages including the story of the killing of the Muslim sorceress by a group of sergeants in the Christian army in 1187 on the eve of Hattin, and the visit of two unnamed priests, one of whom can

Mediterranean and Europe from the Crusades to the Ottomans, ed. Karl Borchardt, Nikolas Jaspert and Helen Nicholson (Aldershot, 2007), pp. 25–37.
[3] Edbury, "French Translation," pp. 73–74.

readily be identified as St. Francis, to the sultan of Egypt in 1219.[4] The five Ernoul manuscripts (but not the three Bernard manuscripts) identify Ernoul, the squire of Balian of Ibelin, as the original author of a particular episode which occurred in 1187.[5] How much else he wrote is difficult to ascertain, although John Gillingham's suggestion that his account ended with the description of the siege of Tyre at the end of that same year would seem to be correct.[6] Balian, and also Conrad of Montferrat, had featured prominently in the events of 1187; thereafter they both disappear almost completely from the story, and it is likely that other, anonymous, writers took over who then used Ernoul's work and perhaps other existing compositions to fashion a history which, like so much other medieval historical narrative, is essentially a composite work. It is possible that the versions of *Ernoul-Bernard* that have been transmitted to posterity were put together in the late 1220s and early 1230s by someone associated with John of Brienne whose immediate purpose was to explain John's by then troubled relationship with Frederick II and how it was that he came to be governing Constantinople.

Whoever first added the continuation to the end of the translation of William of Tyre was undoubtedly working from a Bernard the Treasurer manuscript: it ended in 1231, and it lacked the reference to Ernoul as the originator of the description of the 1187 incident. I am currently engaged in an analysis of all the manuscripts of the *Continuations* in an attempt to establish which stand closest to the Bernard text and which represent later developments, but this task is hampered by the fact that all three surviving Bernard manuscripts are comparatively late, dating to the fourteenth century or, at earliest, the very end of the thirteenth. However, it is already clear that the text of the *Continuations* in the already-mentioned British Library, Henry Yates Thompson ms. 12 (F38) has an extremely close affinity with the Bernard the Treasurer text preserved in the Bern Burgerbibliothek ms. 113 (F24). Unfortunately the British Library manuscript, which, as mentioned, contains one of the earliest, if not the earliest, surviving manuscript of the *Continuations*, has never been used in the preparation of a printed edition, and the Bern manuscript, although known to Louis de Mas Latrie, the nineteenth-century editor of *Ernoul-Bernard*, was largely disregarded by him.[7]

There is no particular reason to assume that all the manuscripts containing the *Ernoul-Bernard* continuation go back to a single original; in preparing the manuscripts of the Old French William of Tyre and its continuations, different scribes could have employed different versions of the *Ernoul-Bernard* text. It may, however, prove significant that, with one exception, all the manuscripts of the

---

[4] See *Chronique d'Ernoul et de Bernard le Trésorier*, ed. Louis de Mas Latrie (Paris, 1871), pp. 163–66, 431–35.

[5] Ibid., pp. 149–50.

[6] John Gillingham, "Roger of Howden on Crusade," in idem, *Richard Coeur de Lion: Kingship, Chivalry and War in the Twelfth Century* (London and Rio Grande, 1994), p. 147, n. 33.

[7] For a recent description of the Bern manuscript and its contents see http://www.hrionline.ac.uk/partonopeus/Bmanuscriptnotes.htm (accessed 21 Feb. 2010).

Continuations share two significant features: they lack the extended description of Jerusalem that is to be found in all the Ernoul and Bernard manuscripts, and they include the story of the election and moral laxity of the Patriarch Eraclius which is repositioned from the pre-1184 portion of the *Ernoul-Bernard* narrative.[8] This one exception, which includes the description of Jerusalem and lacks the Eraclius story, is an Acre manuscript, the Paris BN ms. fr. 9086 (F50); this manuscript at least would therefore appear to belong in an independent tradition, but further investigation is still needed to establish whether the others were all derived from a single *Urtext*.[9]

Investigations into the manuscripts prove what many scholars have long suspected: that we are ill-served by the printed editions. The 1871 edition of *Ernoul-Bernard* by Louis de Mas Latrie failed to take into account two manuscripts containing the earlier versions of the Ernoul text; the editor's choice of the fourteenth-century Brussels Bibliothèque royale ms. 11142 (F18) as his base is questionable, and his use of some of the manuscripts of the William of Tyre *Continuations* and Francesco Pipino's fourteenth-century Latin translation in his apparatus only serves to add further confusion.[10] With regard to the *Ernoul-Bernard* version of the continuation, we are even worse off. It was published by the Maurists, Martène and Durand, as long ago as 1729, and that edition remains the best we have.[11] They chose a manuscript copied in Rome in 1295 – it is now the Paris BN ms. fr. 9082 (F77) – which, although they were not to know, contains a text that is clearly far removed from the original and appears to include a number of quirky readings and chapter divisions that set it apart from all the others. Unfortunately, later editors followed their lead in making use of it. It was re-edited in an inferior edition by Guizot in 1824,[12] and then consigned to the small print in the *Recueil des historiens des croisades. Historiens occcidentaux*, 2, where it is labelled ms. G.[13]

Historians are, of course, most familiar with the *Continuations* of William of Tyre as it is presented in the *Recueil* edition of 1859. The editors chose to base their edition on the Paris BN ms. fr. 2628 (F73), which provided a much fuller narrative than *Ernoul-Bernard* and one that extends as far as 1264. Undeterred by the fact that only one other medieval manuscript contains this text for the period 1184–1231, as against forty-one with the *Ernoul-Bernard* continuation, they printed this account – sometimes known as the *Colbert-Fontainebleau Continuation* – in large

---

[8]   *Chronique d'Ernoul*, pp. 82–87, 188–210.

[9]   For a description of this manuscript, see Jaroslav Folda, *Crusader Manuscript Illumination at Saint-Jean d'Acre, 1275–1291* (Princeton, 1976), p. 175, and see plate 1.

[10]   *Chronique d'Ernoul*, pp. xxiv–xxix.

[11]   *Veterum Scriptorum et Monumentorum ... amplissa Collectio*, ed. Edmond Martène and Ursin Durand, 9 vols. (Paris, 1724–33), 5:581–752.

[12]   François Pierre Guillaume Guizot, *Collection des mémoires relatifs à l'histoire de France* (Paris, 1823–35), p. 19.

[13]   For a description, see Folda, *Crusader Manuscript Illumination*, pp. 200–204 .

print, thus ensuring that it would henceforth be regarded as *the* principal version.[14] In fact, the *Colbert-Fontainebleau Continuation* text represents a later recension, dating at the earliest to the late 1230s or early 1240s. What seems to have happened is that someone working in the Latin East took a version of the *Ernoul-Bernard* continuation and expanded large parts of it. The new author largely left the sections dealing with affairs in the West, such as the rise to power of Frederick II or the account of the Fourth Crusade, alone; what attracted his attention were events in the East from the time of the Third Crusade onwards (p. 126 in the *Recueil* edition) as well as a scattering of earlier episodes including the battle of Hattin. Once we get past the account of the events of 1187 and the end of the section supposedly written by historical Ernoul, we find that the *Ernoul-Bernard*'s treatment of the internal history of the Latin East is for the most part sketchy. The new version filled in the gaps, and from 1205 onwards (p. 305 in the *Recueil* edition) it provided a completely new account. This narrative extended well beyond 1231 to include a description of the civil wars sparked by the crusade of Frederick II.

It is not hard to see why the nineteenth-century editors decided to give the *Colbert-Fontainebleau Continuation* prominence. Quite simply, it is much more informative. Although only two manuscripts give this text for the period before 1231, several more – either copied in Acre or derived from those that were – gave the *Ernoul-Bernard* continuation to 1231 and then pasted on the Colbert-Fontainebleau account of the 1230s, picking it up more or less where *Ernoul-Bernard* left off (at *Recueil*, p. 380). The accounts were subsequently supplemented to bring the story further on into the thirteenth century. Beginning with the year 1248, a version of the *Annales de Terre Sainte* was employed, padded out with other material, some of which would seem to have come from the continuation of the chronicle of Guillaume de Nangis. I suspect that the *Colbert-Fontainebleau Continuation* first made its appearance in the Latin East in the early 1240s. It was certainly in existence by the time Philip of Novara came to write his history of the Ibelin–Lombard wars as he incorporated material from it into the later sections of his own work.[15]

The story, however, does not end there. Further revisions and expansions were being made, probably in Acre later in the 1240s, and these generated the texts to be found in two important manuscripts: the Lyon, Bibliothèque de la Ville, ms. 828 (F72), and the Florence, Bibliotheca Medicea Laurenziana, ms. Pluteus LXI, 10 (F70). Both manuscripts were copied in Acre.[16] To understand how these texts relate to the others we need to keep in mind the propensity of copyists to switch exemplars. Indeed, as I have argued elsewhere, it would seem that in the

---

[14] *L'estoire de Eracles empereur et la conqueste de la terre d'Outremer; c'est la continuation de l'estoire de Guillaume arcevesque de Sur, RHC Oc* 2:1–481.

[15] Filippo da Novara, *Guerra di Federico II in Oriente (1223–1242)*, ed. Silvio Melani (Naples, 1994), pp. 210–40 *passim* (where the shared passages are indicated in bold type).

[16] For an edition of the unique passages in these manuscripts, see *La Continuation de Guillaume de Tyre (1184–1197)*, ed. Margaret Ruth Morgan (Paris, 1982). For a challenge to Morgan's arguments for the primacy of the Lyon *Eracles*, see Peter W. Edbury, "The Lyon *Eracles* and the Old French Continuations of William of Tyre," in *Montjoie*, pp. 139–53.

112

Acre scriptorium copyists worked from unbound signatures that sometimes got muddled.[17] That would explain how it is that the Florence manuscript changes abruptly from following the *Ernoul-Bernard* continuation to the new material for the period 1190–97 and then back again. The Lyon manuscript – often known as the *Lyon Eracles* – provides a text that would seem to have been adapted from the *Colbert-Fontainebleau Continuation*; the account of the years 1187–91 alternates between following that version and providing a new narrative; from 1191 to 1197 it gives us a continuous new narrative, albeit one which in general terms keeps to the already established framework. The *Lyon Eracles* then goes back to following the *Ernoul-Bernard* continuation for the period 1197–1231. It is possible that the author of this recension composed more than has survived, but, because a copyist changed exemplars when relating the events of 1197, this material has been lost. (It should be added that although only two manuscripts give the full text of the *Colbert-Fontainebleau Continuation* for 1184–1231, there is a third manuscript, the Paris BN ms. fr. 2631 (F74) – this is of Italian provenance from the late thirteenth century – that reproduces a section from that recension embedded in what is otherwise a characteristically Acre version of the *Ernoul-Bernard* continuation; sure enough, this section is about the right length to have originally filled an eight-folio signature.)

While later in the thirteenth century those copies of the Old French William of Tyre that were being made in Acre were given further continuations to take the narrative closer to the time of production, in the West a different text, known as the Rothelin Continuation, which described events from the late 1230s to 1261, came to be added to the end of the *Ernoul-Bernard* continuation.[18] This may have been originally conceived as an independent work, but it only survives as an appendage to the Old French William of Tyre. It proved to be particularly popular in France, presumably as it gave a good account of St. Louis's crusade to Egypt; most, if not all, the manuscripts with this continuation are of French provenance, and most of them date from the early decades of the fourteenth century, a period in which there was much talk at the French royal court of launching a new crusade.

These texts do not exist in a vacuum. Between the late 1220s and the late 1240s there was much writing and rewriting taking place to produce the various versions of these narratives that survive. In other words, that was a highly creative period which generated successive accounts of the history of the crusades and the Latin East from the time of the First Crusade to the present. There can be no doubt that the demand for this literature would have been stimulated by, and would have reflected, the crusading endeavours in the West, especially in France. The years 1228–29 had seen Frederick II's belated crusade to the East; in 1234 the pope proclaimed a new crusade which was to become the Barons' Crusade of 1239–41 – recently given

---

[17] Edbury, "French Translation," pp. 83–89, esp. p. 85.

[18] *Continuation de Guillaume de Tyr, de 1229 à 1261 dite du manuscrit de Rothelin*, RHC Oc 2:483–639. See Margaret Ruth Morgan, "The Rothelin Continuation of William of Tyre," in *Outremer*, pp. 244–57.

the prominence it deserves thanks to Michael Lower's fine monograph;[19] from the end of 1244 preparations were afoot for King Louis IX's crusade of 1248–54. The further continuations into the second half of the thirteenth century, and the continued production of manuscripts in both Acre and northern France, reflect a continuing interest in the West in the crusades and fortunes of the Latin East which, at the French royal court, was to remain strong until the outbreak of the Hundred Years' War.

---

[19] Michael Lower, *The Barons' Crusade: A Call to Arms and its Consequences* (Philadelphia, 2005).

XIII

Gerard of Ridefort and the Battle of Le Cresson (1 May 1187): The Developing Narrative Tradition

At the Military Orders Conference held in London in 2005, Malcolm Barber read a characteristically robust essay entitled "The Reputation of Gerard of Ridefort".[1] In it he surveyed what can be known of Gerard's career from the surviving sources, pointing out *inter alia* how historians have had to come to terms with the contentious evidence presented by the various surviving versions of the narrative that came originally from the pen of Ernoul, a squire of Balian of Ibelin. As is well known, Gerard had a meteoric rise within the Templar Order: he had entered it at some point between the end of 1179 and 1183 and was elected master in 1185. He died fighting at the siege of Acre on 4 October 1189. A controversial figure in his own day, he has generally been seen in a negative light. In particular, he is remembered as the man who in 1187 used his position as a close adviser to King Guy of Lusignan to persuade the king to undertake the fatal attempt to relieve Tiberias and so precipitated the Christian defeat at Hattin.[2]

Ernoul's original narrative, which seems to have concentrated on the middle years of the 1180s and extended as far as the end of 1187, does not survive. It described the collapse of the kingdom of Jerusalem while at the same time extolling the reputation of his master, Balian of Ibelin, together with that of Balian's brother, Baldwin of Ramla. Eventually it was incorporated alongside other material into the anonymous text that since the nineteenth century has been known as *La Chronique d'Ernoul et de Bernard le Trésorier*. This work exists in three recensions, which close with the events of 1227, 1229 and 1231 respectively, and which all appear to date from the early 1230s. What then happened was that someone shaved off the pre-1184 sections of this work and stuck the remainder – about three-quarters of the whole – (plus a few earlier passages that were repositioned later in the narrative) on the end of the French translation of William of Tyre's celebrated history. This

---

[1] *MO*, 4, pp. 111–19.

[2] For his career, see Jochen Burgtorf, *The Central Convent of the Hospitallers and Templars: History, Organization and Personnel (1099/1120–1310)* (Leiden, 2008), pp. 539–42; Alain Demurger, "Gérard de Ridefort," in *Prier et combattre: dictionnaire européen des ordres militaires au Moyen Âge*, ed. Nicole Bériou and Philippe Josserand (Paris, 2009), pp. 386–87.

development should probably be dated to the mid or late 1230s. The "Continuation of William of Tyre", as this work had now become, was subsequently expanded and reworked by redactors in both western Europe and the Holy Land to provide us with the complex array of versions that survive to this day. Two particularly important later versions, the Colbert-Fontainebleau text which in the nineteenth century served as the base for the *Recueil* edition and the Lyon text, edited for the period 1184–97 by M.R. Morgan in 1982, originated in the Holy Land and would appear to date from the 1240s.[3] It is important to establish how the various recensions relate to each other, since an understanding of their relationships should affect our approach to them and the stories they tell.

In the medieval centuries the copyists of French vernacular texts regularly modified what was before them, changing the word order, rephrasing whole sentences, and also interpolating or omitting sections as they saw fit. These texts are no exception, and in addition they present various other problems. For example, there is good reason to suppose that some copyists switched exemplars, with the result that a manuscript may begin with a particular recension and then change abruptly to another; in some instances, especially with regard to *Ernoul-Bernard*, it would seem that the earliest versions of the text may only survive in comparatively late copies; trying to establish the original form of the work is therefore not as simple as we might wish.

Bearing these hazards in mind, I want to examine how the texts, or, rather, how some of them, constructed the events surrounding the Battle of Le Cresson, which took place on 1 May 1187, and, in particular, how they present the role of Gerard of Ridefort. The story is well known. Ever since Guy of Lusignan came to power in 1186, Raymond of Tripoli had remained unreconciled to his exclusion from power and had been engaged in what were arguably treasonable dealings with Saladin. In the spring of 1187 it was agreed that a high-level delegation comprising Gerard, the Hospitaller master Roger des Moulins, Archbishop Joscius of Tyre, and two leading lay nobles, Balian of Ibelin and Reynald of Sidon, should go to Raymond, who was at his wife's castle at Tiberias, in an attempt to bring about a rapprochement between him and Guy. It was at this precise moment that Raymond allowed a large Muslim military demonstration to pass through his land; as soon as Gerard, who had reached the castle of al-Fula on his way to Tiberias, learnt that there were Muslims in the vicinity, he got together as many knights as he could – the Ernoul narratives claim that there were 140, of whom 90 were Templars, 10 Hospitallers and 40 from the royal garrison in Nazareth – and battle was joined. Almost all the Christians were killed or captured as were a large number of the inhabitants of Nazareth who, allegedly at Gerard's prompting, had come upon the field of battle in hope of plunder. Gerard himself was one of only three survivors.

---

[3] For further details, see Peter W. Edbury, "New Perspectives on the Old French Continuations of William of Tyre," *Crusades* 9 (2010), 107–13.

XIII

There are two versions of the story printed at the end of this paper. The first is from the *Chronique d'Ernoul*. It is not what I believe to be the earliest form of this text, but is edited from those manuscripts which represent the closest recension to the one used in constructing the William of Tyre Continuation. What is noticeable about this version is the comparative absence of value judgements on Gerard's actions. At sentences 13–15, we see Gerard's prompt action to gather troops to counter a Muslim raid. If there is implied criticism, it is that – so we are told at sentences 18 and 30 – the Muslims had kept their side of their bargain with Raymond and had not done any damage. The Christians then attacked the much larger Muslim force – 140 Christians against 7,000 Muslims – and were soundly defeated (sentences 19–22). There is no apportioning of blame; the one thing that Gerard did which might be intended to be seen as reprehensible was to tell the men of Nazareth to follow in the hope of plunder – an action that was to have tragic consequences (sentences 24–26). Later, at sentence 62, the narrator allows Gerard to give his version of events. It is remarkably dispassionate. Even when Balian of Ibelin, Archbishop Joscius and Gerard set off from Nazareth for the last leg of their journal to Tiberias and Gerard turns back on account of his wounds, the narrator avoids commenting on the hatred Gerard and Raymond had for each other (sentence 66). It is only at sentence 68 when Balian and the archbishop meet Raymond that the narrator attributes the disaster to Gerard's pride (*orgueil*). Even here there is ambiguity as to whether this is to be understood as the view of the author or as Raymond's own perspective.

If this were the only episode in which Gerard was mentioned and this was the only version to have survived, we would not immediately identify this text as being hostile to him. Any criticism is muted, and, after all, Gerard *had* led his men to a major defeat. The reader's attention is drawn more to the ambivalent behaviour of Raymond that prepares us for Gerard's subsequent assertion on the eve of Hattin that Raymond was not to be trusted, and the fortuitous sequence of events which meant that Balian of Ibelin avoided involvement and, in all likelihood, death in the defeat. Indeed, Balian, Ernoul's master, holds centre-stage and emerges with his reputation unscathed, even although his chief role consisted of being somewhere else at the crucial moment.

The second version of this narrative comprises a later recension. The text is based on that given by the so-called "Lyon *Eracles*", the Lyon, Bibliothèque de la ville, MS 828, an Acre manuscript that has been dated to circa 1280. This has been compared with the two manuscripts, and a fragment of a third, of what is sometimes called the "Colbert-Fontainebleau *Eracles*", and which formed the base for the edition that appeared in the nineteenth century in the *Recueil des historiens des croisades: historiens occidentaux*.[4] For this episode the three manuscripts are

---

[4] The two manuscripts are: Paris, Bibliothèque nationale de France, MS français 2628 (Acre: *c.*1260) and Paris, BnF fr. 2634 (France: fourteenth-century). The other manuscript, Paris, BnF fr. 9086 (Acre: late 1250s), begins with the same version of this material but then,

XIII

closely in step with only minor variants, and a close analysis shows that, here at least, it is the Lyon text that preserves readings which are closer to those in the first version of the narrative as edited from the *Ernoul-Bernard* manuscripts. Shortly after this point in the narrative the Lyon *Eracles* goes its own way and preserves a distinctive version of the events for the period to 1197.

What distinguishes these manuscripts from the *Ernoul-Bernard* version and all the other copies of the William of Tyre Continuation is a series of interpolations.[5] These are shown below in bold type. It is important to notice that apart from the highlighted passages, these manuscripts give a text that keeps reasonably close to the *Ernoul-Bernard* version, making no substantive alterations to what is there. It would appear that these interpolations were composed in the Latin East in the late 1230s or 1240s, and that a significant element in their author's agenda in adapting the earlier text was the apportioning of blame for the disasters of 1187. The two figures he has in his sights here are Reynald of Châtillon and Gerard of Ridefort. In the first and third interpolations (sentences 1a and 31a) Saladin's invasion is said to have come about as a direct response to Reynald's capture of a Muslim caravan; it was thus Reynald's irresponsible and intransigent behaviour that set in train the events that led to the loss of Jerusalem. The *Ernoul-Bernard* narrative reports Reynald seizing caravans in 1179 and 1182, but only the three manuscripts of the Continuation under discussion (plus Paris, Bibliothèque nationale de France, manuscrit français 9086) report a further attack in 1186. That episode, and with it the claim that Reynald captured Saladin's sister and then told the new king, Guy of Lusignan, that he would not return his plunder because "he was lord of his land as much as Guy was lord of his", forms another addition made by the same redactor as was responsible for the interpolations in the description of the Battle of Le Cresson.[6]

It is the second interpolation (sentences 18a–18c) that concerns Gerard. The message is simple: just before the battle Roger des Moulins, the master of the Hospitallers, and Jacques de Mailli, the Templar marshal, cautioned prudence only to be roundly accused of cowardice, thereby goading them into joining in the fatal charge. Gerard is presented as being arrogant and impetuous, and the consequences were disastrous. What is more, the marshal's counter-assertion – that it would be Gerard who would flee the field – would seem to be borne out by the fact that Gerard himself was one of the few survivors. It should be noted that Gerard's quip that Jacques de Mailli was too much concerned with saving his own blond head is

---

presumably because the copyist of this manuscript or of an antecedent changed exemplars at this point, switches to a different manuscript tradition.

[5]   Also these three alone have a chapter break between sentences 60 and 61.

[6]   *La Chronique d'Ernoul et de Bernard le Trésorier*, ed. L. de Mas Latrie (Paris, 1871), pp. 54–55, 96–97; *L'Estoire de Eracles Empereur et la Conqueste de la Terre d'Outremer*, in *RHC Occ*, vol. 1.2 (Paris, 1859), p. 34. That Reynald did raid a caravan in 1186 is confirmed by Muslim writers. See Bernard Hamilton, "The Elephant of Christ: Reynald of Châtillon," in *Religions Motivation: Biographical and Sociological Problems for the Church Historian*, ed. Derek Baker, *Studies in Church History* 15 (1978), pp. 106–107 and n. 70.

not in the Lyon manuscript and so could be a further embellishment. Blame for the defeat therefore lay with Gerard's refusal to take advice and his lack of military discretion coupled with his pride. The interpolation thus shows Gerard's behaviour in a much more dishonourable light. Whether blackening Gerard's memory in this way is justified is a moot question: the *Libellus de Expugnatione Terrae Sanctae*, a much more contemporary source, records that Roger des Moulins enthusiastically endorsed the decision to attack the Muslims,[7] and, although other sources mention his death at Le Cresson, as Jochen Burgtorf has recently shown, the interpolator's statement that Jacques de Mailli was the Templar marshal is erroneous.[8]

It might be wondered how modern perceptions of Gerard of Ridefort (and also of Reynald of Châtillon) might differ had the interpolated manuscripts not survived. The point is that while the *Ernoul-Bernard* texts, with their more matter-of-fact even-handed portrayals, are likely to date in their present from to the early 1230s but incorporate narrative material associated with an eyewitness, Ernoul, the interpolations would appear to be have been added some time later by an author who was striving for literary effect by painting the protagonists in more lurid colours. It is hard to know how authentic the memories they preserve may have been, and how much credence they deserve. It is quite possible that the same author also wrote the generally pro-Ibelin account of the 1230s to be found in these same manuscripts. If so, these additions were the work of someone who shared Ernoul's loyalty to the Ibelin family and so was taking the opportunity to denigrate Balian of Ibelin's political adversaries.

Finally, there is a unique variant reading in another manuscript of the Old French William of Tyre and its continuations that merits attention. The manuscript in question was copied in Rome in 1295, but belongs in the textual tradition that would link it to the Acre scriptorium. A minor alteration to sentence 24 to be found in this manuscript changes the sense to meant that Gerard told the men of Nazareth to go to the battlefield after, and not before, his defeat. The addition of the two-word phrase "tot desconfit" has the effect of making his behaviour far more reprehensible.[9] There is no knowing how far back in the manuscript transmission these words had been introduced, but is the fact that it is found in a manuscript copied just twelve years before the arrest of the Templars yet further evidence that, in some circles at least, there were people who were eager to believe ill of the Order?

---

[7] "Libellus de expugnatione terrae sanctae per Saladinum" in Ralph of Coggeshall, *Chronicon anglicanum*, ed. Joseph Stevenson, Rolls Series 66 (London, 1875), pp. 212–13.

[8] Burgtorf, *Central Convent*, pp. 576–77.

[9] Paris, BnF fr. 9082, fol. 276v (= *RHC Occ.*, vol. 2, MS G).

XIII

Appendix

I. The Battle of Le Cresson from the 1231 version of La Chronique d'Ernoul et de Bernard le Trésorier.[10]

F24 – Bern, Burgerbibliothek, MS 113, fols. 131r–132r
F25 – Bern, Burgerbibliothek, MS 340, fols. 40r–42v
F26 – Paris, BnF fr. 12203, fols. 40r–42v

[1]Or vos lairai atant des mesages, et si vos dirai d'un des fix Salehadin qui novelement estoit adoubés. [2]Il manda al conte de Triple qu'il le laissast entrer en la terre as crestiens parmi sa terre et por faire une corsee. [3]Quant li quens oi le mandement, si fu molt dolans, et si se pensa que, s'il li escondisoit cel don qu'il li demandoit qu'il perderoit l'aiue et le consel de Salehadin son pere, et, s'il li otrioit, grant honte et grant blasme en averoit de crestienté. [4]Or se pensa après qu'il le feroit en tel maniere qu'il garniroit si les crestiens qu'il n'i perderoient noient, ne que li fix Salehadin malgré ne l'en saveroit. [5]Donc manda li quens al fil Salehadin qu'il li donoit bien congié d'aler parmi sa terre et entrer en la terre des crestiens par tel covent que a solel levant passeroit le flun et iroit en la terre des crestiens, et de solel luisant riroit et repasseroit le flun ariere; ne que dedens vile ne dedens maison nule chose ne prenderoit ne damage n'i feroit. [6]Ensi le creanta le fix Salehadin a faire et a tenir. [7]Quant ce vint lendemain par matin, si passa le flun et vint par devant Tabarie et entra en la terre as crestiens. [8]Et li quens de Triple fist fermer les portes de Tabarie que cil dedens n'en ississent por iaus faire damage. [9]Or sot bien li quens de Triple le jor devant que li mesage le roi venoient a lui. [10]Il fist faire letres et prist mesages si fist porter ses letres a Nasarel, a chevaliers qui la estoient en garnisons de par le roi, et par toute la terre qu'il savoit que li sarrasin devoient entrer, que por chose qu'il veissent ne qu'il oissent cel jor ne se meuissent des viles ne des maisons, car li sarrasin devoient entrer en la terre et que s'il se tenoient coi qu'il n'ississent des viles il n'aroient garde, et s'on les trovoit as cans on les prenderoit et ociroiot et quanque il troveroient as cans. [11]Ensi garni li quens de Triple ciaus del pais. [12]Aprés ala li mesages a le Feve al maistre de l'Ospital et al maistre del Temple et a l'archevesque de Sur, et si lor porta les letres de par le conte de Triple. [13]Quant li maistres del Temple oi et sot que li sarrasin devoient lendemain par matin entrer en la terre, si prist .i. mesage et l'envoie batant al covent del Temple qui estoit a .iiii. liues d'iluec a une vile qui a non Caco. [14]Et si lor manda par ses letres que, tantost com il aroient oi son commandament, montassent et venissent a lui, car lendemain par matin devoient li sarrasin entrer en la terre.

---

[10]   Previously edited in *La Chronique d'Ernoul*, pp. 144–53. The manuscript numbers F24, F25 etc, refer to the numbering in Jaroslav Folda, "Manuscripts of the History of Outremer by William of Tyre: A Handlist," *Scriptorium* 27 (1973), 90–95.

[15]Tantost com li covens oi le commandement del maistre, si monterent et vinrent la ainscois qu'il fust mie nuis, et se logiererent devant le chastel. [16]Quant ce vint lendemain par matin, si murent et alerent a Nasarel. [17]Et estoient chevalier .iiii.[xx] et .x. del Temple et .x. chevalier de l'Ospital qui estoient avec le maistre, et prisent a Nasarel .xl. chevaliers qui estoient en garnisons de par le roi. [18]Et passerent Nasarel bien .ii. liues vers Tabarie et encontrerent les sarrasin a une fontaine c'om apele le Fontaine del Cresson, qui retornoient ariere por passer le flun sans damage faire les crestiens, car li crestien estoient ensi garni comme li quens lor avoit mandé. [19]Dont vint li maistres del Temple et li chevalier ki avec lui estoient. [20]Si se ferirent entre les sarrasin a l'encontre, et li maistres de l'Ospital ensement. [21]Et li sarrasin les recoillirent hardiement et si les enclosent, si que li crestien ne parurent entr'aus, car li sarrasin estoient encore .vii. mile chevalier a armes et li crestien n'estoient que .vii.[xx]. [22]La ot li maistres de l'Ospital la teste copee, et tot li chevalier del Temple et de l'Ospital ensement, fors solement li maistres del Temple qui eschapa, lui tierc de chevaliers, et li .xl. chevalier qui estoient es garnisons le roi furent tot pris.

[23]Quant li escuier de l'Ospital et del Temple virent que li chevalier s'estoient feru entre les sarrasin, si tornerent en fuies a tot le harnas, si ke del harnas as crestiens n'i ot rien perdu. [24]Or vos dirai que li maistres del Temple ot fait quant il ot passé Nasarel et il aloit encontre les sarrasin. [25]Il envoia .i. sergant a cheval ariere batant et fist crier par Nasarel que tot cil qui poroient armes porter venissent aprés lui al gaaing, car il avoit les sarrasin desconfis. [26]Lors s'en issirent de Nazarel tuit cil qui aler pooient, et viel et jovene, et corurent tant qu'il vinrent la u la bataille fu et troverent les crestiens mors et desconfis, et li sarrasin lor corent sus; si les prendent tos. [27]Quant li sarrasin orent desconfis les crestiens et ocis et pris, si prendent les testes des chevaliers crestiens qu'il avoient ocis; et si les estechierent enson les fers de lor lances; si enmenerent les prisons loiés et s'en passerent devant Tabarie. [28]Quant li crestien, qui dedens Tabarie estoient, virent que li crestien avoient esté desconfit, et que li sarrasin portoient les testes des crestiens sor lor lances qui estoient ocis, et c'on les enmenoit pris et loiés, si orent si grant duel c'onques si grans duels ne fu vue en une cite, de cou qu'il veoient les testes de lor amis porter et trainer et les autres qui estoient pris mener et fer loiés pardevant iaus, et de cou qu'il ne les pooient secorre ne aidier ne vengier. [29]Si en faisoient si grant duel que por poi qu'il ne se tuoient. [30]Ensi passa li fix Salehadin de solel luisant ariere de jors, et il et ses gens, et bien tint al conte de Triple ses couenences; c'onques en chastel ne en vile ne en maison ne fisent point de damage, se de cou non qu'il troverent as cans. [31]Cele bataille fu en venredi, et cel jor fu il feste S. Felippe et S. Jake, le premier jor de mai.

[32]Or vos dirai de Balian qui a Naples estoit. [33]Quant ce vint la nuit, si mut si com il ot en covent al maistre de l'Ospital et al maistre del Temple por aler aprés iaus. [34]Quant il ot erré .ii. liues et il vint a une cité qui a a non le Sabat, si se porpensa qu'il estoit molt haus jors et qu'il n'iroit avant ains aroit oi messe. [35]Donc torna a le maison l'evesque; se le fist lever et sist avec lui et parla desci que la gaite trast le jor. [36]Quant la gaite ot trait le jor, si fist li vesques revestir .i. sien chapelain et li fist

XIII

chanter messe. [37]Quant Balians ot oi messe, si s'en ala grant aleure aprés le maistre de l'Ospital et del Temple et prist congié a l'evesque et erra tant qu'il vint al chastel de le Feve u li maistres de l'Ospital et del Temple avoient la nuit giut. [38]La trova il dehors li chastel les tentes del covent del Temple tendues, et se n'i avoit nului. [39]Et il ala avant, si trova le porte del chastel overte et se n'i avoit nului. [40]Adonc s'esmervella molt de ce qu'il ne veoit home a cui il demandast que cou pooit estre. [41/42/43]Donc fist descendre .i. sien vallet et l'envoia dedens le chastel por savoir et por enquerre s'il troveroit nului dedens le chastel qui li peust dire noveles que ce pooit estre.[11] [44]Et li valles i entra et cerca et cria aval le chastel, ainc n'i vit home qui li poist dire novele, fors solement .ii. malades qui gisoient en .i. lit; cil ne li sorent rien dire. [45]Donc s'en revint ariere a son segnor et dist qu'il n'i avoit nului trové qui novele li seust dire fors .ii. malades qui ne li sorent rien dire. [46]Dont li commanda ses sire qu'il montast et alast aprés lui, et il si fist; dont se partirent d'iluec, si s'en alerent vers Nasarel. [47]Quant il orent .i. poi eslongié le chastel, si issi .i. freres del Temple a cheval et commenca a crier aprés iaus qu'il l'atendissent, et il l'atendirent tant qu'il vint a iaus. [48]Dont vint Balian d'Ibelin; se li demanda, 'Quels noveles?', et il respondi, 'Mavaises'. [49]Et se li conta que li maistres de l'Ospital avoit la teste copee, et il et si chevalier, et tot li chevalier del Temple ensement tot ocis; n'en i avoit que .iii. escapés, le maistre del Temple et .ii. de ses chevaliers. [50]Et li .xl. chevalier que li rois avoit mis a Nasarel en garnisons tot pris. [51]Quant Balian d'Ibelin oi ces noveles, si commenca a crier et a braire et a faire grant duel, il et li chevalier qui avec lui estoient. [52]Et apela .i. sien sergant; et l'envoia ariere a Naples a la roine sa feme por conter ces noveles et por dire qu'ele commandast tos les chevaliers de Naples qu'il fussent la nuit sor nuit aprés lui a Nasarel. [53]Aprés cou que Balians ot envoié a Naples, si s'en ala grant aleure a Nasarel, et quant il vint a mains d'une liue de Nasarel si encontra les escuiers et le harnas les chevaliers del Temple, qui estoient escapé de le desconfiture. [54]Et sachiez vos bien de voir que, s'il ne fust tornés al Sabat por oir messe, il fust bien a tans venus a le bataille. [55]Quant Balian vint a Nasarel, si trova si grant cri et si grant plor en la cité por ciaus de la vile qui avoient esté mort et pris en la bataille, que poi i avoit des maisons qu'il n'en i eust u des mors u des pris. [56]La trova il le maistre del Temple qui escapés estoit. [57]La se herberga Balian et atendi ilueques desci que si chevalier fussent venu de Naples, qu'il n'osa aler avant desi qu'il fussent venu. [58]Puis fist savoir a Tabarie al conte qu'il estoit a Nasarel. [59]Quant li quens oi dire qu'il estoit a Nasarel et qu'il n'avoit mie esté a le bataille, si en fu molt liés. [60]Quant ce vint lendemain, si i envoia bien jusc'a .lx. chevaliers encontre lui por lui conduire. [61]Quant Balian ot trové le maistre del Temple a Nasarel si ala a lui et se li demanda de cele bataille, comment ele avoit esté. [62]Et il li conta, et se li

---

[11] The other Ernoul manuscripts (with minor variants) read as follows:
[41] Dont fist descendre .i. sien vallet qui avoit a non Ernous.
[42] Ce fu cil qui cest conte fist metre en escrit.
[43] Celui Hernoul envoia Balians de Belin dedens le chastel pour cerquier et pour enquerre s'il avoit nului dedens le vile qui li peust dire noveles que cou pooit estre.

dist que molt si estoient bien prové, et molt avoient ocis si chevaliers des sarrasin, et estoient desconfit quant .i. enbussemens qu'il avoient deriere en une montagne les enclost par coi il furent desconfit. [63]Donc prisent consel qu'il envoieroient la ou la bataille avoit esté por les cors des chevaliers faire enfoir. [64]Dont fisent prendre tos les somiers de la cité et les envoierent por les cors, et les firent aporter a Nasarel et enfoir. [65]Quant ce vint lendemain, si mut Balian et li archevesques de Sur et li maistres del Temple por aler a Tabarie. [66]Quant il furent hors de la cité, si retorna li maistres del Temple, qu'il ne pooit chevaucier, si estoit dolereus des cols qu'il avoit eus en la bataille le jor devant. [67]Et Balian et l'archevesque de Sur alerent a Tabarie. [68]Quant li quens de Triple oi dire que Balian et l'archevesques de Sur venoient, si ala encontre molt dolans et molt coreciés de l'aventure qui estoit avenue le jor devant par l'orguel le maistre del Temple. [69]Quant li quens ot encontrés les mesages, si les rechut molt hautement et les mena avec lui en son chastel. [70]Et a cel point vint avec Renaus de Saiete. [71]Quant li mesage furent el chastel avec le conte, si conterent lor message, et li quens lor respondi qu'il estoit molt dolans et molt honteus de cele aventure qui avenue estoit, et quanque il diroient et feroient entraus .iii., il feroit, car il savoit bien qu'il ne le mesconselleroient mie. [72/73]Dont li disent il qu'il mesist les sarrasin fors de la cité et quil les en envoiast, et si en alast avec aus al roi, car tot ensi com il s'estoit mis en aus .iii., si estoit li rois mis de le pais faire. Li quens fist tot ensi com il li disent. [74]Quant li mesage orent l'otroi del conte, si envoierent .i. mesage batant al roi et li fisent savoir qu'il amenoient le conte avec iaus.

Variants

[1] No new *para in* F24. vos lairai atant des] F25 F26: Atant vos lairai ores del

[3] le mandement] F24: cel mandement et si se] F25 F26: si demandoit] F25 F26: demandoit il se pensa consel] F25 F26: secors averoit] F26: avoit

[4] F25 F26 be*gin new para.* aprés] F25 F26: aprés le quens de Triple en tel] F24: sagement en cel garniroit] F25 F26: li garderoit saveroit] F25 F26: savoit

[5] li quens] F25 F26 *lack.* des crestiens] F24: as crestiens riroit] F25 F26: iroit

[6] F24 be*gins new para.* tenir] F25 F26: dir

[7] Quant] F25 F26: et qe

[9] F25 F26 be*gin new para.* le roi] F25 F26 *lack.*

[10] prist] F24: si prist Nasarel] F25 F26: Nazareth (*et passim*) la estoient] F24: estoient veissent] F25: venissent car] F24 *begins new para here.* en la terre] F25 F26 *lack.* il n'aroient] F25 F26: des maisons qe il n'avroient s'on les trovoit] F25 F26: fise nos les tenroit quanque il troveroient] F25 F26: qant il troverent

[11] F25 F26 be*gin new para.* garni] F24: si garni

[12] le Feve] F25 F26: la Feve (*et passim*)

[13] sot] F25 F26: senti lendemain] F25 F26 lack. al covent] F25 F26: as chevaliers estoit] F25: estoient

[14] tantost] F24: si tost

[15] covens] F25 F26: quens

XIII

54

[17] et .x. chevalier de] F25 F26: et .x. de

[18] Cresson] F25 F26: Kerson qui retornoient] F25 F26: et s'en retornerent quens] F25 F26: quens de Triple

[19] F25 F26 begin new para. Dont] F25 F26: Lors

[20] Si se] F24: Si

[21] a armes] F25 F26 *lack.*

[22] estoient] F24 repeats. le roi furent] F25 F26: en Nazareth de par le roy

[23] F24 F25 F26 b*egin new para.* de l'Ospital et] F25 F26 lack. le harnas si ke del] F25 F26: lor arnois car les

[24] ot passé] F24 *corrects from* passa parmi

[25] al gaaing, car il avoit] F25 F26: gaagnier q'il avoient

[26] Lors] F24: dont de Nazarel tuit cil … pooient] F24: tot cil de Nasarel qui armes pooient porter corurent tant] F24: corirent tant

[27] F25 F26 be*gin new para.* si enmenerent] F24: et s'enmenerent

[28] sor lor lances … ocis] F25 F26: qi estoient ocis sor lor lances pris mener et fet] F25 F26 *lack.*

[30] F25 F26 be*gin new para.* de solel luisant … jors] F25 F26: le flum ariere de soleil luisant

[32] No ne*w para in* F24. dirai] F25 F26: dirons

[34] et il] F25 F26 *lack.* Sabat] F25 F26: Sabast porpensa] F24: pensa avant ains] F25 F26: en avant si

[36] sien] F25 F26 *lack.*

[37] F25 F26 be*gin new para.* Quant Balians ot oi messe] F24 *lacks.* Feve] F26: Fave avoient la nuit giut] F24: auoit giut la nen trova nul

[38] F24 be*gins new para.* La trova] F24: Ains trova

[39] F25 F26 lack this sentence.

[40] de ce] F25 F26 *lack.* home] F25 F26: nului home

[41/42/43] descendre] F25 F26: crier laienz et l'envoia dedens le chastel] F25 26 lack. et por enquerre … nului] F25 F26: qe ce fust ne se il poroit trover peust dire] F25 F26: disist que ce pooit estre] F25 F26 *lack.*

[44] F25 F26 be*gin new para.* i entra et … chastel] F25 F26: entra el chastel et cerca et cria aval et amont poist] F25 F26: seust gisoient en .i. lit; cil] F25 F26 *lack.*

[45] F24 begins new para. F25 F26 lack this sentence.

[46] dont se] F25 F26: atant

[47] crier] F25 F26: huier tant] F25 F26 *lack.*

[48] F25 F26 begin new para. Dont vint Balian … demanda] F25 F26: Lors demanda Balians (F26: Balyans) au frere del Temple respondi] F24: dist

[49] tot ocis; n'en i] F25 F26: et n'en chevaliers] F24: chevaliers avec lui

[50] .xl.] F25 F26 *lack.* mis] F25 F26 *lack.*

[51] Balian d'Ibelin] F25 F26: Balyas de Belin et a braire] F24 *lacks.* il et li chevalier] F25: si (F26: et si) chevaliers ensement

[52] sien] F24 lacks. tos] F25 F26 *lack.* sor nuit] F25 F26: tuit

[53] les chevaliers] F25 F26 *lack.*

[54] sachiez vos bien] F24: bien saciés tornés al Sabat] F25 F26: bien tornez au Sabast a tans] F25 F26 *lack.*

55   F25 F26 begin new para. mort et] F24 *lacks.*

57   ilueques desci que si chevalier fussent venu] F25 F26: ses chevaliers desi qu'il vindrent qu'il fussent] F25 F26: che (F26:qe) si chevaliers s'estoient

58   conte] F25 F26: conte de Triple

59   n'avoit mie esté] F25 F26: n'estoit

61   F25 F26 be*gin new para.* a Nasarel] F25 F26: en Nazareth

62   ocis si chevaliers] F25 F26: li cristiens ocis coi il] F25 F26: ou il les

64   Dont fisent] F25 F26: donc vindrent si firent

65   mut] F25 F26: vint Sur] F25 F26: Sur et li arcevesques del Temple de Sur *(blundered reading).*

65/66   por aler a … Temple] F25 F26 *lack (haplography).*

66   F24 begins new para.

68   F25 F26 begin new para.

69   les mena] F24: mena

71   feroient] F24: voroient .iii. il feroit] F25 F26: il tendroit

72/73   F24 be*gins new para.* si en] F25 F26 *lack.* car] F25 F26 *lack.* li disent] F25 F26: s'estoit mis en aus et il distrent sanz contredit

74   25 F26 be*gin new para.* conte] F25 F26: conte de Triple de li (F26: la) pais envoierent] F25 F26: envoient

II. The Battle of Le Cresson from the "Lyon" text of the French Continuations of William of Tyre[12]

F72 – Lyon, Bibliothèque de la ville MS 828 (= *RHC. Occ.,* vol … 2 MS D), fols. 294v–296r

F50 – Paris, BnF fr. 9086 (= *RHC. Occ.,* 2 MS C), fols. 366v–367r (§§1–2 only)

F57 – Paris, BnF fr. 2636 (= *RHC. Occ.,* 2 MS A), fols. 317v–319v

F73 – Paris, BnF fr. 2628 (= *RHC. Occ.,* 2 MS B), fols. 252v–254r

[1]Un des fis de Salahadin, qui novelement estoit adoubés, **que l'on nomoit Noredin Emirhali, qui puis fu sire de Domas, si estoit herbergié outre le flum.** [1b]**Salahadin son pere li manda qu'il deust entrer en la terre des crestiens gagier les por la caravane que le prince Renaut avoit prise et por sa suer qu'il tenoit en prison qu'il avoit prise en la devant dite caravane.** [1b]**Porce que il ne poeit entrer par autre part que par la terre de Thabarie, et la seignorie de Tabarie si estoit dou conte de Triple en cel tens, et por ce que le devant dit conte avoit trives a lui et avoit faites maintes ayes et maintes amors au devant dit Salahadin, ne vost**

---

12   Previously edited in *La Continuation de Guillaume de Tyr (1184–1197),* ed. M.R. Morgan, Documents relatifs à l'histoire des croisades 14 (Paris, 1982), pp. 37–42; English version in Peter W. Edbury, *The Conquest of Jerusalem and the Third Crusade* (Aldershot, 1996), pp. 31–35. Cf. *L'Estoire de Eracles Empereur,* pp. 37–45.

entrer en la terre des crestiens sans son congié. ²**Et porce qu'il savoit qu'il i
avoit discort entre lui et le roi**, porce manda il au conte de Triple qu'il le laissast
entrer en la terre des crestiens parmi sa terre por faire une corse. ³Quant li cuens oi
le mandement, si en fu molt dolent, et penssa que se il li escondissoit cel don que il
le demandoit, que il ne perdist l'aye et le conseill son pere Salahadin, et que se il li
otreiast, grant honte et grant blasme en avroit de la crestienté. ⁴Or pensa aprés que
il le feroit en tel maniere que il garniroit si les crestiens que il n'i perdroient noient
et que li fis Salahadin maugré ne l'en savroit. ⁵Donc manda au fis Salahadin que
bien li donoit congié d'aler parmi sa terre et d'entrer en la terre des crestiens par tel
covent que il au soleil levant passereit le flum et au soleill cochant retorneroit ariere
en sa terre, ne ne girroit dou flum en vers soleill couchant; ne que dedens nule ville
ne dedens maison nule chose ne prendreit ne damage ne fereit. ⁶Ensi le creanta li fis
Salahadin a faire et a tenir. ⁷Quant ce vint a lendemain par matin, si passa le flum et
vint par devant Thabarie et entra en la terre as crestiens. ⁸Et li cuens de Triple fist
fermer les portes de Thabarie, que cil dedens n'en ississent por lui faire damage.
⁹Or sot bien li cuens de Triple le jor devant que li messages venoient a lui. ¹⁰Si fist
faire letres et prist messages et les envoia a Nazareth, as chevaliers qui la estoient en
garnison, et par toute la terre ou il savoit que li sarazin devoient aler, que por chose
que il veissent ne que il oissent ne se meussent cel jor de la ville ne de maison, car
li sarazin devoient entrer en la terre; et que se il se tenoient coi que il n'en ississent
des villes, il n'avoient garde, et, se l'on les trovoit as chans, l'on les prendroit et
ociroit. ¹¹Ensi garni li cuens de Triple ciaus dou pays. ¹²Aprés ala li messages au
chastel de La Feve au maistre dou Temple et del Hospital et a l'arcevesque de
Sur; si lor aporta les letres de par le conte de Triple. ¹³Quant le maistre do Temple
sot que li sarazin devoient lendemain core et entrer en la terre, si prist .i. message
batant et l'envoia au covent dou Temple qui estoit a .iiii. milles d'iluec a une vile
qui a a non Caco. ¹⁴Si lor manda par ses letres que tantost come il avroient veu
son comandement montassent et venissent a lui, que lendemain par matin devoient
entrer li sarazin en la terre. ¹⁵Tantost com il orent oi le mandement dou maistre, si
monterent et vindrent la ains qu'il fust mie nuit, et se logererent devant le chastel.
¹⁶Et quant ce vint lendemain par matin, si murent et alerent a Nazareth. ¹⁷Si estoient
li chevalier dou Temple. lxxxx. et .x. del Hospital, qui estoient avec le maistre,
et pristrent a Nazareth.xl. chevaliers qui estoient en garnisson de par le roi. ¹⁸Et
paserent a Nazareth bien .ii. milles vers Thabarie, et troverent les sarazins a une
fontaine qui a a nom la fontaine dou Creisson; cil tornerent arieres por passer le
flum sans damage faire as crestiens, car les crestiens se tenoient si garni come li
cuens lor avoit mandé. ¹⁸ᵃ**Le devant dit maistre estoit bon chevalier, et seur de
son cors, et mesprisoit toutes autres genz come cil qui estoit trop outrecuidiés.**
¹⁸ᵇ**Il ne vost croire le conseill dou maistre del Hospital, frere Rogier des Molins,
ne de frere Jaque de Mailli qui estoit mareschal dou Temple, ains le ranpona**

et li dist que il parloit come home qui baoit a fouir.[13] [18c]**Dont le mareschal li respondi qu'il ne s'en fuiroit mie de la bataille, ainz remaindroit ou champ come preudome, et il s'en fuiroit come mauvais et recreant.** [19]Donc vint li maistre dou Temple et li chevalier qui estoient aveques lui. [20]Si se ferirent as sarazins, et li maistre del Hospital aussi. [21]Et les sarazins le recurent lieement; si les forsclostrent si que les crestiens ne parurent entreaus, car li sarrazin estoient encores .vii.m. chevaliers armés, et li crestien n'estoient que .c. et .xl. [22]La ot le maistre del Hospital la teste copee, et tuit li chevalier dou Temple ausi, fors le maistre soulement qui eschapa touz seuls, soi tiers de chevaliers; et les .xl. chevalier qui estoient en garnisson de par le roi furent tuit pris. [23]Quant li escuier dou Temple et del Hospital virent que les chevaliers se furent ferus entre les sarazins, si tornerent en fuie o tout le hernois as crestiens, si que del hernois as crestiens n'i ot riens perdu. [24]Or vos dirai que le maistre do Temple ot fait si come il pasa a Nazareth et il aloit contre les sarrzins.[14] [25]Il envoia un sien serjant ariere batant a cheval et fist crier a Nazereth que tuit cil qui armes poroient porter venissent aprés lui au gaaing, car il avoit les sarazins desconfis. [26]Lors s'en issirent cil de Nazareth, tuit cil qui aler i pooient, et corurent tant qu'il vindrent la ou la bataille avoit esté; si troverent les crestiens mors et desconfis, et li sarazin lor corurent sus; si les pristrent tous. [27]Quant li sarazin orent desconfit les crestiens et ocis, si pristrent les testes des chevaliers crestiens qu'il avoient tué; si les atachierent sur les fers des lances; si enmenerent les prisons liez, et s'en passerent devant Thabarie. [28]Quant li crestien qui dedens Tabarie estoient virent que li crestien avoient esté desconfit et que li sarazin porterent les testes des crestiens sor lor lances et que l'on les aveit pris et liez, si en orent grant duel porce qu'il veoient les testes de lor amis porter et les autres qui estoient pris mener liez par devant iaus. [29]Si en firent tel duel qu'a poi qu'il ne se tuoient. [30]Ensi passa li fis Salahadin des le soleill couchant le flum arieres de jor, et bien tint au conte de Triple ses covenances; ne onques en chastel ne en vile ne en maisson ne firent damage fors de ciaus qu'il troverent as chans. [31]Ceste bataille fu faite par .i. venredi; celui jor fu feste Saint Jaque et Saint Phelippe, premier jor de mai. [31a]**Ce fu par l'achaisson de la caravane que le prince Renaut avoit prise en la terre dou Crac; ce fu le comencement de la perte dou reaume.**

[32/33]Balyan qui a Naples estoit quant ce vint la nuit si mut si com il ot en covent au maistre dou Temple et au maistre del Hospital por aler aprés yaus. [34]Quant il ot erré .ii. milles et que il vint a une cité qui a a nom Le Sabast, si s'apensa qu'il estoit molt haut jor, et qu'il n'en iroit avant tant qu'il eust oi messe. [35]Donc torna a la maisson l'evesque; si le fist lever, et sist avec lui et parla tant que la gaite traist le jor. [36]Lors fist li evesque revestir .i. sien chapelain et li fist chanter messe. [37]Quant Balian ot oie

---

[13]   F57 and F73 add: … et li dist, "Vos amez trop cele teste blonde qui si bien la volez garder".

[14]   Paris, BnF fr. 9082, fol. 276v: "Or vouz dirai que le maistre du temple fist quant il passa Nazareth **tot desconfit**. Il envoia a Nazareth .i. serjant …"

XIII

58

messe, si s'en ala grant aleure aprés le maistre dou Temple et ala tant que il vint au chastel de La Feve. [38/39]trova hors dou chastel les tentes dou covent tendues; si n'en i avoit nului. [40]Lors se merveilla qu'il ne trova nelui a cui demander que ce peust estre. [41/42/43]Lors fist un sien valet entrer dedens le chastel enquerre s'il troveroit qui li deist que ce poroit estre. [44]Le vaslez ala et cria par le chastel; onques n'i vit home qui li seust dire noveles que .ii. malades qui gisoient en une chambre, et cil ne li sorent riens dire. [45]Lors vint a son seignor; si li dist qu'il n'i avoit nul trové qui noveles li seust dire. [46]Donc vint ses sires; si li comanda qu'il montast et alast aprés lui; si alerent vers Nazereth. [47]Quant il orent un poi esloignié le chastel, si s'en issi un frere dou Temple a cheval et cria que il l'atendissent; et il l'atendirent tant qu'il vint a eaus. [48]Donc vint Balian; si li demanda quels noveles, et il dist, 'Mauvaisses'. [49/50]Si li dist que le maistre del Hospital avoit le chief copé, et tuit li chevalier dou Temple; si n'en i avoit que .iii. eschapez: le maistre dou Temple et .iii. de ces chevaliers, et les chevaliers que le roi avoit en garnisson a Nazereth tuit pris. [51]Quant Balian de Ybelin oi ces noveles, si en fist grant duel. [52]Si apela un sien serjant, et l'envoia arieres a Naples a la reyne sa feme conter ses noveles et dire que ele comandast a touz ses chevaliers de Naples que il fussent la nuit a Nazereth a lui. [53][…] si encontra les escuiers et le hernois des chevaliers dou Temple qui estoient eschapé de la desconfiture. [54]Or sachiés de voir que, s'il ne fust tornés au Sabast por oir messe, il fust bien venus a tens a la bataille. [55]Quant Balian fu venus a Nazereth, si oi si grant duel en la cité por ciaus de la vile qui avoient esté morz et pris en la bataille; que poi i avoit des maissons dom il n'i eust ou mors ou pris. [56]La trova le maistre dou Temple qui eschapez estoit. [57]La se herberga Balian et atendi ses chevaliers tant qu'il vindrent de Naples; car il n'en osa aler avant tant que ses chevaliers fussent venus. [58]Puis fist savoir a Thabarie au conte que il estoit a Nazereth. [59]Quant li cuens de Triple oi dire que il n'ot mie esté a la bataille, si en fu molt liez. [60]Quant se vint au lendemain, si envoia bien jusques a .l. chevaliers por lui conduire.

[61]Quant Balian ot trové le maistre dou Temple a Nazereth, si ala a lui; si li demanda de cele bataille, coment ele avoit esté. [62]Et il dist que molt s'estoient bien provez, et molt i avoient li crestien ocis de sarazins et estoient ja desconfis quant un enbuschement que il avoient enclos et amenés en une montaigne les ensclostrent, dont il furent desconfit. [63]Lors pristrent conseill que il envoieroient la ou la bataille avoit esté por les cors des chevaliers faire enfoir. [64]Donc firent prendre toz les somiers de la cité et envoierent por les cors; si les firent porter a Nazereth por enfoir. [65]Lendemain vint Balian et l'arcevesque de Sur et le maistre dou Temple, si murent por aler a Thabarie. [66]Quant il furent hors, si s'en retorna le maistre dou Temple, car il ne poeit chevauchier tant par estoit dolanz et dolerous des cos qu'il avoit reseus en la bataille le jor devant. [67]Mais Balian et l'arcevesque de Sur alerent a Tabarie. [68]Quant li cuens de Triple oi dire que Balian et l'arcevesque de Sur venoient, si ala a l'encontre molt dolenz et molt corouciez de l'aventure qui estoit avenue le jor devant, et tout par l'orgueill dou maistre dou Temple. [69]Quant le conte ot encontré les messages, si les resut molt hautement et les enmena avec lui en son ostel. [70]En celui point vint Renaut de Sayete. [71]Quant li messages furent el chastel avec le

conte, si li distrent lor messagerie; li cuens lor respondi qu'il estoit molt dolanz et molt hontous de l'aventure qui avenue estoit, et quant que il diroient et atireroient entr'iaus il feroit, car il savoit bien que il ne le forsconseilleroient mie. [72/73]Lors distrent que il meist les sarazins fors de la cité; puis s'en alast avec yaus au rey; tout ausi com il s'estoit mis en eaus .iii. s'estoit mis li rois de la pais faire. [74]Si envoierent un message batant au roi, et li firent assavoir qu'il avoient le conte avec eaus.

Variants

[1] Un des] F72: Noredin adoubés] F57 F73: adoubés a chevalier Noredin] F50 F57: Noradin Emirhali] F57 F73: Amirail Domas si] F50 F72: Damas qui; F73: Domas si

[1a] gagier les] F57 F73: et gagier les crestiens Renaut avoit prise] F57 F3: Renaus prist

[1b] il ne poeit] F57: cil ne pooient; F72: il n'i poeit; F73: cil ne poeit si estoit] F57: si est; F72: estoit devant dit conte] F50 conte au devant dit Salahadin] F50: a Salaadin; F72: au deuant dit sarazin

[2] qu'il savoit] F57 F73 *lack.* manda il] F72: manda corse] F57: chevauchié; F73: chevauchee

[3] demandoit] F57 F73: demandoit (F57: et) il se doutoit son pere] F57 F73 *lack.*

[4] Or pensa] F57 F73: Et pensa noient] F57 F73: riens et que li fis Salahadin maugré ne l'en savroit] F57 F73 *lack.*

[5] chose] F57 *lacks.*

[8] Thabarie] F57 F73: la cite

[9] de Triple] F57 F73 *lack.*

[10] n'avoient] F 57: n'avroient

[12] au chastel de] F57 F73: a del Hospital] F57 F73: au maistre de l'Ospital

[13] core et] F57 F73 *lack.* .iiii.] F57: .iii.

[14] par ses letres] F57 *lacks.* par matin] F57 F73 *lack.*

[15] il orent] F57 F73: li covens

[17] li chevalier dou Temple] F57 F73 *lack.* lxxxx. et .x. del Hospital] F57 F73: cent meins dis et cil de l'Ospital .x. pristrent] F72 *lacks.*

[18] Creisson] F57 F73: Croisson

[18c] et] F57 F73 *lack.*

[21] lieement] F57 F73: molt lieement parurent entreaus] F72: porent encontre yaus

[22] ausi fors le maistre soulement] F57 *lacks.* qui eschapa touz seuls] F57 F73: dou Temple qui s'en eschapa garnisson] F57: garnison en Nazareth; F73: garnison a Nazareth de par le roi] F57 F73 *lacks.*

[23] se furent] F57: s'estoient; F73: se estoient as crestiens, si] F57 F73: si

[24] F57, F72 and F73 all begin new paragraph here. ot fait] F57 F73: fist

[25] sien] F57 F73 *lack.* a Nazareth] F57 F73: par Nazareth venissent] F57: alaissent; F73: alassent auoit] F73: avoient

[28] avoient esté] F57 F73: estoient pris et des crestiens] F57 F73 *lack.* aveit] F57 F73: enmenoit

XIII

[32/33] F57, F72 and F73 all begin new paragraph here. au maistre del Hospital] F57: a celui de l'Ospital

[34] et que il] F57 F73: si tant qu'il eust oi messe] F57 F73: si avroit messe oye

[35] Donc] F57 F73: Lors si l'evesque] F57 F73: de l'evesque sist] F57: s'assist; F73: se assist

[37] messe] F57 F73: la messe

[37/38] de La Feve … chastel] F57 F73 *lack (haplography)*.

[38] tentes] F72: tendes nului] F57 F73: nului dedens

[40] merveilla] F57 F73: merveilla molt nelui] F57 F73 *lack*.

[41/42/43] enquerre] F57 F73: por enquerre

[44] en une chambre] F57 F73: dedens une chambre riens dire] F57 F73: dire noveles

[46] montast] F57 F73: montast a cheval

[47] il l'atendirent] F57 F73: il atendirent; F72: sil l'atendirent

[47/48] a eaus. Donc vint] F57 F73 *lack (haplography)*.

[49/50] dist] F57 F73: conta chief copé] F57 F73: teste copee et .iii. de ces chevaliers] F57 *lacks*. roi avoit] F57 F73: roi avoit mis a Nazareth] F57 F73 *lack*.

[51] que il] F57 F73 *lack*.

[53] F57, F72 and F73 all appear lack the first half of this sentence as given by the other mss, apparently as a result of haplography following the word 'Nazareth'. des chevaliers] F57 F73 lack.

[55] si grant duel … vile] F57 F73: grant duel mener por ces (F57: ceulz) de la cité

[57] ses chevaliers tant … tant] F57 F73 *lack (haplography)*.

[58] savoir a Thabarie] F57 F73: assavoir

[59] Quant li cuens … dire] F57 F73: et

[61] F57, F72 and F73 all begin new paragraph here. Balian] F57 F73: Balian (F57: Baliam) d'Ybelin

[62] desconfis] F72: ocis desconfis enclos et amenés … ensclostrent] F57 F73: en une montaigne les forclost

[63] faire] F57 F73 *lack*.

[65] si murent] F57 F73 *lack*.

[66] hors] F57 F73: hors de la cité car il] F57 F73: por ice qu'il dolanz et] F57 F73 *lack*.

[68] oi dire] F57 F73: sot venoient] F57 F73: venoient a lui

[69] en son ostel] F57 F73: en son chastel en son ostel

[71] le forsconseilleroient mie] F57 F73: li conseilleroient mie a son damage

[72/73] distrent] F57 F73: si li distrent tout] F57 F73: que tout .iii. s'estoit] F57: ausi estoit; F73: ausi si estoit

XIV

A New Text of the *Annales de Terre Sainte*

In 1884, Reinhold Röhricht and Gaston Raynaud published in parallel two versions of a Latin Syrian narrative they dubbed the *Annales de Terre Sainte*.[1] These texts were written in Old French and, through a series of brief annals, recounted the history of the crusades and the Latin East from 1095 to 1291. It was immediately clear that material from similar versions of these texts was embedded in both the *Gestes des Chiprois* and the late Italian compilation known as the *Chronique d'Amadi*, and (for the 1240s onwards) in the *Estoire de Eracles*.[2] It was also clear that Marino Sanudo had incorporated a Latin translation of substantial sections of these annals into his *Liber secretorum fidelium crucis*.[3] In 1960, Alfonso Sánchez Candeira published a Spanish version that broke off with the entry for 1260.[4] Historians have frequently made use of the information to be found in the *Annales de Terre Sainte* and the associated sources; indeed, for the thirteenth century they comprise an essential series of narratives which, despite their brevity, contain a significant body of otherwise unknown data.

A third Old French version of the *Annales* that can be set alongside the two published by Röhricht and Raynaud is to be found in the Florence, Biblioteca Medicea-Laurenziana, MS Pluteus LXI.10, and it is with particular pleasure therefore that I am able to offer an edition of this text to Benjamin Kedar who has himself so often unearthed hitherto overlooked sources and drawn them to scholarly attention. This manuscript is well known. It contains the Old French translation of William of Tyre's celebrated history. It has attracted attention because it alone preserves a version of the continuation of this work that takes the narrative beyond 1275 to 1277[5] and also because it has a unique section relating to the years 1191–97.[6] Furthermore, it has an impressive series of miniatures. Jaroslav Folda has argued that the manuscript was copied in Acre in 1290 or 1291, on the eve of

---

[1] *Annales de Terre Sainte*, ed. Reinhold Röhricht and Gaston Raynaud in *Archives de l'Orient Latin* 2 (1884) documents, pp. 427–61.

[2] *Les Gestes des Chiprois* in *Receueil des Historiens des Croisades, Arm* 2: 651–872; *Chronique de Amadi* in *Chroniques d'Amadi et de Strambaldi*, ed. René de Mas Latrie (Paris, 1891–93), 1; *Le estoire de Eracles empereur* in *Recueil des Historiens des Croisades, Historiens occidentaux* 2: 436–81.

[3] Marino Sanudo, *Liber secretorum fidelium crucis*, ed. Jacques Bongars in *Gesta Dei per Francos* (Hanau, 1611; repr. Jerusalem, 1972), pp. 206–32.

[4] "Las cruzadas en la historiografía española de la época: traducción castellana de un redacción desconocida de los 'Anales de Tierra Santa'," ed. Alfonso Sánchez Candeira in *Hispania: Revista Española de Historia* 20 (1960), pp. 325–67.

[5] *Eracles*, pp. 473–81.

[6] Louis de Mas Latrie, *Histoire de l'île de Chypre sous le règne des princes de la maison de Lusignan* (Paris, 1852–61), 3: 591–97; *La Continuation de Guillaume de Tyr (1184–1197)*, ed. Margaret Ruth Morgan (Paris, 1982), pp. 9–14, 108–98.

146

the city's capture by the Muslims.[7] The text of the *Annales* occupies folios 1^r–8^r. The nineteenth-century editors of the Continuations of William of Tyre considered it to be a summary of their main text, and alluded to it as such in their edition of the section covering the years 1275–77. In fact, it is not a summary but an independent text, which, as these same editors acknowledged, included snippets of information that are not to be found elsewhere.[8] The nineteenth-century edition of the Continuations of William of Tyre appeared in 1859, but since then, so far as I am aware, only Jaroslav Folda has mentioned the presence of the *Annales* text in this manuscript.[9]

The Florence version of the *Annales* ends with the events of 1277. It is written in the same hand as the bulk of the William of Tyre text that follows[10] and so, assuming that Folda's dating is correct, it predates the fall of Acre and therefore predates both the versions published by Röhricht and Raynaud, each of which concludes with the events of 1291. While the language differs markedly, the information it contains generally parallels the others closely, although, from the late 1250s onwards, it sometimes diverges appreciably. It is closer to the text preserved in Röhricht and Raynaud's MS B than that in their MS A, but, in common with the other versions, its contents become steadily more significant as the thirteenth century progresses. There is, however, not a vast amount of material that is to be found here and nowhere else. A few examples of unique information may, however, serve to give the flavour of what it has to offer, although it should be emphasized that this list is by no means exhaustive. The Florence *Annales* alone notes that in 1260 the Christians destroyed the church of St. Nicholas outside the walls of Acre when preparing to defend themselves against an anticipated Mongol assault; that in 1268 Guy, the new archbishop of Nazareth, had previously been prior of the same church; and that Balian of Ibelin lord of Arsur's death in 1277 occurred on 29 September.

The discovery of this text raises important questions about the interrelationship of the various versions and the other associated narratives, and also about the process of composition. Where, when and how these texts were assembled deserve further consideration, and by placing them in their cultural context it may be possible to gain fresh insights into the intellectual *milieu* of the Latin East in the thirteenth century. These are complex issues and ones to which I hope to return on another occasion.

---

[7] Jaroslav Folda, *Crusader Manuscript Illumination at Saint-Jean d'Acre, 1275–1291* (Princeton, 1976), pp. 111–16, 192–96 and plates 140–65.

[8] *Eracles*, p. 473 n. e, p. 478 nn. a, e.

[9] Folda, *Manuscript Illumination*, p. 111.

[10] Folda, *Manuscript Illumination*, p. 116 n. 201.

Note

In the edition that follows I have kept textual emendations to a minimum. I have made no attempt to correct mistakes in personal names, although a number are present, for example, the text confuses 'Bohemond' and 'Raymond' in the princely house of Antioch, and calls the short-lived Pope Innocent V (1276) 'Clement'.

148

Florence: Biblioteca Medicea-Laurenziana, Ms Pluteus LXI.10, fos. 1r–8r

Bien est droit et raison que chascun doit savoir en quel tens et en que saison et en quel an de l'incarnation Nostre Seignor Jhesu et quant les granz meutes des Crestiens ont esté emprises et faites por la sainte terre de Jherusalem, ou le dous beneoit Jhesu Crist, fiz de la beneoite Vierge Marie, se deigna tant humilier que por nos sauver vost recevoir mort et passion en la crois, laquel avoit esté ou servage des mescreanz .cccc. et .lxxxx. anz, une horre bien et autre horre mal, le peuple Crestien qui abitoit selonc ce que les seignages chamoient. Desquelz meutes fu la premiere esmeute[1] par Pierre li Ermites, a qui Deu dona grace en ce fait.

A mil et .lxxxxv. anz de l'incarnation Nostre Seignor Jhesu Crist Urbain qui lors <...> assembla un grant consille a Clermont ou qu'il fit doner la cruis as pelerins por passer en la terre sainte.

A mil et .lxxxxvi. anz murent les pelerins por passer en Surie et firent leur chevetaine Godefroi de Buillon duc de Loherene.

A mil et .lxxxxvii. anz fu prise Nique par les pelerins.

A mil et .lxxxxviii. anz fu prise Antioche.

A mil et .lxxxxviiii. anz fu prise la sainte cité de Jherusalem et Godefroi de Buillon fu esleu a roi. Et en cest an meismes desconfirent noz genz les Turs de Babiloine devant Escalone.

A mil et cent anz morut Godefroi de Buillon et fu roi apres lui Baudoin son fere qui fu apellé le premier roi de Jherusalem.

A mil et .c.i. an fu prise Cesaire.

A mil et .c.ii. anz fu la segonde bataille de ciaus de Babiloine es plains de Rames qui Baudoyn le premier roi desconfist.

A mil et c.iii. anz fu prise Accre.

A mil et .c.v. anz fu la tierce bataille de ciaus de Babiloine et de noz genz. Et en cest an morut Raymont le conte de Toulouse.

A mil et .c. et .vii. anz pelerins qui aloient de Japhe en Jherusalem desonfirent les Turs d'Escalone.

A mil et .c. et .viii. anz Hue de Saint Homer sire de Thabarie ferma le Thoron en la terre de Sur. Et en cest an Bertrant fiz le conte de Tholouse ariva devant Triple. Et en cest an vindrent les Geneveis et pristrent Gibelet.

A mil et .c.viiii. anz fu prise Triple[2] et en fist seignor Bertran fiz le conte de Tholouse, qui en fist homage au roi de Jherusalem.

A mil et .c.x. anz fu prise la cité de Barut et celle de Seete.

A mil et .c.xiii. anz fu la quarte bataille que le roi Baudoyn desconfi les Sarrasinz a Thabarie.

A mil et .c.xv. anz fu fermé le chastel de Mont Real.

---

[1] Manuscript: esmthue
[2] Manuscript repeats: Triple

XIV

A mil et c.xviii. anz Baudoyn le premier roi de Jherusalem morut en la terre d'Egypte entre Faramie et Laris, et fu coronés a roi Baudoyn de Borc qui fu le segont roi de Jherusalem.

A mil et .c.xxiii. anz fu la quinte bataille de ciaus de Babiloine que Baudoyn le segont roi desconfist vers Jherusalem.

A mil et .c.xxiiii. anz fu prise Sur.

[1v] A mil et .c.xxvi. desconfist le roi Baudoyn les Sarrasinz a Margesafar, et ce fu la siste bataille.

A mil et c. et .xxxi. morut Baudoyn le segont roi, et fu roi apres lui Fouque d'Anjo qui estoit baron sa fille.

A mil et .c.xliii. fu mor le roi Fouque, et en son leuc fu coronés Baudoyn son ainz né fiz.

A mil et .c.xlvii. Conrat l'emperere d'Alemaigne et Loys le roi de France qui estoient passés en Surie assegererent Domas et ne la pristrent mie.

A mil et .c.liiii. anz fu pris de Sarrasinz Baudoyn le quart roi.[3]

A mil et .c.lxiii. anz morut Baudoyn le quart.

A mil et .c.lxiiii. anz fu fait roi Amauri son frere.

A mil et .c.lxv. fu rendu le chastel de Harenc. Et en cest an fu desconfit Buemont prince d'Antioche et le conte de Triple et asses des barons et menés en prison a Halape.

A mil et c.lxvii. anz ala le roi Amauri en Egypte et prist Alixandre et Belbeis. Et au segont an chassa il Salahadin de champ. Et au tiers an il asseia Damiate par l'aye des Grex de Costantinople mes la prist mie. Et les Sarrasinz pristrent Belinaz des Crestiens.

A mil et .c.lxx. anz fu le grant crolle qui abati moult de terres de Crestiens et de Sarrazins; ce est asaveir Triple, Arche, Valenie, Gibel, La Liche, Antioche et pluisors autres cités, et ce avint a la feste Saint Pierre et Saint Pol.

A mil et .c.lxxiiii. morut le roi Amauri, et fu roi apres lui Baudoyn son fiz qui puis fu mesel.

A mil et .c.lxxvii. anz le segont jor de delier Baudoyn li roi mesiau par la vertu de la sainte crois desconfist Salahadin a Mongisart.

A mil et .c.lxxviiii. anz se combati le roi Baudoyn et Salahadin a Margelyon, et ne lor avint pas bien porce qu'il laissierent la voire crois a Thabarie. Ainz furent desconfit. Et fu en celle desconfiture frere Eudde de Saint Amant maistre del Temple et Baudoyn de Ybelin et pluisors autres chevaliers.

A mil et .c.lxxx. anz morut Loys le roi de France, et fu roi apres lui Phelippe son fiz.

A mil et .c.lxxxi. an fu coronés a roi de Jherusalem Baudoyn le petit qui fu fiz dou marquis Guillaume Longue Espee et de Sebille suer le roi mesel.

A .m. et .c.lxxxv. anz morut le roi Baudoyn le mesel.

---

[3] Evidently a blundered reading: other versions note Baldwin's capture of Ascalon s.a. 1154.

150

A .m. et .c.lxxxvi. anz morut le petit roi, et fu coronee Sebille sa mere et Gui de Lesignan son mari.

A mil et .c.lxxxvii. anz le premier jor de mai fu occis le maistre de l'Hospital frere Rogier des Molins et le mareschal dou Temple frere Jaques de Mailli devant Casal Robert. Et au quart jor de juignet furent desconfit les Crestiens a Quarne Hatin, et fu la perdue la sainte crois et fu pris le roi Gui. Et cel jor meismes fu Accre rendue as Sarrasinz et a Salahadin. Et au quart jor de septembre li fu rendue Escalone, et en celui jor oscursi le souleill. Et au segont jor de octovre li fu rendue la sainte cité de Jherusalem et tot le roiaume fors Sur.

A .m. et .c.lxxxviii. anz vint le marquis de Monferar a Sur.

A .m. et .c.lxxxviiii. ans le rei Gui, [2r] apres ce qu'il fu delivré de la prison Salahadin, asseia Accre.

A .m. et .c.lxxxx. anz fu neé l'emperor Fedric au flum dou Salef, et fu enterrés en Antioche. Et pape Celestin corona Henri son fiz a empeeor. Et en cel an le roi Phelippe de France et le roi Richart d'Engleterre vindrent au siege d'Accre. Et le roi Richart prist en son venir l'isle de Chypre de Kyrsac. Et en cel an comensa l'ordre de l'Hospital des Alemanz.

A .m. et .c.lxxxxi. an le roi de France et celui d'Engleterre recovrerent Accre des Sarrasinz a .xi. jors de juing.

A .m. et .c.lxxxxii. anz le roi Gui acheta Chypre dou roi Richart et si en fu saisi. Et les Haississins tuerent le marquis. Et le conte Henri espousa Ysabel, la fille le roi Amauri, qui fu feme Hamfroi dou Thoron.

A mil et .c.lxxxxiii. le roi Richart fist trives a Salahadin et recovra Japhe, Arsur, Cesaire et Cayphas. Et en cel an il s'en ala outremer, et fu agaitie et pris en Osteriche.

A mil et .c.lxxxxiiii. anz morut le roi Gui, et son frere Heymeri fu coronez de Chypre apres lui. Et Lyvon le sire d'Ermenie prist Buemont prince d'Antioche et le tint en prison.

A mil et .c.lxxxxv. anz ala le conte Henri en Ermenie et delivra Buemont le prince d'Antioche de prison, et fist mariage de la fille Rupin, qui estoit mere de Lyvon et de Raimont l'ainz né fiz dou prince. En cel an le conte Henri chassa les Pisanz d'Accre, et en cel an meismes s'acorderent a lui et retornerent en Accre.

A mil et .c.lxxxxvi. anz morut Salahadin. Et Seiffedin son frere toli le roiaume de Babiloine et de Domas de ces nevous. Et en cel an morut le patriarche Heymeri d'Antioche, et fu fait patriarche Pierre d'Engolesme qui estoit evesque de Triple.

A mil et .c.lxxxxvii. anz rendirent les Sarrasinz Gibelet as Crestiens. Et en cel an fu fait pape Innocent. Et maistre Fouque preescha la crois en France. Et l'empeeor Henri prist Puille et Cesille. En cel an manda il le secors en la terre de Jherusalem. Et le conte Henri de Champaigne chay de la fenestre dou chastel d'Accre aval et morut. Et le Heidel prist Japhe.

A mil et .c.lxxxxviii. anz le roi Heimeri de Chypre espousa la royne Ysabel de Jherusalem. Et l'arcevesque de Maience corona Lyvon a roi d'Ermenie. Et en cel an fu recoverte la cité de Baruth, et les Alemans assegierent le Thoron et ne le pristrent mie. Et adonc morut l'empereor Henri.

A mil et .cc.i. morut Buemont le prince d'Antioche, et fu fait prince Raymont son fiz qui estoit conte de Triple. Et en cel an secha le flum d'Eygpte, et y ot en la terre grant famine et grant cherestie.

A mil et .cc.ii. fu le crolle qui abati Sur, Accre, Gibelet, Arches et une partie de Triple et moult autre cités de Crestienz et de Sarrasinz cheytent.

A mil et .cc.iii. entra le roi Lyvon en Antioche devers le chastel le jor Saint Martin et prist jusques au Temple et demora dedenz .iii. jors.

A mil et .cc.iiii. anz l'estoire dou conte de Flandres et dou duc de Venise amenerent le fiz l'empereor Kyrsac et le mistrent en Costantinople si que Marchofle le tua, dont le conte [**2v**] de Flandres et le duc de Venise assegierent Marchofle et pristrent lui et la cité, et le firent saillir dou pillier aval, et eslurent le conte Baudoyn a empereor. Et en cel an mandi le roi Heymeri l'estoire de Chypre et de Surie en Egypte et destrurent Fouhé et en amenerent grant gaain.

A mil et .cc.v. morut le roi Heymeri.

A mil et .cc.vi. prist le prince Buemont Nefin et Gibelacar dou sire de Nefin qui estoit revelé contre lui.

A mil et .cc.vii. fu coronés lempereor Othes, et le roi Phelippe d'Alemaigne fu tué.

A mil et .cc.viii. se revela la comune d'Antioche contre le prince Raymont par le conseill dou patriarche Pierre d'Angolesme, et mistrent en Antioche les chevaliers que le prince avoit chassiez, si que le prince dessendi de son chastel tos armés et desconfi les chevaliers et la comune et prist le patriarche et le mist ou chastel en prison dont il en morut.

A .m. et .cc. et .x. anz vint le roi Johan en Accre et espousa la royne Marie, et le patriarche les corona a Sur.

A mil et .cc.xi. le roi Hugue de Chypre espousa la reyne Aalis. Et en cel an Gautier de Monbeliart ala par mer en Damiate et prist Borge et amena grant gaain.

A mil et .cc.xii. l'avant dit Gautier de Monbeliart ala en Romanie et prist Satalie et illeuc fu occis.

A mil et .cc.xiii. fu la bataillle d'Espaigne. Et en cel an desconfi Lascre le soudan dou Coine et l'occist el champ. Et en cel an tuerent les Hasissisins Raymont le prince d'Antioche.

A mil et .cc.xiiii. anz fu tué le patriarche Aubert en la procession dedenz l'iglise de Sainte Crois en Accre. Et fu fait patriarche Raoul evesque de Saiete. Et en cel an desconfist le roi Phelippe de France l'empereor Othes au pont de Bovines, et Loys son fiz desconfist le roi Johan en Peito. Et en cel an le roi Johan d'Engleterre devint home de l'yglise de Rome et dou pape et li dona treu d'Engleterre.

A mil et .cc. et .xv. anz pape Innocent le tiers tint consile general por le secors de la terre de Jherusalem et trova la campane devant Corpus Domini.

A mil et .cc.xvi. anz fu rendue Antioche a Rupin par l'atrait de Acharie le seneschal d'Antioche. Et en cel an morut l'empereor Othes et le roi Johan d'Engleterre.

XIV

152

Et Federic qui l'on apeloit l'enfant de Puille fu esleu a empereor et coroné a roi d'Alemaigne. Et morut aussi pape Innocent, et fu fait pape Honoire. A mil et .cc.xvii. anz le roi de Hongrie et le duc d'Osteriche alerent en Surie. Et la grant croisiee des Hongres et des Alemans alerent au Gor et a Monte Tabor. Et les Templiers fermerent Chastiau Pelerin. Et le roi Johan et le patriarche firent fermer le chastel de Cesaire.

A .m. et .cc. et .xviii. anz morut le roi Hugue de Chypre en la cité de Triple et fu enterés en l'yglise de l'Hospital de Saint Johan. Et en cel an ala l'ost de Surie en Damiate. Et en cel an vint maistre Pelage, qui estoit evesque d'Albane et legat de l'yglise de Rome et le prince des Romains.

A mil et .cc.xviiii. pristrent les Crestiens Damiate des Sarrasinz, et le prince Buemont toli Antioche a [3r] Rupin son nevou par l'atrait de Guillaume Farabel. Et cel an morut le roi Lyvon d'Ermenie.

A mil et .cc.xx. anz fu coronés Federic a empereor.

A mil et .cc.xxi. perdirent les Crestiens Damiate a l'issue d'aoust.

A mil et .cc.xxii. anz retorna le legat a Rome. Et le roi Johan et le patriarche Raoul et le maistre de l'Hospital, frere Garin de Mont Agu, alerent o lui. Et lors parla le roi Johan au pape dou mariage de sa fille a l'empereor, et la fu otroie par la dispensacion de pape Honoire. Et Phelippe, fiz de Raymont le prince d'Antioche, espousa la fille dou roi Lyvon d'Ermenie. Et apres avint que le baill d'Ermenie le prist et le mist en sa prison dont il morut. Et en cel an fu le crolle en Chypre qui abati Baphe.

A mil et .cc.xxiii. retorna de Rome le patriarche Raoul. Et Phelippe le roi de France morut en cel an, et Loys son fiz fu coronés a roi.

A mil et .cc.xxiiii. vint l'evesque de Pact et aporta l'anel a Ysabel la fille le roi Johan de par l'empereor Federic. Et en cel an morut le patriarche Raoul, et apres lui fu esleu a patriarche Girot. Et le baill d'Ermenie prist le roi Phelippe fiz dou prince Et en cel an Buemont fiz dou prince espousa Aaliz la royne de Chypre.

A mil et .cc.xxv. anz fu coronee la fille dou roi Johan a Sur, et passa la mer a l'empereor, et ala o lui Symon l'arcevesque de Sur et Belleem seignor de Seete.

A mil et .cc.xxvi. anz vint le conte Thomas en la Surie, et fu baill d'Accre de par l'empereor Federic. Et lors comensierent les Alemans a fermer le chastiau de Monfort.

A mil et .cc.xxvii. anz le patriarche Girot, qui estoit legat general, et le duc de Lambro et l'arcevesque de Vincestre et l'evesque de Excestre vindrent en Surie. Et en cel an morut Phelippe de Ybelin, et fu fermés le chastiau de Seete, et morut frere Garin de Mont Agu, maistre de l'Hospital, et aussi morut Coreidin qui estoit soudan de Domas.

A mil et .cc.xxviii. vint l'empereor Federic et ferma Japhe. Et la royne Aalis se parti dou mariage de Raymont le fiz le prince d'Antioche.

A mil et .cc.xxviiii. anz l'empereor Federic fist la trive au Quemel, et li fu rendu Jherusalem et Lidde et Nazereth. Et l'empereor vendi le roiaume de Chypre a .v. baills et si dona feme au roi et puis s'en ala. Et en cel an fu la bataille de Chypre, que le seignor de Baruth desconfist les .v. baills, et si y fu occis Gautier de Cesaire et Girart de Mont Agu.

A mil et .cc.xxx. anz fist faire le patriarche Girot les .ii. tours de Jahpe devers Escalone. Et cel an fu reconsiliee l'yglise dou Sepulcre. Et vint le patriarche d'Antioche qui estoit legat de la court de Rome.

A mil et .cc.xxxi. vindrent les Lomguebars et pristrent Baruth, et assegierent le chastel sanz prendre, et si s'en partirent hontousement.

A mil et .cc.xxxii. anz alerent les Longuebars en Chypre par le conseill de Amauri Barlais et de Heymeri de Bessan et de Hue de Gibelet, si que le sire de Baruth et ses enfanz alerent [3v] apres, et les Geneveis aveuc eaus, et les desconfirent. Et se fu la segonde bataille de Chypre. Et la royne Aalis ala de Chypre en France por recouvrer le conté de Champaigne. Et le patriarche Girot ala a Rome porce que l'empereor Federic l'avoit acuzé au pape et si avoit perdue la legacion. Et puis, quant il vint devant le pape, il li dona la legacion perpetuelment en son patriarchie.

A mil et .cc.xxxiii. Buemont le prince d'Antioche morut, et fu prince son fiz Buemont. Et fu rendu le chastel de Cherines au seignor de Baruth.

A mil et .cc.xxxiiii. anz vint l'arcevesque de Ravene en la legacion. Et le prince Buemont espousa la fille au conte Pol de Rome. Et en cel an fu ars Mumusart.

A mil et .cc.xxxv. revint la royne Aalis de Champaigne.

A mil et .cc.xxxvi. morut Johan de Ybelin, seignor de Baruth. Et son nevou Johan de Cesaire et le Temple et l'Ospital alerent assegier Monferant.

A mil et .cc.xxxvii. furent desconfit les Templiers a Trepessac. Et le patriarche Girot vint de Rome. Et Hue l'arcevesque de Nazereth morut, et aussi Pierre l'arcevesque de Cesaire morut, et le Sseiraf, seignor de Domas, morut aussi.

A mil et .cc.xxxviii. morut le patriarche Girot, et aussi le Quemel qui estoit seignor de Domas et de Babiloine. Et le Johet si fu seignor de Domas.

A mil et .cc.xxxviiii. vindrent en Accre le roi de Navarre et le conte de Bertaigne et le conte de Montfort et le duc de Borgoigne et le conte de Bar et le conte de Nevers et autres chevaliers asses. Et en cel an meismes les desconfi le Roc, un grant amiraill, entre Gadres et Escalone, et fu pris le conte de Montfort, et le conte de Bar morut, et asses autres chevaliers y ot que pris que mors. Et Raoul de Saisson espousa lors la royne Aalis.

A mil et .cc.xl. anz fu faite la trive o le Salah qui estoit sire de Domas et a rendi Saphet au Temple et Biaufort et tote la terre de Jherusalem. Et en cel an vint le conte Richart. Et morut Belleem le seignor de Seete. Et s'en retorna le roi de Navarre et le conte de Bertaigne. Et adonc ferma le conte Richart Escalone.

A mil et .cc.xli. an Johan de Ybelin, fiz dou sire de Baruth, fist fermer le chastel d'Arsur. Et le conte Richart aferma la trive o le soudan et delivra le conte de Monfort et les autres chevaliers qui le Roc avoit pris a la desconfiture dou roi de Navarre. Puis s'en retorna en son pays. Et morut pape Gregoire, et le souleill oscurzi, et le siege demora un an et .viiii. mois sanz pape.

A mil et .cc.xlii. anz alerent les Templiers et sire Jofrei de Sargines et le Melec Johet a Escalone ensi que le Nasser et l'ost de Babiloine assaillirent la herberge dou

154

Temple et y ressurent les Sarrasinz grant domage, et les Crestiens guerpirent de nuit leur herberges et alerent a Japhe. Et en cel an requist la royne Aalis le roiaume de Jherusalem et l'ot.

A mil et .cc.xliii. les Templiers et Joffrei de Sargines tindrent herberge a Japhe, et le Salah qui estoit seignor de Domas vint as molins [4r] des Turs por afermer la trive a noz genz. Mais il les engingna et ne fist point. Et lors asseia le sire de Baruth l'Ospital de Saint Johan. Et en cel an fu grant guerre en Accre entre les Franceis et les Suriens.

A mil et .cc.xliiii. anz fu fermee la trive au seignor de Domas et o le Nasser son nevou, et rendirent Jherusalem et le Temple Domini et tote la terre dou flum en sa fors Naples et Jerico. Et en cel an vint le patriarche Robert. Et fu feru adonc des Haississins le sire de Baruth dont il fu mahaignies dou destre bras. Et en cel an vindrent les Horesmins qui desconfirent noz genz a Forbie, et fu pris le maistre de l'Hospital, frere Guillaume de Chastiau Nuef, et le conte Gautier et son nevou Jaque, et Pierre arcevesque de Sur, et Raoul evesque Saint Jorge, et les .ii. fiz dou sire dou Boutron, et frere Hugue de Monlai mareschal dou Temple, et pluisors autres chevaliers y furent que mors que pris. Et fu prise la cité de Jherusalem, et mis a l'espee tos les Crestiens qui dedenz estoient.

A mil et .cc.xlv. pape Innocent le quart desposa l'empereor Federic. Et en cel an morut Aubert le patriarche d'Antioche.

A mil et .cc.xlvi. anz morut la royne Aalis, et son fiz le roi de Chypre prist la seignorie d'Accre.

A mil et .cc.xlvii. vint le soudan de Babiloine et prist Tabarie et asseia Escalone par mer et par terre, et manderent lors cil de Surie querre secors en Chypre. Et le roi de Chypre manda .viii. galees et .ii. galions et .c. chevaliers, et en fu chevetaine Johan de Ybelin seignor d'Arsur, et alerent a Escalone, et Deu manda une fortune de tens dont .xxi. galees de Sarrasinz et une nave rompirent devant Escalone. Et en cel an morut Belleem de Ybelin le seignor de Baruth le quart jor de setembre. Et les Sarrasinz pristrent Escalone en la moitie de octovre.

A mil et .cc.xlviii. anz ariva en Chypre le roi Loys de France a .xxviii. jors de setembre.

A mil et .cc.xlviiii. anz a .xxx. jors de mai mut le roi de France de Chypre por aler a Damiate, et si ariva au quart jor de juing, et au quint jor prist la terre, et au siste jor li fu rendue la cité de Damiate. Et le roi de Chypre tolli la baillye d'Accre a sire Johan Foinon. Et au septembre apres fu une guerre de Pisanz et de Geneveis qui dura .xxii. jors. Et en cel mois fu une grant tempeste en mer dont .lxxii. vaissiaus que granz que petis brisierent au port d'Accre. Et devant Damiate furent brisiees .xxii. naves et .x. vaissiaus sanz les autres qui brisierent par la riviere. Et a .xxviii. jors de novembre mut le roi de France de Damiate por aler a la Mensorre, et y parvint la a .xxii. jors de delier. Et a .viii. jors de genvier brisierent noz genz a Bessan une herberge de Turquemanz. Et a .viii. jors de fevrier vint un Bedoyn au roi de France si enseigna le gué dou flum de Tenis, dont noz genz passerent et pristrent la Mensorre, car les Sar[4v]rasinz l'abandonerent. Robert le conte d'Arteis et le Temple, qui fesoient l'avant garde, s'embatirent dedenz la ville et leur genz corurent au gaain. Les Sarrazins, qui virent leur mauvais contenement, lor corurent sus et asses en occistrent, car le conte Arteis, frere le rei de France, y fu perdu, que om ne sot qu'il devint. Et y fu occis le conte de Salebiere et Raou de Cossi. Si recovrent les Sarrazins la Mensorre.

A mil et .cc.l. anz a l'entre d'avrill faillirent les viandes en l'ost. Et au quint jor s'en parti li rois o tot son ost por venir en Damiate, et come il furent venuz a un casal qui a nom Sarmensac fu le roi desconfit et pris et tote la chevalerie. Si avint que la meismes fist il pais as Sarrazins, et por la raenson de lui et des autres rendi il Damiate et tos les prisoniers qui avoient esté pris en celle guerre et par dessuz .c. .m. mars d'argent. Et les Sarrasinz delivrerent le roi et ses freres et tos les prisoniers qui avoient esté pris dou tens l'empereor jusques alors. Et le segont jor de mai les Turs de Babiloine occistrent leur soudan, et covint que le roi lor jurast la trive si come il avoit fait au soudan, et ensi fu delivré. Et a .xiii. jors de may vint le roi et ses .ii. freres en Accre et ferma le borc. Et a l'entree d'aost se partirent d'Accre por aler en leur pays Amfous le conte de Poitiers et Charle le conte d'Anjo et Guillaume le conte de Flandres. Et ou mois de setembre Henri le roi de Chypre espousa Plaisence fille de Buemont le prince d'Antioche et conte de Triple. Et le maistre de l'Hospital frere Guillaume de Chastiau Nuef fu delivré de la prison de Babiloine et vint en Accre a .xviii. jors de octovre. Et en cel an le jor Sainte Lucye morut l'empereor Federic. Et le premier jor de fevrier fu desconfit le soudan de Halape en Egypte, et perdi .xxvii. .m. homes, et de cil d'Egypte morurent .ii. m. Turs.

A .m. et .cc.li. an a .xviii. jors de mars le roi de France mut d'Accre et ala fermer Cesaire. Et en cel an pape Innocent le quart se parti de Lyon sur le Rone et ala en Gene. Et Nicolle Arcir fu fait arcevesque de Sur et vint en Surie. Et a .viii. jors de genvier morut Buemont prince d'Antioche, et fu fait prince Buemont son fiz.

A mil et .cc.lii. anz a .xv. jors d'avrill ala le roi de France fermer Japhe. Et en cel an sa mere, la royne Blanche, morut. Et Buemont le prince d'Antioche ala a Japhe au roi de France aveuc sa mere Lucie porce que le roi le feyst chevalier, et il le fist. Et en cel an Julien le seignor de Seete espousa la fille Heiton le roi d'Ermenie.

A mil et .cc.liii. anz le soudan de Domas fist pais a ciaus d'Egypte, et engignierent le roi de France. Et au mois de mai vindrent ciaus de Domas devant Accre et abatirent Doc et Recordane. Et puis alerent a Seete et la pristrent et occistrent bien .viii. cenz persones et enmenerent bien .cccc. en prison a Domas. Et a l'issue de meis de juign le roi de France ala fermer Seete. Et en cel an [**5r**] morut le roi Henri de Chypre et aussi Nicolle l'arcevesque de Sur. Et si fu esleu arcevesque Gille qui avoit esté vesque de Damiate. Et morut aussi Gui de Mimars qui estoit evesque de Baphe, et Gautier qui estoit evesque d'Accre morut aussi. Et Haiton, le roi d'Ermenie, ala a Tatars.

A .m. et .cc.liiii. anz le roi Loys de France vint en Accre a .xxiiii. jors de mars et fist chevalier Belleem de Ybelin le fiz dou sire d'Arsur, qui puis espousa Plaisence la royne de Chypre. Et a .xxiiii. jor d'avrill le roi de France et la royne s'espouse et ses enfanz monterent sur mer, et lendemain qui fu le jor Saint Marc a l'orre de

XIV

vespres firent voille dou port d'Accre. Et a .xxiiii. jors de mai morut le roi Conrat. Et a .x. jors de juing Marguerite la dame de Seete morut. Et a .viii. jors de juignet morut Robert patriarche de Jherusalem. Et a .xxii. jors de juignet ariva le patriarche d'Antioche en Accre. Et a .xxvii. jors de setembre Heudde evesque de Tosquelane, qui vint legat aveuc le roi de France en Surie, monta sur mer et s'en ala outremer. Et Buemont le prince d'Antioche espousa Sebille la fille dou roi d'Ermenie le quart jor de octovre. Et le pape Innocent morut au meis de decembre, et Renaut l'evesque d'Oiste si fu pape et fu apelé Alixandre. Et comferma a l'Hospital de Saint Johan Mont de Tabor.

A mil .et. cc.lv.[4] anz fu faite la trive dou soudan de Domas et dou conte de Japhe, Johan de Ybelin, qui adonc estoit baill dou reiaume de Jherusalem, et fu hors de la trive Japhe et la seignorie de Rames. Et en cel an le cardenal Octevien entra en la terre de Puille aveuc l'ost dou pape, et si li fu rendu Sciege et Sipont et Saint Lorens et Mont Angle et tote la terre jusqu'a Optrente.

A mil et .cc.lvi. anz maistre Florens ariva en Accre tot sacré evesque d'Accre le jor de Saint Johan. Et en cel an por la maison Saint Sabbe comensa la meslee entre les Geneveis et les Veniciens, et furent desconfit les Veniciens par les Pisanz, qui lor furent encontre qui estoient jurés as Geneveis, et fu leur rue corrue et robee. Et frere Renaut de Vigier qui estoit maistre dou Temple morut, et frere Thomas Berart fu maistre.

A mil et .cc.lvii. anz ou mois de juignet le seignor d'Arsur qui estoit baill dou roiaume de Jherusalem por lui et por les homes de la seignorie, et les conselles do comun de Gene d'Accre por eaus et por leur comun jurerent ensemble d'aidier et de maintenir et de deffendre l'un l'autre contre totes genz par mer et par terre de leur cors et de leur gent et de leur avoir. De quei il avint que les Geneveis se partirent dou sairement qu'il avoient as Pisanz, et se ralierent les Pisanz et les Veniciens ensemble. Et fist tant le seignor o l'aye de Geneveis qu'il assegierent les Pisanz et les Veniciens et furent a ce menés que les Pisanz rendirent leur tors au sire d'Arsur. Et apres ce vint en Accre conselle des Pisans un vaillant home de Pise qui avoit nom Siguer de la Sacete. Et de Venise vint chevetaine Lorens Teuple qui amena o lui .xiiii. galiees et .ii. naves, et maintenant comensa [5v] la grant guerre en Accre des Pisanz et Veniciens o les Geneveis. Et furent au comensement encloz les Pisanz et les Veniciens par le seignor. Mes apres vint Buemont prince d'Antioche et amena o lui sa suer la royne Plaisence de Chypre et son fiz Huguet, qui esteit heir dou reiaume de Jherusalem, et par l'atrait dou maistre dou Temple et de Johan de Ybelin conte de Japhe tindrent la partie des Pisanz et des Veniciens, et furent encloz les Geneveis. Apres vint le Rous de la Turque, chevetaine de .xlviii. galees et de .iiii. naves devant Accre la vigille Saint Johan, et les Pisanz et les Veniciens armerent .xlii. galiees, et lendemain qui fu le jor Saint Johan le Baptiste se combatirent ensemble et furent desconfit les Geneveis et perdirent .xxviii. de leur galiees. Et lors fu finee la guerre, et se partirent les Geneveis d'Accre, et les Pisans

[4] Corrected in manuscript from: lxxv

et les Veniciens abatirent leur tor et presque tote leur rue. Et en cel an pristrent les Tatars Baudac et tote la terre de Perce et occistrent le halife. Et adonc fu occis Johan l'Alemen le sire de Cesaire en son chastel de Cesaire si come il dormeit en son lit. Et morut lors Johan de Ybelin seignor d'Arsur.

A mil et .cc.lviiii. anz a .xviii. jors d'avrill vint en Accre legat, frere Thomas de Lentin de l'ordre des Preeschors et evesque de Beleem. Et la royne Plaisence vint en Accre le premier jor de mai et fist baill de la terre Jofroi de Sargines qui estoit seneschal dou roiaume. Et cel an ala a Rome Jaque le patriarche de Jherusalem por delivrer Saint Ladre de Betaine des mains de l'Hospital de Saint Johan, que le pape lor avoit doné.

A mil et .cc.lx. anz pristrent les Tatars Halape par force et mistrent a l'espee quanqu'il troverent, et tote la terre de Haman de la Chamelle et de Domas, et vindrent ou reiaume de Jherusalem, et alerent vers le Crac, et pristrent le soudan, et puis pristrent Saete. Et por paor d'iaus cil d'Accre taillierent tos les jardins qui estoient pres de la ville et abatirent totes les murailles et tors qui estoient dehors la ville et l'yglise Saint Nicolaz et les vaz⁵ qui estoient ou sementire, et comensierent afaire une barbecane entor la ville. Et en cel an meismes par l'enortement de ciaus d'Accre issirent cil de Babiloine et estoit lors soudan un qui anomoit en surnom le Goutous et se combatirent as Tatars ou plain de Thabarie et les desconfirent le tiers jor de setembre, et depuis la desconfiture, si come il tornoient en Babiloine, un Turc qui anomoit Bendoudar occist le soudan, et quant il l'ot occis si fu fait soudan de Babiloine. Et Julien le seignor de Seete vendi lors Seete et Beaufors au Temple, dont Haiton le roi d'Ermenie se tint mal apaie, porce qu'il avoit sa fille a feme, et vost rendre au Temple ce qu'il avoient doné. Et en cel an Johan de Ybelin le sire de Baruth et les Templiers et la chevalerie d'Accre alerent brisier un herberge de Turquemanz qui estoit au Thoron des chevaus outre le Saphet .xii. milles, et furent desconfit et fu pris le sire [6r] de Baruth et frere Mahé le Sauvage comandor dou Temple et autres freres et chevaliers dou sciecle asses, et asses en y ot de mors. Mes il furent mis a raenson et delivrés dedenz .xv. jors.

A mil et .cc.lxi. aliena le sire d'Arsur Arsur a l'Hospital de Saint Johan. Et en cel an morut pape Alixandre le jor de Saint Urbain, et fu fait pape a .xxviiii. jors d'aoust maistre Jaque qui estoit patriarche de Jherusalem. Et en cel an Pallialogue prist Costantinople. Et la royne Plaisence morut, et Hugue de Lesignan ressut le bailliage de Chypre.

A mil et .cc.lxii. anz fu Antioche assegiee de Sarrasinz. Mais par l'atrait dou roi d'Ermenie les Tatars s'esmurent contre eaus si qu'il laissierent le siege et s'en partirent. Et en cel an Charle le conte d'Anjo et de Provence, frere le roi Loys de France, asseia Marseille, et cil dedenz se tendirent a lui par force dont il en fu seignor, et mist bailli et justisier en la ville de par lui.

A mil et .cc.lxiii. anz Bendocdar le soudan de Babiloine vint devant Accre a .xiiii. jors d'avrill et lendemain corut jusque es portes de la ville et par force mist la

---

⁵ Manuscript B: vaisiaus. Cf. Sanudo (p. 221): lapides cimiterii

158

gent dedenz. Et fu navrés Jofrei de Sargines, et pluisors autres chevaliers et sergenz y ot asses mors et navrés. Et fu la ville en grant aventure. Et l'achaison por quei il vint fu porce que le Temple et l'Ostpital ne vodrent rendre leur esclas si come il l'avoient otroie por la trive faire, et le soudan voloit aussi rendre les siens. Mes le conte de Japhe rendi ses esclaz au soudan par quoi il li tint bien la trive. Et en cel an vint Henri le fiz dou prince Raymont d'Antioche en Accre et sa feme Ysabiau qui fu fille dou rei Henri de Chypre et de la royne Aalis, par qui la seignorie dou reiaume li escheeit, et requistrent as seignors d'Accre le baillage dou reiaume de Jherusalem et l'orent sanz ce que om lor feyst homage ne sairement, porce qu'il n'avoient amené aveuc eaus l'eir. Si s'en retorna la dite Ysabel en Chypre et laissa son baron baill en Accre. Et lors s'en parti d'Accre por aler outremer l'evesque de Beleem qui estoit legat en Surie. Et a .xxiiii. jors de setembre vint en Accre Guillaume patriarche de Jherusalem et legat de tote Surie. Et Henri frere dou prince d'Antioche fu fait baill en Accre.

A mil et .cc.lxiiii. anz vindrent de Venise .lviii. que galiees que tarides et alerent devant Sur et combatirent la cité, mais il n'i forfirent neent ainz s'en retornerent sanz riens faire, car Phelippe de Montfors qui lors en estoit seignor se defendi bien et biau d'iaus. Et morut lors pape Urbain le quart. Et Johan de Ybelin seignor de Baruth et Huet qui estoit heir de Cesaire et Ysabel feme de Henri fiz dou prince morurent aussi. Et fu fait pape maistre Gui le cardenal evesque de Sabine qui fu evesque de Nerbone, et fu apelé Climenz le quart. Et Charles le conte de Provence fu fait senator de Rome perpetuelment et manda a Rome son vicaire. Et lors desconfist le roi de Castelle celui de Grenate ou il occist moult de Sarrasinz. Et adonc vint en Accre Olivier de Termes.

A mil et .cc.lxv. anz Bendocdar le [6v] soudan de Babiloine a .viii. jors de mars prist la cité de Cesaire et a .xv. jors de mars asseia le chastel d'Arsur et tant le combati que le dereain jor d'avrill le prist par force. Et lors apparut l'estoile de colmete. Et Hugue de Lesignan qui estoit baill de Chypre vint en Accre por secors, et amena o lui bien .c. et .xxx. que chevaliers que sergenz a cheval. Et en cel an Symon de Montfort qui estoit conte de Lexestre et avoit a feme le suer le roi d'Engleterre porchassa tant vers les barons de la terre qu'il prist le roi et son frere le conte Richart, qui estoit apelez roi d'Alemaigne, et Odoart fiz le roi, et les tint en prison. Mes Odoart issi de prison et se ralierent o lui ses homes, et il se combati a Symon de Montfort et le desconfi et occist. Et en cel an meismes Charle le conte d'Anjo et de Provence fu coroné a Rome a roi de Cesille par le comandement de pape Climenz et entra en Puille et se combati a Manfrei a Bonivent et le desconfi et occist. Apres vint a Saint Germain Laguillier et la occist asses de la gent de Mamfrei. Et adonc vint en Accre le conte de Nevers et sire Erart de Nantueill et Erart de Valeri et furent bien .lx. chevaliers.

A mil et .cc.lxvi. Bendocdar le soudan de Babiloine vint devant Accre le segont jor de juing et demora .viii. jors; puis se parti et ala assegier le Saphet et le prist a .xxii. jors de juignet, car cil dedenz se rendirent sauve leur vies. Mais il lor tint mal covenances, car il lor fist a tos coper les testes. Apres se parti un amiraill de l'ost dou soudan qui avoit nom Semelmot, et en mena partie de l'ost et entra en la terre d'Ermenie par force et la corut et fist grant domage, car un des fiz le roi y fu occis et l'autre pris et mené en prison en Babiloine. Et en cel tens morut le conte de Nevers de quei grant domage fu en la terre d'Accre. Et el meis d'aoust vint en Accre Hugue de Lesignan baill de Chypre qui amena o lui belle compaignie de genz d'armes. Puis firent une chevauchee, lui et le Temple et l'Ospital et les Alamanz et les chevaliers franseis et moult autres genz a cheval et a pie, et alerent vers Thabarie. Le cri se leva par la terre, et les Turs dou Saphet vindrent et s'enbuschierent vers le plain d'Accre en un leu qui a nom le Caroublier, et si come les nostres retornoient il ferirent a l'avant garde qui chevauchoit bien .iii. liues devant les autres, c'est asaveir l'Ospital et les Alemans et la compaignie sire Jofrei de Sargines, et les desconfirent et asses en occistrent. Et en celle saison morut Johan de Ybelin conte de Japhe. Et Joceaume arcevesque de Cesaire morut aussi. Et Gille arcevesque de Sur morut outremer.

A mil et .cc.lxvii. le <.ii.>[6] jor de mai Bendocdar le soudan de Babiloine corut devant Accre soudainement et occist moult de genz, et lendemain s'en parti et ala au Saphet, et a .xv. jors de mai revint arieres devant Accre et fist taillier tos les jardins qui estoient devant la ville et abatre les tors des jardins. Et a .xvi. jors d'aoust ariverent au port d'Accre .xxviii. galies de Geneveis et fu chevetaine Luque de Grimaut et ardi[7r]rent .ii. naves de Pisanz et y demorerent .xii. jors. Et en ce vindrent .xxviii. galiees de Veniciens et troverent une partie des galiees de Geneveis au port d'Accre, car les autres estoient a Sur; si en pristrent .v. aveuc tote la gent. Et en celle saison morut Hugue le dreit heir de Chypre ou meis de novembre, et apres fu coroné a roi Hugue de Lesignan le jor de noel. Et le corona le patriarche Guillaume de Jherusalem qui se trova lors en Chypre. Et en cel <an> se croisa le roi Loys de France et ses enfanz et le roi de Navarre et moult d'autres contes et barons de France et d'Engleterre et d'Alemaigne et d'Espaigne por passer en Surie.

A mil et .cc.lxviii. morut le pape Climenz le quart. Et en cel an Charles le roi de Cesille desconfist Coradin o tot son ost qui estoit venuz d'Alemaigne par l'atrait des Pisanz, et li fist coper la teste. Et en cel <an> Bendocdar prist Japhe et laissa aler la gent. Et puis se parti de Japhe et ala devant Biaufort et le prist par force des Templiers a .xv. jors d'avrill. Puis s'en ala en Antioche et la prist de venue et moult y ot perdu grant peuple dedenz la cité que mors que pris. Et adonc fu delivré de la prison de Babiloine Lyvon fiz dou roi d'Ermenie en eschange de Sangor, qui estoit parent Bendocdar, que les Tatars avoient pris. Et en cel an morut Henri arcevesque de Nazereth, et fu fait arcevesque Gui qui estoit prior de Nazereth.

A mil et .cc.lxviiii. fu un crolle en Ermenie qui fondi .v. chastiaus et .iii. abayes d'Ermins et bien .xii. casaus. Et adonc morut Jofrei de Sargines en Accre. Et en cest an fu coronés Hugue de Lesignan a roi de Jherusalem. Et fu lors si grant cherestie en Surie que le mui dou froment valut bien .viii. besanz. Et le mecredi devant noel Robert de Cresetes et Olivier de Termes et le sire de Passi et bien .cc. chevaliers

---

[6] Supplied from manuscript B

160

alerent en enbuschement bien a une liue fors d'Accre, si que l'ost dou Saphet les
surprist et ferirent sur noz genz, et tant y ot des Sarrazins que les noz ne <le>s
porent soufrir, car l'on dit que Bendocdar le soudan y fu en persone o .iiii. m.
chevaucheors, et si i fu occis Robert de Creseques et le frere Olivier de Termes et
auquanz chevaliers.

A mil et .cc.lxx. anz a .xxi. jor d'avrill morut Guillaume qui estoit patriarche
de Jherusalem et legat de Surie et evesque d'Accre. Et ou mois de juing mut le roi
de France et ses enfans et le roi de Navarre et pluisors autres contes et barons et
asses chevaliers et sergenz por venir en Surie, et alerent a Tunes. Et morut devant
Tunes le roi de France[7] et son fiz Johan Tristan et le roi de Navarre et pluisors autres
vaillanz homes. Puis se parti l'ost de Tunes par grant avoir que le roi Charles en
ot, et vin<t> a Trapes et la orent si grant fortune de tens que presque totes les nes
perirent. Et en cel an occistrent les Haissisins Phelippe de Montfort en sa chapelle
a Sur. Et en cest an Bendocdar le soudan de Babiloine vint en la terre de Triple et
corut tote la terre et vindrent au borce dou Margat et mistrent le feuc. Puis alerent
a chastiau et assegierent la tor et la prirent [7v] par force. Ce est de Chastel Blanc
et pristrent bien .iii. .m. persones dedenz dont le fiz dou soudan qui se nomoit en
surnom Melec Sayt les mena devant le Crac et la les delivra et laissa aler porce que
ce estoit le premier gaain qu'il avoit fait et si plot moult au soudan son pere.

A mil et .cc.lxxi. asseia il le chastel dou Crac de l'Hospital et tant destrainst cil
dou chastel que par enginz que par mines que par combatre qu'il se rendirent a
lui sauve leur vies et fu a .viii. jors d'avrill. Et a .viiii. jors de mai Odoart fiz dou
roi d'Engleterre ariva en Accre, et Johan fiz le conte de Bertaigne, et Guillaume
de Valence, oncle de Odoart, et Thomas de Clarre. Et en setembre vint en Accre
Eymont le frere Odoart. Et a .xviii. jors de mai fu rendu le chastiau de Gibelacar
as Sarrasinz. Et en juing par la volenté de Deu brisierent .xi. galiees de Sarrasinz
a Lymesson. Et a .viii. jors de juing asseia Bendocdar Montfors des Alemans, et
a .xii. jors de juing se rendirent cil dedenz a lui sauve leur vies. Et a .vi. jors de
juignet vint le soudan Bendocda devant Accre et lendemain s'en ala. Et a .xx. jors
de juignet Odoart et sa gent et les gens d'Accre alerent brisier Saint <Jorge>[8] et y
forfirent poi. Et a .x. jors de Novembre s'en parti d'Accre Theobalde qui fu esleus a
pape de Rome. Et a .xxiiii. jors de novembre alerent noz genz brisier Quaquo et .ii.
herberges de Turquemans et occistrent bien .m. et .v. cenz Sarrazins, et amenerent
moult de bestes groces et menues.

A mil et .cc.lxxii. anz a .xxii. jors d'avrill fu faite la trive de Hugue de Lesignan,
roi de Jherusalem et de Chypre, et de Bendocdar le soudan de Babiloine, et n'i avoit
en la trive a Crestiens que le plain d'Accre sanz plus et le chemin de Nazereth. Et en
mai s'en ala Eymont frere de Odoart. Et a .xxviii. jors de juign fu navré Odoart en sa
chambre des Haississis. Et a .xii. jors d'aoust Guillaume de Valense son oncle s'en
passa outremer. Et a .xiii. jors de setembre s'en ala Johan fiz le conte de Bertaigne.

---

[7] Manuscript: roi de Tunes
[8] Supplied from Manuscript B

Et a .xxii. jors de setembre s'en passa Odouart. Et a .viii. jors de octovre ariva en Accre frere Thomas de l'ordre des Preeschors patriarche de Jherusalem et legat de tote Surie et en leuc de evesque d'Accre. Et ou meis de delier Bendocdar passa les Aigues Freides et chassa les Tatars qui avoient assegiee la Birre, mes il perdi de sa gent bien .iii. m. Turs. Et a .xxi. jor de mars Eymont l'Estrange espousa la dame de Baruth.

A mil et .cc.lxxiiii. anz ou meis de mai fu le consille dou pape et des prelaz a Lyon sur le Ronne. Et adonc morut Olivier de Termes.

A .m. et .cc.lxxv. anz morut Buemont le prince d'Antioche et conte de Triple. Et a .xxv. jors de mars Bendocdar corut la terre d'Ermenie et mist a l'espee quanque il trova. Et en cest an vint en Accre Guillaume de Rossillon chevetaine de serjans le roi de France. Et lors morut Julien qui fu sire de Seete.

A mil et .cc.lxxvi. anz a .x. jors de jenvier morut maistre Gedair pape de Rome qui ot non Gregoire. [8r] Puis fu fait pape Climens le quint et il morut le tiers jor apres a Arles. Et a .xviii. jors de juing fu neé devant Sur Henri le pere dou roi Hugue de Jherusalem et de Chypre. Et en cest an morut pape Climens, et puis fu fait pape Adrian, et morut en cest an meismes.

A mil et .cc.lxxvii. anz a .viii. jors de mai vint en Accre le conte Rogier de Saint Severin o .vi. galiees de par le roi Charle, et li fu livré le chastel d'Accre, et li jurerent les frairies et les homes liges dou roiaume. Et ou mois de juing fu occis en Chypre Nicolle sire de Cesaire. Et ou mois de juignet morut Bendocdar a Domas. Et a .xxvi. jors de setembre morut frere Thomas qui estoit patriarche de Jherusalem et legat de tote Surie. Et a .xxviiii. jors de setembre morut Belleem de Ybelin sire d'Arsur.

XV

Redating the Death
of King Henry I of Cyprus?

So first, your memory I'll jog,
And say: A CAT IS NOT A DOG.

T.S. Eliot: *Old Possum's Book of Practical Cats*

Every modern scholar who has had occasion to mention the death of King Henry I of Cyprus has dated it to the year 1253. There survive several annalistic sources, all of which are agreed on this point. Four texts, the *Estoire de Eracles*, MS B of the *Annales de Terre Sainte*, the Spanish *Anales de Tierra Santa*, and Marino Sanudo give simply the year,[1] but the late medieval Italian compilation known as the *Chronique d'Amadi* and following it, the sixteenth-century author, Florio Bustron, specify the date as 18 January.[2] Amadi also notes that he died at Nicosia, was buried at the Templar church and left a son named Hugh. All these sources are clearly related to one another and to an appreciable extent repeat the same information. Their unanimity on any particular point is therefore only to be expected. They are all ultimately derived from annals originating in the Holy Land, although the *Chronique d'Amadi*, which is written in a Venetian dialect of Italian from around 1500 and which betrays clear signs of having been translated from an earlier French text, preserves historical traditions from the kingdom of Cyprus not found in the others.

Describing the death of King Hugh III of Cyprus some three decades later, another much-used narrative from the Latin East, the *Gestes des Chiprois*, makes a specific statement about the mode of dating the year:

Et quant vint a .xxiiii. jours dou mes de mars, que define en l'an de M et CC et LXXXIII et comense a M et CC et LXXXIIII, trespassa le tres noble roy Hugue de Lezingniau....[3]

In other words, for this author the year began on 25 March, the feast of the Annunciation of the Blessed Virgin. As is well known, it was a practice that was

---

[1] "Eracles," 2:441; *Annales de Terre Sainte*, ed. Reinhold Röhricht and Gaston Raynaud in *AOL* 2 (1884) documents, p. 445; "Las cruzadas en la historiografía española de la época: traducción castellana de una redacción desconocida de los 'Anales de Tierra Santa,'" ed. Alfonso Sánchez Candeira in *Hispania: Revista Española de Historia* 20 (1960), 364; Marino Sanudo, *Liber Secretorum Fidelium Crucis*, ed. Jacques Bongars in *Gesta Dei per Francos* (Hanau, 1611), p. 220.

[2] *Chronique d'Amadi*, in *Chroniques d'Amadi et de Strambaldi*, ed. René de Mas Latrie (Paris, 1891–93), 1:202; Florio Bustron, *Chronique de l'île de Chypre*, ed. René de Mas Latrie, Collection des documents inédits sur l'histoire de France: Mélanges historiques 5 (Paris, 1886), p. 109.

[3] *Les Gestes des Chiprois* in *RHC Arm* 2:791.

widespread in the middle ages, but it does prompt the question whether, by modern computation, Henry's death as recorded by *Amadi* occurred in the opening days of 1253, as is generally assumed, or at beginning of 1254. It is therefore particularly unfortunate that, due to a substantial lacuna covering the years 1249–57, the *Gestes des Chiprois* does not record Henry's death.[4] There can, however, be no doubt that by the middle of the thirteenth century the Cypriot royal chancery began the new year in March. An act of King Henry I survives dated 26 February 1248 in which the king records a transaction agreed between John of Ibelin, count of Jaffa, and Archbishop Eustorgue of Nicosia. Present on that occasion was the papal legate, Odo of Châteauroux. But, as is well known, Odo, who had been active in promoting the crusade of King Louis IX in the west, had only arrived in Cyprus in September 1248 in the French king's company. The document must therefore belong to February 1249.[5] A similar argument can be applied to a Cypriot royal charter bearing the date January 1286. Here King Henry II of Cyprus endows masses for his maternal uncle, Baldwin of Ibelin the Constable, who had recently died. But from the *Gestes des Chiprois* we know that in July 1286 Baldwin had accompanied the king on his visit to Syria, and after Henry's coronation as king of Jerusalem in August that year he had remained behind in Acre as the royal *bailli*. Henry's endowment clearly belongs to the beginning of 1287.[6] Two fourteenth-century examples can serve to confirm this point. Following Henry II's return to Cyprus in late August 1310 after the death of his usurping younger brother, Amaury of Tyre, it proved necessary to issue a *remède* to regularize legal matters transacted during the period of Amaury's rule. The text of this document bears the date January 1310, but clearly January 1311 is intended.[7] Then again, King Peter I of Cyprus was murdered in January 1369, but the *remède* issued on that occasion to correct the abuses that had precipitated his death bears the date January 1368.[8]

However, as Jean Richard has shown, at least by the fourteenth century the Cypriot chancery followed Byzantine practice and began the year not on the Feast

---

[4] See *Les Gestes des Chiprois*, p. 742 note a.

[5] *The Cartulary of the Cathedral of Holy Wisdom of Nicosia*, ed. Nicholas Coureas and Christopher Schabel (Nicosia, 1997), no. 48, pp. 144–47); *RRH* no. 1156. For Odo's movements at this time, Jean Richard, *Saint Louis: Crusader King of France* , trans. Jean Birell (Cambridge, 1992), pp. 113–15.

[6] *The Cartulary of the Cathedral of Holy Wisdom*, no. 57, pp. 160–62; *RRH* no. 1461; *Les Gestes des Chiprois*, pp. 792–93.

[7] Codex vaticanus latinus 4789, fo. cclxii^v: "a mois de Jenvier de iii^c & x de Crist." Cf. *Bans et Ordonnances de rois de Chypre* in *RHC Lois* 2:368. For these events, see Peter W. Edbury, *The Kingdom of Cyprus and the Crusades, 1191–1374* (Cambridge, 1991), pp. 124–31.

[8] Codex vaticanus latinus 4789, fo. cclxix^v: "le mardi a xvi jours de Jenvier l'an de M.iii^c.lxviii de Crist." 16 Jan. 1369 was indeed a Tuesday. The printed text (*Bans et Ordonnances*, p. 378) is corrupt. See Jean Richard, "La révolution de 1369 dans le royaume de Chypre,", *BEC* 110 (1952), 110–11.

of the Annunciation as the *Gestes des Chiprois* would have it, but on 1 March.[9] There is ample evidence for this mode of dating. On 2 March 1328 King Hugh IV issued letters of appointment dated both by the indiction and by the year *anno domini* which taken together demonstrate that 1328 and not 1329 is indeed the year.[10] In a document dated 5 March 1363 King Peter I confirmed the privileges Henry I had given the Genoese in 1232, and, as is clear from other evidence, the king was present in Genoa on that date, making his way from Venice to the papal court at Avignon.[11] Two documents are known with the date March 1378 in which the indiction is given, thereby confirming 1378 as the year. In one of them, dated 7 March, the chancery clerk has even felt it necessary to add the significant phrase, *secundum cursum regni Cipri*.[12] Finally, as Richard has noted, Leontios Makhairas, writing of events in the 1380s, gives a clear indication that the year ran from 1 March to 28 February.[13]

To return to the 1250s. There is good reason to suppose that the practice of beginning the year on the Feast of the Annunciation or perhaps on 1 March was employed elsewhere in the Latin East at that time. For example, as Professor Hans Mayer has indicated, Julian lord of Sidon clearly followed this policy as is shown in documents from his lordship of 1256 (1257 n.s.).[14] J. Delaville le Roulx similarly suggested that John of Ibelin count of Jaffa's grants in favour of the Hospitallers and dated January and February 1256 were in fact issued at the beginning of 1257.[15] Furthermore, Mayer has pointed out that a joint meeting of the High Court of the kingdom of Jerusalem and the *cour des bourgeois* of Acre

---

[9] Jean Richard, *Chypre sous Les Lusignans. Documents chypriotes des archives du Vatican (XIVe et XVe siècles)* (Paris, 1962), p. 21, cf. p. 76; idem, "La révolution," p. 110; idem, "Freedom and Servitude in Cyprus and Rhodes. An Assize dating from 1396," in Benjamin Arbel, ed., *Intercultural Contacts in the Medieval Mediterranean* (London, 1996), p. 272.

[10] Louis de Mas Latrie, *Histoire de l'île de Chypre sous le règne des princes de la maison de Lusignan* (Paris, 1852–61), 2:140.

[11] Mas Latrie, *Histoire* 2:248–49. George Hill, *A History of Cyprus* (Cambridge, 1940–52), 2:325.

[12] Richard, *Chypre sous les Lusignans*, p. 21 (citing Louis de Mas Latrie, *Trésor de chronologie, d'histoire et de géographie pour l'étude et l'emploi des documents fu moyen âge* [Paris, 1889], col. 21); Mas Latrie, *Histoire* 2:371–72.

[13] Leontios Makhairas, *Recital Concerning the Sweet Land of Cyprus entitled 'Chronicle,'* ed. Richard M. Dawkins (Oxford, 1932), § 621. Cf. *Chronique d'Amadi*, p. 416.

[14] *Tabulae ordinis Theutonici*, ed. Ernst Strehlke (Berlin, 1869), nos. 108–11, pp. 88–91; RRH nos. 1253–56; Hans E. Mayer, "Ibelin *versus* Ibelin: The Struggle for the Regency of Jerusalem 1253–1258," *Proceedings of the American Philosophical Society*, 122 (1978), 48 n. 126; idem, *Varia Antiochena: Studien zum Kreuzfahrerfürstentum Antiochia im 12. und frühen 13. Jahrhundert*, MGH Studien und Texte 6 (Hanover, 1993), p. 31.

[15] *Cart Hosp* nos. 2845, 2853, vol. 2:833–35, 837–38; RRH nos. 1245–46. Cf. Peter W. Edbury, "John of Ibelin's Title to the County of Jaffa and Ascalon," *English Historical Review* 98 (1983), 127–28. *Contra*, Hans E. Mayer, "John of Jaffa, His Opponents and His Fiefs", *Proceedings of the American Philosophical Society* 128 (1984), 152–53.

ascribed in the text recording this occasion to February 1250 ought properly to be dated February 1251.[16]

If then beginning the year on either 1 March or 25 March was widespread in the Latin East, where does that leave *Amadi*'s obit for Henry I? Did our annalist follow this practice? It may seem all too obvious, but the point nevertheless needs to be stressed — and hence the quotation at the head of this paper — that an annal is not a legal document. There are no grounds for assuming *a priori* that whoever composed this entry was trained in the chancery practice of the Latin East or was in any way influenced by people who were. He may have been, but, if so, that remains to be demonstrated.

The first question therefore is to ask how the annalist drawn on by the compiler of the *Chronique d'Amadi* operated. Here the entry for 1253 provides a useful point of departure. The other annals mentioned in the opening paragraph of this discussion are very similar to one another, although not totally identical. Even so, the text found in MS B of the *Annales de Terre Sainte* will serve for purposes of comparison:

> A M et CC et LIII, fist pais le soudan de Damas a ceaus d'Egypte, et engignierent le roi de France, et li fauserent le sairement qu'il li avoient juré par pluisors fois, et vindrent cil de Damas devant Acre, et abatirent Doc et Recordane; et d'enqui alerent à Saite et la prisent, et ocirent bien viij^c persones, et en menerent bien iv^c en prison à Damas; et quant li rois ot fremee Japhe, il ala fremer la cité de Saiete, et Henris, li roys de Cippre, morut en cel an; et Nicole Larcar, archevesques de Sur, morut, et fu esleüs archevesques Gilles, qui avoit esté evesque de Damiete, et Guis de Mimars, evesques de Balfe, morut, et Gautiers, evesques d'Acre; et Heitons, roys d'Ermenie, ala as Tartars.[17]

Seemingly the most important events of the year were (1) the reconciliation of the Ayyubid sultan of Damascus with his erstwhile rivals, the Mamluk junta that had taken power In Egypt in 1250, despite the promises made to King Louis, who, as we know, was hoping to profit from the divisions in the Muslim world at that time; (2) the sultan of Damascus's military demonstration outside Acre which included destruction of the nearby mills at Doc (Da'uk) and Recordane (Khirbat Kurdana)[18] and his damaging attack on Sidon which entailed the slaughter of 800 people and the captivity of a further 400; and (3) the restoration of the fortifications at Sidon by King Louis.[19] There then follows the necrologies: King Henry, the archbishop of Tyre (and his replacement by Giles, titular bishop of Damietta),[20] and the bishops of Paphos and Acre. Finally we are

---

[16] *Abrégé du Livre des Assises de la Cour des Bourgeois* in *RHC Lois* 2:246–49; Mayer, "Ibelin *versus* Ibelin," p. 33 n. 60.

[17] *Annales de Terre Sainte*, p. 445.

[18] For Doc and Recordane, see Denys Pringle, *Secular Buildings in the Crusader Kingdom of Jerusalem: an Archaeological Gazetteer* (Cambridge, 1997), nos. 85, 133, pp. 47, 62–64.

[19] Richard, *Saint Louis*, pp. 134–39.

[20] Bernard Hamilton, *The Latin Church in the Crusader States: the Secular Church* (London, 1980), p. 266.

informed of King Hetoum I of Cilician Armenia's personal visit to the Mongol khan. By contrast the *Chronique d'Amadi* describes the same year in these words:

El re de Franza fortificò la cità de Saeto. Morite Henrico re de Cypro, a Nicossia, a dì 18 zener, et ful sepulto al Tempio; ha lassado uno figliolo chiamato Huget. Morite Guido, vescovo di Bapho. La terra che era interdita per l'arcivescovo Hugo Pisan, per la rissa che era tra lui et el re Henrico;[21] intesa la morte del re, vene d'oltra mare et reconciliò la terra. Gatier, vescovo de Acre, morite; Nicolo Larcar, arcivescovo de Sur, morite; dapo lui fo elletto per arcivescovo de Sur Giglio, che era vescovo de Damiata. Haetonte, re de Armenia, andò alhora a li Tartari. [22]

It is immediately apparent that the emphasis is completely different. The necrologies and the king of Armenia's visit to the Mongols are still there and are sufficient to prove that the texts are related, but the events in the Muslim world and the attacks on the environs of Acre and Sidon are omitted, leaving only the reference to Louis IX's fortification of Sidon. Instead, the notice of Henry death is expanded and we are informed about the archbishop of Nicosia's interdict and its lifting. What has happened is that the annal has been re-written by someone, presumably in Cyprus, from a Cypriot standpoint. Events that are of no consequence to Cyprus are left out, and this is fully in keeping with the *Amadi* annalist's tendency to omit or compress references to the events in the Muslim world in these years; other material relating to the island is introduced.

Many of the adjacent annals in *Amadi* are far closer to those found in the *Annales de Terre Sainte* or the other related texts than the annal for 1253. In fact, for the middle decades of the thirteenth century this text has comparatively little Cypriot-related information not found in the earlier sources, although the anonymous author is alone in recording the death of Archbishop Eustorgue of Nicosia on 28 April 1250 and the death of Baldwin of Ibelin, the seneschal of Cyprus, on 21 February 1267.[23] It is only later, when dealing with the events that occurred after 1291 and in particular with the political crisis of 1306–10, that *Amadi* comes into its own as a major independent source. For the mid thirteenth century *Amadi* might therefore be described as a version of the *Annales de Terre Sainte* with a Cypriot slant. That being so, it is worth asking whether the individual pieces of information are presented in chronological sequence, and, more importantly, how all the other annalistic texts date events from other years which occurred in the period between 1 January and 25 March.

Joinville provides sufficient information to obtain a chronological framework for 1253. He indicates that Louis left Jaffa for Sidon "que li Sarrazin avoient abatue" at the end of June and arrived in Sidon to find the bodies of the slain still unburied; the French king then seems to have remained at Sidon until shortly

---

21   As the editor notes: "La phrase reste en suspens."
22   *Chronique d'Amadi*, p. 202.
23   *Chronique d'Amadi*, pp. 200, 208.

before his departure for the west in April 1254.[24] That would put the sultan's raid in June, and the start of Louis's sojourn in Sidon in July. If indeed the events are being recorded in chronological order, then Henry's death would have occurred after Louis took up residence in Sidon, thereby supporting the date January 1254. We have no way of establishing the precise dates of the deaths of the three bishops, although Giles, Archbishop Nicholas of Tyre's successor, was named as archbishop-elect (and so not yet enthroned) in September 1254.[25] Hethoum, however, is unlikely to have set off for Qaraqorum in the middle of winter, and the Armenian sources, while not specifying exactly when he went, agree that his departure occurred in 1253.[26] Maybe the annalist placed this event last either because Armenia lay outside his immediate field of vision or because he only learnt of its significance when Hethoum returned three years later and so added it as an afterthought. At most, the order in which the events are listed in the annal suggests that Henry could have died in 1254 rather than 1253, but by itself this argument is far from conclusive.

When we turn to the question of how the various annals date other events, which occurred in the first three months of any year, we find a striking lack of consistency. In several instances the sources place the events in the year as if it began in January. Thus in February 1250 we are told that King Louis IX's army crossed "le flun de Thenis" (the Bahr as-Seghir) and engaged the Muslims in battle at Mansurah.[27] We learn that it was in 1260 that the Mongols occupied Aleppo. (Aleppo in fact fell in January that year, its citadel surrendering the following month.[28]) In January 1264 the Hospitallers and Templars raided al-Lajjun.[29] Early in March 1268 Baybars took Jaffa,[30] and in February 1271 he began the siege of Crac des Chevaliers.[31] There are, however, a number of cases in which annalists have put events belonging to the period 1 January — 24 March with the events of the previous year in a way, which suggests that they were adopting the Feast of the Annunciation as the start of the year. For example, several narratives agree in placing the Egyptian victory over the sultan of Aleppo,

---

[24] John of Joinville, *Histoire de Saint Louis*, ed. Natalis de Wailly (Paris, 1872), caps.110–20.

[25] *Annales monasterii de Burton, 1004–1263*, ed. Henry R. Luard in *Annales monastici* (London, 1864–69), 1:368–69; *RRH* no. 1221.

[26] *La Chronique attribuée au Connétable Smbat*, trans. Gérard Dédéyan (Paris, 1980), p. 98 and n. 33; Hayton, *La flor des estoires de la terre d'orient* in *RHC Arm* 2:163–64, 296.

[27] "Eracles," p. 437; *Annales de Terre Sainte*, p. 443; *Anales de Tierra Santa*, p. 361; Marino Sanudo, *Liber*, p. 218.

[28] "Eracles", p. 444; *Annales de Terre Sainte*, p. 449; *Anales de Tierra Santa*, p. 366; Marino Sanudo, *Liber*, p. 221. For the date, Reuven Amitai–Preiss, *Mongols and Mamluks: The Mamluk-Ilkhanid war, 1260–1281* (Cambridge, 1995), p. 26.

[29] *Annales de Terre Sainte*, p. 451; Marino Sanudo, *Liber*, p. 222.

[30] "Eracles," p. 456; *Annales de Terre Sainte*, p. 453; Marino Sanudo, *Liber*, p. 223.

[31] *Annales de Terre Sainte*, p. 455; *Les Gestes des Chiprois*, p. 777; Marino Sanudo, *Liber*, p. 224.

al-Nasir Yusuf, which took place in February 1251, in February 1250.[32] Two annals specify that Bohemond V of Antioch died on 8 January 1251, although the context leaves no doubt that the year 1252 is intended.[33] *L'estoire de Eracles* and Marino Sanudo record the arrival in Acre of Bohemond VI of Antioch, his sister Plaisance and Plaisance's son, King Hugh II of Cyprus, in what proved to be a major turning point in the War of Saint Sabas on 1 February 1257, although here again the context points unmistakeably to 1258.[34] The *Annales de Terre Sainte* and Marino Sanudo indicate that Caesarea fell to Baybars on 26 January 1264. It is clear that they mean 1265 and the town in fact surrendered on 5 March of that year.[35] The *Annales de Terre Sainte* dates the start of the siege of Arsur to 21 March 1264 (1265 n.s.), but it should be noted that other sources simply give the date as 1265.[36] The *Annales de Terre Sainte* also places the battle of Benevento in February 1265, though the context demands that 1266 is understood.[37] Some entries seem to contain anomalies. For example, whereas the annals all begin their entry for 1250 with King Louis's advance in February, they end their entry for the previous year by recording a raid in Palestine led by the lord of Arsur in January.[38] Even the *Gestes des Chiprois*, the narrative that specifies that the year began in March, is inconsistent. On some occasions it appears to begin the year in January—for example when reporting the start of the siege of Arsur in 1265 or the siege of Crac des Chevaliers in 1271—but elsewhere it appears to begin the year in March: for example, the arrival of Bohemond VI in Acre in February 1257 (1258 n.s.), the battle of Benevento in February 1265 (1266 n.s.) or the death of Humphrey of Montfort on 2 February 1283 (1284 n.s.).[39]

    Unlike the other annals, which incorporate the whole date into the text, the author of the text that has been preserved as the *Chronique d'Amadi* recorded only

---

[32] "Eracles," p. 440; *Annales de Terre Sainte*, p. 445; *Anales de Tierra Santa*, p. 363; Marino Sanudo, *Liber*, p. 220. Robert Irwin, *The Middle East in the Middle Ages* (London, 1986), p. 28.

[33] *Annales de Terre Sainte*, p. 445; *Anales de Tierra Santa*, pp. 363–64. "Eracles," p. 440, and Marino Sanudo, *Liber*, p. 220, both give the year as 1251 without specifying the actual date.

[34] "Eracles," p. 443; Marino Sanudo, *Liber*, p. 220. The *Annales de Terre Sainte*, pp. 447–48, gives the date as 1257 without specifying the month. Cf. *Les Gestes des Chiprois*, pp. 743–44. See Jonathan Riley-Smith, *The Feudal Nobility and the Kingdom of Jerusalem, 1174–1277* (London, 1973), pp. 216–17, 313.

[35] *Annales de Terre Sainte*, pp. 451–52; Marino Sanudo, *Liber*, p. 222. *Les Gestes des Chiprois*, p. 758, records this event as occurring in 1265.

[36] *Annales de Terre Sainte*, p. 452. Cf. "Eracles," p. 450; *Les Gestes des Chiprois*, p. 758; Marino Sanudo, *Liber*, p. 222.

[37] *Annales de Terre Sainte*, p. 452. Cf. "Eracles," p. 454; *Les Gestes des Chiprois*, p. 763. Other examples include the death of Archbishop Lociamus of Caesarea in 1266 (1267 n.s.) and the marriage of Haimo Le Strange in 1272 (1273 n.s.). "Eracles," p. 455; *Annales de Terre Sainte*, p. 456.

[38] "Eracles," p. 437; *Annales de Terre Sainte*, p. 443; *Anales de Tierra Santa*, p. 361; Marino Sanudo, *Liber*, p. 218.

[39] *Les Gestes des Chiprois*, pp. 790–91.

the day and the month as part of his narrative account (as in the entry for 1253 quoted in full above), with the year appearing simply in the margin. Even so, he repeated several of the events mentioned in the previous paragraph in such a way as to leave no doubt that he was drawing on common material. But as has been seen, his sources were decidedly wayward when it came to pinpointing when the year began and so provided no coherent guide. None of the annals appears to follow any coherent or consistent pattern. So when the *Amadi* author introduced additional material, such as the date of King Henry I's death, there would be no certainty as to which practice he would follow. He found a report of the king's death in the version of the annals that formed the basis for his history and re-wrote it to include the precise date and some other details which he had obtained from some other source. Accordingly the question whether Henry died in January 1253 or January 1254 cannot be established for certain from internal evidence alone, even if the balance of probability points to 1254.

So if internal arguments from the annals do not admit a satisfactory solution, what about the evidence of other sources? Placing Henry's death in January 1254 would be convenient for various reasons. In the first place, it would solve a chronological problem signalled a number of years ago by Professor Hans Mayer. There is in existence a charter issued by King Henry dated October 1253, several months after the supposed date of his demise.[40] Mayer is confident that the text is authentic and well-preserved, and he proposed that the date had been wrongly transmitted as a result of scribal error, suggesting that it should in fact be attributed to 1252.[41] But if Henry died at the beginning of 1254 the need to assume that a mistake had been made disappears and the integrity of the charter is vindicated. Another problem that redating Henry's death would seem to solve is one originally noted by Louis de Mas Latrie and commented on further by Sir George Hill.[42] Almost immediately after recording Henry's death, *Amadi* reports that Archbishop Hugh Fagiano of Nicosia had previously placed Cyprus under an interdict as a result of a quarrel with the king, and after his death he had returned from overseas and "reconciliò la terra." But papal letters dated 30 March 1254 have Pope Innocent IV assigning the revenues of the diocese of Nicosia to the patriarch of Antioch, something that would have been unthinkable had the archbishop then been resident in his see.[43] Clearly in March 1254 Archbishop Hugh was not yet back in Cyprus, although in July of that year the pope was making alternative provision for the patriarch. The implication could well be that Hugh was now back and the pope's earlier instructions had therefore to be set

---

[40] *Tabulae ordinis Theutonici*, no 105, pp. 84–85; *RRH* no. 1208.

[41] Hans E. Mayer, *Das Siegelwesen in den Kreuzfahrerstaaten* (Munich, 1978), p. 66 n. 192; cf. idem, *Die Kanzlei der lateinischen Könige von Jerusalem*, Schriften der *MGH* 40 (Hanover, 1996), 2:680.

[42] Hill, *History of Cyprus* 3:1057 n. 3.

[43] *Chronique d'Amadi*, p. 202. For the papal letters, Innocent IV, *Registres*, ed. Elie Berger (Paris, 1881–1921), nos. 7393–96.

aside.[44] If indeed Hugh returned to Cyprus soon after Henry's death, having the king die in January 1254 and not 1253 would seem more plausible in the light of the pope's interventions. One of Pope Innocent's letters of 30 March 1254 is addressed to an unnamed king of Cyprus.[45] The pope could, of course, have been addressing the infant heir to the throne, King Hugh II, but that is unlikely, especially as there are no other papal letters addressed to the young king who was die in 1267 without having reached his majority. It would seem more likely that the pope was addressing King Henry and that at the time the papal chancery was unaware of Henry's death ten weeks previously. We have in fact to wait until 18 January 1255 before we find independent evidence, again in a papal letter, that the king was indeed dead.[46]

Amadi's story of Hugh of Fagiano could, if it is accepted at face value, prove decisive. According to *Amadi*, the king and the archbishop had quarrelled; Hugh placed the kingdom under an interdict, and then, on Henry's death returned from overseas and lifted it. In other words, Hugh was absent from Cyprus at the time of Henry's death. As we have just seen, the sequence of papal letters would indicate that Hugh was away from Cyprus in March 1254, but was back by the following July. But there is also evidence to show that he was in Nicosia in June 1253, in which case it is possible that his quarrel with the king and the beginning of his absence from Cyprus only occurred after that date. What is more, this piece of evidence consists of the archbishop issuing an order threatening excommu-nication against any individual "whoever he might be" (*quicumque fuerit ille*) and his accessories who should disrupt divine service.[47] It could be that this order represents a move in an escalating dispute between the king and the archbishop and that Hugh's interdict as recorded by *Amadi* was then imposed when the threat of excommunication proved insufficient. But even if the threatened excommunication had nothing to do with the archbishop's relations with the king, it could still be argued that Hugh absented himself from Cyprus at some point between June 1253 and March 1254 and so was away when the king died — on 18 January 1254.

It is time to draw some conclusions. Having Henry die a year later than is generally supposed is in itself of no particular significance, although it could have implications for our understanding of the politics of a period for which the evidence is comparatively limited. What this discussion does highlight, however, is the need for a far greater analysis of this group of annals, which together constitute a major element in the sources for the history of the Latin East in the middle years of the thirteenth century. Questions such as how they are related to each other and how and when they were composed deserve serious consideration. It is important to know how far the annals were originally composed close to the

---

[44]   Innocent IV, *Registres*, no. 7873.
[45]   Innocent IV, *Registres*, no. 7395.
[46]   *The Cartulary of the Cathedral of Holy Wisdom*, no. 90, p. 177.
[47]   *Cartulary of Nicosia*, no. 29, pp. 115–16.

XV

date of the events themselves and which passages should be seen as later interpolations. Only then can a critical understanding of the material be obtained. Relying on information for these sources without first considering their mode of composition and their general reliability is perilous.

XVI

The De Montforts in the Latin East[1]

It is a well known fact that Simon de Montfort the Elder took the cross as a participant in the Fourth Crusade, but that he left the main expedition, which in 1202 had seized the Adriatic port of Zara in defiance of the papal prohibition, and made his own way to the Holy Land. He was accompanied by his younger brother, Guy. What is less well known is that Guy chose to remain in the East where he married a young widow named Helvis (or Heloise) of Ibelin. Helvis's first husband, Reynald lord of Sidon, had been a man much her senior, and she had born him a son named Balian and two daughters. Her marriage to Guy, which took place in 1204, was equally fruitful: a son named Philip and two more girls. It was only after her death, which occurred some time in the early 1210s, that Guy returned to the West, taking his children with him.[2]

Guy's son, Philip de Montfort, grew to manhood in France, where he married and had children.[3] However, his wife died, and in 1239 he returned to the land of his birth as a participant in the crusade led by Thibaud IV, count of Champagne and king of Navarre. His kinsmen in the East evidently welcomed him with open arms. At that time his elder half-brother, Balian lord of Sidon, was a leading figure in the politics of the kingdom of Jerusalem. His cousins, his mother's nephews, were among the most powerful aristocrats in the East. His mother's brother, John of Ibelin lord of Beirut, had died a few years earlier, but, of John's children, the eldest, another Balian, was lord of Beirut and constable of Cyprus, a second, John, was lord of Arsuf and was soon to become constable of Jerusalem, while two others, Guy and Baldwin, were prominent in the kingdom of Cyprus. Another cousin, the son

---

[1]   Originally published in *Thirteenth Century England* 8, Proceedings of the Durham Conference 1999, eds M. Prestwich, R. Britnell and R. Frame. Woodbridge: Boydell, 2001, pp. 23–31. This essay has been reset with the original page numbers given in square brackets within the text.

Thanks are due to my colleagues Clive Knowles and Helen Nicholson for help on various points.

[2]   For further discussion and references, P.W. Edbury, *John of Ibelin and the Kingdom of Jerusalem* (Woodbridge. 1997), 25.

[3]   A son. also named Philip, had a distinguished career in the West, rising high in the service of Charles of Anjou in Sicily.

A simplified table illustrating the Latin Syrian branch of the de Montfort family

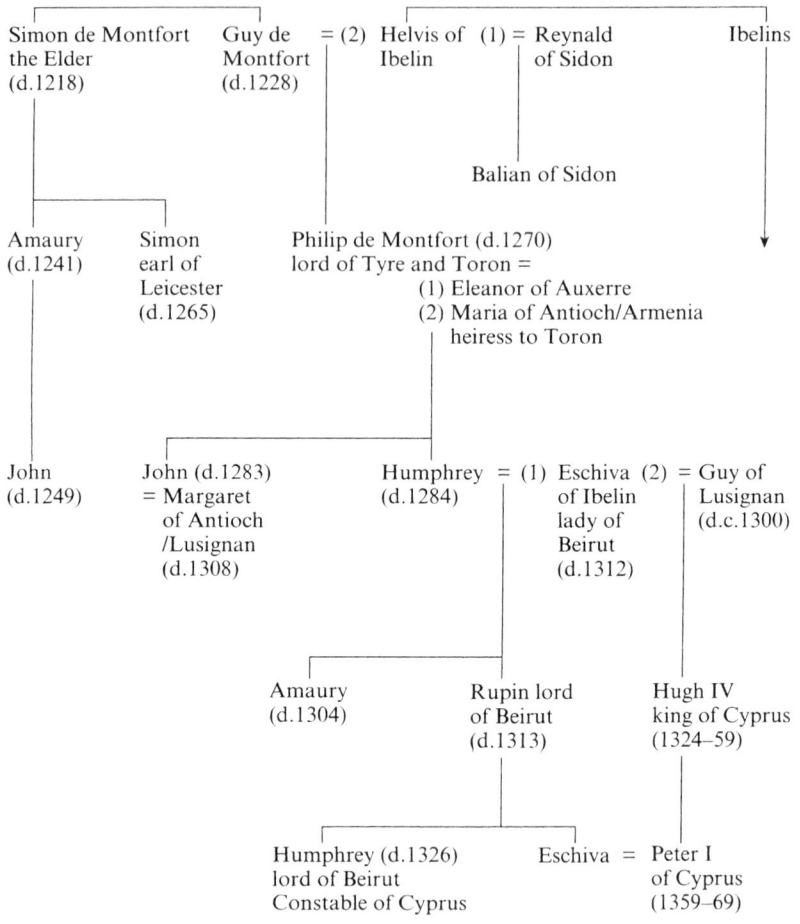

of his mother's other brother, was John, later to become famous as count of Jaffa and author of the celebrated legal treatise. Yet another cousin was lord of Caesarea. All were closely linked by marriage and kinship to the royal dynasties of both Cyprus and Jerusalem.

Philip de Montfort can be seen as a pivotal figure in a wide-ranging kinship-nexus. He was the first cousin of Simon earl of Leicester – their fathers were brothers – and, as is well known, Simon was the king of England's brother-in-law and Simon's wife's sister was married to the emperor Frederick II. On

The De Montforts in the Latin East   3

his mother's side, as has been seen, Philip's cousins were the Ibelins, and through them he was related to most of the leading nobility in the East. What was more, **[24]** the Ibelins had their own links with western nobles. For example, John of Ibelin count of Jaffa's mother had been a member of the Montbéliard family, and this meant he was related to a number of leading families in Champagne and eastern France including the counts of Brienne and the lords of Joinville. John was married to the sister of the king of Cilician Armenia, and his wife's sister was queen of Cyprus.[4]

In 1240, soon after his arrival in the East, Philip married afresh. His new wife was Maria of Armenia, the heiress to the lordship of Toron which lay inland to **[25]** the east of Tyre. Maria's father had had claims to both the kingdom of Cilician Armenia and the principality of Antioch, and Maria also would have had a claim to the crusader lordship of Outrejourdain should ever it pass back into Christian hands. Toron itself, which was in Christian control at this period, was said to be worth 60,000 Saracen bezants. It is not surprising that a man with as many connections as Philip quickly made his presence felt in the politics of the Latin East. By 1240 the Ibelins and their associates, with whom Philip had been quick to identify himself, had for several years been in rebellion against the titular king of Jerusalem, Conrad of Hohenstaufen, and his father, the emperor Frederick II. The Ibelins controlled Acre and much of the rest of the kingdom of Jerusalem while Frederick's officers held Tyre. All attempts at a settlement had proved futile. In 1241 the Ibelin group tried to break the deadlock by proposing that Simon de Montfort earl of Leicester, who himself had been on crusade in the East earlier that same year, should act as Frederick's lieutenant in the East and that bygones should be bygones. The proposal never came to anything, but Philip must surely have had a hand in it.[5] As we have seen, Simon was linked to the emperor by marriage and, through his cousin, to the leading figures in the opposing camp in the East.

The next year, 1242, the Ibelins changed tactics and with Venetian assistance seized control of Tyre from the Hohenstaufen officers in a swiftly executed military action. The legality of this move was decidedly questionable, although the Ibelins' apologists did their best to pretend otherwise. They now had to decide what to do with their prize. Tyre was a city in the royal domain, and provision had to be made for its defence and day-to-day administration. They were reluctant to hand it over to the nominal regent, Alice of Champagne, lest she and her husband became too powerful. Instead it first passed into the

---

4   See Edbury, *John of Ibelin*, 62–7.
5   See ibid., 67–9.

hands of Philip's cousin, Balian of Ibelin lord of Beirut, and then, in 1246, the new Ibelin-backed regent, King Henry I of Cyprus, gave custody of it to Philip. Contemporaries were well aware that Philip had no permanent legal title to Tyre. In theory he was guarding it at the behest of the regent until a king of Jerusalem should come to take over, but in practice he treated it as his own and before long took to styling himself 'lord of Tyre and Toron'.[6]

Philip had become one of the most powerful men in the East. Together with his kinsmen he was a member of the ruling clique that dominated the kingdom of Jerusalem. After his acquisition of Tyre all went well for a number of years, although in 1250 he was to share captivity with St Louis during his Egyptian campaign. The turning point, as I have argued elsewhere, came in 1258 when he broke with his relatives over the War of St Sabas. In the first instance this was a war between Venice and Genoa, although it was largely fought in the East. Philip aligned himself closely with the Genoese and took advantage of the fighting to expel the Venetians from Tyre. In Acre, however, Venetian victories resulted in the Ibelin-dominated regime, which initially had favoured Genoa, turning against the Genoese, and they were to lead ultimately to the end of the Ibelin dominance which had obtained since the early 1230s. After 1258, and until Philip's death in 1270, Venetian Acre faced Genoese Tyre.[7] **[26]**

In 1268 there was. for the first time since the 1220s, a resident king of Jerusalem in the East. The execution of Conradin of Hohenstaufen after Tagliacozzo meant the end of the absentee Hohenstaufen monarchy, and King Hugh III of Cyprus came forward to claim the throne as the representative of a cadet branch of the royal house. The question of Philip's title to Tyre would now inevitably arise. Hugh was, however, in too weak a position to expel Philip, and indeed he needed Philip's support to consolidate his own rule and stage an effective resistance to the Muslims who in the previous years had been making major gains at the expense of the Christians. Soon after Hugh's accession, Hugh and Philip came to an agreement. Indeed, it may be that it was Philip who took the initiative and that, even before Hugh became king, there were plans afoot for Philip's son John to marry Hugh's sister Margaret. Be that as it may, John now wedded Margaret, and the king formally enfeoffed John with the lordship of Tyre to be held by him and his descendants by his new wife. For his part Philip agreed to hand control of Tyre to his son.[8] Philip was then in his sixties and had outlived his kinsmen in his own generation. In

---

[6]   See ibid., 70–75, 79.

[7]   See ibid., 91–4.

[8]   P.W. Edbury, *The Kingdom of Cyprus and the Crusades* (Cambridge, 1991), 91.

1270 he died, stabbed by an Assassin who was allegedly acting at the behest of the Mamluk sultan, Baybars.[9]

John de Montfort, lord of Tyre and Toron and brother-in-law of King Hugh III of Cyprus and Jerusalem, clearly outclassed all the other nobles of his day in what was by now the rapidly dwindling kingdom of Jerusalem. Like his father he issued his own coins[10] and.made his own truces with the Muslims. In 1277 Hugh's government in Acre collapsed, and Acre itself was taken over by the representatives of his rival in the East, Charles of Anjou, king of Sicily. If Hugh was to stage a recovery he would need John's help, but, although John gave him loyal support, the Angevins remained ensconced in Acre for the rest of Hugh's life. John died towards the end of 1283. His marriage had been childless, and by the terms of the settlement agreed between Hugh and his father Tyre should have escheated to the king. But a further clause agreed in 1268 had laid down that in the event of an escheat the de Montfort family was to be indemnified to the tune of 150,000 Saracen bezants for its expenses in fortifying and guarding Tyre. There was no way that Hugh could produce this sum, and he came to an agreement with John's younger brother and next of kin, Humphrey, to the effect that Humphrey should have control of Tyre until Hugh paid up, and if Hugh had not paid by the following May he should hold Tyre permanently. In fact Hugh and Humphrey de Montfort both died before the May deadline arrived. It would seem that the de Montfort rights to Tyre thereupon lapsed (or. possibly, that Hugh's heirs paid the indemnity). By the late 1280s Tyre had been granted to the new king of Cyprus's younger brother as his appanage.[11]

In about 1274 Humphrey de Montfort had married Eschiva of Ibelin, the younger sister of Isabella, lady of Beirut.[12] Isabella had died childless in the **[27]** early 1280s leaving Eschiva as her heiress. So Humphrey, in the brief period between the death of his brother John in 1283 and his own death a few months later would have held both Tyre and, through his wife, Beirut. His descendants, Rupin, named presumably after his Cilician Armenian great grandfather, and Rupin's son Humphrey, inherited the title 'lord of Beirut' and employed it until the line died out in the second quarter of the fourteenth

---

[9]   'Gestes des Chiprois', *Rented des historiens des croisades. Documents arméniens*, 2 vols (Paris, 1869 –1906), ii, 775–7.

[10]   D.M. Metcalf, *Coinage of the Crusades and the Latin East in the Ashmolean Museum Oxford* (London. 2nd edn. 1995), 96.

[11]   Edbury, *The Kingdom of Cyprus*, 96, 98.

[12]   W.H. Rudt de Collenberg. 'Les dispenses matrimoniales accordées a l'Orient latin selon les registres du Vatican d'Honorius III a Clement VII (1223–1385)', *Melanges de l'Ecole francaise de Rome* 91 (1979), no. 12.

century. From 1291 Beirut itself was in Muslim hands, and henceforth the family resided in Cyprus where they held the town of Lapithos.[13] Humphrey's widow, Eschiva of Beirut, subsequently married Guy of Lusignan, a younger son of King Hugh III,[14] and, although it would not have been anticipated at the time, it was their son, another Hugh, who eventually mounted the throne of Cyprus as King Hugh IV (1324–59). The close ties between the de Montforts and the Cypriot Lusignans were thus reinforced.

On Humphrey's death in 1326 the family failed in the male line. Only Humphrey's sister, Eschiva, remained. In 1339 Pope Benedict XII turned down a request for a dispensation for her to marry her cousin, the future King Peter I of Cyprus. The papacy was reluctant to sanction the marriage of first cousins, and in this case the age difference between them was cited as an additional reason: Eschiva would have been born in about 1310, while Peter was not yet of age and was about twenty years her junior, having been born as recently as 1328. But in 1342 the new pope, Clement VI, agreed to grant a dispensation. He did so at the instance of Cardinal Jean de Comminges, Eschiva's second cousin.[15] It is unfortunate that there is no evidence for what happened next, and so whether the marriage actually took place is unknown: certainly there were no children. In 1339 Peter had been the king's second son, and it looks as if his father was trying to provide for him at no expense to himself by marrying him to a wealthy heiress. However, in 1343, not long after the dispensation was granted, his elder half-brother died and so Peter was now in line for the royal succession. In due course he married a foreign princess. We do not know whether Eschiva was discarded or simply passed away. She simply disappears from our sources.

The genealogy of this branch of the de Montfort family has a certain intrinsic interest. For a hundred years, from 1239 until 1342, and through four generations the de Montforts had been among the wealthiest and most prominent nobles in the kingdoms of Jerusalem and Cyprus, first in Syria as lords of Tyre and Toron and then in Cyprus as titular lords of Beirut. We know more about them than space allows, although not a huge amount. Philip de Montfort, Simon earl of Leicester's first cousin, is the one who emerges

---

[13] 'Gestes de Chiprois', pp. 790–91, 856–7; 'Chronique d'Amadi', in *Chroniques d'Amadi et de Strambaldi*. ed. R. de Mas Latrie (Paris, 1891–93), 1, 267, 294–8, 354, 357, 361, 362, 384, 395, 403. Rupin testified in the Templar trial in Cyprus. K. Schottmüller, *Der Untergang des Templer-Ordens* (Berlin. 1887), 2, 158.

[14] W.H. Rudt de Collenberg, 'Les Lusignan de Chypre', *Epeteris* 10 (1979/1980), 113–14.

[15] Rudt de Collenberg, 'Les Lusignan', 127–8.

most clearly from our sources, and there can be no doubt that he shared his cousin's abilities and ambition. What he made of his cousin's demise is not recorded, but there does survive from the Latin East an account of the Barons' War in England written by someone who was for a time in the late 1260s in the service **[28]** of Philip's son, John de Montfort (an English translation follows as an appendix). The *Gestes des Chiprois,* as it is known, is a composite narrative in French which survives in a single medieval manuscript copied in Cyprus in the 1340s. It is much used by historians of the Latin East. The section covering the second half of the thirteenth century is by an anonymous author, who has been misleadingly dubbed the 'Templar of Tyre'.[16] He was writing in Cyprus apparently in the second decade of the fourteenth century. He was not a Templar, but he does appear to have been in the employ of the Templar master, William of Beaujeu, in Acre in the 1270s and 1280s. More importantly from our point of view he explicitly tells us that he had been a member of Margaret of Antioch/Lusignan's entourage at the time of her marriage to John de Montfort in 1268 and served her for a year after the marriage.[17] He was clearly well informed about the Latin Syrian branch of the family, and his history is a major source of information for it.

In drawing attention to this account of the Barons War, I am not suggesting for one moment that it provides any new information about the events in England between 1258 and 1265 or that the author was well informed. What it does is to tell us is what an intelligent man at the opposite extremity of Latin Christendom was prepared to believe or wanted his readers to believe. There are a number of points that are perhaps of interest, and it might be worth asking whether any of the elements that are clearly fanciful or erroneous turn up elsewhere. There are silly mistakes – Simon de Montfort, for example, is said to be earl of Gloucester – and it is odd that, although the author refuses to name the principal battles (Lewes and Evesham), he does state – wrongly – that Henry III rounded up the rebels when he was at Salisbury. Perhaps it is significant that the author avoids mentioning the fact that the prime object of the original complaint was the acquisitiveness of the Lusignans, the western cousins of the Cypriot royal house which included his own mistress, Margaret of Antioch/Lusignan. A possible source of information was the entourage of the Lord Edward who was in the East in 1271–72, and it could be that the romanticised account of his escape from captivity reflects stories put

---

[16]   There are two editions, one edited by G. Raynaud (1887), and the other (cited here) by G. Paris, L. de Mas Latrie and C. Kohler in *Recueil des historiens des croisades. Documents arméniens,* ii. A new edition by L. Minervini and a translation into English by P. Crawford are currently in preparation.

[17]   'Gestes', 774. See pp. ccxl–ccxlvi.

about at that time. But there is much else that seems to betray a Montfortian slant: Simon's initial refusal to get involved in a dispute that was primarily about royal patronage; the importance to Simon of his oath; Edward's ruse with the banners; the personal accolade afforded Simon – 'he was a worthy knight, bold and courageous'; the story of his capture and execution and the attempt to make it appear he had died in battle; then the use of this story to explain the vendetta which culminated in the murder of Henry of Almain; the assertion that many of the Montfortians were put to death or died in prison after Evesham. Much of this is factually wrong – for example, Henry of Almain was not at Evesham but still held in custody at the time, and so that part of the story is demonstrably false – but the message is clearly exculpatory with Simon portrayed as the victim of the dispute rather than as its cause. It is the product **[29]** of a man who consistently held the Latin Syrian branch of the de Montfort family in high regard.

One last footnote: John de Montfort, the son of Earl Simon's elder brother Amaury and grandson of Simon the Elder, was a member of St Louis's crusade which wintered in Cyprus in 1248/9 before embarking on the disastrous Egyptian campaign. But he never reached Egypt, for in 1249, while the expedition was still on the island, he died and was buried at Nicosia. By the fifteenth century his tomb had become a centre for pilgrimage, and he was reverenced as a saint and miracle-worker.[18]

Appendix

An Account of the Barons' War Written in Cyprus

(from 'Les Gestes des Chiprois', in *Recueil des historiens des croisades. Documents arméniens*, 2, 759–62)

§329 In this same year (1265) it happened that an important man named Simon de Montfort, who was in England and who had the king of England's sister as wife by whom he had several children and who was earl of Gloucester, had a great war with the king of England as I shall now describe for you.

---

[18]   G. Grivaud, *Excerpta Cypria Nova, voyageurs occidentaux à Chypre au XVème siècle* (Nicosia, 1990), 25, 86, 90, 100, 119, 129; N. Coureas, *The Latin Church in Cyprus, 1195–1312* (Aldershot, 1997), 197, 206.

§330 It happened that this king of England had nothing that he did not give away. Often there came to him foreign people from various provinces whom he received and favoured in all things. Even though he could do all this as lord, all the same most of the knights of England were greatly angered, and they discussed it among themselves and in the end they came to the king and told him politely that he should no longer welcome foreign people into the land. Because they had made their request in such a friendly manner and had shown him by many arguments that it was both to his advantage and to that of the land, the king agreed to their petitions and promised in the presence of them all that he would no longer give fiefs nor land to anyone in the world except with the agreement of his men. He sent for Earl Simon de Montfort and wanted him to be head of his men in this affair. But he made many excuses; he did not want this role and greatly discouraged the king until the king forced him to agree to it and swear on the gospels. Earl Simon then said that he would take care not to go against his oath since [the king] had made him swear. This had happened a good while previously, and when it was far in the past the king failed to keep his promises to his men. So it happened that the knights asked Earl Simon de Montfort to be their leader in this crisis in accord with the oath that he had made, and because of his oath to come to the aid of the knights of England. When the king of England got to hear of it, they – he and his brother, Earl Richard who was called king of Germany, and a son of his who was named Edward and who was by now grown up and was a big, fine-looking knight – took counsel together to seize hold of the earl of Montfort and some other earls **[30]** and vavassors, and then others would come out on top. But before they could put their scheme into operation, Earl Simon de Montfort and the others departed and left the city where the king was and raised a host against him. On seeing them coming against him, the king went out to meet them with such few men as he could muster. But the earl's men comprised a large enough force, and the battle did not last very long. In the end the king and his supporters were defeated, and a number died on both sides. The king was taken prisoner and so was his son, the Lord Edward, and the king's brother, Richard known as the king of Germany, and some other knights. Many escaped the battle, and they held and maintained the king's castles and fortresses.

§331 So the king of England and his son, the Lord Edward, were in the prison of Earl Simon de Montfort of Gloucester, and because they were very closely related to the countess, Earl Simon's wife, they were in a spacious prison and not held under harsh conditions. The Lord Edward, who was a young knight, went riding every day with the earl. And when the Lord Edward saw that the earl trusted him, he arranged to obtain a strong, speedy and robust horse, and he who got it presented it to him. Once he had possession of this horse and had ridden it and had proved its worth, he ordered his men – the knights of his party to come to a particular place near the castle where he was and when they got there to tell him immediately and to remain there all night. They did just as he had instructed, and there were 300 knights armed and well mounted on their horses but without any other retinue. They spent the night in that place and immediately they let the Lord Edward know using a servant and by prearranged signals.

§332 When it was dawn Earl Simon de Montfort rode out as usual, and the Lord Edward, mounted on this horse of his, was with him. He started galloping off to the right and to the left, all the time getting further away from the road taken by the earl. When he was a good distance away he set off at speed, saying 'Farewell earl of Montfort!', and went to the place where the knights were lying in wait. They immediately sallied forth and received him. The earl and his people went after him but could not catch up with him, and, when they saw the knights issue from their embuscarde, they turned back. They took the Lord Edward away, and so he was freed as you have heard.

§333 The Lord Edward assembled as many men, both horse and foot, as he could and went against Simon de Montfort. When he was near he sent a few people on horseback ahead carrying banners with the de Montfort arms.

§334 Earl Simon had told his two sons, who were in another castle, how the Lord Edward had escaped from his prison and how he was assembling many men to come against him and ordered them to come to his aid. Because of this, when Earl Simon saw the approach of the Lord Edward's people bearing the de Montfort banners, he went out to meet them, and, although he and his men went out armed, they were in no sort of order as they had taken no precaution against this ruse. If he had gone out in military formation it would not have gone ill for him, for he was a worthy knight, bold and courageous. So it happened that when he was outside with only some of his men, he found himself deceived as you have heard. For the Lord Edward's men who were leading the way threw the de Montfort banners on the ground and, raising the arms of the Lord Edward, attacked Earl Simon de Montfort and his men. So battle was joined, and the Lord Edward came up after and rushed into the fray. **[31]**

The battle was very bitter and many men were killed on each side. In the end Earl Simon de Montfort was defeated, he and his men, and the earl was taken alive. Once he had come from the battle, the Lord Edward sought counsel from his cousin who was named Henry of Almain and who was also cousin to Earl Simon's children, the children of two sisters, as to what he should do to Earl Simon. The Lord Henry advised him that if he wanted peace and an end to the war, he should cut off Earl Simon's head and have it said that he was killed in the battle since it would have been regarded as shameful to have killed him after he had been captured. So that night the Lord Edward, on the advice of the Lord Henry of Almain, had Earl Simon de Montfort's head cut off and had him thrown on the field among the other dead bodies. You should know that in the battle many knights and other men of whom some were earls and barons were killed. The land was greatly weakened in consequence.

§335 After this mortal battle all those belonging to Earl Simon de Montfort's party were very downcast and bereft of further hope. They freed the king of England, his brother, the king of Germany, and the others who were in prison.

§336 When the king was in Salisbury (*Salibiere*), he seized his adversaries. Some he killed. Many other he held in prison where they died of hunger, disease or distress.

§337 Now I shall tell you what happened after this war. This nobleman, the Lord Henry of Almain, came to a town named Viterbo on his way to Rome to be made emperor of Germany. There, in a church in Viterbo, he was hearing mass. Guy de Montfort, the son of Earl Simon de Montfort of whom I have told you, came to Viterbo and entered the chapel and struck Henry of Almain right through his body with a staff in revenge because he had counselled his father's execution as you have heard. Then he left and went to Tuscany.

§338 This Guy de Montfort had as wife the daughter of Count Rosso of Tuscany (Rosso Aldobrandini), and he had brought with him fifty of his lord's knights and other mounted men to do this deed. The pope excommunicated him for a while, and then he was absolved. You should know that this Henry of Almain was his cousin – they were the children of two sisters as I have told you before. But now I shall stop telling you about this and tell you about another event.

The Arrest of the Templars in Cyprus

At the beginning of June 1308, the Templars who were living on Cyprus were placed under arrest. Modern scholarly descriptions of this episode all rely heavily on just one narrative source, the so-called *Chronique d'Amadi*.[1] This is an anonymous work which provides what I believe is by far the most detailed account of the arrest of members of the order anywhere in Latin Christendom, and so, before turning to the events themselves, some explanation of its nature and provenance is called for.

Amadi, as it is usually referred to for sake of convenience, is written in Italian and survives in a single manuscript dating from the mid-sixteenth century. This manuscript belonged to a Venetian bibliophile named Francesco Amadi – hence the name – and is now in the Marciana Library. It comprises a compilation spanning the history of the crusades and Lusignan rule in Cyprus from the First Crusade to the year 1442. Almost all the material in the sections covering the period before the middle of the first decade of the fourteenth century can be readily identified as having been drawn from extant sources: the Old French translation of William of Tyre and its continuations,[2] a version of the *Annales de Terre Sainte*,[3] Philip of Novara's account of the civil war between the Ibelins and the adherents of Frederick II (1220s–1242), and the narrative conventionally, if misleadingly, attributed to the

---

[1] 'La Chronique d'Amadi', in *Chroniques d'Amadi et de Strambaldi*, ed. René de Mas Latrie, 2 vols (Paris, 1891–93; repr. Nicosia, 1999), vol. 1, pp. 280, 283–91. For modern accounts, George Hill, *A History of Cyprus*, 4 vols (Cambridge, 1940–52), vol. 2, pp. 232–6; Peter W. Edbury, *The Kingdom of Cyprus and the Crusades, 1191–1374* (Cambridge, 1991), p. 121; Nicholas Coureas, *The Latin Church in Cyprus, 1195–1312* (Aldershot, 1997), pp. 139–40; Pierre-Vincent Claverie, *L'ordre du Temple en Terre Sainte et à Chypre au XIIIe siècle*, 3 vols (Nicosia, 2005), vol. 2, pp. 273–8; Malcolm Barber, *The Trial of the Templars*, 2nd edn (Cambridge, 2006), pp. 252–4.

[2] The *Amadi* compiler used the 'Colbert-Fontainebleau' version of the Old French Continuation of William of Tyre, which is to be found in only two of the 45 surviving manuscripts of that work. This is the main text edited in RHC Oc 2.

[3] Scattered through the material drawn from the 'Annales de Terre Sainte' are a few entries of Cypriot interest not found in the earlier versions. Two French texts of the *Annales de Terre Sainte* have long been known (Reinhold Röhricht and Gaston Raynaud, eds, *AOL*, 2 (1884), documents, pp. 427–61). For a third French text, see 'A New Text of the Annales de Terre Sainte', ed. Peter W. Edbury, in *In Laudem Hierosolymitani: Studies in Crusades and Medieval Culture in Honour of Benjamin Z. Kedar*, ed. Iris Shagrir, Ronnie Ellenblum and Jonathan Riley-Smith, (Aldershot, 2007), pp. 145–61.

'Templar of Tyre'.[4] All these earlier narratives were written in French, and so *Amadi* represents a translation into Italian.

When we come to the early fourteenth century, we find that *Amadi* has a detailed narrative of the events surrounding the period in which the lord of Tyre, Amaury of Lusignan, held power. In 1306, Amaury, the brother and heir-presumptive of the ill and incompetent King Henry II of Cyprus, assumed control of the kingdom. Henry was suspended from office in a *coup d'état* which at least initially commanded wide support. Amaury held power until 1310 when he was assassinated. The king then returned to power, and a number of his brother's adherents were imprisoned, never to regain their liberty. The events of the years 1306–10 occupy 150 pages in the published edition of *Amadi*. By comparison, the section dealing with the years 1218–42, the material drawn from Philip of Novara's well-known account of the civil war in Cyprus, fills only 80 pages, whilst the thirty-five-year reign of King Hugh IV (1324–59) is dismissed in a mere eight pages. There can be no doubt that the 1306–10 narrative, which was evidently written by a partisan of King Henry, was composed within a few years of the events themselves and, like the earlier materials, was originally written in French. But in this instance the French version has not survived. Besides giving a detailed description of the politics of the period, it contains an invaluable account of the start of the Hospitaller conquest of Rhodes,[5] as well as of the arrest of the Templars. *Amadi*, however, makes no mention of the formal interrogation of the Templars arrested in Cyprus or of the non-Templar witnesses who were called to give evidence, and for these the historian must consult the records preserved in the papal archives.[6]

There are, however, important questions relating to the *Chronique d'Amadi* that have not been sufficiently addressed. Did the translator also assemble the compilation, or did the work previously exist in its entirety in French? An answer to that question might help decide further questions about the relationship of *Amadi* to two other important narratives for medieval Cypriot history: those by Leontios

---

[4]   Philip of Novara's history is edited as Filippo da Novara, *Guerra di Federico II in Oriente (1223–1242)*, ed. and trans. Silvio Melani (Naples, 1994). The *Amadi* compiler evidently used a text of Philip of Novara's narrative that differed at certain points from the extant French version, and the apparatus to Melani's edition indicates points at which the texts diverge. For the 'Templar of Tyre', see *Cronaca del Templare di Tiro (1243–1314)*, ed. and trans. Laura Minervini (Naples, 2000); English translation: *The 'Templar of Tyre': Part III of the 'Deeds of the Cypriots'*, trans. Paul Crawford (Aldershot, 2003). Whereas *Amadi* contains a full translation of Philip's text, the material from the 'Templar of Tyre' is often summarized, and, as there appears to be little or no use of the latter for the period from 1242, where Philip ends, to the late 1260s, it is quite possible that the compiler was not working from a text such as the *Gestes des Chiprois* in which Philip of Novara and the 'Templar of Tyre' are juxtaposed, but knew of them separately.

[5]   'Chronique d'Amadi', pp. 254–9.

[6]   For the trial of the Templars in Cyprus see *UT*, vol. 2, pp. 147–400; *The Trial of the Templars in Cyprus: A Complete English Edition*, ed. and trans. Anne Gilmour-Bryson (Leiden, 1998); Barber, *Trial*, pp. 254–8.

Makhairas and Florio Bustron. Bustron was working in the sixteenth century;[7] the Italian of his *Historia overo Commentarii de Cipro* is far more literary than *Amadi*'s and the content more sophisticated; whereas we can certainly rule out the possibility that *Amadi* derived his material from Bustron, it is not clear whether Bustron utilized *Amadi*'s Italian text or a putative lost French original. The relationship of *Amadi* and Leontios Makhairas's Greek-language *Recital Concerning the Sweet Land of Cyprus* is even more problematic. There is no doubt that their narratives from the second half of the fourteenth century onwards are textually related. But precisely how awaits elucidation, as does the question of how much of the work that goes under his name was actually originated by Leontios. Then again there is the problem of precisely when and where the *Amadi* compiler was at work...[8] But rather than pursue these matters, we should return to our story.

As is well known, King Philip IV had ordered the arrest of the Templars in France on 13 October 1307, and on 22 November Pope Clement V, in what is generally seen as an attempt to wrest the initiative away from Philip, issued the bull *Pastoralis praeeminentiae* in which he instructed the European monarchs to arrest the Templars within their respective kingdoms and take control of their lands in the name of the papacy. In this letter the kings were informed that the pope had himself heard from a Templar knight that, at his reception into the order in Cyprus which had taken place in the presence of the master, Jacques de Molay, and 200 brothers, half of whom had been of knightly rank, he had been obliged to deny Christ.[9] Presumably, however, as a result of the closing of the sea routes to the east with the onset of winter, *Pastoralis praeeminentiae* did not arrive in Cyprus until the following May.

By then Amaury of Tyre had been in power for two years. According to *Amadi*, the popularity of his rule among the nobility was now beginning to show the first signs of crumbling, although our author also insists that, since his seizure of power, the Templars had consistently given him their backing. Thus *Amadi* records Jacques de Molay loaning Amaury 50,000 bezants in 1306 at the beginning of his

---

[7] Florio Bustrone, 'Historia overo Commentarii de Cipro', ed. René de Mas Latrie as 'Chronique de l'île de Chypre', *Collection de documents inédits sur l'histoire de France: Mélanges historiques*, 5 (1886), pp. 1–531 (repr. Nicosia, 1998).

[8] Gilles Grivaud believes that *Amadi* was composed around the middle of the sixteenth century and has offered the hypothesis that the author may have been a Cypriot nobleman named Hector Podocataro. From the evidence he adduces, it seems likely that the Podocataro family owned a copy of *Amadi*, but beyond that it is difficult to go: Gilles Grivaud, 'Ο πνευματικός βίος και η γραμματολογία κατά την περίοδο της Φραγκοκρατίας', in Ιστορία της Κύπρου, ed. Theodore Papadopoulos, vol. 5 (Nicosia, 1996), pp. 881, 1147–53.

[9] Pierre Dupuy, *Traittez concernant l'histoire de France: Sçavoir la condemnation des Templiers avec quelques actes* (Paris, 1654; repr. Paris, 1978), fols 189r–190v (for the version sent to the future King Robert of Naples); *Foedera, conventiones, litterae et acta publica*, ed. Thomas Rymer et al., new edn, 4 vols in 7 parts (London, 1816–69), vol. 2.1, cols 16–17 (for the version sent to Edward II of England).

rule, and the author notes that Jacques then helped in negotiations to determine the financial provision needed to support the now suspended King Henry. By the early months of 1308 relations between Amaury and his brother had reached a new low, and we hear of the marshal of the Temple, Aymon (or Ayme) d'Oiselay, taking an active part in Amaury's efforts to separate Henry from those nobles, knights and servants who had remained loyal to him and to force the king to designate Amaury as governor of Cyprus for life.[10]

In the late spring of 1307, in a bid to shore up his support by gaining papal endorsement for his rule and counter allegations he feared were being made to the pope by envoys from King Henry, Amaury had sent Het'um, lord of Gorhigos, who was both a member of the Cilician Armenian royal family and a canon of the Cypriot Praemonstratensian monastery at Bellapaïs near Kerynia, to the papal *curia*. Protracted negotiations, however, failed to persuade Pope Clement to give Amaury the backing for which he had hoped. Het'um returned in May 1308 to report his lack of success and brought with him the papal instructions for the arrest of the Templars.[11]

It is at this point that the *Amadi* narrative comes to the fore. But before embarking on a detailed account of the circumstances of the arrest in late May and early June 1308, the author provides a close paraphrase of a passage to be found in the narrative by the 'Templar of Tyre' summarizing events in France from the arrest of the Templars there until the suppression of the order five years later. In this section, he repeats this earlier author's scepticism about the validity of the charges and the Templar guilt.[12] The 'Templar of Tyre', however, has nothing of what follows.[13]

According to *Amadi*, on 12 May, Amaury, in execution of the papal mandate, sent Balian of Ibelin, prince of Galilee and one of his most prominent supporters, to the Templar headquarters at Limassol. The message was that the Templars should surrender their arms and horses and accept confinement in the archbishop's house at Nicosia. Clearly the authorities were reluctant to use force and were hoping that a peaceful surrender could be effected. The senior Templar officer in Cyprus was the marshal, Aymon d'Oiselay,[14] and he attempted to negotiate, offering to allow himself and the other members of the order in Cyprus to be held under guard on one of their rural estates while refusing to relinquish control of either their arms or their treasure. But if the Templars imagined that Amaury would be satisfied with a pretence of taking them into custody, they were mistaken. On 19 May, Amaury

---

[10]   'Chronique d'Amadi', pp. 248, 251, 260–61, 262, 266.

[11]   Edbury, *Kingdom of Cyprus*, pp. 118–21.

[12]   'Chronique d'Amadi', pp. 280–82; cf. *Cronaca del Templare di Tiro*, pp. 340–43.

[13]   The unique manuscript of the 'Templar of Tyre' is mutilated at the end, breaking off just four paragraphs further on in the middle of a description of the events that date to 1309. Florio Bustron (pp. 164–70) provides a parallel and self-evidently derivative account.

[14]   *Amadi* normally gives his name as 'Heme d'Ussellet' or similar.

issued orders that no-one was to receive a salary from the Templars or to pay a salary on behalf of the order, and anyone who had received payment from the order should keep it and be quit of any further obligation. At the same time he sent a canon of Nicosia cathedral named Baldwin to the Templars at Limassol with the message that they should come at his command and submit themselves to the judgment of the Church; if they refused he would come and arrest them by force, and any who resisted would be killed. This time they replied that they would submit in four months time, in other words in September, and in the meantime the lord of Tyre should send a galley to the pope for further instructions which they would then obey.[15]

Amaury then sent a canon of Limassol cathedral named Andrea Tartaro,[16] who encountered Aymon d'Oiselay and the Templar turcopolier[17] at the village of Nissou which lay on the main road south from Nicosia. It was there that on 24 May talks were held with a group consisting of Aimery of Lusignan, who was the constable of Cyprus and Amaury's younger brother, Balian of Galilee, Baldwin the canon of Nicosia and Raymond Viscount, the owner of Nissou. After lengthy discussions Aimery and Balian returned to Nicosia to get Amaury to agree to the deal they had negotiated. The upshot was that on 27 May the Templars arrived in Nicosia under a promise of safe conduct. Amaury summoned a large assembly of knights and clergy, and a notary read a statement on behalf of the Templars in which they made an orthodox profession of faith. Baldwin the canon then translated it into French for the benefit of the people and made a statement to the effect that the Templars were good Christians who believed what they had professed; he added that they had in the past shown themselves ready to die in defence of the Christian religion and that they had fought alongside the kings of Jerusalem and the crusaders from the west against the Muslims, mentioning in particular the events at Safed. (Safed had fallen as long ago as 1266, and the Templars in the garrison, who seem to have been tricked into believing that they were surrendering on terms, preferred to die rather than be forced into apostasy.[18]) Then the senior Templar officers who were present, the marshal, the commander of Cyprus, the draper and the treasurer,[19]

---

[15]   'Chronique d'Amadi', pp. 283–5.

[16]   *Amadi* states that Andrea was a canon of Famagusta, but documents of the period show that he was a canon of Limassol. *Notai genovesi in oltremare atti roggati a Cipro da Lamberto di Sambuceto*, ed. Romeo Pavoni (Genoa, 1987), no. 158 (1302); *Notai genovesi in oltremare atti roggati a Cipro*, ed. Michel Balard (Genoa, 1984), pp. 312–13 (nos 25–7) (1309).

[17]   Bartholomew of Gordo: see *Trial in Cyprus*, ed. Gilmour-Bryson, pp. 118–19 and n. 241.

[18]   The memory of this incident was subsequently recalled by two of the lay witnesses who participated in the Templar trial in Cyprus: *Trial in Cyprus*, ed. Gilmour-Bryson, pp. 71, 422–3.

[19]   The commander of Cyprus, Raimbaud de Caromb, had been arrested in France. The man referred to here was James of 'Doumanin' or 'Doymalin' who appears to have

254

together with a brother knight from each *langue* and two Templar sergeants swore their adherence to these statements both on their own behalf and on behalf of all the other members of the order in Cyprus. These were said by *Amadi* to total 83 knights and 35 sergeants. But while all this was happening, Amaury had secretly ordered a force comprising knights, other mounted men, infantry and marines to move from Famagusta to occupy Limassol. The following day (28 May), Amaury again convened an assembly of clergy, knights and burgesses and had the papal letters read out, specifying that he should confine the Templars and take possession of their treasure and movable goods because, on the basis of the examination of the Templars that the king of France had already made within his own kingdom, they had been found to be heretics.[20]

On 29 May, Amaury ordered the viscount of Nicosia to take a force of knights, together with the Hospitaller prior and members of the Franciscan and Dominican orders who were presumably needed as witnesses to what would ensue, to make an inventory and seal everything in the Templar house in Nicosia including the silver and gold vessels and the treasure. There was, so we are told, not much there because the Templars had had most of their valuables secretly taken to their Limassol headquarters. Although *Amadi* does not say so explicitly, it would seem that this act was in contravention of the agreement that had been hammered out at Nissou. Aymon d'Oiselay was very upset and immediately returned with his whole company to Limassol, leaving only the commander of Cyprus and another knight and three sergeants who followed shortly afterwards.[21] The viscount and his companions made a thorough inventory of the contents of the Templar church in Nicosia, which they then closed, even going to the trouble of removing the bell rope so that the bell could not be rung. Amaury ordered similar inventories to be made at the Templar houses in Paphos and Famagusta and in all their rural estates.[22]

The closing of the Templar church in Nicosia led King Henry to reprove the men of religion who had consented to it; although he was suspended from power, he ordered that it be re-opened, on the grounds that there was an endowment there that stipulated that two chaplains should say mass for his ancestor and namesake, King Henry I.[23] We thus have the paradoxical situation in which Amaury, who had enjoyed the support of the Templars, was acting against them, while the king, whose relations with the order had been poor for much of his reign, was apparently making

been acting in his absence; the draper was John of 'Villa' or 'Vilaers': Claverie, *L'ordre du Temple*, vol. 2, p. 254; *Trial in Cyprus*, ed. Gilmour-Bryson, pp. 117, 139 and nn. 238, 343.

[20]   Clearly a description of *Pastoralis praeeminentiae*: 'Chronique d'Amadi', pp. 285–7.

[21]   The knight is named as 'Piero Cadel', but in the trial documents Peter 'Cadelli' is described as a sergeant: *Trial in Cyprus*, ed. Gilmour-Bryson, pp. 140, 367.

[22]   'Chronique d'Amadi', pp. 287–8.

[23]   Although *Amadi* does not say so here, he had previously (p. 202, s.a. 1253) reported that Henry I was buried in the Templar church.

a gesture of support.[24] It should be added that the Templar church in Nicosia would seem to have been a substantial building: it was there in 1324 that Henry II's body was laid in state before his burial at the Franciscan church.[25]

Amaury now ordered what would appear to have been a general mobilization of his armed forces. At the same time the Templars armed themselves, but the Cypriot captains managed to avoid a full-scale engagement and instead succeeded in laying siege to the Templar headquarters in Limassol. They demanded that the Templars surrender their horses and arms, and, after a brief show of resistance, they capitulated on 1 June. The Cypriot captains thereupon gained entry to the building and took possession of their goods, making a full inventory of the considerable store of arms and equipment they found there. These were removed to the royal house at Limassol along with the foodstuffs that were surplus to the Templars' immediate requirements. In the treasury they found valuables with an estimated value of 120,000 white bezants together with 1,500 marks worth of silver plate. This was all inventoried and placed under seal, and a guard was set.[26] It was believed that the majority of the Templar wealth had been hidden secretly, although subsequent enquiries yielded nothing. So in Cyprus at least, stories of hidden Templar treasure started to circulate almost at once.[27]

The Templars themselves were divided into two groups. Half of them with the marshal, Aymon d'Oiselay, were sent to the Templar estate at Khirokitia; the other half, with the Templar commander of Cyprus, to another Templar property not far away at Yermasoyia. There they were well supplied with food and kept under guard. The treasure was moved to Nicosia; the horses and other beasts of burden, the supplies and furniture were all sold; the arms were taken to the royal armouries at Famagusta, and slaves belonging to the order were put to work on the fortifications at Famagusta, a major building project that was in progress at the time.[28]

Amadi concludes his account by recording that word later reached Amaury that the marshal and commander had written to friends in Genoa and were plotting to have ships brought secretly to Cyprus so that they could make their escape. Accordingly he ordered that the high-ranking officials, namely the marshal, the commander, the draper, treasurer and the commander of Apulia, should all be taken to the royal village of Lefkara and kept there under guard.[29]

---

[24] 'Chronique d'Amadi', p. 288.

[25] 'Chronique d'Amadi', p. 402. See Gilles Grivaud and Christopher Schabel, 'La ville de Nicosie', in *L'art gothique en Chypre*, ed. Jean-Bernard de Vaivre and Philippe Plagnieux (Paris, 2006), p. 107.

[26] 'Chronique d'Amadi', pp. 288–90. The degree of detail given in the text suggests that the original author would have had access to the inventories compiled at the time.

[27] 'Chronique d'Amadi', p. 290.

[28] 'Chronique d'Amadi', pp. 290–291. For the fortifications at Famagusta, see *Reg. Clem. V*, no. 2736; 'Chronique d'Amadi', pp. 326–7.

[29] 'Chronique d'Amadi', p. 291.

That is not quite the end of the Templars so far as *Amadi* is concerned. The narrative makes no mention of the Templar process in Cyprus, but it does record that on 7 November 1312 the papal legate assembled the clergy and leading laity in Nicosia cathedral and read out letters from the pope announcing that all the Templars' possessions were to pass to the Hospitallers.[30] *Amadi* records two other incidents involving the Templars that may come as something of a surprise. It might be imagined that Amaury's firm stance in securing their arrest and sequestrating their possessions would have left little room for further goodwill and co-operation between his regime and the order. However, in 1310, following Amaury's murder, the knights who were working for the restoration of the king evidently feared that the Templars held at Khirokitia would be recruited by their opponents, who were now led by Amaury's brother, Aimery of Lusignan, in what could well have developed into an armed struggle. Then, in 1311, Aymon d'Oiselay was named as a leading member of a group of erstwhile supporters of Amaury who were plotting to seize the kingdom in the name of Amaury's son, Hugh, who was then in Cilician Armenia. The plot was nipped in the bud, but it would seem that it was that episode rather than his position as a leading officer in the order that resulted in his incarceration in Kerynia castle where he died in 1316. *Amadi* asserts that many Templars died at Kerynia, although other evidence indicates that at least some of those arrested in Cyprus were allowed back to their places of origin and treated with leniency.[31]

As most of the senior officers who had not been rounded up in France at the time of the arrests there were in Cyprus, these events were significant. Many of the members of the order on the island should probably be regarded as being on active service. Certainly, as Alan Forey has shown, there was a much higher proportion of Templars in Cyprus who had been in the order for less than 10 years than is true of those arrested in the west, and we have to assume that these men were indeed younger.[32] Their numbers were substantial – 83 knights and 35 sergeants according to *Amadi* of whom 42 knights, 2 priests and 32 sergeants gave testimonies which survive in the trial documents[33] – and the quantity of arms and armour found in the headquarters at Limassol was appreciable. All this suggests that they could have been well able to defend themselves in the event of a military showdown, especially as it would seem that many of them were together in Limassol and not scattered around their estates. There is no hint in our sources that news had reached Cyprus of the arrests in France before Het'um arrived with the papal letters in May

[30] 'Chronique d'Amadi', p. 395.

[31] 'Chronique d'Amadi', pp. 360, 392, 398. For Templars repatriated from Cyprus, see Alan Forey, *The Fall of the Templars in the Crown of Aragon* (Aldershot, 2001), pp. 216, 243 n. 53; Peter W. Edbury, 'The Suppression of the Templars in Cyprus', *St John Historical Society Proceedings* (2003), 37–8 (for a French Templar, William of 'Valdreys' or 'Vadres', who reappeared in Burgundy in the 1330s).

[32] Alan Forey, 'Towards a Profile of the Templars in the Early Fourteenth Century', in *MO*, 1, pp. 198–200.

[33] *Trial in Cyprus*, ed. Gilmour-Bryson, p. 31.

1308, and so there is no way of knowing if either the government or the members of the order had made any contingency plans. It was of course conceivable that Amaury would choose to defy papal instructions rather than proceed against his own political allies at a time when his authority was beginning to be challenged by elements within the Frankish elite in Cyprus. As Helen Nicholson has pointed out, had 'the ruler of Cyprus supported the order, it would have been difficult for the pope to dissolve it'.[34]

But the ruler of Cyprus chose not to support the order. Maybe Amaury realized he could escape repaying the loan he had received in 1306; maybe he hoped to get his hands on Templar property; maybe he was glad to be rid of what was, after all, a substantial force of armed men on Cypriot soil not under his control, but it seems to me that there are two other, far more important reasons than these. Firstly, for Amaury to defy both the pope and the king of France was to invite intervention that could lead to the end of Lusignan rule in Cyprus altogether. As it was, the Angevin kings of Naples claimed the Lusignans' other royal title, that of king of Jerusalem, and in making this claim they could count on the support of both the king of France and the pope. What is more, the idea seems to have had currency in some circles in the west that the French king could acquire the rather tenuous Brienne claim to the Cypriot crown – this dated from a disputed succession in the 1260s – and use it to endow a junior member of the French royal family with the throne. What all this meant was that in the event of a French-led crusade to the east, the king of Cyprus would have good reason to feel apprehensive. In August 1308, the pope indeed proclaimed just such a crusade to begin the following year.[35] Quite possibly Het'um, on his return to Cyprus the previous May, had been able to tell Amaury that talk of a crusade was already in the air at the papal court. So reluctance to antagonize the papacy and fear of a French-led crusade, combined with signs that his rule was becoming unpopular, may have been sufficient to convince Amaury that he had no choice but to fall in with the papal mandates. Amaury's letter to the pope reporting that he had indeed carried out the instructions to arrest the Templars – a letter which incidentally corroborates many of the details recorded by *Amadi* – has survived, as has another letter which shows Pope Clement forwarding Amaury's missive to Philip the Fair. The surviving copy of Amaury's letter lacks the date, but the fact that it had reached the pope, who was then at Lusignan in Poitou, by 20 August 1308 shows that it must have been dispatched almost immediately after the arrests were effected.[36] It would thus seem that Amaury was making a virtue out of necessity and using the arrests to ingratiate himself with the pope.

The second principal reason is that, although the Templars had supported Amaury's rule, they were not integrated into Cypriot society. The trial documents

[34] Helen Nicholson, *The Knights Templar: A New History* (Stroud, 2001), p. 228.

[35] Edbury, *Kingdom of Cyprus*, pp. 107, 123.

[36] *Vitae Paparum Avenionensium*, ed. Etienne Baluze, new edn by Guillaume Mollat, 4 vols (Paris, 1914–27), vol. 3, pp. 84–6; cf. Claverie, *L'ordre du Temple*, vol. 3, p. 618, no. 715.

258

show that some individual Templars had been received into the order in the Latin East, but it appears that these men were invariably from western Europe, and that the Templars did not recruit from among the members of the Frankish nobility. So there were no prominent families who might want to come to the defence of the order because their relatives were Templar brothers.[37] Although it is true that none of the lay witnesses called to testify in the Templar process in Cyprus were prepared to corroborate the charges levelled against them, positive support was clearly lacking. Indeed, the Ibelin family, which at this time was by the far the most prominent noble house in Cyprus, had, back in the 1270s, been attempting to hijack part of the Templar tradition. According to the version of the *Lignages d'Outremer* which was assembled at that time in Ibelin circles, Barisan, the founder of the house in the early twelfth century, had been given the castle of Ibelin because of his work in escorting pilgrims from Jaffa to Jerusalem.[38] The tradition of ill-feeling between the Templars and the Cypriot monarchy which extended back at least to the 1270s would also have affected the stance taken by the nobility, as would the criticisms of the order the nobles would have found embedded in literary works such as the Old French translation of William of Tyre's celebrated history.[39] Amaury of Lusignan and his associates who had seized power in 1306 counted the Templars among their political allies; they evidently did not count them among their friends.

[37] According to *Amadi* (p. 267) the Templar marshal, Aymon d'Oiselay, was the cousin of the prominent Cypriot nobleman, Rupin of Montfort. Rupin was among the first of the nobles to oppose Amaury, and in the summer of 1307 Aymon intervened to release him from confinement, whereupon Amaury banished him to internal exile on his mother's estate at Lapithos. The genealogy of the Montfort family is well known; if indeed the two men were related, their kinship cannot have been close. Aymon was himself a Burgundian: Claverie, *L'ordre du Temple*, vol. 1, p. 111. Rupin was named as one of the partisans of Henry II against whom Aymon was said to be plotting in 1311: 'Chronique d'Amadi', p. 392.

[38] *Lignages d'outremer*, ed. Marie-Adélaïde Nielen (Paris, 2003), p. 60, cf. pp. 22–3. For the circumstances of the grant of Ibelin in 1144, see Peter W. Edbury, *John of Ibelin and the Kingdom of Jerusalem* (Woodbridge, 1997), pp. 4–5.

[39] Claverie, *L'ordre du Temple*, vol. 1, pp. 86–97; vol. 2, pp. 242–71; Peter W. Edbury, 'The Old French William of Tyre and the Origins of the Templars', in *Knighthoods of Christ: Essays on the History of the Crusades and the Knights Templar presented to Malcolm Barber*, ed. Norman Housley (Aldershot, 2007), pp. 151–64; idem, 'The Old French William of Tyre, the Templars and the Assassin Envoy', in *The Hospitallers, the Mediterranean and Europe: Festschrift for Anthony Luttrell*, ed. Karl Borchardt, Nikolas Jaspert and Helen J. Nicholson (Aldershot, 2007), pp. 25–37.

XVIII

Latins and Greeks on Crusader Cyprus

Lord, your holiness must know that our fathers did not leave their homes and their kinsmen and their heritages to go to dwell on a rock in the midst of the sea until they had made agreements and assizes for their support and comfort.[1]

These are words put into the mouth of a Cypriot knight named Raymond Babin by the Cypriot Greek historian, Leontios Makhairas. It was 1360, and Raymond was at the court of Pope Innocent VI arguing for the legitimacy of the accession of the new king, Peter I, against the challenge of his nephew, the son of Peter's deceased elder brother.

By 1360, and indeed for the previous seventy years, Cyprus was the most easterly outpost of Latin Christendom in the Mediterranean. Except for the crumbling kingdom of Cilician Armenia to the north in what is now part of southern Turkey, all the mainland areas of Anatolia, Syria and North Africa were under Muslim rule. So, though an island defended by the sea, Cyprus lay on an exposed frontier of Christendom. In 1191, during the Third Crusade, King Richard the Lionheart had conquered the island from its Byzantine ruler and established Western rule there. Henceforth Cyprus was regarded as a springboard for campaigns against the Muslims in the Levant. For substantial periods in the thirteenth century the king of Cyprus was also ruling in what was left of the kingdom of Jerusalem and made use of the resources of the island to support the dwindling Christian territories along the Levantine coast. Despite the lengthy periods of peace, there was no doubting the latent hostility of the Cypriot regime towards the Muslims of Egypt, Syria and southern Turkey, and in 1365 this hostility was to erupt in the famous Cypriot-led campaign that sacked Alexandria, thereby initiating a war with the Mamluk sultanate that lasted until 1370. The end of Christian rule in Syria and Palestine in the course of the latter part of the thirteenth century meant that Cyprus was more vulnerable to Muslim naval attack than previously, and from time to time there were genuine, if

---

1   Leontios Makhairas, *Recital Concerning the Sweet Land of Cyprus Entitled 'Chronicle'*, ed. R.M. Dawkins (Oxford, 1932), §106.

unfulfilled, scares that the Mamluks were preparing an invasion fleet. In fact no large-scale Muslim assault on the island occurred until the 1420s, but fears of the possibility of an invasion would have lain constantly in the minds of the leading figures in the island.[2]

But if Cyprus lay at the periphery of Christendom, there was also another sense in which it can be considered a frontier society. Since the end of the twelfth century the island had been ruled by an elite made up of men of Western European extraction who dominated the far larger population of indigenous Greeks. Language, religious observance and social custom served as a barrier, separating the new rulers from their subjects. But this barrier was not impenetrable, nor did it remain unchanging during the centuries of Western rule. How Latins and Greeks, Catholic and Orthodox, rulers and ruled interacted, and whether the development of their relationships reflected the external threat, are big questions, and it is on these issues rather than on the subject of how Cyprus faced its Muslim neighbours that I want to concentrate attention.

Raymond Babin's statement that the Cypriots 'dwelt on a rock in the midst of the sea', with its unspoken rider that they were surrounded by enemies, was undoubtedly true. On at least one occasion in the fourteenth century Cypriot envoys had used this same argument to justify a petition to the pope for a dispensation to allow a marriage within the prohibited degrees.[3] The self-image that the Latin rulers wanted to project was of a society that was dedicated to the defence of Christendom and was imbued with a thoroughly Western, chivalric outlook. We can see this when, in the thirteenth century, at a time when the Christians still held substantial sections of the coastlands of the Levant, the Cypriot knights could claim – controversially – that they had often seen military service in the Holy Land 'in the service of God' rather than because their king had commanded them to go and fight there.[4] In the fourteenth century the kings appear on their coins wearing characteristic Western attire and holding a sceptre or a drawn sword, while on the reverse is the Cross of Jerusalem. At the same period the stylized portraits of knights and their ladies on the engraved tomb slabs, as illustrated at the end of the nineteenth century by Major Tankerville J. Chamberlayne, or which can be seen today in the museum in the castle at Limassol, again emphasise the European image that they present.[5] We know that the Cypriot nobles were obsessed

---

2   For that topic, see P.W. Edbury, *The Lusignan Kingdom of Cyprus and its Muslim Neighbours*, Bank of Cyprus Cultural Foundation Ninth Annual Lecture on History and Archaeology (Nicosia, 1993).

3   W.H. Rudt de Collenberg, 'Les dispenses matrimoniales accordées à l'Orient latin d'Honorius III à Clément VII (1223–1385)', *Mélanges de l'École française de Rome (moyen âge, temps modernes)*, 89 (1977), 10–93, no. 111 (79); cf. no. 59 (on 69).

4   'Document relatif au service militaire', *R[ecueil des] h[istoriens des] c[roisades]. Lois*, vol. 2, 430, 432, 434.

5   D.M. Metcalf, *Coinage of the Crusades and the Latin East in the Ashmolean Museum Oxford* (2nd edn, London, 1995), 199–224 and plates 26–33; T.J. Chamberlayne,

with hunting and falconry,[6] that they enjoyed the romances of the Round Table and of William of Orange and the like. Indeed, according to Maurice Keen, the earliest known instance of knights dressing up as characters from the Arthurian cycle occurred in Cyprus in the mid-1220s at the jousts held as part of the celebrations surrounding the knighting of the sons of the Lord of Beirut.[7] That these people sought to conform to Western chivalric ideals is beyond doubt. Joinville, whose opinion cannot be ignored, tells us that Guy of Ibelin, the Constable of Cyprus in the mid-thirteenth century, was 'one of the most accomplished knights that I have ever seen'.[8] Moreover, Lusignan Cyprus made its own contribution to Western knightly culture. There is good reason to suppose that Robert de Boron, the author of the *Roman de l'Estoire dou Graal*, spent some time in Cyprus in the early years of the thirteenth century and that he introduced ideas current in Eastern Christian traditions into his narrative, while Philip of Novara's treatise on knightly *mores*, *Les Quatre Ages de l'Homme*, would seem, if the number of surviving manuscripts is a guide, to have circulated in the West to a far greater extent than any of his other writings.[9]

How did the Latins – in particular the Latin laity – view their Cypriot Greek subjects? In fact Frankish writers living in the East have little to say on this matter. The various versions of the French continuation of William of Tyre are shrill in their denunciation of Greek perfidy when describing the circumstances of Richard the Lionheart's conquest of the island in 1191, but it has to be remembered that they were determined to leave their readers in no doubt that the conquest was thoroughly justified: the Greeks treated the shipwrecked mariners 'most cruelly'; Isaac, the last Byzantine ruler of the island, commanded 'his evil Greeks' to execute the pilgrims, 'For the Greeks regard the Franks as heretics and reckon killing a Latin to be very

---

Lacrimae Nicossienses. Recueil d'inscriptions funéraires la plupart françaises existant encore dans l'île de Chypre (Paris, 1894).

6 J. Richard, 'La Fauconnerie de Jean de Francières et ses sources', *Le Moyen Age*, 69 (1963), 893–902, at 898–9; D. Jacoby, 'Knightly values and class consciousness in the crusader states of the eastern Mediterranean', *Mediterranean Historical Review*, 1 (1986), 158–86, at 164.

7 Philip of Novara (Filippo da Novara), *Guerra di Federico II in Oriente (1223–1242)*, ed. S. Melani (Naples, 1994), 72, 150; 'Les Gestes des Chiprois', *RHC. Documents arméniens*, vol. 2, 672, 702, 793; M.H. Keen, *Chivalry* (New Haven and London, 1984), 93; Jacoby, 'Knightly values', 163, 166–7.

8 John of Joinville, *Histoire de Saint Louis*, ed. N. de Wailly (Paris, 1868), ch. 66.

9 K.N. Ciggaar, 'Robert de Boron en Outremer? le culte de Joseph d'Arimathie dans le monde byzantin et en Outremer', in *Polyphonia Byzantina: Studies in Honour of Willem J. Aerts*, ed. H. Hokwera et al. (Gröningen, 1993), 145–59; *eadem*, 'Le royaume des Lusignan: terre de littérature et de traductions. Échanges littéraires et culturels', in *Les Lusignans et l'Outre Mer* (Poitiers, 1995), 89–98, at 91–2; Philip of Novara, *Les Quatre Ages de l'Homme*, ed. M. de Fréville (Paris, 1888), xiv–xvii. Cf S. Painter, *French Chivalry* (Baltimore, 1940), 31, 33, 36, 137 (where the author did not think it necessary to point out that Philip was not French and was not writing in France).

pleasing in the sight of God.' One mid-thirteenth-century recension of this text portrays the conquest as a divinely-inspired act 'to establish the Holy Church and Roman Christianity on the aforesaid isle and eradicate the evil root of the wicked Greeks'.[10]

In his account of the civil wars on Cyprus in the late 1220s and early 1230s, Philip of Novara allows the Greek population of the island to remain totally invisible. It is the Frankish knights who are regularly described as *chiprois*. Perhaps significantly, the only mention of a Greek comes in one of Philip's poems. It is a passing reference to a Greek falconer and, far from carrying any pejorative connotation, would seem, if anything, to mark Frankish respect for Greek expertise in this field.[11] More revealing, however, are Philip's remarks about Greeks to be found in his legal treatise which dates from around the middle of the thirteenth century and which was written explicitly with Cyprus in mind. Philip and his audience took it as axiomatic that society on the island was hierarchic, with class, race and religion all having a bearing on legal status and privilege. At the top of the scale were the Frankish vassal-knights and, so Philip informs us, a knight could not be appealed against in a case which could end in trial by battle by a sergeant or by a burgess, or indeed by anyone who was not a knight.[12] So while the vassals were not above the law, it would be hard for anyone else to gain redress from one of their number in the courts. This advantageous legal position was reinforced by a rule that said that no one could testify as a bearer of warranty against a Frank in the High Court (and so be liable to fight a judicial battle) if he were not a Catholic ('of the law of Rome'). That of course immediately ruled out the Greek majority in the population. Moreover, no one could testify against a Frank if his testimony was suspect on the grounds that he had lost a lawsuit in the past, or was a perjurer or guilty of breach of faith. Also barred were defeated champions, apostates and men who had served the Muslims in arms against the Christians for more than a year and a day. Philip adds that he is uncertain whether men who had served the Greeks – presumably he means the Byzantines – in arms against the Franks fell under the same exclusion. He then lists bastards, serfs of whatever religion and clergy who had renounced their orders as also disqualified from bearing testimony.[13] But if the

---

10   'L'Estoire de Eracles Empereur et la conqueste de la terre d'Outremer', *RHC Historiens occidentaux*, vol. 2, 159–69; *La Continuation de Guillaume de Tyr (1184–1197)*, ed. M.R. Morgan (Paris, 1982), 112–21 (quotation at 119).
11   Philip of Novara, *Guerra di Federico II*, 142, line 179.
12   Philip of Novara, 'Livre de Philippe de Navarre', *RHC. Lois*, vol. 1, 486.
13   Philip of Novara, 'Livre', 501–2; cf. John of Ibelin, 'Livre de Jean d'Ibelin', *RHC Lois*, vol. 1, 114, where the parallel passage in John's treatise is ambiguous, but could possibly be construed as meaning that men who had served the Byzantines against the Franks were barred from testifying. For Franks serving in Muslim and Byzantine armies, see J. Richard, 'An account of the Battle of Hattin referring to the Frankish mercenaries in Oriental Muslim states', *Speculum*, 27 (1952), 168–77, at 171–5.

law made it hard for people of other confessions to proceed successfully against a Frank, there was still plenty of scope for litigation between members of the ruling elite, and it is with how disputes among the feudatories were to be conducted that Philip's work is primarily concerned. The Cypriot vassals formed a close-knit caste, and their exclusivity is underlined by Philip in the passage that follows the one I have just described:

> If the lord has given a fief[14] to a serf or someone disqualified for one of the reasons mentioned above and wants to have him sit in his court saying that he is his liege man, and if the court or one of the parties to a dispute wants to bar him, he may well say to the lord, 'Sire, you have the right to enfranchise him since that is your wish, and if he is your vassal you will keep faith with him as you ought, but you are not keeping faith with us. With due respect, neither can you nor should you enfranchise him, nor can you make him our peer.'[15]

Philip makes it clear that lower down the social scale there was a legal pecking-order determined by religion. If a party to a legal dispute had an *essoin*, he should report the matter to the court using a Latin Christian as his messenger whenever possible. But if that were not possible, he could use a non-Latin Christian and, failing that, a Muslim.[16] In cases of assault, compensation of 100 sous was due to the victim if he were a Frank and another 100 bezants to his lord, but if he were a Syrian, a Greek or a serf, the compensation was only 50 sous to the victim though 50 bezants were still payable to the lord.[17] The fullest expression of this social stratification comes in Philip's chapter describing the procedure for establishing property boundaries in cases where it would be necessary to rely on local knowledge taken on oath. If possible the group to whom the enquiry had been delegated would take evidence from a Latin Christian. If no one could be found who could testify, they could take evidence from a Syrian; failing that from a Greek, then a Christian of another Eastern confession and finally a Muslim. The reference to Syrians – Arabic-speaking Christians – is noteworthy. It means that Philip is describing a procedure that had come to Cyprus from the mainland of Latin Syria, as he says at the beginning of the chapter. However, there would have been communities of Syrian Christians in the towns on the island at the time he was writing, and, if indeed this passage means that in Cyprus the testimony of a Syrian was to be preferred to that of a Greek, then it can serve as a forceful illustration of the low esteem in which the ruling class viewed the overwhelming majority of the indigenous population.[18] Not that Philip had a particularly

---

14   Following the variant reading at 502 and n. 9.
15   Philip of Novara, 'Livre', 502.
16   Philip of Novara, 'Livre', 499; cf. John of Ibelin 98–9.
17   Philip of Novara, 'Livre', 546–7; cf. John of Ibelin 186–7.
18   Philip of Novara, 'Livre', 532–4; this chapter is included in the later recensions of John of Ibelin's treatise (394–5).

138

high opinion of Syrians either. Elsewhere in his treatise he lambasts them for being more credulous than any other people when it came to believing in astrology.[19]

So the Greeks of Cyprus appear but rarely in Philip's treatise. Apart from the instances to which I have just alluded, there are a few scattered references to 'vilains'. It is clear that Philip uses this word to denote the unfree rural population, the *paroikoi* of the Byzantine texts. They were regarded as a type of chattel. 'Vilains on the land or other things that pertain to a fief' can be the subject of litigation, and the lord may demand from his vassal 'land, vilains, a sum of money or anything else that the vassal holds'.[20] 'Vilains' who abscond from the land should be returned, although they too can give rise to disputes between landowners, and the 'vilain' who strikes a knight will loose his right hand.[21] If a 'vilain' dies without heirs, the lord will take two-thirds of his effects, leaving the remainder for his widow. If she is unable to continue to pay the levies on the land the lord will take her plough and her donkey.[22]

What little Philip does tell us suggests that the Lusignan regime pressed heavily on the indigenous population. Whether the mass of the peasantry was any worse off under the Franks than it had been under the Byzantines is difficult to know. I suspect that for the individual *paroikos* the change of masters had made little difference. But for those higher up the social ladder the Frankish conquest may have had far-reaching consequences. Speaking of those vassals whose fiefs consisted of scattered parcels of land, Philip lets slip the information that some of them at least had been endowed with the sequestered lands of churches or abbeys or with the holdings of former Greek *archontes*, a class which otherwise seems to have disappeared totally from the sources for thirteenth-century Cyprus.[23]

The problem is that the situation was never so simple. The Franks needed the Greeks. Whether as administrators, merchants, artisans or peasants, their presence and their labour was essential for the continued existence of the Lusignan regime, and

---

19   Philip of Novara, 'Livre', 567.
20   Philip of Novara, 'Livre', 496, 519 (following variant B at n. 5).
21   Philip of Novara, 'Livre', 535–6, 547.
22   Information from a hitherto unpublished chapter from Philip's work found only in Munich: Bayerische Staatsbibliothek: Codex Gallus 771, f.162r–v. P.W. Edbury, 'Philip of Novara and the *Livre de forme de plait*', *Praktika tou tritou diethnous Kuprologikou sunedriou*, vol. 2, ed. A. Papageorgiou (Nicosia, 2001), 555–69, at 566. On agrarian conditions on Cyprus, see J. Richard, 'Agriculture in the kingdom of Cyprus', in *A History of the Crusades*, ed. K.M. Setton (Philadelphia and Madison, 1955–89), vol. 5, 267–84; P.W. Edbury, 'La classe des propriétaires terriens franco-chypriotes et l'exploitation des ressources rurales de l'île de Chypre', in *État et colonisation au Moyen Age*, ed. M. Balard (Lyon, 1989), 145–52; *idem*, 'Le régime des Lusignan en Chypre et la population locale', in *Coloniser au Moyen Age*, ed. M. Balard and A. Ducellier (Paris, 1995), 354–8, 364–5.
23   Philip of Novara, 'Livre', 536 ('artondes' is evidently a bad reading for 'arcondes' = *archontes*); cf. Edbury, 'Le régime des Lusignan en Chypre', 355–7.

it is clear that the sharp lines of division indicated by Philip of Novara broke down over the course of time and that by the fifteenth century acculturation was proceeding apace. The Frankish landowning class was reinforced both by refugees from the Frankish principalities in Syria during the thirteenth century and by newcomers from the West, but it was not generally possible for members of the indigenous population to join this elite. It is only in the late fourteenth century that we begin to find Cypriot Greeks or Syrians becoming knights, and the earliest examples known to me – Thomas Barech and Thibault Belfarage – were both converts to Catholicism.[24] In the fifteenth century, however, many members of the ruling class were coming to prefer the Greek language and Greek religious observance in their daily lives, while members of the indigenous burgess community – the Audeth family being perhaps the best-known example – were able to obtain landed estates and Latin ecclesiastical benefices.[25]

But even in the thirteenth century when it would seem that the Franks formed a rigidly closed caste from which Greeks were systematically excluded, Greeks were nevertheless employed in positions of responsibility and individual Greeks could and did prosper. It is clear that Greeks were regularly used as estate officials and comprised the staff of the *secrète*, the royal finance office whose very name betrays its Byzantine antecedents. By the late fourteenth century, when the sources allow us to see something of the personnel at the *secrète*, we find that it was staffed by members of a close-knit group of 'civil-service families' which included relatives of the historian, Leontios Makhairas.[26]

In 1191 Richard's conquest had been swift and decisive. His campaign had lasted just one month, and there is no reason to suppose that it was particularly destructive. The sources tell of two popular outbreaks in the course of 1191–92 – one against Richard's officers, the other against the Templars who for a brief period had had charge of the island in 1191–92[27] – but after that there is no evidence for the local populace engaging in armed insurrection. True we hear of riots in the 1310s and the 1360s against Latin attempts to force the Greeks into religious conformity, but these entailed no significant loss of control by the authorities and seem to have been

---

24 Leontios Makhairas, §§568, 579, 599.

25 J. Richard, 'Une famille de "Vénitiens blancs" dans le royaume de Chypre au milieu du XVème siècle: les Audeth et la seigneurie du Marethasse', *Rivista di Studi Bizantini e Slavi*, 1 (1981), 89–129; *idem*, 'Culture franque et culture grecque: le royaume de Chypre au XVème siècle', *Byzantinische Forchungen*, 11 (1987), 399–415; W.H. Rudt de Collenberg, 'Le déclin de la société franque de Chypre entre 1350 et 1450', *Kypriakai Spoudai*, 46 (1982), 71–83.

26 See P.W. Edbury, *The Kingdom of Cyprus and the Crusades, 1191–1374* (Cambridge, 1991), 191–2

27 For references, Edbury, *Kingdom of Cyprus*, 7–8.

no more than short-lived spontaneous outbursts of anger over a specific issue.[28] By contrast, it would seem that at the time of the Genoese war of 1373–74 the Cypriot Greeks took the side of their Frankish masters, supporting them in their struggle against the invaders. It was only with the breakdown of normal governmental control during the Mamluk invasion of 1426 and the captivity of King Janus in Egypt that we find the subject population trying to take power for itself.[29] In other words, the Lusignan regime was effectively established and was not confronted by the sort of endemic resistance that was to dog the Venetians for long periods after their occupation of Crete early in the thirteenth century. Other evidence supports this view: there was no network of fortifications in Cyprus designed to overawe the indigenous population; we do not hear of Frankish landlords being killed or held to ransom by the islanders; the feudatories had rural residences,[30] but they did not have to fortify them against their own peasants. All this implies an acceptance – a reluctant acceptance perhaps, but an acceptance nevertheless – of Frankish rule. I can suggest three possible explanations for why this might be: the Greeks lacked the sort of people who could lead an opposition movement; the Latins had settled in the island in sufficient numbers to give them a firm control and make their regime viable; and, thirdly, the Lusignans were clever enough to avoid provoking too much hostility.[31]

But there is a further dimension. It would seem that the Latin and Greek populations on Cyprus went beyond simply reaching a measure of accommodation. There were, at least by the close of the Frankish period, signs of the emergence of what Gilles Grivaud in a recent paper has termed 'la nation *chyproise*'.[32] Eventually Frankish society went into decline: the nobility suffered from recurrent periods of plague – Grivaud has counted nine outbreaks between 1347 and 1471 – and from the political upheavals attendant on the Genoese invasion of 1373–74 and the civil war of the 1460s; the Latin Church hierarchy, always recruited heavily from Western Europe, never fully recovered from the corrosive effects of the papal schism of 1378.[33] The elite, now as much Italian or Catalan as French, and increasingly

---

28   1310s: *Acta Ioannis XXII (1317–1334)*, ed. A.L. Taūtu (Vatican City, 1952), no. 36; 'Chronique d'Amadi', in *Chroniques d'Amadi et de Strambaldi*, ed. R. de Mas Latrie (Paris, 1891–93), vol. 1, 395–6. 1360s: Philippe de Mézières, *The Life of St Peter Thomas*, ed. J. Smet (Rome, 1954), 92–3; Leontios Makhairas, §101.

29   1370s: Leontios Makhairas, §§395, 398–9, 433–4, 436, 440–41 and *passim*; but see §§445, 448, 468. 1426: Leontios Makhairas, §§696–7.

30   For example, 'Les Gestes des Chiprois', 692.

31   For a discussion of these three points, Edbury, 'Le régime des Lusignan en Chypre', 355–8.

32   G. Grivaud, 'Éveil de la nation *chyproise* (XIIIe–XVIe siècles)', in *Kyprios Character: Quelle identité chypriote?*, ed. P. Gontier (Paris, 1995), 105–16.

33   Grivaud, 'Éveil de la nation *chyproise*', 109; W.H. Rudt de Collenberg, 'Le royaume et l'église de Chypre face au Grand Schisme (1378–1417) d'après les registres des

assimilated into Greek society through intermarriage, allowed their older exclusiveness to break down. For example, even as early as the late thirteenth century we find examples of Latins commissioning Greek artists to paint altarpieces using a Byzantine style and technique, albeit adopting certain Western characteristics.[34] In all likelihood the legal advantages that Philip of Novara had described the Latins enjoying lost their vigour. In the fourteenth century the growth of the chancery court and the court of the auditor – what in England would be labelled prerogative courts – probably put the Greeks, or at least the wealthier Greeks, on a more even footing with the Franks, and it may be significant that in a fifteenth-century manuscript of the legal treatise by Philip of Novara's contemporary, John of Ibelin, that is known to have been kept in Cyprus the word 'Grex' has been heavily crossed out from the list of categories of people who may not bear warranty in the high court against a Frank.[35] For their part the Greeks were prepared to borrow from the Latins. Thus in the fourteenth century the new Orthodox cathedral in Famagusta was built not in the traditional Byzantine style but following Italianate Gothic forms complete with flying buttresses. Grivaud makes the important point that those historians who seek to construct the history of the Greeks of Cyprus simply in terms of their struggle to preserve their identity in the face of successive oppressors – Crusaders, Venetians, Turks, British – are, despite the validity and attractiveness of their approach, in danger of losing sight of the nuances.

Something of the assimilation that was taking place is exemplified by Leontios Makhairas, the author quoted at the beginning of this chapter. Leontios, writing towards the middle of the fifteenth century, believed in the Byzantine world order in which the legitimate ruler was the emperor, but at the same time he respected his Frankish masters. As an articulate and educated Greek from a prominent family, he also recognised that the Greek language had changed under the influence of the French-speaking ruling class, and the loan words and Gallicisms in his own writings abundantly bear out what he says. To quote a well-known passage:

> And because there are two natural rulers in the world, the one lay and the other spiritual, so in this little island there were the emperor of Constantinople and the patriarch of Antioch the Great until the Latins took the land. For this reason we were obliged to know good Greek, for sending letters to the emperor, and to be perfect in the Syrian language … And when the

---

archives du Vatican', *Mélanges de l'École française de Rome (moyen âge, temps modernes)*, 94 (1982), 621–701.

34   J. Folda, 'Crusader Art In The Kingdom of Cyprus, c. 1275–1291: reflections on the state of the questions', in *Cyprus and the Crusades*, ed. N. Coureas and J. Riley-Smith (Nicosia, 1995), 209–37, at 216–21.

35   Edbury, *Kingdom of Cyprus*, 190, 192–3. For the deletion of the word 'Grex', see Biblioteca Apostolica Vaticana, Cod. Vat. Lat. 4789 f. 53v (cf. John of Ibelin, 114 at n. 18.)

142

Latin period began men began to learn French, and their Greek became barbarous in such a way that no one in the world can now say what our language is.[36]

Elsewhere Leontios could put into the mouth of King Peter II (1369–82) the idea that the island rightly belonged to the Byzantine emperor and the Franks had only gained control by default.[37] On religious matters Leontios was markedly restrained. He was clearly proud of the Orthodox traditions and the Orthodox saints of Cyprus, but apropos of Thibault Belfarage, a convert from Orthodoxy to Catholicism, he has this to say:

> I am not condemning the Latins, but what is the need for a Greek to become a Latin? For should a good Christian despise the one faith and betake himself to the other? And do you, my reader, despise the former faith? ... The Latins derive from the Apostle [i.e. Saint Peter]; the Greeks are a catholic [that is, true/universal] church.[38]

Leontios, though he wrote in Greek, was evidently conscious that he would have members of the Frankish community among his readers.[39] But would the assimilation and the mutual respect that Leontios's history reveals have developed to the same degree had Cyprus not been exposed to the ever-present threat of Muslim invasion?

---

36   Leontios Makhairas, §158.
37   Leontios Makhairas, §527 (at 521). See C. Kyrris, 'Cypriot identity, Byzantium and the Latins, 1192–1489', *History of European Ideas*, 19 (1994), 563–73, at 563.
38   Leontios Makhairas, §579. See C. Kyrris, 'Some aspects of Leontios Makhairas' ethnoreligious ideology, cultural identity and historiographic method', *Stasinos*, 10 (1989–93), 167–281, at 183 n. 42.
39   Kyrris, 'Some aspects', 205 and n. 90.

XIX

The Templars in Cyprus

Our knowledge of Templar activity in Cyprus between the Latin conquest in 1191 and the suppression of the Order in the years 1307–12 is, to say the least, patchy. Templars feature in comparatively few episodes: they purchased the island from King Richard of England in 1191 and ruled it until the early months of 1192; in the 1270s they quarrelled with the king of Cyprus, Hugh III, over their recognition of his rival, Charles of Anjou, as King of Jerusalem, and Hugh confiscated their Cypriot lands; they participated in some Cyprus-based military operations around the year 1300 which culminated in their occupation of Ruad; and, finally, there exists some interesting material from Cyprus on the circumstances of the suppression of the Order.

Moving from political and military activities to the question of endowments, we find that the evidence is even thinner: not a single charter or confirmation recording grants of property has survived. However, it is possible from the sources at our disposal to obtain an impression of the significance of what must have been one of the wealthiest and most powerful corporations on the island.

Richard the Lionheart conquered Cyprus in May 1191 en route for Palestine and the siege of Acre. Scholars disagree as to whether his conquest was premeditated or more a matter of opportunism,[1] but there is little doubt that the English king was not interested in acquiring the island for its own sake but merely wanted to raid the island for supplies and as much cash as possible to help pay for his campaign in the Holy Land. Having seized what he could at the time of the invasion, he quickly sold Cyprus to the Templars for 100,000 gold dinars, of which 40,000 were paid immediately. But the Templars either underestimated the resources that were needed to administer the island or simply

---

[1] P.W. Edbury, *The Kingdom of Cyprus and the Crusades, 1191–1374* (Cambridge, 1991), p. 8 and n. 17.

XIX

lacked the manpower to do so. According to one version of the French Continuation of William of Tyre, they

> ... wanted to rule the people of the island of Cyprus as they would the people in a village in the land of Jerusalem. They wanted to rob, beat and ill-treat them, and they aimed to control the island of Cyprus through twenty brother knights....

At Easter 1191 the people of Nicosia rose in revolt. Another version of the same narrative tells us that the Templars mustered all the available Latins and that the total came to fourteen knights, twenty-nine other mounted men and seventy-four foot soldiers. They sallied forth from their stronghold and butchered large numbers of insurgents.[2]

The Order had clearly taken on more than it could manage. Had it succeeded in turning Cyprus into a Templar sovereign state, its subsequent history would have been very different. But it was not to be. The Templars found that they could neither govern the island nor pay their debt to King Richard. The answer to their difficulties lay in the politics of Latin Syria. To cut a long story short, Richard decided that Conrad of Montferrat should rule the remnants of the kingdom of Jerusalem while the King of Jerusalem, Guy of Lusignan, should have Cyprus. The Templars seem to have been happy to fall in with this solution to what had become an extremely fraught political conflict. Unfortunately the fullest accounts of the transaction concerning Cyprus contradict each other at vital points. One version of the *Continuation* of William of Tyre states that Guy reimbursed the Templars the 40,000 dinars they had paid Richard and accepted responsibility for the balance of 60,000 still owed.[3] But another version – the one which is probably closest to the events and which also gives some plausible circumstantial details – claims that Guy paid Richard 60,000 dinars and that, although he owed a further 40,000, the king did not insist on payment; this version makes no mention of Guy paying the Templars anything.[4]

These two accounts cannot both be right. Elsewhere I have followed the second,[5] but on reflection I am no longer sure. The English sources claim that Richard gave Cyprus to Guy, and this would seem to be more in keeping with the implication of the first version that Guy paid Richard nothing. The *Itinerarium peregrinorum* speaks of the 'condition of the Templar sale having been exchanged', and this too would appear to support the first account. What may have happened is that Guy compensated the Templars for their outlay, accepted that he now owed Richard the balance, but then succeeded in avoiding having to make any payments.[6]

---

[2] *Cont WT*, pp. 135, 137; *Eracles*, 2, pp. 189–91.
[3] *Eracles*, p. 191.
[4] *Cont WT*, pp. 137, 139, cf. pp. 136, 143. The later versions (*Eracles*, pp. 187–8 var. CG; *Ernoul-Bernard*, p. 286) say that Guy bought Cyprus from Richard.
[5] Edbury, p. 9.
[6] 'Itinerarium Peregrinorum et Gesta Regis Ricardi' in *Chronicles and Memorials of the Reign of Richard I*, ed. W. Stubbs (RS 38), 1, p. 351.

In the light of the circumstances in which he had acquired the island, it is possible that Guy found himself under moral, and perhaps financial, obligation to the Templars and that his indebtedness to the Order was one reason for its generous endowment there. Unfortunately, we do not know the full extent of the Templars' holdings in the island, although we can identify some of their estates. Still less do we know when they obtained them. What is certain, however, is that almost all their properties passed to the Hospitallers in the second decade of the fourteenth century after the Order's suppression, and we do have a fairly accurate idea of the extent of the Hospitaller estates in Cyprus after the transfer. In the fourteenth century the Knights of Saint John held a number of properties that are not attributable to either Order in the thirteenth. Whereas it is possible that some may have been fresh acquisitions, the probability is that almost all the fourteenth-century Hospitaller estates had been obtained before the end of the thirteenth by one or other of the two Orders. As some of the documentation recording gifts to the Hospitallers in Cyprus survives, and so our knowledge of the thirteenth-century Hospitaller estates seems likely to be more complete, it may well be that a majority of these unattributable estates had in fact belonged to the Templars.[7]

If I am right, then it is probable that the Templars would have been among the richest landholders in Cyprus after the Crown. Apart from the Hospitallers, only the archbishop of Nicosia and the greatest of the lay lords such as John of Ibelin, Count of Jaffa, who in the mid-thirteenth century is known to have held Episkopi and Peristerona, can have had comparable incomes. Whether the Templars were wealthier than the Hospitallers is hard to judge. In the mid-thirteenth century the archbishop of Nicosia made agreements with both Orders in respect of the tithes they owed. In 1255 the Hospitallers undertook to pay the archbishop 300 white besants annually in lieu of tithe, plus a silver mark for their cemetery rights, while in 1261 the Templars agreed to pay 190

---

[7] Known Templar estates: Khirokitia, Yermasoyia, Phasouri, Psimolophou (and the dependent settlements at Tripi and Kato Deftera), Gastria and Temblos, together with properties in Limassol, Nicosia, Paphos and Famagusta. Known Hospitaller estates from before 1300: Kolossi, Plataniskia, Monagroulli, Phinikas, Palekhori, Kellaki, Louvaras and Trakhoni, together with properties at Nicosia, Limassol and Mora, and unidentified localities: *Esteriga*, Nostra Dame de *Combos* and St George. Additional estates in the possession of the Hospitallers by 1319–20: *Mons Esquillate*, Apsiou, Yerasa, Paramytha, Mathikoloni, *Sirincocie* (= Syrianokhori?), Sanidha, Anoyira, Akoursos, Ayios Konstantinos, *Androclio*. J. Richard, *Chypre sous les Lusignans. Documents chypriotes des archives du Vatican (XIVe et XVe siècles)* (Paris, 1962), pp. 111–20, cf. p. 68; J. Riley-Smith, *The Knights of St John in Jerusalem and Cyprus, c. 1050–1310* (London, 1967), p. 505; Edbury, pp. 77–8. *Mons Esquillati*, unidentified by Richard, could be an attempt at Latinizing 'the Mountain of Kellaki'; if so, it presumably denotes a group of Hospitaller estates in the Troodos to the north of Kellaki (see the map in Richard, p. 71). Later medieval lists name many more Hospitaller properties, some of which, however, were probably settlements dependent on the estates mentioned in this note. L. de Mas Latrie, *Histoire de l'île de Chypre sous le règne des princes de la maison de Lusignan*, 3 (Paris, 1852–61), pp. 502–3; Florio Bustron, 'Chronique de l'île de Chypre' ed. R. de Mas Latrie, in *Collection des documents inédits sur l'histoire de France: Mélanges historiques*, 5 (1886), pp. 170–71, 246–7.

besants as tithe and, again, a silver mark for cemetery rights. These settlements provide the only indications of the relative wealth of the Orders of which I am aware, but they raise more problems than they solve. Although at first sight, they might seem to indicate that the Hospitallers were wealthier, the Templars may have driven a harder bargain. In any case, both Orders seem to have held most of their possessions outside the Nicosia diocese.[8]

Although they were richly endowed, the Templars are unlikely to have maintained a substantial military establishment in Cyprus before 1291. They had acquired the fort at Gastria to the north of Famagusta by 1210, but from the little known of its structure it would not appear to have required a substantial garrison.[9] The same would have been true of the fortified towers they owned at Limassol, Yermasoyia and Khirokitia. They would have used the income from their estates to help support their obligations in Syria rather than assist in the defence of the island. By the same token, an absence of Templar military strength in Cyprus would have meant that the Order played little part in the politics of the Lusignan kingdom, and so would have tended to obviate the danger of confrontation with the secular authorities.

It is with this thought in mind that we come to the breach between King Hugh III and the Templars in the mid-1270s. Hitherto there had been no recorded conflict between the Order and the royal dynasty. Although it is true that, in 1210, the disgraced regent of Cyprus, Walter of Montbéliard, had sought refuge with the Templars, and it may be significant that Hugh I, who came into his inheritance at this time, is known to have been a patron of the rival Order, the Hospitallers,[10] there is no evidence that any coolness that may have developed at that time amounted to anything. Indeed, a few years later the Templars and the Ibelin-dominated regime in Cyprus united in opposition to the Emperor Frederick II and his officers.[11]

In the 1270s King Hugh III of Cyprus and Charles of Anjou, King of Sicily, were both laying claim to the kingdom of Jerusalem. Hugh had possession of Acre, the one remaining royal city, and in 1269 had been crowned and anointed king. But as his reign progressed and dissatisfaction grew in various quarters, so the fact that his title was disputed came to acquire greater significance. Initially he seems to have had Templar support, but, with the election of William of Beaujeu as master in 1273, the Order moved decisively into Charles's camp. So far as is known, Hugh had done nothing in particular to antagonize the Templars, but William was a relative of the Angevin royal house and, before

---

[8] *CH*, no. 2762; J.L. La Monte, 'A Register of the Cartulary of the Cathedral of Santa Sophia of Nicosia', *Byzantion*, 5 (1930), nos. 90, 92. Cf. Riley-Smith, pp. 432–3.

[9] *Eracles*, p. 316; C. Enlart, *Gothic Art and the Renaissance in Cyprus*, tr. and ed. D. Hunt (London, 1987), pp. 473–5.

[10] Edbury, pp. 44, 46.

[11] A. Demurger, *Vie et mort de l'ordre du Temple*, 2nd ed. (Paris, 1989), pp. 235–6. Cf. Pope Gregory IX, *Registres*, ed. L. Auvray (Paris, 1890-1955), no. 1037.

his election, had been Templar commander in Apulia. It is also worth noting that many Templars were from France, where Charles's brother, and now his nephew, had each ruled as king, and so there may well have been a natural sympathy for his claims, and it was also true that the Templar establishments in the East had come to depend heavily on the ports of Charles's kingdom for their supplies of food, arms and horses. In 1276, with both the Templars and the Venetians, who had their own reasons for disaffection, ranged against him, Hugh found that his authority in Syria was undermined to such an extent that he retired to Cyprus, leaving Acre to fall into the hands of Charles's officers. Later he regretted his surrender and, in 1279 and again in 1283–84, vainly attempted to re-establish his position. William of Beaujeu had eased the Angevin assumption of power in Acre and continued to give Charles's agents his full support.[12] Not surprisingly, Hugh retaliated by taking reprisals on the Templars' Cypriot properties. In the aftermath of his first abortive attempt to re-occupy Acre in 1279, he ordered the confiscation of their estates and the destruction of their house at Limassol.[13] How long this confiscation lasted is not clear: in the early 1280s Pope Martin IV ordered Hugh to stop harming the Templars and not to touch their possessions, and it may have been at about the same time that the pope had the archdeacon of Tortosa and the bishop of Sidon, both of whom, incidentally, were beneficed in Templar-controlled cities, pronounce sentence against him.[14]

The antipathy between the Templars and the Lusignan kings continued until the Order's suppression. With the fall of Acre in 1291 the Templars moved their headquarters to Cyprus, and henceforth the number of Templars stationed on the island would have been far greater than before. A Chapter General held in Nicosia in 1291 is said to have been attended by 400 brothers of the Order; in 1300 the Order was able to send 120 knights, 500 archers and 400 servants to garrison the island of Ruad; one deposition made at the Templar trial mentions an assembly of 120 brothers or more held at Limassol in 1304; in 1308, 38 brother knights and 35 sergeants are reported to have been arrested when the members of the Order were rounded up.[15] With far larger forces now in the island, tension apparently remained high. Early in his reign, King Henry II sent an embassy to the pope to complain about the Order, and in 1298 the pope

---

[12] Edbury, pp. 93–6; A.Forey, *The Military Orders from the Twelfth to the Early Fourteenth Centuries* (Basingstoke and London, 1992), p. 133; M. Barber, 'Supplying the Crusader States: The Role of the Templars', in *The Horns of Ḥaṭṭīn*, ed. B.Z. Kedar (Jerusalem and London, 1992), pp. 325–6.

[13] 'Annales de Terre Sainte', ed. R. Röhricht and G. Raynaud, *AOL*, 2 (1884), p. 457, cf. p. 456; 'Les Gestes des Chiprois', *RHC DArm*, 2, p. 784.

[14] *Veterum Scriptorum et Monumentorum … Amplissima Collectio*, ed. F. Martène and U. Durand (Paris, 1727–33), 2, col. 1300; L. de Mas Latrie, 2, p. 109.

[15] *Procès*, 1, p. 562; 2, p. 139; 'Chronique d'Amadi', in *Chroniques d'Amadi et de Strambaldi*, ed. R. de Mas-Latrie, 1 (Paris, 1891–93), pp. 239, 286. At the Templar trial in Cyprus 76 members of the Order, of whom at least 38 were brothers, were examined. M. Barber, *The Trial of the Templars* (Cambridge, 1978), p. 219.

194

told the king and the Master, James of Molay, to resolve their differences. Continued Templar contacts with the Sicilian Angevins may have contributed to the difficulties; disputes over the right of the Order to acquire property and claim exemption from taxes further soured relations; and there is evidence, too, to suggest that disagreements between the king and the military orders impaired the effectiveness of the Christian response to the Mongol invasion of Syria in 1299. In 1306, when the Cypriot nobles forced King Henry to relinquish his authority to his brother, Amaury, lord of Tyre, the Templars gave them strong support, and, even after their arrest two years later, members of the Order persisted in expressing their hostility towards the king.[16]

It would, however, be misleading to give the impression that, after the retreat from mainland Syria in 1291, the Templars did little in Cyprus other than quarrel with the king. For example, in 1302 the Master, James of Molay, acted decisively in ransoming the count of Jaffa and members of his family who were seized by Greek pirates from his estate at Episkopi.[17] In 1300 the Templars joined the Cypriots and Hospitallers in a naval raid on Egypt and Syria, and the following year they participated in the occupation of the island of Ruad, remaining there in force, after the Cypriot and Hospitaller withdrawal, until the Egyptian sultan moved against them in 1302, and most of the Templar garrison was killed or taken captive.[18] Futile as these military actions may seem in retrospect, the Order's commitment to the recovery of the Holy Land was none the less very real. In about 1305 James of Molay submitted a proposal to the pope calling for a full-scale crusade to win back Jerusalem in which he envisaged that Cyprus would be used as a forward base.[19] At the same time the Order had been building up its fleet, and the surviving registers of a Genoese notary working in Famagusta at this period provide evidence for Templar involvement in the vigorous commercial life of that city.[20] Furthermore, despite the Order's constant arguments with the Crown, the people of Cyprus themselves evidently held them in high regard, for, when Cypriot lay witnesses were called to testify in the Templar trial, not one of them was prepared to condemn the Order, and many spoke openly in its favour. Even those nobles – such men as the seneschal Philip of Ibelin, Baldwin of Ibelin, Rupen of

---

[16] L. de Mas Latrie, 2, pp. 108–9; Boniface VIII, *Registres*, ed. G. Digard et al. (Paris, 1884–1939), nos. 2438–9, 2609, 3060–62; *Notai genovesi in Oltremare: Atti rogati a Cipro da Lamberto di Samuceto*, ed. R. Pavoni (C[ollana] S[torica di] F[onti e] S[tudi]) 49 (Genoa, 1987), no. 202; Edbury, pp. 111–13, 121.

[17] 'Amadi', p. 238.

[18] M. Barber, 'James of Molay, the Last Grand Master of the Temple', *Studia Monastica*, 14 (1972), pp. 98–9; Edbury, pp. 105–6.

[19] S. Schein, *Fideles Crucis: The Papacy, the West and the Recovery of the Holy Land. 1274–1314* (Oxford, 1991), pp. 201–2.

[20] *Notai genovesi in Oltremare: Atti rogati a Cipro da Lamberto di Sambuceto*, ed. V. Polonio (CSFS 31) (Genoa, 1982), nos 148, 166, 171, 219, 258, 413; ed. R. Pavoni, (CSFS 32) (Genoa, 1982), no. 206; ed. Pavoni (CSFS 49) (Genoa, 1987), nos 104, 150, 155, 162.

Montfort and Aygue of Bethsan – who had been close to the king and so might have been tempted to avenge themselves on the Templars for their support of Amaury of Tyre, chose not to do so.[21]

I should like to conclude by offering some hypotheses. It is my belief, although there is insufficient evidence to prove it, that the Templars received most of their lands in Cyprus in the immediate aftermath of the Lusignan establishment in the 1190s. So long as the Order was content to transfer the income from its estates to Latin Syria and not involve itself in the island's politics, all went well – or at least nothing happened that was sufficiently dramatic to leave a mark on the sources. However, in the 1270s the Order's espousal of Charles of Anjou's claims brought it into conflict with the Lusignans, and the lingering ill-will thus generated came to acquire greater significance when, after 1291, the Templars moved their headquarters to Cyprus and thereby increased their numbers on the island. In Cyprus they never managed to acquire the sort of autonomy they had enjoyed in their lordships at Sidon, Tortosa, Château Pèlerin and elsewhere in Syria, and in all probability successive kings tried to keep them at arm's length and to prevent them from having influence in the affairs of their realm. Rich, militarily powerful and yet constricted by royal authority, Templar relations with the Crown remained poor. In 1295 Pope Boniface VIII issued a bull stating that they were to enjoy the same privileges in Cyprus as they had had in the Holy Land.[22] What exactly that meant is not clear, but almost certainly it should be taken as evidence of Templar aspirations to free themselves from both secular and ecclesiastical jurisdiction. Maybe a desire for greater freedom also lay behind their support for the 1306 revolution. Old habits die hard. Just as James of Molay, in 1305, could advocate a type of crusade which arguably was already anachronistic, so, too, may he have been striving for the sort of role in Cypriot political affairs that his predecessors had played in the kingdom of Jerusalem as far back as the third quarter of the twelfth century.

---

[21] Barber, *Trial of Templars*, pp. 218–19; Edbury, p. 125 n. 94.
[22] Boniface VIII, nos. 487, 1937.

XX

The 'Cartulaire de Manosque': a Grant to the Templars in Latin Syria and a Charter of King Hugh I of Cyprus[1]

AMONG THE manuscripts which once belonged to the French virtuoso and antiquarian, Nicolas-Claude Fabri de Peiresc (1580–1637), and which are now in the Bibliothèque Inguimbertine at Carpentras is a bound volume of the early seventeenth century comprising copies of documents relating to French religious houses, the Society of Jesus and the Knights of St. John (Carpentras MS. 1816).[2] The collection of Hospitaller documents was used by J. Delaville Le Roulx in his *Cartulaire général*,[3] but both he and other modern historians have overlooked two pieces to be found there: the précis of a *vidimus* or confirmation of a grant of the village of Cabor to the Templars, and a charter of King Hugh I of Cyprus dated September 1210. This oversight is all the more extraordinary as the documents were accurately described in the library's catalogue published as long ago as 1899,[4] and both appear twice in the manuscript. On fos. 688v and 672 there are what seem to be rough copies, evidently derived from now lost earlier manuscripts, perhaps the originals, and on fos. 522 and 544r–v there are carelessly executed transcriptions of the rough copies. This edition of these documents is based on the readings as preserved on fos. 688v and 672.

Bibliothèque Inguimbertine, Carpentras MS. 1816 fo. 688v

[PRÉCIS OF A *VIDIMUS* OR CONFIRMATION BY JOSCIUS, ARCHBISHOP OF TYRE, OF THE SALE OF CABOR TO THE TEMPLARS BY JOSCELIN III OF EDESSA, APPARENTLY BETWEEN OCTOBER 1186 AND JOSCELIN'S DEATH AT AN UNKNOWN DATE AFTER SEPTEMBER 1190 (UNDATED)]

Joscius Tyrensis[5] archiepiscopus notum facit quod comes Joscelinus, quondam regni Jerusalem senescallus, concessit domui templi in perpetuam eleemosinam[6] Chabur cum omnibus suis pertinentiis sub tali ratione quod fratres[7] templi mille bisantios pro dextris suis exsolvent;[8] eum testem de eo esse rogaverunt[9] fratres templi; sine [?] die. Sigillum

[1] I wish to thank M. le conservateur, Bibliothèque Inguimbertine, Carpentras, for his kindness in supplying photographs of the manuscript discussed and for permission to publish extracts from it. Thanks are also due to Dr. Pierre Chaplais and Dr. Jonathan Riley-Smith for their invaluable assistance.
[2] For a description see L. Duhamel, J. Liabastres and L.-H. Labande, *Manuscrits de la Bibliothèque de Carpentras* (Catalogue général des manuscrits des bibliothèques publiques de France: Départements, xxxiv–xxxvi, Paris, 1899–1903), ii. 563–82.
[3] *Cartulaire général de l'ordre des Hospitaliers de S. Jean de Jérusalem, 1100–1310* (4 vols., Paris, 1894–1906), nos. 5, 20, 45 etc. (Delaville Le Roulx used the older catalogue number and referred to the manuscript as MS. Peiresc 48.)
[4] Duhamel, ii. 572, 574.
[5] Fo. 522: *Tyensis*
[6] Fo. 522: *elemosynam*
[7] Fo. 522: *tres*
[8] Fo. 522: *exsoluerit*
[9] Fo. 668v: *rogaverint*

plumbeum appensum serico rubro; ab una parte archiepiscopus[10] in pontificalibus et inscriptum: 'Joscius Dei gratia Tyrensis[11] archiepiscopus'; ab altera parte apostolus et inscriptum:[12] 'Joannes[13] apostolus et evangelista'.

Carpentras MS. 1816 fo. 672

[KING HUGH I OF CYPRUS CONFIRMS THE GRANT OF A PIECE OF LAND TO THE KNIGHTS OF ST. JOHN BY JOHN OF LA BAUME (SEPTEMBER 1210)]

In nomine sanctae et individuae Trinitatis, Patris et Filii et Spiritus sancti, amen. Ego Hugo, per Dei gratiam rex Cypri, notum facio omnibus praesentibus et futuris quod Johannes de Balma, assensu et concessione dominae Agnetis matris suae, pro salute animae suae animarumque parentum suorum dedit et in perpetuam eleemosinam concessit fratri Garino de Monte Acuto, venerabili magistro sanctae domus hospitalis sancti Johannis, et fratribus eiusdem domus auctoritate mea et concessione unam peciam terre coherentem terre casalis hospitalis quod vocatur More in territorio Nicoss', et ex alia[14] parte coherentem prastiae Sancti Sergii, et ex alia parte Crionerou[15] et terre prastie fratris raicii Johannis. Hanc autem praedictam totam terram distinctam a locis prescriptis usque ad flumen quod dicitur Pechea[16] pretaxatus Johannes praedictae domui hospitalis dedit et in perpetuam eleemosinam concessit. Instanter inde supplicans quatenus ego pernotatam donationem suam domui hospitalis factam praesenti scripto ac sigilli mei impressione confirmo et subscriptorum virorum testimonio corroboro, quorum haec sunt nomina: Galterius Cesar', regni Cypri connestabulus, Aymericus de Rivet, Cypri senescallus, Reynaldus Suessionensis, Cypri marescallus, Galterius de Bethsan, Laurentius de Morfo, Symon Paphensis, Marinus de Bombel, Galterius Bellus, Petrus Chaperon. Factum est hoc anno ab incarnatione Domini M.CC X mense Septembri. Sigillum est regis sedentis; in circulo, 'Hugonis regis Cypri'. In altera parte turris eminens inter minores duas clausas; in circulo, 'Civitas Nicossie'. Appensum est serico rubro.

The latinity of both documents shows the influence of post-medieval tendencies as is frequent in manuscripts copied at about the beginning of the seventeenth century. The précis of the Templar document is probably late, and although its text is far from satisfactory, it helps fill a major gap in our knowledge of the history of the estate concerned. The descriptions of the *bullae* are of interest. That of Joscius of Tyre accords with another description inserted at the end of a copy of a document of 1187 and with the only, albeit fragmentary, example known to be extant.[17] That of Hugh I, however, is at variance both with a surviving *bulla* of his and with descriptions of two others known from copies of documents of 1217. On these the legends read 'HUGO DEI GRA REX CIPRI' instead of '[Sigillum] Hugonis regis Cypri', and 'CASTELLUM NICOSSIE' instead of 'Civitas Nicossie'.[18] The legend 'CIVITAS NICOS[S]IE', however, was borne by *bullae* of both King Aimery (1196–1205) and King Henry I (1218–53).[19]

---

[10] Fo. 522: *actum*
[11] Fo. 522: *Tyensis*
[12] The last 3 words omitted on fo. 522.
[13] Fo. 668v: *Johs* erased. Fo. 522: *Johannes*
[14] Fo. 672: corrected from *altera* [?]
[15] Fo. 544: *Coionerou*
[16] *Lege Pediea* [?]
[17] *Codice Diplomatico della Repubblica di Genova*, ed. C. Imperiale di Sant'Angelo (3 vols., Rome, 1936–42), ii. 320; F. Chandon de Briailles, 'Bulles de l'Orient latin', *Syria*, xxvii (1950), 293 and plate XIV, no. 12. See F. Chandon de Briailles, 'Bulle de Clérembaut de Broyes, archevèque de Tyr', *ibid.*, xxi (1940), 82.
[18] G. Schlumberger, F. Chalandon and A. Blanchet, *Sigillographie de l'Orient latin* (Paris, 1943), pp. 144–5.
[19] *Ibid.*, pp. 143–4, 146.

The sole historian to have noticed these documents and to have made use of them was Du Cange. Both are referred to by him in his *Les familles d'Outre-mer*, and on both occasions he gave as his source a certain 'Cartulaire de Manosque'.[20] Manosque was the headquarters of a Hospitaller commandery in the Priory of St. Gilles. E.-G. Rey, the nineteenth-century editor of Du Cange's study, was unable to identify this cartulary,[21] but from a careful comparison of all the documents that Du Cange cited as belonging to it with the contents of the Carpentras 1816, there can be no doubt that our manuscript is a version of it. Besides documents from the Latin East it also contains a number relating to the commandery of Manosque itself. Whether this was the actual manuscript that Du Cange used is unknown, though he is known to have relied on another of Peiresc's manuscripts for his knowledge of the legal treatise by John of Ibelin.[22]

To place the grant to the Templars in its context it is necessary to establish as far as possible both the date of Joscius's confirmation or *vidimus* and also the date of the original grant by Joscelin III of Edessa. Joscius was already arch-bishop of Tyre in October 1186,[23] and he died at an unknown date between October 1200 and May 1202.[24] The fact that Joscelin is described as 'quondam regni Jerusalem senescallus' in the précis strongly suggests that he was dead at the time Joscius's instrument was issued or at least that he had ceased to be seneschal. Joscelin is known to have died before October 1200,[25] but in all likeli-hood his death occurred shortly after September 1190, the date of his last appearance as witness to a surviving privilege.[26] Joscelin is almost certainly the 'comes Iocelinus' mentioned by the author of the *Itinerarium peregrinorum* among those who died during the siege of Acre (1189–91),[27] and this idea is supported by the evidence of the charters issued by Guy of Lusignan during the siege. Joscelin was a regular and prominent witness before September 1190,[28] and the abrupt disappearance of his name thereafter is most readily explained by his death.[29] He was still seneschal, a post he had held since 1176, when last heard of; the next known occupant of that office, Ralph of Tiberias, had acquired it by 5 January 1194.[30] The date of Joscius's instrument thus belongs to the period, September 1190–May 1202.

The question of the date of Joscelin's sale of Cabor to the Templars raises a number of problems. The transaction must have taken place after 21 October 1186, for on that day King Guy of Lusignan issued two privileges mentioning Cabor. In one he confirmed Joscelin's possession of it, stating that Joscelin had

[20] C. du Fresne Du Cange, *Les familles d'Outre-mer*, ed. E.-G. Rey (Collection de documents inédits sur l'histoire de France, Paris, 1869), pp. 520, 751.

[21] See *ibid.*, p. 974.

[22] M. Grandclaude, 'Classement sommaire des manuscrits des principaux livres des Assises de Jérusalem', *Rev. historique de droit français et étranger*, 4th ser., v (1926), 471–2.

[23] *Tabulae ordinis Theutonici*, ed. E. Strehlke (Berlin, 1869), p. 19.

[24] *Ibid.*, p. 31; *Urkunden zur älteren Handels- und Staatsgeschichte der Republik Venedig mit besonderer Beziehung auf Byzanz und die Levante*, ed. G. L. F. Tafel and G. M. Thomas (3 vols., Vienna, 1856–7), i. 425–6 (wrongly dated 1203).

[25] *Tab. ord. Theut.*, p. 31.

[26] *Ibid.*, p. 22.

[27] *Das Itinerarium peregrinorum*, ed. H. E. Mayer (Stuttgart, 1962), p. 317.

[28] *Regesta Regni Hierosolymitani, 1097–1291*, ed. R. Röhricht (2 vols., Innsbruck, 1893–1904), nos. 690, 693, 696, 697. (No. 697 should be dated 24 Apr. 1190; see H. E. Mayer, *Marseilles Levantehandel und ein akkonensisches Fälscheratelier des 13. Jahrhunderts* (Tübingen, 1972), pp. 183–6.)

[29] See *Reg. Hier.*, nos. 698, 701, 702. The attempt by R. L. Nicholson (*Joscelyn III and the Fall of the Crusader States, 1134–99* (Leyden, 1973), p. 198) to date his death to after 26 Aug. 1199 is insufficiently supported by the evidence.

[30] *Cartulaire général*, no. 972.

purchased the fief of Cabor, consisting of the village itself (present-day Kabul, a few miles east-south-east of Acre) and the house at Acre which went with it, for 5,000 besants.[31] In the other Guy announced that he had agreed with Joscelin that Cabor was to be part of the marriage portion for Joscelin's elder daughter whom it was proposed to marry to Guy's brother, William of Valence.[32] This projected marriage came to nothing, although for how long after October 1186 hopes of its conclusion were still entertained is unknown. The sale must therefore belong to the period between the collapse of the marriage proposals and Joscelin's death which, as has been argued, was after, but perhaps not long after, September 1190.

In attempting to get closer to the date of the sale, three or four other dates are relevant: Cabor was lost by the Christians in the immediate aftermath of the battle of Hattin (4 July 1187), not to be recovered until after the capture of Acre (July 1191) at the earliest; in October 1187 Cabor and other properties in and around Acre were given to the Pisans by Conrad of Montferrat.[33] Joscelin is unlikely to have sold Cabor to the Templars before Conrad's grant, since several Templars, including the grand preceptor, at that time the Order's senior officer who was both alive and at liberty,[34] gave their support to Conrad's grant. It is doubtful whether, even in the period of crisis of late 1187, they would have agreed to losing their rights to an estate which had changed hands for 5,000 besants not long before, or that Conrad would have risked antagonizing them by alienating it. Furthermore, if Joscelin sold Cabor before Hattin, we have to assume that the marriage project was abandoned soon after it had been agreed and that there was good reason why he should be prepared to sell for 1,000 besants what he had recently bought for 5,000 besants; once Cabor was in Muslim hands, however, it would not be surprising if he were prepared to sell his rights to it should it be recovered at a discount. The sale would scarcely date to the period July–October 1187, since, quite apart from Templar support for the grant to the Pisans, the Order would presumably have lacked the desire, authority or money to make what at that time must have seemed an extremely speculative purchase.

Placing the sale of Cabor after October 1187 is not without difficulties. It would still mean that the Templars would be buying lands not in Christian hands, and, in addition, there would be the prospect of litigation with the Pisans once it was recovered. On the other hand, our knowledge of political developments lends some plausibility to a post-1187 date. Joscelin had been among the Frankish lords who had made their way to Tyre after Hattin and was said to have been one of those who had welcomed Conrad of Montferrat when he arrived at Tyre at about the end of July 1187.[35] He then disappears from view until 10 April 1190 when he witnessed a privilege of Guy of Lusignan issued at the siege of Acre.[36] Any explanation of the silence of the sources is necessarily a matter for conjecture, but the most likely reason why Joscelin does not appear as a witness to any of the privileges issued by Conrad of Montferrat is that he, like a

[31] Tab. ord. Theut., p. 20.
[32] Ibid., p. 21. There appears to be no other record of this member of the Lusignan family.
[33] Documenti sulle relazioni delle città toscane coll'Oriente cristiano e coi Turchi fino all'anno 1531, ed. G. Müller (Florence, 1879), p. 30.
[34] See M. L. Bulst-Thiele, Sacrae Domus Militiae Templi Hierosolymitani Magistri: Untersuchungen zur Geschichte des Templerordens, 1118/9–1314 (Göttingen, 1974), p. 117.
[35] Cod. dip. Genova, ii. 318–19; Annali Genovesi di Caffaro e de' suoi continuatori dal 1099 al 1293, ed. L. T. Belgrano and C. Imperiale di Sant'Angelo (5 vols., Rome, 1890–1929), i. 145.
[36] Reg. Hier., no. 690.

number of prominent Palestinian feudatories, had opposed Conrad's regime in Tyre from its early stages.[37] Conrad, who from the outset seems to have intended to displace the captive Guy of Lusignan, would have seen Joscelin, the man who had engineered Guy and Sibylla's *coup d'état* of 1186, as an enemy,[38] and it is possible that it was in the spirit of personal malice that he chose Cabor as one of the properties with which to solicit the much-needed help of the Pisans. Certainly it was not his to dispose of legally. In July 1188 Guy of Lusignan and Gerard of Ridefort, the master of the Temple and Joscelin's old political ally, were released from captivity, and by September of that year the Templars had withdrawn their support from Conrad.[39] With the beginning of the siege of Acre in August 1189, the prospects of recovering Cabor must have seemed brighter, and so the idea of its purchase not so far-fetched, especially if the Templars were prepared to help Joscelin out of the financial straits in which he may well have found himself.

In the mid twelfth century Cabor had belonged to a woman named Joiette and in 1175 it was in the possession of her grandson, Rohard.[40] In 1183 King Baldwin IV ratified the purchase of Cabor by his mother, Agnes of Courtenay,[41] and on her death[42] it would have passed by inheritance to her daughter Sibylla, the wife of Guy of Lusignan. Guy then sold it to Joscelin for 5,000 besants, confirming his sale in October 1186 and agreeing at the same time that it was to be part of the marriage portion for Joscelin's daughter. In October 1187 Conrad of Montferrat granted Cabor to the Pisans and at some point before his death Joscelin sold his rights to the Templars for 1,000 besants. There were thus two claimants and the situation cannot have been simplified by the fact that on 19 November 1189 Guy of Lusignan confirmed Conrad's grant.[43] Guy needed Pisan support both against Saladin and against Conrad, and, if confirmation of Conrad's acts was the price, he was probably in no position to quibble. It may be significant that of all the surviving privileges issued by Guy between his release and the end of 1190, this confirmation and another privilege for the Pisans of the same date[44] are the only ones for which Joscelin did not act as a witness. At some point during the eleven-nineties the Templars sought to enhance their claim by having Joscius, who besides being archbishop of Tyre was chancellor of the kingdom, endorse their rights. No more is known of Cabor until May 1238 when it is mentioned in a papal letter among a group of properties belonging to the Hospitallers.[45] Unfortunately there is no evidence as to how the Hospitallers came by it—conceivably they acquired it directly or indirectly from the Pisans.

In May 1262, in a general agreement settling a number of disputes between the Orders, the Templars renounced their rights to Cabor in favour of the Hospitallers.[46] Presumably they handed over any written title they may have had

---

[37] H. E. Mayer, 'On the beginnings of the communal movement in the Holy Land: the commune of Tyre', *Traditio*, xxiv (1968), 451, 453.

[38] For a recent discussion of these events see J. S. C. Riley-Smith, *The Feudal Nobility and the Kingdom of Jerusalem, 1174–1277* (1973), pp. 109–14.

[39] See Mayer, 'Communal movement', pp. 455–6.

[40] *Cartulaire général*, no. 480. For Rohard of Cabor see *Tab. ord. Theut.*, p. 10; *Cartulaire général*, no. 579.

[41] J. Delaville Le Roulx, 'Inventaire de pièces de Terre-Sainte de l'ordre de l'Hôpital', *Rev. de l'Orient latin*, iii (1895), 36–106, no. 262.

[42] Before Oct. 1186, *Tab. ord. Theut.*, p. 20.

[43] *Documenti delle città toscane*, pp. 38–9.

[44] *Ibid.*, pp. 36–8.

[45] *Cartulaire général*, no. 2199. See also no. 2661 (another reference to Cabor as a Hospitaller property, Dec. 1253).

[46] *Ibid.*, no. 3028. See J. S. C. Riley-Smith, *The Knights of St. John in Jerusalem and Cyprus, c. 1050–1310* (1967), pp. 449–50.

to the property which would explain how Joscius's instrument recording a sale to the Templars found its way into the Hospitaller archives. What we have therefore is a clue to the beginnings of one of these disputes between the Orders. It originated some seventy years earlier in the period following the collapse of the Kingdom of Jerusalem and was connected with the struggle for power between Guy of Lusignan and Conrad of Montferrat.

Hugh I's charter records a grant of land by a certain John of La Baume to the Hospitallers. In Cyprus feudatories were not permitted to alienate their feudal holdings to religious corporations without royal permission,[47] nor could they authenticate such alienations;[48] hence the instrument takes the form of an announcement by the king that the transfer of title has been effected and stresses royal permission for the grant to be made. Nothing is known of John of La Baume (de Balma), nor of Agnes his mother with whom he is associated in this grant. Members of the La Baume family, however, were among the earliest Latin settlers in Cyprus in the eleven-nineties,[49] and the family name continues to appear in the sources until the early fifteenth century. The La Baumes were not prominent members of the aristocracy, although in the late fourteenth century members of the family were appointed to the largely honorific posts of constable and marshal of Jerusalem.[50] The approximate location of the land in question can be established. Mora (More), the only one of the three neighbouring villages shown on modern maps, is situated about ten miles due east of the centre of Nicosia;[51] Crionerou was near another vanished settlement, Loukkomiatis (Lefcomiati), shown on Lord Kitchener's map published in 1885 as being about three and a half miles east of Nicosia;[52] St. Sergius is otherwise unknown,[53] but it may have lain to the south as the River Pedhieos flows north of Mora and the site of Loukkomiatis in an easterly direction. Both manuscript copies read 'Pechea' as the name of the river, but there can be little doubt that the emendation to 'Pediea'—hence the modern Pedhieos—is justified. The land referred to in this grant was thus to the west of Mora, itself a Hospitaller possession, and was presumably administered with it after 1210.

The reference to a rays ('raicius') is of interest since no other mention of this officer is known from Cypriot sources of the thirteenth century.[54]

The witness list may provide a clue explaining one aspect of the background to the political crisis in Cyprus in 1210 which resulted in the fall of the regent,

[47] Philip of Novara, 'Livre', Recueil des Historiens des Croisades (hereafter R.H.C.) (16 vols., Paris, 1841–1906), Lois, i. 530–1.
[48] This is implicit in the fact that no Cypriot feudatory seems to have the right of coins. This right, together with those of court and justise, is only mentioned once by the Cypriot jurist, Philip of Novara (ibid., p. 541), and then not in a specifically Cypriot context. See F. Chandon de Briailles, 'Le droit de "coins" dans le royaume de Jérusalem', Syria, xxiii (1942–3), 244–57.
[49] See Reg. Hier., nos. 723, 737, 780.
[50] For an incomplete account of the family see Du Cange, pp. 520–2.
[51] For further evidence that Mora was in Hospitaller possession by 1210 see Cartulaire général, no. 1354. It was still owned by the Order in the 16th century. L. de Mas Latrie, Histoire de l'île de Chypre sous le règne des princes de la maison de Lusignan (3 vols., Paris, 1852–61), iii. 502.
[52] For references to Crionerou where it is mentioned together with Loukkomiatis see Mas Latrie, iii. 511; Chypre sous les Lusignans. Documents chypriotes des archives du Vatican, XIVe et XVe siècles, ed. J. Richard (Paris, 1962), p. 146 and n. 8.
[53] Unless it was the 'San Sergi' given with, among other properties, 'il casal Rionero' (Crionerou?) to Gioan Cercasso in the reign of James II. Florio Bustron, 'Chronique de l'île de Chypre', ed. R. de Mas Latrie, Mélanges Historiques, v (Collection de documents inédits sur l'histoire de France, Paris, 1886), p. 418. The Ayios Seryios to the north of Famagusta is clearly another place of the same name.
[54] For the rays in the Kingdom of Jerusalem see J. S. C. Riley-Smith, 'Some lesser officials in Latin Syria', Eng. Hist. Rev., lxxxvii (1972), 1–15.

Walter of Montbéliard. Only four other formal charters from the Cypriot chancery are known from the reign of Hugh I (1205–18), one of which, a general confirmation of Hospitaller rights and properties in Cyprus, dates from the same month (September 1210) as this new charter and has an identical witness list, while another, a grant to the Holy Sepulchre, dates from November of that year.[55] Together these documents are the earliest surviving *acta* of King Hugh after his coming of age and the witnesses to them give some indication of who Hugh's leading counsellors were at that time. On Hugh's majority, Walter of Montbéliard, called upon to give account of the finances of his regency, fled into exile.[56] His flight probably occurred not long before September, since by the time he had made his way via Tripoli to Acre, John of Brienne, who himself had reached the East only in mid-September,[57] was there to welcome him. According to the principal account of these events, Walter had incurred the young king's displeasure by keeping him short of funds during his minority, but the fact that he fled is evidence not so much for any financial maladministration as for his realization that a party strongly opposed to him had gained control. Hugh, who would have been aged fifteen at the time, may or may not have been able to formulate his own policies, but though there is no direct evidence that he was dominated by his advisers, it is unlikely that he would have been able to act without them. The witness lists of all three charters of 1210 are headed by the constable, Walter of Caesarea, followed by the seneschal, Aimery of Rivet, and the marshal, Raynald of Soissons; in fourth place on each occasion was Walter of Bethsan. Aimery and Raynald, as well as Simon of Paphos and Walter Le Bel, had been prominent in Cyprus since the eleven-nineties.[58] Lawrence of Morf, too, was said to have been numbered among the first settlers.[59] Though Walter of Caesarea is not previously recorded in Cyprus, he was a member of a long-established Jerusalemite family and heir presumptive to the lordship of Caesarea.[60] Walter of Bethsan's brothers had been prominent in Cyprus earlier,[61] and his nephew, Gremont the titular lord of Bethsan, witnessed the grant to the Holy Sepulchre. Thus of the nine witnesses to the Hospitaller charters of September 1210, only two, Marinus of Bombel and Peter Chappe, are possible newcomers to the Latin East.[62]

Walter, however, was a newcomer. On the death of King Aimery in 1205 he had become regent because Aimery's only surviving son, Hugh I, was a minor and he, as the husband of Hugh's elder sister and then heiress, Burgundia, was his closest adult male relative.[63] Little is known of his career before 1205. He was the second son of Amé of Montfaucon, count of Montbéliard;[64] in 1199 he took the cross in response to the preaching of the Fourth Crusade, but in the spring of

[55] *Cartulaire général*, no. 1354; *Cartulaire de l'église du Saint Sépulcre de Jérusalem*, ed. E. de Rozière (Paris, 1849), pp. 314–15; *Reg. Hier.*, nos. 844, 846. The others date to 1217. *Reg. Hier.*, nos. 900, 903, see no. 896.
[56] 'L'estoire de Eracles empereur et la conqueste de la Terre d'Outremer', *R.H.C., Historiens Occidentaux*, ii. 315–16. See G. Hill, *A History of Cyprus* (4 vols., Cambridge, 1940–52), ii. 77.
[57] 'Eracles', p. 310.
[58] *Reg. Hier.*, nos. 723, 729, 737, 780; J. Richard, 'L'abbaye cistercienne de Jubin et le prieuré Saint-Blaise de Nicosie', 'Επετηρὶς τοῦ Κέντρου 'Επιστημονικῶν 'Ερευνῶν, iii (Nicosia, 1969–70), 69.
[59] 'Les Lignages d'Outremer', *R.H.C., Lois*, ii. 472.
[60] Du Cange, p. 280.
[61] *Reg. Hier.*, nos. 723, 729. See 'Eracles', p. 213 (var. D).
[62] Two other witnesses to the charter of Nov. 1210, Walter of St. Bertin and Walter Juvenis, are likely to have been members of families well established in the East by that date.
[63] Hill, ii. 73–4.
[64] *Documents et mémoire pour servir à l'histoire du territoire de Belfort*, ed. L. Viellard (Besançon, 1884), pp. 211, 356 n. 1.

1201 accompanied his kinsman, Walter of Brienne, on his expedition to Italy.[65] What evidence there is seems to suggest that it was not until after this that he went to the East and married Burgundia. Aimery of Lusignan is said to have made him constable of Jerusalem at the time of his marriage;[66] the marriage must therefore date to the years 1197–1205, the period of Aimery's reign in Jerusalem, but, as Walter is known to have been in the West in the years 1199–1201 and as John of Ibelin is known to have been constable until at least as late as 1200,[67] it would appear to belong to the closing years of his reign. In other words, Walter had achieved a rapid rise to power; it is not unreasonable to suppose that the older established vassals in the East resented him.

---

[65] Geoffrey de Villehardouin, *La conquête de Constantinople*, ed. and trans. E. Faral (2 vols., Paris, 1961), i. 7, 35.

[66] 'Eracles', p. 316.

[67] *Docs. de Belfort*, pp. 358–60, 361, 363–4; *Reg. Hier.*, no. 776.

XXI

The Crusades and their Critics

Abstract

Crusading expeditions and the concept of crusading have always been controversial. But why should the crusades have a negative image in the West as well as in those lands targeted by the crusaders? Many crusades ended in failure or enjoyed limited success, and after what was perceived as the God-given success of the First Crusade contemporaries could only assume that God had then withheld support. The loss of Jerusalem and, in the late thirteenth century, the expulsion of the crusaders from Syria and Palestine gave further pause for thought. Later centuries could see the crusades as the instrument of a corrupt papacy, an expression of superstition and barbarism or an opportunity for colonial exploitation. The crusades continue to hold political resonances in today's world, and so what are we to make of the futility and atrocities or the heroism and piety that attended the crusading movement?

1999 saw the 900th anniversary of the crusaders' conquest of Jerusalem. I was in Israel at the time of the actual anniversary, attending an academic conference that had been deliberately timed to mark that occasion, and, while I was there, various groups of westerners - mostly I think from English-speaking countries: Britain, America, Canada - had come to the Near East with the intention of apologizing for the crusades. I am not sure how they got on or whether much notice was taken of them, but their actions set me thinking. We cannot, of course, undo what has been done, but should we apologize for past events - especially for episodes that occurred long before our own time? There is no doubt that these people were well motivated: trying to heal present hurts; trying to break the cycle of violence and hatred. But should I, as

This article was published as part of the proceedings of the Round Table "Archaeology and the Crusades" organised within the framework of the project "Crossings: Movements of People and Movement of Culture: Changes in the Mediterranean from Ancient to Modern Times" which was supported by the European Union Framework Programme, Culture 2000.

a professional historian, be imbued with a sense of guilt, or, for that matter, a sense of pride, when viewing the past?

Back in the 1960s when I was an undergraduate in Scotland at the University of St Andrews I took a course on the philosophy of History taught by members of the university's Moral Philosophy Department. At that time the influence of Oxford philosopher A.J. Ayer was considerable. Ayer had been a follower of Wittgenstein and was the leading British exponent of Logical Positivism. So far as history was concerned, there were two main points from that school of thought that we students had to take on board: first, it is not the job of historians to pass moral judgements on the past, and, accordingly, they should eschew the use of emotive language and the making of value judgements, and, secondly, however hard they might try, scholars cannot escape from the context of their present cultural environment when interpreting historical events.

Let me take these points in reverse order. Bearing in mind Benedetto Croce's famous dictum that 'All History is Contemporary History', historians can do no more than describe how, here and now, we perceive the surviving evidence from the past. In part we see the past through the writings of other historians, but even when we turn to the primary sources, however objective we may try to be, our perceptions are inevitably going to be coloured by the sum of our intellectual baggage and by our contemporary environment.

So what about moral judgements? In a sense the people who wanted to apologize were themselves making a moral judgement on the past. Clearly they believed that the Crusades were a 'Bad Thing' and were responding to what they considered a moral imperative to try to do something to mitigate their memory. A.J. Ayer and his followers took the view that the historian's role is to describe what happened in the past and offer a balanced explanation of why things turned out as they did; but in their view - and indeed in the view of most modern scholars engaged in historical research - the making of value judgements is at odds with the intellectual rigour that should be brought to bear on the discipline.

It is of course getting a 'balanced explanation' that is the problem. It is no part of my purpose to set out to justify the crusades, but I wonder whether the people who wanted to apologize for them realized that when the crusaders arrived in Jerusalem in 1099 the majority of the population of Syria and Palestine were Christians who had been ruled by a Muslim minority since the seventh century, and so when the propagandists for the crusade spoke of 'liberating the Church in the East' or 'liberating the Christians in the East' this was not just spin. (The fact that the crusaders then went on to treat the indigenous Christians rather badly is another matter.) Then again, while it is true that the crusaders were intruders in the Muslim heartland in the Near East, the Dar al-Islam, it is also true that the credentials of many of the regimes they supplanted or attempted to supplant were suspect: Egypt and southern Palestine were ruled by the Shiite Fatimid Caliphate based in Cairo, although, so far as I can make out, most of the caliph's Muslim subjects were Sunnis; in Damascus and Aleppo the military elite that held power were Turks, who had only arrived and displaced Arab rule in the course of the previous half century; Antioch, which was also under Turkish control when the crusaders arrived there in 1097, had been ruled by the Christian Byzantine empire as recently as 1084.

Be that as it may, the fact remains that for many people the crusades have a negative image. You will recall that George W. Bush's advisers told the president very firmly to excise the 'C' word from his vocabulary in the run-up to the Second Iraq War for fear of antagonizing those Arab governments that were sympathetic to his plans to topple Saddam Hussein. For those on the receiving end - Muslims and, with the broadening of the scope of the crusades, Greeks - the crusades are perceived as vehicles of violence and oppression. But in the West too the whole idea has come to acquire negative connotations, especially among people of liberal persuasion, and I want to spend the rest of this lecture exploring further why that should be. Why should the crusades have a negative image in the West as well as in those lands targeted by the crusaders?

The First Crusade was without doubt a huge success. It had begun in 1095 when, at the ecclesiastical council held at Clermont in central France, Pope Urban II had called for an army to aid Byzantium and win back Jerusalem for Christendom. The response was enormous; the contingents converged on Constantinople and went on to aid the emperor, Alexios Komnenos, recover Nicaea; they then advanced across Asia Minor to Antioch, which they captured after a long and difficult siege, and in 1099 they marched south and took Jerusalem. It was a remarkable achievement. Contemporaries regarded it as nothing short of miraculous, and so it was that when in the years immediately after the crusade various western clerics took it upon themselves to record these events, they wrote of them in terms of a God-given victory in which the crusaders, or Franks, were God's chosen instruments. Inspired by biblical examples such as Gideon's defeat of the Midianites (Judges 7), they saw these events as 'The Deeds of God operating through the Franks' or, to use their own Latin phrase, they were the 'Gesta Dei per Francos'.

Constructing a view of the crusade in these theological terms had two major implications: it was almost inevitable that the exercise would be repeated, and, secondly, if a later crusade were to fail - and fail they most certainly did - that failure would also have to be explained in theological terms.

During the twelfth and thirteenth centuries there were many more crusading expeditions, and as the movement developed so it became defined. A crusade had to be initiated by the pope, for the pope, and only the pope, could offer the necessary incentives. On the one hand there was the spiritual incentive - the indulgence - which was variously seen as the remission of penance, the forgiveness of sin, or the assurance of eternal salvation for those who died on the expedition. On the other, there were more mundane inducements: church protection for lands and family members while the crusader was away; the suspension of lawsuits; and, later, financial help from the church to help pay the very considerable expenses of going. The crusaders took a vow to complete the campaign and wore the badge of the cross.

In calling a crusade the pope utilized ideas then current about the Just War and the Holy War, for the crusade had to be both justifiable and holy. The formulation of Christian ideas about 'just war' - the circumstances in which warfare is licit for Christians - went back to St Augustine, and his theses continue to have modern resonances. There were three main points:

1. War had to be defensive, or, by extension of that idea, either fought with the intention of recovering what had been lost, or designed to pre-empt threatened attack. There is of course ample scope here for a broad interpretation: the point is that naked aggression was not allowable.

2. War had to be called by the legitimate authority. Kings could rightly wage war to defend their kingdoms, but wars in defence of Christendom - and that was how the crusades were presented - were matters for the pope. There are two points here: it was not open to just anybody to start a war, and so private warfare or vendetta was ruled out; and secondly, it was the pope and not the emperor who could claim to be the legitimate authority when it came to defending Christendom. There are clear echoes here of the controversies between the pope and the western emperor that had convulsed much of western Europe in the second half of the eleventh century, and the First Crusade can be seen as an assertion by the pope that it was he, and not the emperor, who was ultimately in control.

3. War had to be fought with the right intention. Crusaders were to go on crusade, not because they liked killing people or because they were out for selfish gain, but because they believed in the righteousness of what they were doing: liberating their Christian co-religionists from oppression, and freeing the places made sacred by Christ's presence on earth from the control of unbelievers. So the crusades were supposed to be motivated by love: love for one's fellow Christians; love for Christ. That of course was the theory: what really passed through the minds of the crusaders is much harder to establish, and what actually happened in practice might well seem to have been at variance with this ideal.

So the crusades had to conform with contemporary ideas about the just war. More difficult to analyze is the idea of Holy War, and medieval theologians and canon lawyers were rather reticent about trying to define what was meant by this phrase. In the Old Testament, though not in the New, we find the idea of warfare waged at God's command, and so, in the context of medieval warfare against the enemies of Christendom, whoever they might be, it fell to the pope as Vicar of Christ and Successor of St Peter to declare God's command. There is

XXI

184

no doubt that, in the centuries before the First Crusade, Christian thinkers seem to have taken the view that warfare against unbelievers was praiseworthy and not subject to the same censure reserved for war against one's fellow Christians.

There was thus a crusading ideology promoted by the Church. But did the lay knights and the other warriors who went actually subscribe to it? This is a question that is largely unanswerable, and it is easy to be cynical about their motivation. Even so, there is reason to believe that many participants in the crusades did accept the church's view. Certainly many crusaders believed that their task was to cleanse the world of unbelief. This goal goes some way to explaining why, at the start of the First Crusade, certain groups of crusaders set about massacring the Jewish communities in parts of western Europe. (It has been claimed that these atrocities were the most devastating attacks on the Jews in western Europe at any time before the twentieth century.) The need to rid the world of unbelief may also explain the crusaders' refusal to allow Muslims or Jews to reside within the walls of Jerusalem after its conquest. On the other hand, evidence for the once popular idea that men went on crusade to win land or wealth proves to be at best dubious. Some crusaders undoubtedly intended to remain in the East for the rest of their lives, but, although crusaders could win renown for their exploits, there is little ground for supposing that many returned richer than when they set off. Although peer pressure may have helped persuade many to take part, it would seem that most crusaders were convinced of their moral duty to do what they were doing, and that freeing Jerusalem and the other places made sacred by Christ's presence on Earth was a worthy and meritorious activity.

In the centuries that followed the events of 1095-99 there were many more crusades, and, although in popular thinking their primary goal was often identified with the Holy Land, in fact the objectives of the crusades were diverse. From the twelfth century onwards crusaders could defend Christian Europe against its external enemies in other theatres, notably Spain and the Baltic lands. From around 1200 crusades against the internal enemies of Christendom began; these might be against heretics, such as in the Albigensian Crusades of the early decades of the thirteenth century, or, as became increasingly frequent later in the thirteenth century and in the fourteenth, against the enemies of papacy in Italy and elsewhere. Eventually there were to be crusades against Protestants: indeed, the Spanish Armada of 1588 was a crusading expedition intended to topple the Protestant regime in England and so create political conditions suitable for inducing the English to return to the bosom of the Catholic Church.

Before I go any further there are two common misconceptions about the crusades that need to be cleared out of the way. Firstly, the crusades were not wars of conversion intended to force unbelievers into accepting Christianity. It was only much later - in the mid-thirteenth century - that we find a pope suggesting that one of the several potential benefits of a crusade was that, by conquering territory inhabited by unbelievers, missionary activity would be easier. To begin with, the crusaders were less concerned with the spiritual health of non-Christians than with inducing the Orthodox and members of the other eastern Christian confessions in the lands they conquered to accept papal jurisdiction. Ultimately the crusades achieved precisely the opposite of what had been intended: far from uniting all Christians under papal leadership, relations between western and eastern Christendom sank to a new low. The crusading movement did not in itself cause the schism between the Catholic and Orthodox churches, but it did contribute significantly to the creation of a situation in which any genuine reconciliation became impossible.

Secondly, the crusades did not mark the beginning of mutual antipathy between Islam and Christendom. Christians and Muslims had been fighting each other ever since Islam had appeared in the seventh century of the Christian Era. Initially the Muslims had been very successful, conquering a huge swathe of territory previously under Christian rule, but gradually Christendom began to stage a come-back. The tenth century had witnessed Byzantine advances against the Muslims in Anatolia and the recovery of Crete and Cyprus. In the West there were considerable Christian gains in the eleventh century in Spain, and then, between 1060 and 1091, we see the conquest of Sicily. So the First Crusade need not be viewed a bolt from the blue but rather as the culmination of a long process of Christian expansion at Muslim expense all around the Mediterranean.

So to return to my main point: why the negative image? Even in the middle ages there were people in the West who questioned the sense of going on crusade. If the First Crusade was a major triumph, it is equally true that all the later crusades to the Holy Land and many of those fought in other theatres as well either ended in complete failure or, at best, had only very limited success. After 1187 Jerusalem remained in Muslim hands except for a period of precarious Christian rule from 1229-1244, and eventually, at the end of the thirteenth century, the westerners were expelled from the Holy Land altogether. There were of course good reasons why that should have been so. We could, for example, explain these failures in terms of superior Muslim resources or the erratic behaviour of particular crusaders. But contemporary Christians did not necessarily see things in such terms. After the God-given victory of the First Crusade, how was the absence of divine intervention to ensure further successes to be explained? Clearly God had withheld victory. But why? The most usual explanation was that it was 'because of our sins': God who is just and holy will not give His support to those whose lack of righteousness and holiness renders them unworthy in His sight. (This of course was nothing new: it is an idea that can be found, for example, in Solomon's prayer at the dedication of the Temple as recorded in II Chronicles 6.) Indeed, explaining the failure of crusading expeditions as the consequence of sin became a cliché, endlessly repeated. And so people began to associate crusading with sinfulness and failure and to conclude that, if God was not going to give the expeditions His blessing, crusading was not worth the effort: why go to all the trouble and expense, not to mention the physical danger, of going on crusade if God was going to withhold His support, thereby ensuring that the enterprise would fail anyway? The failure of the crusades was thus a moral failure with the finger of blame pointing at the sinfulness of the crusade leadership and, more generally, at the sinfulness of western Christendom as a whole.

There were plenty of people in the middle ages who were critical of the crusades, but on close analysis it turns out that in most cases they were critical of the aims, organization or conduct of the particular expedition that happened to be at the forefront of their minds at the time, rather than sceptical about the principle of crusading. Even so, the diversification of the aims of the crusades - especially those that were intended to crush the defenders of heretics or those that were against individuals who opposed papal ambitions for political reasons - contributed to bringing the whole idea into disrepute. Crusades against heretics did command widespread support, but, in the event, too many ordinary Christians were the victims of such warfare - I am thinking here in particular of the Albigensian crusades of the early thirteenth century - and when later papal appeals for new crusades elicited scant response that in itself encouraged cynicism. The upshot was that when western Christendom did need defending, as for example in 1241 when the Mongols invaded Poland and Hungary, there was no coordinated response. On that occasion the bitter conflict between the pope and the western emperor, Frederick II of Hohenstaufen, rendered the raising of a crusading army impossible. In the event the Mongols withdrew in 1242 of their own volition, but there were fears that they would return, and so, when a few years later the king of France, Louis IX, led an expedition to Cyprus, Egypt and the Holy Land, there were those in eastern Europe who complained that his forces would have been better deployed nearer home.

Criticism of crusading acquired a new lease of life with the Protestant Reformation of the sixteenth century. To the Protestants, the crusades were yet another example of the misuse of power by the papacy. Much of what they said had an obvious polemical tone; the earliest history of the crusades written in English, Thomas Fuller's *History of the Holy Warre*, which appeared in the 1630s and quickly went through four editions, belongs in this tradition. Fuller, who was a puritan clergyman and fellow of Sydney Sussex College Cambridge, shared the medieval view that the crusaders' failure was a moral failure: in his eyes the movement, conceived by a corrupt papacy and implemented by people whose sinfulness was all too obvious, stood no chance of success.

In one respect, however, there was a definite link between the crusading movement and the origins of Protestantism. The Protestant revolution had started in 1517 with Luther's famous Ninety-Five Theses against the traffic in indulgences nailed to the door of the church in Wittenberg. I am not sure how far Luther was aware of this fact, but in the course of the previous four centuries the traffic in indulgences had largely developed in the context of the crusades. What had started as a promised remission of penance for those who went on crusade came to be seen as the assurance of salvation for those who died during the campaign. But that struck some people as being grossly unfair: it favoured the spiritual welfare of the warriors over those people who would have liked to have taken part in the crusades but who for various reasons could not. We might, for example, include here the elderly, the disabled, the clergy, and, of course, women. So from early in the thirteenth century the offer of the indulgence was extended to those who would pay for someone else to go at their expense. Those entrusted with organizing a crusade knew they would need all the money they could get, and so were only too happy to accept money in exchange for indulgences along with money from other sources such as the fees for releasing men from their crusading vows. What this meant was that crusading and getting people to part with their money became inextricably linked in the minds of many, and so the whole thing came to acquire a distinctly mercenary flavour. As the novelty wore off and failure became the norm, so spontaneous enthusiasm waned. Before long we find partial indulgences - the promise of days off purgatory - having to be offered to those who merely turned up to listen to crusade sermons. At the same time the indulgence was broadened to include other worthy objectives. For example, one of the earliest surviving examples of printing with moveable type from Gutenberg's workshop in Mainz is the 1455 prospectus for indulgences offered to those who would contribute to rebuilding the walls of Nicosia. Other objectives were less worthy, and the whole thing was in danger of getting out of control. The church found itself caught in what Sir Richard Southern described as an 'inflationary spiral', and Luther's Ninety-Five Theses attacked what he regarded as an abuse that betokened both theological perversion that gave a false answer to that essential question, 'What good thing must I do that I may have eternal life?' (Matthew 19:16), and moral depravity. So in trying to place the crusading movement in a wider context, we might conclude that, if one road from the 1095 Council of Clermont had led to Jerusalem, another led to Wittenberg.

As we move nearer the present we come to the Enlightenment of the eighteenth century. Now the spirit of age called on sensible people to put superstitious nonsense behind them and try to think in rational terms. It was an important moment for History, for it was then that

History was redefined as a humanistic discipline. In the middle ages, and for long after, it had been acceptable to explain events in terms of God's will or the operation of divine providence. Back in the twelfth century the great historian of the crusades, Archbishop William of Tyre, had not seen anything incongruous in ascribing rational explanations to particular events and then moving on to invoke God's will to explain others. But after Gibbon, Voltaire and their contemporaries such an approach was anachronistic; History henceforth was to be the record of human achievement and folly, and the crusades could be condemned as part of the superstitious and barbarous middle ages - that dismal period that lay between the glories of Ancient Greece and Rome and the equally glorious present.

At the beginning of the nineteenth century Napoleon's celebrated presence in Egypt helped created a fresh intellectual climate that allowed for a much more positive view to emerge. True, the crusades to the Holy Land had ultimately failed and they had been attended by a lot of misconceived religiosity, but there were positive spin-offs that had benefited the material culture of western Europe. In a society that prized mercantile endeavour, it was now pointed out - with some justice - that, among other things, the crusades had encouraged trade with the East with the result that previously rare or unheard of commodities - Asian silks, spices, precious stones - were made available in the West. So although initially the Enlightenment had denigrated the crusades, room was now found for a re-appraisal. There can be no doubt that the crusades did indeed provide a catalyst for advances in navigation and ship-building techniques, as well as in mercantile activity; technology and business skills improved, while at the same time curiosity about what lay beyond the European horizons was stimulated. It was against this background that the voyages of discovery around southern Africa and to the New World were made possible, and so it can be claimed that the crusades had some part in creating the conditions that eventually were to lead to the European world hegemony of the eighteenth and nineteenth centuries. At the end of the fifteenth century Columbus had evidently believed that finding a direct route westwards to the 'Indies' would so enrich his patron, the king of Spain, that he would have the wherewithal to defeat the Ottomans and Mamluks and regain the Holy Land for Christendom.

It is only as late as the 1830s and 1840s that we first encounter the idea that the crusades were an essentially French enterprise, and that the kingdoms and principalities founded in the East in the aftermath of the First Crusade were the first French overseas empire. While it is true that a lot of French people had taken part and French had become the language of choice among the upper-class settlers, there were plenty of other nationalities besides, and so this view, which, needless to say, was fostered by patriotically-minded Frenchmen, who regarded themselves as being particularly well suited to governing other peoples, was distinctly one-sided. There had of course always been those in France and throughout Catholic Europe who had regarded the crusades as a genuine work of piety, and in post-Napoleonic France - the France of the restored monarchy - what we might think of as a Catholic view of the crusades found powerful support in the romantic medievalism of the age. In the 1830s King Louis Philippe had part of the palace of Versailles redecorated with murals depicting the crusading exploits of his ancestors and the coats of arms of those noble families who were known to have participated. It led to a storm of protest from those members of the nobility who were left out, some of whom promptly supplied evidence that their forebears too had been crusaders. It was only much later that it transpired that much of this fresh evidence was forged.

The view of the crusades as a French-led movement and of the crusader states as the first French colonial empire was stimulated by the French conquest of Algeria in 1830s and 1840s. So it was that the crusades, French chauvinism and romantic ideas of chivalry got mixed together. People in Britain, Germany and elsewhere were not impressed, and the installation of Marochetti's statue of Richard the Lionheart in its present position outside the Houses of Parliament in London in 1860 was, in part at least, a conscious riposte to this French conceit. (Richard was the most celebrated king of England to have gone on crusade, but in the course of a ten-year reign he had only spent a few weeks actually on English soil, and so it may seem a trifle strange for the Victorians to want to transform him into an English national hero.) But in Britain too the romantic medievalism fostered in the nineteenth century by Sir Walter Scott and his followers instilled a widespread positive view of the crusades. There, as in France, the sense of a civilizing mission as a justification for imperialism drew strength from the crusading imagery popular at the time.

So the crusades came to be perceived as an early form of colonial imperialism. For a Frenchman living, say, at the time of the Second Empire in the mid-nineteenth century this would have seemed a 'Good Thing', but in today's post-colonial world many have drawn the opposite conclusion. This French view of the crusade received a further shot in the arm after 1918 with the League of Nations' mandate that placed Syria and the Lebanon under French control.

It was also after 1918 that Britain received Palestine. That brings us naturally to the creation of the state of Israel. Part of the problem is that the present-day borders of Israel and the occupied territories are rather similar to those of the kingdom of Jerusalem in the twelfth century. It is easy to draw parallels and condemn both the crusaders and the Israelis as intruders in the world of Islam who displaced and oppressed the indigenous population. It is also true that back in the twelfth century the crusader regimes in Syria and Palestine relied to an appreciable extent on the financial, military and moral support of Christians in the West. Pilgrims from the West came in large numbers; some, who were warriors, stayed on to fight with the king's forces as volunteers for a limited period; the major shrine churches received grants of lands in the West thereby enhancing their incomes; the Military Orders, which had both a charitable and a military role, looked to the West for much of their income and most of their recruits; when danger threatened or when disaster overwhelmed the Frankish settlers, western Europe responded to appeals for aid. Making parallels with the Israel's reliance on western diplomatic support; on the income generated by tourism, and on the considerable inward investment may seem facile, but such parallels are made nonetheless.

Finally there is promotion of Saladin as a role model by certain political leaders in the Near East, notably Saddam Hussein. Saladin - Salah al-Din - recaptured Jerusalem in 1187 and almost, but not quite, expelled the Christians from the Holy Land. Like Saddam he was born in Tekrit in present-day Iraq. They have other things in common as well. Saladin was a military commander who was appointed vizier of Egypt in 1169. In 1171 he turned the tables on his patrons and abolished the Shiite Fatimid Caliphate that had ruled there since the tenth century. So he was no friend of Shia Islam. In 1174 he seized power in Damascus from the heirs of Nur al-Din on whose behalf he had gone to Egypt in the first place, and in 1183 he deprived Nur al-Din's family of Aleppo as well. He was thus a usurper who through an opportunistic use of force had built up an empire comprising a large slice of the Near East. It will come as no surprise to find that the Sunni Abbasid caliph in Baghdad needed quite a bit of persuasion before he would recognize the legitimacy of Saladin's regime. Saladin's power was feared and resented by his Muslim neighbours, and in course of time he came to rely heavily on members of his own family who were entrusted with the top military commands and other governmental responsibilities. His biographers were at pains to portray him as an idealized Muslim ruler, although, rather to their embarrassment, it transpired that he had never performed the hajj. In three respects, however, Saladin differed from his modern admirer: most obviously he had considerable success in his avowed intention of expelling the unbelievers from the Dar al-Islam; after his death in 1193 his memory was held in high regard in educated literary circles in the Christian West, and, thirdly, he was a Kurd.

So were the crusades reprehensible? Ought we to be apologizing? That there were atrocities is beyond doubt - the crusaders' sack of Constantinople in 1204 is a prime example - although it is a moot point whether crusading armies were more prone to committing atrocities than were other European warriors at the same time. It is true that many Christians and many Muslims died, and, caught in the war zones, the civilian populations suffered grievously. But at the end of the day there was little to show for all the effort. The crusaders failed to do in the Holy Land what their contemporaries did manage to accomplish in Sicily and Spain: turn their conquests into an enduring part of Christian Europe. A huge amount of effort achieved little. Yet for well over two centuries after 1095 the crusades were of central importance for the history of western Europe. Every king of France from the mid-twelfth century to the early fourteenth vowed to go on crusade, and almost all them did so. So too did all the German rulers of the Hohenstaufen dynasty between 1138 and 1250. Every English monarch from Henry II to Edward II - in other words between 1154 and 1327 - took the cross, although only Richard the Lionheart and, shortly before he ascended the throne, Edward I actually went to the Holy Land. It is pointless trying to imagine what would have happened had there been no crusades to the eastern shores of the Mediterranean, just as it is pointless trying to imagine what would have happened if the crusaders' gains had proved permanent. The fact is that after 1291 there was no longer a western presence in Syria and Palestine. The repeated failures gave rise to soul-searching at the time, and, I would suggest, to questioning ever since. The failure of the crusades could be seen in theological and moral terms as signifying a withdrawal of divine support; for sixteenth or seventeenth-century Protestants it could be seen in the context of a perceived perversion of papal spiritual authority accompanied by a false view of what sinful humans have to do in order to gain eternal life; in the secular environment that owes so much to the eighteenth-century Enlightenment the failure of the crusading movement could be seen as the concomitant of a denial of rational behaviour. Then again, the crusades could be viewed as having been partly responsible for the preconditions that meant that western Europe came to outdistance the other great old-world civilizations and go on so that by the late nineteenth century every part of our planet lay under European dominance. They could be touted as an early manifestation of European colonialism, or as a foreshadowing of the creation of the state of Israel. The negative connotations that mention of the crusades arouses in very many people are readily understandable. But what about me - the professional historian who has made a career out of studying the crusades and the lands they conquered? There are plenty of us: as a subject for research in universities and elsewhere the history of crusading has during the last thirty or so years flourished as never before. The crusades were a movement of central importance in the history of medieval Europe, and despite, or perhaps because of, their failures and their less savoury aspects they hold an abiding fascination. Can we - should we - aim to do more than just describe and, with due recognition of our own bias, explain what happened? Are we to adopt the role of the moralist and praise the heroism, the piety and the self-sacrifice that the crusading movement entailed, or, conversely, condemn the atrocities, the in-justice and the futility that attended this episode in human history? Or do we try to remain detached? Nowadays students studying the phi-losophy of history are probably not much concerned with A.J. Ayer and Logical Positivism; the applications of post-modernism to histori-cal enquiry has come to be far more alluring. But here too we are taught to turn our backs on moralizing and value judgements. When we do that, are we avoiding a legitimate issue, or are we safeguarding the autonomy of an intellectually rigorous discourse? To that extent the question of whether or not to apologize for the crusades is just another example of the dilemma of our contemporary *Zeitgeist*.

Looking Back on the Second Crusade: Some Late Twelfth-Century English Perspectives

It was as long ago as 1953 that Giles Constable published his seminal study, "The Second Crusade as seen by Contemporaries".[1] By contrast, my concern is to consider very briefly not what contemporaries knew or thought, but how people writing a generation or so later viewed the crusade, and ask what, if anything, they have to say that is distinctive, and whether subsequent events influenced their perceptions. As we might expect, English writers of the late twelfth century or early thirteenth tended to rely heavily on histories composed nearer the events. Two authors were especially influential: Henry of Huntingdon, who must have composed his account of the crusade by 1155 — in other words within seven years of the expedition itself — and the Norman abbot of Mont St. Michel, Robert of Torigni, who would seem to have been writing rather later. Roger of Howden, for example, lifted his account of the crusade verbatim from Henry of Huntingdon, while the description of these events in the annals of the Cistercian abbey of Waverley in Surrey is copied word for word from Robert of Torigni. Roger of Howden's lack of originality is especially disappointing in view of his importance as a source for the Third Crusade. Another invaluable writer, Ralph of Diceto, mentioned only the preliminaries to the crusade, not the crusade itself. What has happened is that his *Abbreviationes Chronicorum* breaks off in 1148; his *Ymagines Historiarum* begins in the same year, and the events of the crusade would appear to have been lost in the hiatus between these works.[2] It also came as something of a disappointment to discover that neither of those two late twelfth-century gossips, Walter Map and Gerald Wales, has any comments on the crusade. Gerald, it is true, does have what I take to be an oblique reference: recalling his own preaching of the Third Crusade at Haverfordwest in 1188, he compared his success at moving an audience made up of Welshmen while speaking in a language they did not understand to Bernard's earlier success in preaching in French to the Germans.[3]

Gerald's memory of St. Bernard's role as a crusade preacher, though mentioned by Robert of Torigni, found few other echoes among the English writers of my period. Of the historians I have seen, only Ralph of Diceto made any significant allusion to his role. Ralph described Louis VII's conflict with the Church over the archbishopric of Bourges. The affair was resolved thanks to Bernard's mediation, and the king agreed to back down and go to Jerusalem to atone for the sacrilegious oath he had sworn during the quarrel. He thereupon took the cross and prepared for his crusade. The idea that Louis was concerned principally with a pilgrimage for the expiation of his sins rather than with undoing the damage wrought by the Muslim capture of Edessa has been discussed elsewhere by Aryeh Graboïs; Ralph of Diceto is the only one of these English writers to suggest that the motivation for the crusade was anything other than the needs of the Holy Land.[4]

Henry of Huntingdon and Robert of Torigni had followed the papal bull *Quantum Predecessores* in linking the crusade to the Muslim capture of Edessa, but it was William of Newburgh, writing in the late 1190s, who gave this theme its most full and most sophisticated treatment.[5] William was in no doubt that the crusade had come about as a direct response to the fall of Edessa, and he described the circumstances at length: Edessa had long been a bastion of Christendom; the faith of the people had stood firm at the time of Valens — here William has a historical tradition deriving ultimately from the *Historia Tripartita* — and the city had never at any time fallen to the Muslims — a misconception which may originate in the reference in *Quantum Predecessores* to the idea that Edessa had escaped Turkish occupation during the period of Byzantine collapse in the decades before the First Crusade. The fall of Edessa was blamed on its ruler, Joscelin, who had seduced the daughter of a certain Armenian; the father had then taken revenge by letting the Turks into the city. Where this story came from is not known — the idea that Edessa fell as the result of the treachery of one of its inhabitants is at variance with our other information — but William's account may not be entirely without foundation: William of Tyre similarly had heard reports of Joscelin's unsavory sexual behavior.[6]

No English author made any reference to the crusade on the eastern marches of Germany, but several followed Henry of Huntingdon or Robert of Torigni in mentioning the successes at Lisbon and in Spain. Henry had contrasted the absence of God's grace at the siege of Damascus with the divine aid that had attended the more lowly crusaders in Spain and Portugal and quoted the first epistle of St. Peter (5 v.5): "For God resisteth the proud, but giveth grace to the humble." He took evident pride in noting that the greater part of these men had come from England. But despite this English involvement, no one could add anything; Gervase of Canterbury, for example, was content simply to record the victories at Lisbon and Almeria, stripping away all Henry's theology.[7] It was the expeditions of Louis VII and Conrad III that continued to hold the center of attention.

So what went wrong? For Henry of Huntingdon, God had spurned the efforts of the crusaders: their fornication, adultery and other wickedness had earned His displeasure, and so it was that the armies were betrayed by the emperor of Constantinople and harried by the sword of the enemy; Louis' hope of restoring his reputation at Damascus had come to nothing as he lacked God's grace. Robert of Torigni was scarcely less theological in his explanation. He preferred not to dwell on the hardships, pestilence and enemy attacks suffered during the passage through the Byzantine empire, ascribing them to the oppression of the poor and the spoliation of churches that had attended the start of the expedition.[8] But of the later writers, only William of Newburgh, his near contemporary Gervase of Canterbury, and the early thirteenth-century Cistercian, Ralph of Coggeshall, attempted an answer that was not totally derivative.

Gervase and Ralph are notable for their secular tone. Gervase mentioned the foolhardiness of the crusaders and the efforts of the Saracens before going on to recount the story of how the Damascus expedition was frustrated by the treacherous dealings of the Templars, who accepted a huge bribe from the citizens to raise the siege only to discover too late that what they had thought were gold coins were in fact copper. Ralph of Coggeshall also reported that the siege was raised when the Templars accepted a bribe, although in his case he believed that it had been paid by Nūr al-Dīn.[9] The idea that Templar venality was to blame was not new — earlier writers including John of Salisbury and the Wurzburg Annalist had already repeated the allegation[10] — while other authors, notably William of Tyre and Michael the Syrian, alluded to a bribe which turned out to be in counterfeit money.[11] So far as I am aware, Gervase is the earliest writer to link the counterfeit bribe with the Templars, although the tale may have had a wide circulation; there is another version in the early thirteenth-century *Chronique d' Ernoul*.[12] But despite their popularity among later writers, it is most unlikely that these stories have any factual basis. The accusations against the Templars are clearly a further symptom of the mounting antipathy towards the Order which elsewhere in the later twelfth century found expression in the writings of, among others, William of Tyre and Walter Map,[13] while the story of the valueless bribe probably appealed to clerical writers because of its moral dimension, showing that avarice and treachery do not prosper. Both Gervase and William of Tyre spoke of the frustrated expectations of the recipients as nothing short of miraculous, although in Gervase's case there is more than a hint of sardonic irony.

William of Newburgh is very different. In his account we find theological and mundane explanations for the failure of the crusade juxtaposed at almost every turn.

> After entering Asia Minor . . . [the crusaders] experienced the treachery of the Greek emperor. Our forces, however, had indulged in certain excesses and had incurred his displeasure, and by their arrogant and uncontrolled behavior, they had fired the anger of Almighty God as well against them.[14]

There is here an extraordinary evenhandedness: Greek perfidy, under-standable ill-will, divine retribution. All go together. William proceeds to discuss God's disfavor: alluding to the story in Joshua, ch. 7, of the sin of Achan and the Israelite's failure before Ai, he explains how the secret crime of just one man could turn God against His people. In the case of the crusade it was licentiousness in the camp that lay at the root of divine displeasure. Secondly, the crusaders were trusting in their own strength rather than relying on God, and William quotes the same verse from I Peter that Henry of Huntingdon had employed: "God resisteth the proud, but giveth grace to the humble." He then returns to mundane explanations: the crusaders plundered the Greeks; the emperor became hostile and withdrew food supplies; the army wasted away through hunger; it was prey to Muslim ambushes; the weather aggravated the crusaders' plight. Essentially what we have is a reworking of the material to be found in Henry of Huntingdon's account. But, unlike Henry, William was unable to see these events wholly in theological terms. As Professor Partner has remarked, "It is not that his stated critical and theological assumptions are very different from Henry's, but he feels greater trepidation about applying them."[15]

Having brought the remnants of the French and German armies to Jerusalem, William ended his account of the crusade abruptly: "They then returned ingloriously, having achieved nothing of note."[16] There is no reference at all to the Damascus campaign. Instead he described the death of Prince Raymond of Antioch in battle — this was in 1149 — and King Baldwin III of Jerusalem's rescue mission to northern Syria, and he then mentioned the capture of Gaza (c.1150) and Ascalon (1153). Once again God, who resisteth the proud, had given grace to the humble. Interestingly, William has nothing but praise for the Latins settled in the East.

So what conclusions, if any, can we draw? Clearly these late twelfth-century writers had only a limited fund of information at their disposal. New elements, such as Joscelin of Edessa's seduction of the Armenian woman, or the Templars' bribe that turned out to be of copper and not gold, are the sort of tales that could conceivably have found their way back to England with the crusaders returning from the Third Crusade, but it would be unwise to insist on this point.[17] John of Salisbury, the ablest and best-informed English commentator on the Second Crusade, was not writing in England and left no mark on later authors. So, for example, Richard of Devizes is alone in alluding to the allegation, which John had featured prominently, that Eleanor of Aquitaine had an adulterous and incestuous relationship with Raymond of Antioch. Other writers of his generation, Walter Map and Gerald of Wales, preferred to comment on Eleanor's supposed adultery with Henry II's father, Count Geoffrey of Anjou, while William of Newburgh decried her presence in the host during the crusade on the grounds that many other women had followed her lead in joining the expedition, with the result that the chastity which should have prevailed in the camp was compromised.[18]

There was also a distinct lack of curiosity. None of the English historians who described the Second Crusade, nor, so far as I am aware anyone else, addressed the question of why, if the fall of Edessa had been the occasion of the crusade, there had been no attempt at its recovery. More significantly, it is difficult to detect any impact on their accounts of the Second Crusade from the events of 1187-92. Thus no one suggested that the sinfully obstructive behavior of the Latins in the East in the late 1140s prefigured the wickedness which led to the loss of Jerusalem, and no one seems to have drawn any parallels or contrasts between the fortunes of Louis or Conrad and those of Richard, Philip Augustus and Frederick Barbarossa. William of Newburgh, with his multiplicity of human and theological reasons for the failure of the expedition, and his appreciation that successes in the East in the years after 1148 did much to efface the disasters, is by far the most interesting, but even

168

he is circumscribed by his limited information and by an inability to see these events in a broader historical perspective. Substantial numbers of Englishmen and Normans had joined the expedition, but echoes of their recollections are conspicuous only by their absence. It was not that later twelfth-century writers were unaware of the events of the Second Crusade: Ralph Niger, writing at the time of the Third Crusade, reminded his readers that the Muslims habitually curtailed the crusaders' sources of supply and obstructed their routes, and he cited the experiences of Louis and Conrad as proof; elsewhere he lampooned Bishop Otto of Freising for his part in persuading Conrad to participate in the expedition.[19] Interestingly, St. Bernard escaped his stricture. Nor are accounts of the Third Crusade completely devoid of references to the Second: Roger of Howden, for example, had the crusaders tell the Muslims in 1191 that they intended restoring the Christian possessions to the frontiers as at the time of Louis' sojourn in the East.[20] But the English writers were either locked in a historiographical tradition that precluded any original investigation of events before their own lifetime, or presumably took the view that the crusade had been too painful a failure for them to want to explore it any further.

NOTES

1. Constable, "Second Crusade". I wish to thank David Bates and Jonathan Riley-Smith for their comments on an earlier draft of this chapter.
2. Henry of Huntingdon, pp. 279-81; Robert of Torigni, *Chronicles*, pp. 152, 154-55; Roger of Howden, vol. 1, pp. 209-10; *Ann. Waverleia*, pp. 231-33; Ralph of Diceto, vol. 1, pp. 256-58 (cf. p. 291). For Roger of Howden's singular account of the First Crusade, see: Gillingham "Howden", p. 60.
3. Gerald of Wales, vol. 1, p. 76 (cf. vol. 2, p. 152).
4. Ralph of Diceto, vol. 1, pp. 256-57; Graboïs, "Crusade".
5. Wm. of Newburgh, vol. 1, pp. 84-87.
6. Wm. of Tyre, *Chronicon*, p. 635.
7. Henry of Huntingdon, p. 281; Gervase of Canterbury, vol. 1, p. 138.
8. Henry of Huntingdon, pp. 280-81; Robert of Torigni, *Chronicles*, p. 154.
9. Gervase of Canterbury, vol. 1, pp. 137-38; Ralph of Coggeshall, p. 12.
10. John of Salisbury, p. 57; *Ann. Herbipolenses*, p. 7.
11. Wm. of Tyre, *Chronicon*, p. 769; Michael the Syrian, vol. 3, p. 276. Cf. Tritton & Gibb, p. 299; Bar Hebraeus, p. 274. I am indebted to Martin Hoch for these references.
12. *Chron. d'Ernoul*, p. 12.
13. For William, see: Edbury & Rowe, pp. 125-26; Walter Map, pp. 62-7, 72-3.

14. Wm. of Newburgh, vol. 1, pp. 92-5, at p. 92.
15. Partner, p. 59.
16. Wm. of Newburgh, vol. 1, pp. 94-7, at p. 94.
17. Both Roger of Howden and Ernoul record another story of this type: Louis visited Roger of Sicily on his way home from the crusade, and Roger allegedly induced him to place a crown on his head, thereby validating his kingship (*Gesta Regis Henrici II*, vol. 2, p. 202; *Chron. d'Ernoul*, p. 13).
18. John of Salisbury, pp. 11-12, 52-9, esp. pp. 52-3; Richard of Devizes, pp. 25-6; Walter Map, pp. 474-77; Gerald of Wales, vol. 8, p. 300; Wm. of Newburgh, vol. 1, pp. 128-29.
19. Ralph Niger, pp. 80 (cf. p. 70), 224.
20. *Gesta Regis Henrici II*, vol. 2, p. 174.

Bibliography

Ann. Waverleia	*Annales monasterii de Waverleia*. Ed. Henry Richard Luard. In: *Annales monastici*, vol. 2 of 5 vols. RS, vol. 36. London, 1864-69, pp. 129-411.
Bar Hebraeus	Bar Hebraeus [Gregory Abû'l-Faraj]. *The Chronography of Gregory Abû'l-Faraj, commonly known as Bar Hebraeus*. Ed. & tr. Ernest A. Wallis Budge. 2 vols. Oxford, 1932.
Chron. d'Ernoul	*Chronique d'Ernoul et de Bernard le Trésorier*. Ed. Louis, comte de Mas-Latrie. Paris, 1871.
Constable, "Second Crusade"	Constable, Giles. "The Second Crusade as Seen by Contemporaries." *Traditio*, vol. 9 (1953), pp. 213-79.
Edbury & Rowe	Edbury, Peter W. & John Gordon Rowe. *William of Tyre: Historian of the Latin East*. Cambridge, 1988.
Gerald of Wales	Gerald of Wales. *Opera*. 8 vols. Ed. J.S. Brewer, et al. RS, vol. 21. London, 1861-1891.
Gervase of Canterbury	Gervase of Canterbury. *Historical Works*. 2 vols. Ed. Wm. Stubbs. RS, vol. 73. London, 1879-80.
Gesta Regis Henrici II	*Gesta Regis Henrici Secundi* (attr. to Benedict of Peterborough). 2 vols. Ed. William Stubbs. RS, vol. 49 (1867).
Gillingham, "Howden"	Gillingham, John B. "Roger of Howden on Crusade." In: *Medieval Historical Writing in the Christian and Islamic Worlds*. Ed. D.O. Morgan. London, 1982, pp. 60-75.

Henry of Huntingdon	Henry, archdeacon of Huntingdon. *Historia Anglorum*. Ed. T. Arnold. RS, vol. 74. London, 1879.
John of Salisbury	John of Salisbury. *Historia Pontificalis: Memoirs of the Papal Court*. Ed. & tr. Marjorie Chibnall. Nelson, 1956 (rpt. with corrections: Oxford Medieval Texts, Oxford, 1986).
Michael the Syrian	Michael I, Jacobite patriarch of Antioch. *Chronique de Michel le Syrien, patriarche jacobite d'Antioche (1166/99)*. Ed. & tr. Jean Baptiste Chabot. 4 vols. Paris, 1899-1924.
Partner	Partner, Nancy F. *Serious Entertainments: the writing of history in twelfth-century England*. Chicago, 1977.
Ralph Niger	Ralph Niger. *De re militari et triplici via peregrinationis Ierosolimitane*. Ed. Ludwig Schmugge. Beiträge zur geschichte und Quellenkunde des Mittelalters, vol. 6. Berlin-New York, 1977.
Ralph of Diceto	Ralph of Diceto. *Opera historica*. 2 vols. Ed. William Stubbs. RS, vol. 68. London, 1876.
Richard of Devizes	Richard of Devizes. *Chronicon de tempore Regis Richardi Primi*. Ed. J. T. Appleby. London, 1963.
Robert of Torigni, *Chronicles*	Robert of Torigni (Robert de Monte), abbot of Mont St. Michel. "The Chronicle of Robert of Torigni." In: *Chronicles of the Reigns of Stephen, Henry II, and Richard I*. Vol. 4. Ed. Richard Howlett. In: RS, no. 82. London, 1889.
Roger of Howden	Roger of Howden. *Chronica*. 4 vols. Ed. William Stubbs. RS, vol. 51 (1868-71).
Walter Map	Walter Map. *Courtiers' Trifles [De nugis curialium]*. Ed. & tr. M.R. James. 2nd ed. Eds. C.N.L. Brooke and R.A.B. Mynors. Oxford, 1983.
Wm. of Newburgh	William of Newburgh. *The History of English Affairs*. Ed. in progress. Eds. P.G. Walsh & M.J. Kennedy. Warminster, 1988-.
Wm. of Tyre, *Chronicon*	William, archbishop of Tyre. *Willelmi Tyrensis archiepiscopi chronicon*. 2 vols. Ed. Robert B.C. Huygens. Corpus Christianorum, Continuatio Mediaevalis, vols. 63-63A. Turnholt, 1986.

XXIII

Preaching the Crusade in Wales

In Lent 1188 Archbishop Baldwin of Canterbury toured Wales preaching the Third Crusade. He was accompanied in his travels by Gerald, Archdeacon of Brecon, the man whom posterity has dubbed 'Giraldus Cambrensis'. Gerald was a scholar of considerable literary ability, and he has left us a vivid narrative of their activities and experiences at that time. Moreover, he had completed the first version of his account, which he entitled the *Itinerarium Kambriae*, before the end of 1191, and so he was writing very soon after the events he described. The *Itinerarium* is a celebrated work, packed with entertaining anecdotes. It is a true forerunner of the modern *genre* of travel books replete with stories about the places visited on the way, information about natural history, tales of the supernatural, descriptions of the countryside and its inhabitants, and digressions to bring in further anecdotes on similar themes but from other parts of the world or from other ages. As a compendium of information about Wales in the late twelfth century it is outstanding, and its appeal remains so strong that a modern English translation is readily available.[1] But although the *Itinerarium* has been used extensively by historians of medieval Wales and the Welsh Marches, its connecting thread—the preaching of the crusade—has often been overlooked. Yet it is a unique example of a record of a preaching mission intended to attract volunteers. I want to begin by seeing what it has to tell us about recruiting men to join the expedition which was then, in the aftermath of the fall of Jerusalem in 1187, being organized to recover the Holy Places and what it has to say about the

[1] The standard Latin edn. of the *Itin[erarium Kambriae]* remains that of J. F. Dimock in *Giraldi Cambrensis Opera* (Rolls Series, 21, 1861–9), vi. 1–152. The English trans. is by L. Thorpe in Gerald of Wales, *The Journey through Wales and the Description of Wales* (Harmondsworth, 1978).

preaching of the Cross at that particular stage in the development of the crusading movement.

Wales at that time was divided between various native
Welsh princes and the Anglo-Norman Marcher lords who for
a century or more had occupied Usk valley up to and including Brecon and the whole of the south coast of Wales as far
as Pembroke and Haverfordwest. In the early twelfth century
King Henry I had kept a close hold on the territory under
direct Norman rule and had succeeded in imposing his
overlordship on the indigenous Welsh princes. But the equi-
librium he had achieved broke down during the Anarchy,
and it took his grandson, Henry II, about twenty years to
restore the situation. In the early 1170s Henry managed to
establish a *détente*. The Welsh rulers were confirmed in their
gains at the expense of the Anglo-Norman lords, while the
Marchers were guaranteed against further attacks; both
groups were obliged to acknowledge the king's ultimate authority over the whole of Wales. In 1177 Henry demonstrated his dominance when at Oxford he took the fealty and
liege homage of the two most powerful Welsh princes, Rhys
ap Gruffydd of Deheubarth and Dafydd ab Owain of Gwynedd. At the same time the king apparently gave his approval
to the suzerainty these two men had been asserting over the
lesser Welsh lords. So by keeping the predatory instincts of
the Marchers in check and by letting the Welsh princes attain
at least some of their ambitions, Henry was able to secure an
unwonted degree of peace which was to last throughout the
latter part of his reign.[2]

In 1188, therefore, Archbishop Baldwin was able to move
around without any difficulty. He and his party entered
Wales from Hereford. After making contact with Rhys ap
Gruffydd, they travelled to Brecon and then, keeping to the
Anglo-Norman controlled areas, moved down the valley of
the Usk and along the south coast to St Davids. Turning
north, they entered Welsh Wales—the *pura Wallia* of the
native princes—and were met by Rhys ap Gruffydd at Cardigan. He accompanied them as they made their way through
his lands, bidding them farewell at his northern border, the

---

[2] R. R. Davies, *Conquest, Coexistence and Change: Wales 1063–1415* (Oxford,
1987), 290–2, cf. 53–5. See also W. L. Warren, *Henry II* (London, 1973), 159–
69.

estuary of the River Dyfi. From there they hastened to Bangor, and, having made a brief excursion to the island of Anglesey, met the Prince of Gwynedd, Dafydd ab Owain, at Rhuddlan. After that they continued east to the Anglo-Norman city of Chester and thence south back to Hereford, pausing at Oswestry and Shrewsbury. The whole of this *laboriosum iter* had taken seven weeks.[3]

At suitable places the archbishop and members of his entourage preached to whoever had gathered to hear them. Presumably messengers had gone ahead to call the people together for the appointed day—in another of his works Gerald explicitly referred to a summons to hear the crusade preached at Haverfordwest[4]—and Baldwin clearly demanded that the rulers should attend. In the *Itinerarium* Gerald recorded one instance of a Welsh lord coming too late for the sermon and asking the archbishop's pardon for not having arrived on time. This man duly took the Cross, but Owain Cyfeiliog, the ruler of a part of Powys who alone of all the Welsh princes, so we are told, had made no attempt to come in person with his men to hear the archbishop, was excommunicated.[5] Coercive sanctions including the threat of anathema for those who refused to turn up to listen to the preaching of the Cross were part of the armoury of the preachers, and English evidence proves that these sanctions continued to be available far into the thirteenth century. On the other hand, the days when indulgences were offered as an inducement for people to attend the preaching of the Cross still lay in the future.[6]

In addition to the sermons that were preached at predetermined places and times, Archbishop Baldwin also signed people with the Cross following private interviews.[7] But it was clearly the public preaching that had the greatest impact.

---

[3] *Itin.*, 146. For a map and reconstruction of the chronology, see Thorpe, 30–6.

[4] *De rebus a se gestis*, ed. J. S. Brewer, *Giraldi Cambrensis Opera*, i. 74.

[5] *Itin.*, 48–9, 144. Having recorded Owain's excommunication, Gerald then, without any apparent sense of incongruity, gave his wisdom as a ruler a glowing accolade (144–5).

[6] For indulgences for hearing crusade sermons from the time of Pope Innocent III onwards, see J. A. Brundage, *Medieval Canon Law and the Crusader* (Madison, 1969), 154. For coercive powers to get people to attend in 13th-century England, see S. Lloyd, *English Society and the Crusade: 1216–1307* (Oxford, 1988).

[7] *Itin.*, 16, 48–9, 119.

224

The archbishop took the lead in speaking to the people, but frequently his sermons were supplemented by addresses from his colleagues. The Bishop of Llandaff preached at Usk, the Abbot of Strata Florida in Anglesey, and Gerald himself shared in the preaching at Haverfordwest, St Davids (where the archbishop left him to get on with it while he travelled ahead), and Shrewsbury. At Lampeter, after the archbishop had preached, there were sermons from Gerald and from the Cistercian abbots of Whitland and Strata Florida.[8] The role of the Cistercians is noteworthy and calls to mind the lead given by St Bernard at the time of the Second Crusade. Archbishop Baldwin was himself a Cistercian and had been Abbot of Ford Abbey in Somerset for a few years until 1180. In Wales the Cistercian Order had grown rapidly during the half century before 1188, especially in Deheubarth and the Marches, and had come to occupy a prominent position in monasticism there.

The preachers had a particular problem, that of language. The indigenous population spoke Welsh; the Marcher lords and their retinues would have conversed in French; in parts of the Marcher-controlled lands English would have been spoken. At Llandaff Gerald noted that the Welsh stood together on one side and the English on the other. At Haverfordwest he himself preached in Latin and French and then was amazed to see how many people who understood neither language flocked to take the Cross. Recalling this instance in a later work, he compared his experiences to those of St Bernard who, when preaching in French to the Germans before the Second Crusade, allegedly moved his audience to tears. On other occasions Alexander, Archdeacon of Bangor, interpreted the archbishop's exhortations into Welsh.[9]

It is unfortunate that Gerald gives no real indication as to what was actually said in the crusade sermons. Presumably the preachers concentrated on the loss of Jerusalem, the atrocities perpetrated by the Muslims, the heroism of earlier

[8] *Itin.*, 55, 82–3, 110, 119, 126, 144.
[9] *Itin.*, 55, 67, 83, 126; cf. 14; *De rebus a se gestis*, 76. It has been suggested that Gerald himself could not speak Welsh fluently. R. Bartlett, *Gerald of Wales 1146–1223* (Oxford, 1982), 14–15.

crusaders, and the indulgence and the assurance of salvation available to all who participated, but there would also have been *exempla*, tales of what might lie in store for those who remained deaf to the preachers' appeal and examples of how individual acts of devotion were rewarded. However, Gerald leaves us in no doubt that the preachers' appeal was strongly emotive and that the sermons ended with the insistence that men should come forward immediately to take the Cross in the sight of all. At Haverfordwest he split his own address into three parts, each of which ended with a call for people to take crusading vows there and then.[10] It would also seem that, where possible, prominent individuals were persuaded beforehand to take the lead in responding to the appeal. At Radnor, the first place in Wales at which the Cross was preached, Gerald himself and Peter, Bishop of St Davids, were the first to respond. Gerald admitted that he was acting on the king's instructions; it was only in a later recension of the *Itinerarium* that he added that he had acted of his own freewill to avenge the injuries inflicted upon the Cross of Christ. At Radnor Rhys ap Gruffydd was persuaded to particpate in the crusade, but it would seem that it was agreed that he should wait until the archbishop arrived in his own territory before taking the Cross. Presumably he would do so at a public ceremony designed to encourage as many of his men as possible to follow his example. However, by the time Baldwin's party reached his lands, he had changed his mind and decided not to go.[11]

Something of the flavour of the preachers' *exempla* as well as of the mentality of the age is doubtless preserved in some of the anecdotes Gerald recorded. The young men of Rhodri ab Owain's household in Anglesey who steadfastly refused to respond to the preaching were killed soon afterwards in a skirmish with brigands. A woman at Cardigan who forcibly prevented her husband from taking the Cross overlay her child in her sleep three nights later and so smothered him. On the other hand turf from the spot where the archbishop had stood at Haverfordwest restored a woman to sight and

---

[10] *De rebus a se gestis*, 75.   [11] *Itin.*, 14–15.

miracles were later performed at the place where he had preached at Cardigan.[12]

Responses varied. At Hay-on-Wye men came running to take the Cross, leaving their cloaks in the hands of wives or friends who were trying to hold them back. Einion, son of Einion Clud, sought permission from his father-in-law and suzerain, Rhys ap Gruffydd, before taking his vows. Rhys's own sons were even more circumspect. After some debate they agreed that one of them should go with the archbishop when he returned to the king to find out whether or not they were actually wanted. At Bangor Gerald recorded that Baldwin compelled rather than per-suaded the local bishop to take the Cross and that this led to an outcry and loud expressions of grief from among his people.[13] Rhys ap Gruffydd was persuaded against going on crusade partly by his wife and partly by a kinsman, who himself was about to take the Cross, who commented that the worst thing that could happen to a crusader would be to come back alive. Clearly Rhys did not share this 'gung ho' attitude. The remark of course drew attention to a major consideration: as the First and Second Crusades had amply demonstrated, the chances of returning safe and sound were limited.[14] The likelihood of death on crusade as well as the expenses that participation entailed no doubt explains why the friends or relatives of would-be recruits tried to dissuade them from responding. The old woman at Cardigan who gave thanks to God that her only son had been deemed worthy in His sight to take crusading vows may indeed have been exceptional.[15]

There were other strands in crusade recruitment. At Whitland, Archbishop Baldwin obliged twelve archers from a nearby castle to take the Cross as a penance (*in poenam*) for the murder of a Welsh youth.[16] At Cruker a man raised the issue of a subsidy, apparently undertaking to join the crusade if he could have half his sustenance provided. The question

[12] *Itin.*, 83, 113, 126. Such stories can be compared with the miraculous anec-dotes recorded by Caesarius of Heisterbach apropos the preaching of the Fifth Crusade in Germany. *Testimonia minora de Quinto Bello Sacro*, ed. R. Röhricht (Geneva, 1882), 162–8, 175–9.
[13] *Itin.*, 14–15, 20, 119, 125–6.   [14] *Itin.*, 15.
[15] *Itin.*, 113.   [16] *Itin.*, 82; cf. 55.

of subsidies for crusaders was important, and from the time of the Third Crusade it came to have a far greater prominence since it was now accepted that hardly anyone would be able to finance himself unaided.[17] At Swansea an old man offered a tithe of all he possessed in return for half the indulgence (*poenitentiae remissio*) available to the crusaders; then, when his offer was accepted, he offered a further tithe for the other half. Later that year, in May 1188, Pope Clement III allowed bishops in France and England to grant half the full crusade indulgence to non-crusaders who gave a tithe of their goods towards the costs of the expedition. It is interesting to find an example of this faculty being anticipated.[18] The practice of allowing people who wished to benefit from the indulgence but who had no intention of actually taking part in a crusade to take vows and then commute them was a feature of crusading which still lay in the future.

At Abergavenny the archbishop told a man who had said he wanted to discuss with his friends whether or not to take the Cross that he ought rather to ask his wife for her consent. Here Baldwin, who was evidently a canonist of some standing, was behaving with complete propriety by alerting the man to his wife's rights in the matter. The separation necessitated by going on crusade entailed the abrogation of marriage vows, and canon lawyers had long recognized that the wife was therefore entitled to give or withhold her agreement to her husband's absence. Indeed, as early as the First Crusade Pope Urban II had insisted that men should not set off without their wives' consent. It was only later, in a statement of 1201 which has been regarded as something of an aberration, that Pope Innocent III allowed that a man could take the Cross without his wife's permission.[19] What is significant about this incident, however, is the remaining part of Gerald's account of the conversation. The man replied to the archbishop's remark by saying that the crusade was an

[17] *Itin.*, 16.
[18] *Itin.*, 73–4. Ph. Jaffé, *Regesta pontificum Romanorum*, 2nd edn. (Leipzig, 1881–8), no. 16252; cf. Brundage, *Medieval Canon Law and the Crusader*, 154.
[19] *Itin.*, 49. See J. A. Brundage, 'The Crusader's Wife: A Canonistic Quandary', *Studia Gratiana*, 12 (1967), 428–42. For Baldwin as a canonist, see C. Duggan, *Twelfth-Century Decretal Collections and their Importance in English History* (London, 1963), 110–15.

issue for men and should not depend on the advice of women; thereupon he immediately took the Cross. Gerald recorded this exchange in a way which seems to show that he approved of the man's sentiments, and, as we have seen, elsewhere he made it clear that he was not sympathetic towards women who tried to obstruct their menfolk from joining the expedition. Perhaps unintentionally he managed to leave the impression that the archbishop, in accepting the vows of a man who on his own admission had not obtained his wife's consent, had connived at a breach of this rule. One wonders how generally crusade preachers let men who had not talked the matter over with their wives take crusading vows, or how often they bothered to enquire whether a recruit's wife had in fact been consulted.

It is time now to consider this preaching tour in its wider context. Why should Archbishop Baldwin go to Wales of all places to preach the crusade? The four dioceses which together comprised Wales were part of the province of Canterbury, but no archbishop had ever visited them or in fact was to do so again for about another century. It has frequently been suggested that Baldwin had an ulterior motive in going to Wales: preaching the crusade povided him with a pretext for asserting his ecclesiastical jurisdiction. Several years later Gerald was to champion the idea that the Welsh dioceses ought to form a separate province with an archbishop at St Davids—an office to which he himself aspired—but in the *Itinerarium* he made no direct mention of this issue.[20] Quite the contrary, he was careful to note in his account of the events of 1188 that Baldwin celebrated mass at the high altar of each of the four cathedrals in turn, and he also described how Baldwin ordered the local bishop to remove the body of Owain Gwynedd who had died excommunicate in 1170 from its place of burial in Bangor cathedral.[21] So the archbishop does seem to have used the opportunity afforded by the

---

[20] For Gerald's ambitions, see M. Richter, *Giraldus Cambrensis: The Growth of the Welsh Nation*, 2nd edn. (Aberystwyth, 1976). The allusion to the disputed rights of Canterbury over St Davids in *Itin.*, 15–16 is a later interpolation.

[21] *Itin.*, 67, 110, 125, 133, 137. Owain had been excommunicated by Archbishop Thomas Becket.

preparations for the crusade and by the political hegemony established in Wales by Henry II to give visible expression to Canterbury's rights in the Welsh dioceses. But it would be unwise to make too much of this point. As Gerald was later to note, Baldwin went to Wales because the king had sent him there. Moreover, Gerald himself seems to have accompanied Baldwin on Henry's orders.[22]

Gerald's role is readily understandable: he was a clerk in the king's service, and as a member of an Anglo-Norman family long-established in south Wales—and one moreover which had ties of blood with the key figure among the Welsh princes, Rhys ap Gruffydd of Deheubarth—he knew the country and could liaise with the local lords.[23] Baldwin too was a sensible choice, and not just because of his exalted status in the Church. He had had previous dealings with Rhys and in 1187 had conducted a legatine visitation which had brought him at least as far as the borders of Wales.[24] In addition, he must have been one of the very few people in England at the time who had some experience of crusade preaching. In 1185 he had preached the Cross with Eraclius, the Patriarch of Jerusalem, at Clerkenwell, and immediately before going to Wales in 1188 he had preached at the king's council at Geddington.[25] It is also possible that Baldwin was strongly motivated. Almost certainly it was to him that Peter of Blois addressed his appeal for crusade preaching to go ahead, and, as Richard of Devizes noted, he was one of only two English bishops who actually fulfilled their vows to go to the East.[26]

---

[22] *Itin.*, 14; *De rebus a se gestis*, 73; Giraldus Cambrensis, *Expugnatio Hibernica: The Conquest of Ireland*, ed. and trans. A. B. Scott and F. X. Martin (Dublin, 1978), 254. The wording in the *Expugnatio* can be understood to mean that it was Gerald who went at the king's instruction—this is the view of the editors—or that it was Baldwin.

[23] Bartlett, *Gerald of Wales*, 12–15; cf. 19–20.

[24] *De rebus a se gestis*, 57; *Epistolae Cantuarenses*, ed. W. Stubbs in *Chronicles and Memorials of the Reign of Richard I* (Rolls Series, 38, 1864–5), ii. 61, cf. 67, 76. Gervase of Canterbury, *Chronica*, in *The Chronicles of the Reigns of Stephen, Henry II and Richard I*, ed. W. Stubbs (Rolls Series, 73, 1879–80), i. 365.

[25] *Expugnatio Hibernica*, 203; *Gesta Regis Henrici Secundi Benedicti Abbatis*, ed. W. Stubbs (Rolls Series, 49, 1867), ii. 33.

[26] For Peter of Blois, see R. W. Southern, 'Peter of Blois and the Third Crusade', *Studies in Medieval History presented to R. H. C. Davis*, ed. H. Mayr-Harting and R. I. Moore (London and Ronceverte, 1985), 213–14. Richard of Devizes, *Chronicon de Tempore Regis Richardi Primi*, ed. J. T. Appleby (London, 1963), 15.

It is important to set Baldwin's tour of Wales in the context of King Henry's preparations for the crusade in England and France. Together with King Philip Augustus, Henry had taken the Cross at Gisors in January 1188. He had then immediately gone to Le Mans where he had decreed the famous tax known as the Saladin Tithe— a levy of one-tenth on all movable property to be paid by all who were not themselves participating in the expedition. After that the king crossed the Channel and moved rapidly to Geddington in Northamptonshire where at a council held in February the Saladin Tithe was imposed on England. The chroniclers agree that the response to the preaching of the Crusade at Gisors and at Geddington was considerable.[27] Roger of Howden noted that after the Council of Geddington priests and laymen were sent to collect the tithe in each county in England, and there is plenty of evidence for the resentment that this tax provoked.[28] But there is no evidence for any attempt to preach the crusade in each county in England. Gerald mentioned that Bishop Reiner of St Asaph had been preaching the Cross in his diocese in north Wales, but I am not aware of any other reference to the casual preaching of the crusade in England or Wales, or for that matter in Scotland.[29] The silence of the sources need not surprise us. No one, neither the king nor the Pope, wanted non-combatants taking the Cross and then getting in the way of the professional warriors. Indeed, burghers and peasants who took the Cross without their lord's permission were to be made to pay the tithe in full. The last thing Henry wanted was a Peter the Hermit or a Fulk of Neuilly taking the common people by storm. The preaching at Gisors and at Geddington had been addressed to the king's barons and

---

[27] *Gesta Regis*, ii. 29–33, 58–9; *Das Itinerarium peregrinorum*, ed. H. E. Mayer (Stuttgart, 1962), 276–8. For other references to the preaching at Geddington, see B. N. Siedschlag, *English Participation in the Crusades* (privately printed, 1939), 26; Warren, *Henry II*, 607.

[28] *Gesta Regis*, ii. 33. See S. K. Mitchell, *Taxation in Medieval England* (New Haven, 1951), 87, 119–22.

[29] *Itin.*, 142. I am indebted to Dr Simon Lloyd for confirming my suspicion that evidence for any systematic attempt to organize crusade-preaching in England is lacking. For Scotland, see A. Macquarrie, *Scotland and the Crusades, 1095–1560* (Edinburgh, 1985), 27–31 *passim*. Gervase of Canterbury, *Chronica*, i. 421 (cf. 426) refers to Baldwin's preaching in Wales in 1188.

retainers. Henry wanted the social and military élite to go on crusade accompanied by their men at arms. The civilian population was to make its contribution by paying the Saladin Tithe.

So if there was no attempt to send preachers the length and breadth of England to recruit men for the crusade, why did King Henry send Baldwin to preach the Cross in Wales? Why was Wales to be treated differently? Baldwin, Gerald, and their party set off almost as soon as the Council of Geddington was over. So while the tithe was being collected in England, they were making a systematic circuit of what was a rather backward and by twelfth-century Angevin standards uncentralized region. The fact was that Wales *was* different. Royal administration on the English model was unknown. Politically fragmented, Wales comprised a society of frontier lords and temporarily overawed but potentially hostile native princes. Of one thing Henry could be absolutely certain: neither the Marchers nor the Welsh princes would readily agree to the Saladin Tithe being collected from their people, and indeed the Marcher lords were to remain exempt from royal taxation for long afterwards.[30] If there was to be a Welsh contribution to the crusade at all, it would have to be in the form of warriors. In fact Henry may have been anxious to recruit archers from Wales for his expedition. He had frequently employed them in the past, and during the closing years of his reign they are found fighting for him in France in his conflict with the Capetians. In this connection it may be noted that the only recorded incident concerning a Welshman in the Holy Land during the Third Crusade is told to illustrate the man's prowess as an archer.[31]

It is also true that Wales was a potential trouble-spot. The Marcher lords and the Welsh princes were independently minded men whose propensity for engaging in private warfare was well known and whose capacity to use their power to

---

[30] Davies, *Conquest, Coexistence*, 286–7.

[31] For Welsh mercenaries in Henry II's service, see J. Boussard, 'Les mercenaires au XIIe siècle: Henri II Plantagenêt et les origines de l'armée de métier', *Bibliothèque de l'école des Chartes*, 106 (1945/6), 193. For their use at the end of the reign, see *Gesta regis*, ii. 46, 50, 68. For the Welshman in the Holy Land, see Ambroise, *L'Estoire de le Guerre Sainte*, ed. G. Paris (Paris, 1897), lines 3731–70; *Das Itinerarium peregrinorum*, 344–5.

affect the political life of England remained potent long afterwards. It could well be that Henry hoped that the more who went on crusade the less likelihood there would be for conflict to break out while his own back was turned. Gerald himself later claimed that John, Count of Mortain (the future King John), upbraided him for emptying the earldom of Pembroke of all its strength, so great was the response to his own preaching at Haverfordwest. More to the point, the fragility of Henry's *détente* in Wales was laid bare when Rhys ap Gruffydd began attacking some Anglo-Norman strongholds in the south almost immediately after the king's death in 1189.[32]

Finally, what did Baldwin's preaching achieve? Gerald draws his account to a close by noting that he had signed about 3,000 men with the Cross, 'all of them skilled with the lance and the arrow and most warlike in their martial endeavours'.[33] But he was also aware of the delays that followed. Conflict in France and Henry's death prevented the main English expedition leaving until the spring of 1190. By then Wales was once again disturbed by warfare, and we may reasonably surmise that many of Baldwin's recruits never set sail. The one Welshman mentioned as participating in the siege of Acre must, if the incident recording his exploit is correctly located in the narrative, have travelled to the East ahead of the main army.[34] Towards the end of 1189 Gerald himself was absolved from the vow he took at the beginning of his tour. He preserved the notification issued by the papal legate which cited his poverty as the grounds for absolution, but perhaps the real reason for his withdrawal from the crusade was that King Richard wanted him back in Wales as part of his attempts to restore peace there.[35] But although Gerald never went to the East, he did not waver in his belief in the importance of the crusade. It is clear from his writings

[32] *De rebus a se gestis*, 76; Davies, *Conquest, Coexistence*, 292.

[33] *Itin.*, 147.

[34] For references, see n. 31. Someone called Simon 'de Wale' was drowned at Acre, *Gesta regis*, ii. 149.

[35] *De rebus a se gestis*, 84–5, cf. 80–1. See Bartlett, *Gerald of Wales*, 15. Richard of Devizes, *Chronicon*, 6, noted that the Pope allowed the king to release men from their crusading vows if he wanted them to remain in England in his service while he was away.

that towards the end of his life he became insistent on the idea that Henry II's refusal to respond to the pleas of Patriarch Eraclius when he visited England in 1185 was the turning-point in the king's career and precipitated his humiliation at the end of his reign.[36] Archbishop Baldwin, on the other hand, arrived in the East in the autumn of 1190 and died at the siege of Acre on 19 November.[37]

[36] Bartlett, *Gerald of Wales*, 67, 77–86; J. B. Gillingham, 'Roger of Howden on Crusade', *Medieval Historical Writing in the Christian and Islamic Worlds* (London, 1982), 60 and n. 60.

[37] Among studies bearing on Gerald and the preaching in Wales to have come to my attention after this paper was read, I should particularly like to note H. Pryce, 'Gerald's Journey through Wales', *Journal of Welsh Ecclesiastical History*, 6 (1989); C. Tyerman, *England and the Crusades 1095–1588* (Chicago and London, 1988); and P. J. Cole, *The Preaching of the Crusades to the Holy Land, 1095–1270* (Cambridge, Mass., 1991).

XXIV

Celestine III, the Crusade and the Latin East

When Celestine was elected pope at the end of March 1191 the Third Crusade was in full swing. In 1187 Saladin had conquered Jerusalem and most of the Latin Kingdom, and he had followed up these successes with further gains in 1188. Celestine's predecessors had called a new crusade to regain what had been lost, but things had not gone to plan. Frederick Barbarossa had died in 1190 while making his way across Anatolia, and only a comparatively small section of his forces actually reached the Holy Land. The kings of France and England, largely because of their mutual rivalries, had delayed setting out until the summer of 1190, and at the time of Celestine's election were still en route for Palestine. Since the summer of 1189 those crusaders who had responded more promptly to the call for the crusade had, together with the surviving followers of the king of Jerusalem, Guy of Lusignan, been engaged in the siege of Acre, but well before Celestine's accession this enterprise had become bogged down in a military stalemate.

In one sense the papacy was at the very centre of crusading affairs: only a pope could inaugurate a crusade, and successive popes had frequently involved themselves in the spiritual, political and military needs of the Latin East. But there was much that happened without the popes' participation or, indeed, awareness. Popes could not control crusades once they were in train – the classic example is Innocent III's inability to prevent the Fourth Crusade's assaults on Zara and Constantinople – and in any case they were handicapped by the delays in getting news to the Curia. To repeat some well-known examples relating to the year 1187: by 3 September Pope Urban III knew about the clash at Cresson which had occurred on 1 May when the master of the Hospital had been killed, but not about the much greater defeat at Hattin on 4 July; news of Hattin reached the pope on 18 October, but by then things had moved on and Saladin had already entered Jerusalem. Reports of the surrender of Jerusalem on 2 October travelled more speedily, reaching the papal Curia at the end of November. But even so, when at the end of October Pope Gregory VIII announced the Third Crusade in his encyclical, *Audita tremendi severitate*, he did so in ignorance of the loss of the Holy City. Similarly, when Frederick Barbarossa convened the diet of Strasbourg on 1 December to consider his response to the papal crusade summons, he too would have been unaware of this crucial development.[1]

---

1   R. Hiestand, 'Some Reflections on the Impact of the Papacy on the Crusader States and the Military Orders in the Twelfth and Thirteenth Centuries', in *The Crusades and the*

It is perhaps not surprising therefore that there is no evidence to suggest that Celestine attempted to intervene directly to influence the conduct of the crusade: if he wrote congratulating the crusaders on the capture of Acre in July 1191 or expressing a view on the truce Richard agreed with the Muslims in September 1192, the correspondence has not survived. In December 1191 he sent a letter to the English bishops in which he mentioned his understandable anxiety that the present political turmoil in England would undermine Richard's efforts to aid 'the land of Jerusalem',[2] and in March 1192 he asked the doge of Venice to facilitate the transportation of the grain that his legate had collected to alleviate shortages in the East.[3] Otherwise there is nothing until 11 January 1193 when Celestine wrote again to the English bishops at some length setting out his views on the subject of the crusade. The pope was by then aware of the truce with the Muslims which marked the cessation of hostilities but not, it would seem, of Richard's arrest in Austria the previous month. What is striking about this letter is the absence of specific references to the contemporary situation. Instead the pope concentrated on generalities: despite all the efforts to recover the Holy Land and wrest Jerusalem and the Holy Sepulchre back from the Muslims, the propensity of the Christians to trust in their own strength rather than in God had provoked God's judgment against them; discord among the Christians rather than seeking after God's mercy with a humble and contrite heart had precluded the possibility of a God-given victory; the pope therefore called on all Christian rulers to set aside their rancour and put their minds to the preservation of that little bit (*tantillum*) of the land of the Lord that was still in Christian hands and to the liberation, if possible, of the Holy Sepulchre; there could be no rejoicing while the land where stood the feet of the Lord was occupied by 'gentiles', and accordingly the pope forbade tournaments, which were a source of joy: instead anyone who might wish to wage war should do so in the Holy Land; peace and a common purpose were needed, and the letter ends with the instruction that the bishops were to excommunicate any who disobeyed.[4] In short the pope's message was that, though the campaigning may have ceased, the crusade goes on.

Celestine may have hoped that as soon as Richard had sorted out the domestic problems in his lands and had had a chance to recuperate and raise more money, he would return to the East, as, it was being said, he had promised.[5] But as is well known, that was not to be: on his way home Richard was arrested by the duke of Austria and held to ransom – he was incarcerated from December 1192 until February 1194 – and he then spent much of the remainder of his life attempting

---

Military Orders: expanding the frontiers of Medieval Latin Christianity, ed. Z. Hunyadi and J. Laszlovszky (Budapest, 2001), 5–7.

2   [Roger of Howden], *Gesta Regis Henrici Secundi Benedicti abbatis*, ed. W. Stubbs, 2 vols, RS 49 (London, 1867), ii, 221–2.

3   R. Hiestand, *Vorarbeiten zum Oriens Pontificius* iii: *Papsturkunden für Kirchen in Heiligen Lande* (Göttingen, 1985), no. 166.

4   Roger of Howden, *Chronica*, ed. W. Stubbs, 4 vols, RS 51 (London, 1868–71), iii, 200–202.

5   Ambroise, *The History of the Holy War*, ed. and trans. M. Ailes and M. Barber, 2 vols (Woodbridge, 2003), i, 198 (text), ii, 193 (translation); *La Continuation de Guillaume de Tyr (1184–1197)*, ed. M. R. Morgan (Paris, 1982), 143.

to regain those parts of his French possessions that Philip II had occupied during his captivity.[6] Richard had made too many enemies among the other crusaders, and a warning of what lay in store came in the form of the propaganda offensive directed against him by Philip II on his return from the East in 1191. According to Roger of Howden and William of Newburgh, when in October that year Philip met Celestine on his way back to France, he asked the pope to release him from his oath not to attack Richard's lands, and the pope refused.[7] Philip and Celestine certainly met, but we can never know whether that part of their conversation was anything more than an imaginative reconstruction by supporters of King Richard; Roger of Howden certainly embellished his version of what transpired on that occasion when, with the benefit of hindsight, he later re-wrote his account.[8] If the subject had been raised, there can be no doubt that Celestine would have told Philip to desist. The Church was supposed to protect the lands of absent crusaders – Gregory VIII's bull proclaiming the Third Crusade, *Audita tremendi severitate*, had said as much – and in 1192 Celestine had accordingly lifted an interdict on Normandy imposed by his own legate.[9] Complaints that the lands of those absent on crusade had been invaded were taken seriously, as is clear from a papal letter of 1195 which mentioned Adolf of Schauenburg's claim that, in the course of a dispute over his newly built castle – the affair seems strongly reminiscent of Richard's later dispute with the archbishop of Rouen over the building of Château-Gaillard – the archbishop of Bremen had occupied his property while Adolf had been crusading with Frederick Barbarossa.[10] But although Roger of Howden claimed that Celestine threatened Philip with anathema unless he stopped attacking Richard's lands,[11] it would seem that the pope did not do so and refused to involve himself in the rights and wrongs of the ensuing struggle.

The pope similarly seems to have adopted contrasting approaches towards Richard's captors, Duke Leopold V of Austria and then, from March 1193 onwards, the emperor. We know that Hubert Walter, soon to be nominated to the see of Canterbury, visited the Curia shortly after news of Richard's arrest became known, and it is assumed that he urged the pope to intervene to secure his release. There is also a report of another of Richard's envoys at the papal Curia at the beginning of October 1193.[12] Letters survive from Queen Eleanor and Archbishop Walter of

---

6   For the fullest modern account, see J. Gillingham, *Richard I* (New Haven and London, 1999), chapters 13, 16, 17.

7   [Howden]. *Gesta Regis Henrici*, ii, 228–9; William of Newburgh, 'Historia Rerum Anglicarum', in *Chronicles of the Reigns of Stephen, Henry II and Richard I*, ed. R. Howlett, 4 vols, RS 82 (London, 1884–89), iii, 358–9. See Gillingham, *Richard I*, 223–4, 226–7, 229–30.

8   Howden, *Chronica*, iii, 166–7.

9   [Howden], *Gesta regis Henrici*, ii, 18–19, 249–50; see Duggan, above, Ch. 1, at n. 86.

10   *PL*, ccvi, 1070–72. Adolf was count of Holstein and was to be a prominent participant in Henry VI's crusade in 1197–98; C. Naumann, *Der Kreuzzug Kaiser Heinrichs VI* (Frankfurt am Main, 1994), 146–7, 247.

11   Howden, *Chronica*, iii, 208.

12   *AASS* July iii, 322.

132

Rouen, all of them penned by Peter of Blois, calling on the pope to act, but they are of interest more as examples of epistolary rhetoric than as analyses of the situation or proposals for practicable action; it is unlikely that they had any effect on papal policy, and we may wonder whether Celestine ever actually read them.[13] What in fact Celestine did was to excommunicate Leopold of Austria but leave Henry VI alone. In June 1194 the pope intervened in an attempt to get Leopold to release the hostages he was holding as surety for the payment of the remainder of Richard's ransom, making it clear that the sentence of excommunication would not be rescinded until he let them go and set off for the Holy Land and spent as long there in the service of Christ as Richard had spent in captivity.[14] In the event Leopold was only reconciled to the Church on his deathbed at the very end of 1194, and the pope later wrote to Archbishop Adalbert of Salzburg to express his approval of his handling of the affair.[15] Although Roger of Howden wanted his readers to believe that the pope threatened to put the emperor and the whole of his realm under interdict unless he released Richard quickly, there is no evidence that Celestine carried out that threat, if indeed he ever made it.[16] The simple fact was that the political situation in Italy would render any such gesture futile. There was nothing Celestine could do to prevent Richard being ransomed and Henry using the proceeds of the ransom to tighten his hold on Italy.

Celestine also had to keep in mind the situation in the Holy Land. Richard's truce with Saladin would expire in the spring of 1196, and, although the Muslims appear to have observed it faithfully, it was far from certain that the Christians in the East would be able to defend themselves unaided when it ended. In March 1195 Henry announced his intention of organizing a crusade and called on the pope to authorize its preaching. Celestine responded in a letter dated 27 April in which he praised Henry's concern for the Holy Land and announced that he was dispatching two papal legates; at the same time he upbraided the emperor for the harm he had done to the Church.[17] With the conquest of Sicily, Henry's power had reached its zenith. However threatened Celestine may have felt by this rapid expansion of imperial power in Italy, he had no choice: the defence of the Holy Land and the recovery of Jerusalem had to be his priority. The problem was that a successful crusade which restored the Kingdom of Jerusalem to something resembling its pre-1187 borders would have enhanced Henry's standing throughout western Christendom enormously and left the papacy in the imperial shadow; moreover, success in the East would have made it virtually impossible to thwart Henry's ambition to make the imperial title

13 *PL*, ccvi, 1262–72; R. Hiestand, *Vorarbeiten*, iii, no. 169. Duggan, above, Ch. 1, n. 59, considers them rhetorical exercises which were never sent.

14 Ralph de Diceto (Diss), 'Ymagines Historiarum', in *Radulfi de Diceto decani Lundonensis opera historica*, ed. W. Stubbs, 2 vols, RS 68 (London, 1876), ii, 119.

15 'Chronicon Magni Presbiteri', *MGH SS*, xvii, 521–3. Leopold died of gangrene; for the *Schadenfreude* of English writers, see Howden, *Chronica*, iii, 276–8; Ralph of Coggeshall, *Cronicon Anglicanum*, ed. J. Stevenson, RS 66 (London, 1875), 65–6; Roger of Wendover, *Flores Historiarum*, ed. H.G. Hewlett, 3 vols, RS 84 (London, 1886–89), i, 236–9.

16 Howden, *Chronica*, iii, 208; see Duggan, above, Ch. 1, at n. 85.

17 *PL*, ccvi, 1089–91; part translated by Duggan, above, Ch. 1, at n. 124.

hereditary.[18] Presumably these were prices that Celestine would have to accept, and if the measured tones of his response betray his weakness in the face of Henry's commanding position in Italy, the promptness with which he replied is testimony to his commitment to the crusading ideal.

Henry's crusade was not like previous expeditions. For a start there was no papal encyclical calling on Christians everywhere to take part. It is likely that many people regarded it as a delayed continuation of the Third Crusade to complete what the earlier campaigning had failed to achieve; Barbarossa had died with his vow to go to Jerusalem unfulfilled, and so maybe it was appropriate that his son should take the lead. Then again, its preparation was, so it would seem, entirely out of the hands of the papacy; Henry gathered an army that would be strictly under the control of the commanders he appointed, and it was he who arranged finance and transport. Celestine wrote on 1 August 1195 to the German bishops to encourage recruitment, but it would appear that the essential work of organization was sorted out at a series of imperial diets.[19] The campaign was to be fought entirely by men who were subjects of the empire, and even the papal legate who accompanied the expedition, Cardinal Conrad von Wittelsbach, archbishop of Mainz, was drawn from a leading family closely allied to the Hohenstaufen.

Celestine attempted to involve the English in the planned crusade. On 25 July 1195 he sent a crusading bull to the archbishop of Canterbury and the bishops and other prelates of his province instructing them to preach the cross. The archbishop was told specifically to get King Richard to send knights and foot soldiers to the East. There is no mention of the impending end to the truce in the East or of Henry VI's planned crusade. Much of the letter is taken up with a lament over the desecration of the Holy Places and exhortations to repentance and prayer; in particular the pope wanted those warriors who had hitherto been engaged in warfare against other Christians to turn instead to the defence of the land of Christ's birth, passion, resurrection and ascension. The letter aroused sufficient interest for Ralph of Diceto, the dean of St Paul's cathedral in London, to incorporate it into his historical writings,[20] but, so far as is known, it elicited no positive response. The pope stopped short of suggesting that Richard should go to the East in person, and in retrospect it is not surprising after the events of the previous seven years that nothing seems to have come of this papal initiative. It has been suggested that Celestine was trying the dilute the German character of the planned crusade by encouraging men from elsewhere to participate,[21] but, as Henry and Richard were now allies and Henry was said to be encouraging Richard in his war on Philip II in the early summer of 1195 and offering support,[22] it is unlikely that the pope would have thought that the presence of an

---

18 See Naumann, *Der Kreuzzug*, 106–19; R. Hiestand, 'Kingship and Crusade in Twelfth-Century Germany', in *England and Germany in the High Middle Ages*, ed. A. Haverkamp and H. Vollrath (Oxford, 1996), 255.

19 JL 17274. See Naumann, *Der Kreuzzug*, 74–83, 86–9; Hiestand, 'Kingship and Crusade', 257, 258, 261.

20 Diceto, ii, 132–5; see Duggan, below, Ch. 9, at n. 126.

21 For example, J. Prawer, *Histoire du royaume latin de Jérusalem*, 2 vols (Paris, 1969–70), ii, 113.

22 Gillingham, *Richard I*, 292.

English contingent working in conjunction with Henry's expedition would impair the emperor's control.

In the event the main part of Henry's crusade sailed from Italy in September 1197 without the emperor being present. The total number of participants is believed to have been in excess of 16,000, and they required approximately 244 ships to transport them. Once in the East, the crusaders had some successes, including the recovery of Beirut and Jubayl from the Muslims, but their siege of Toron failed. News of Henry's death, which occurred just a few weeks after his fleet had sailed, meant that the crusade came to a premature halt, and most of the crusaders returned to the West in the early spring of 1198. But the absence on crusade of so many high-ranking nobles and clergy, the majority of whom were supporters of the Hohenstaufen family, not to mention the absence of the large numbers of imperial *ministeriales*, was to have significant consequences for the succession crisis that now ensued.[23]

It is not easy to establish Henry's motivation in organizing the crusade. The sheer size of the expedition suggests that he genuinely wanted to win back Jerusalem and was not simply using the crusade as a means of outflanking the papacy in the intricate game of political manoeuvring in Italy. The matter is complicated further by the question of Henry's designs on the Byzantine empire. Whereas Henry used the threat of invasion in an attempt to extort money from the Byzantines, the fact that his expedition was destined for the Holy Land and not Constantinople is a further indication of the seriousness with which he prosecuted the crusade. The Greek historian Nicetas Choniates indicated that the pope helped to deflect Henry from attacking the Byzantine world, but, as Charles Brand argued, his story lacks corroboration and is inherently unlikely. Our knowledge of the diplomatic exchanges between Celestine and successive Byzantine emperors is fragmentary, but, as Celestine made clear in a letter of 1196, the pope regarded the Orthodox Church as prey to error and needing to be recalled from schism to unity. It is therefore not a foregone conclusion that he would have attempted to curb Henry's designs.[24]

Celestine's attitude to crusading was conservative. To him it was axiomatic that the places made sacred by Christ's presence should be under the control of Christians and the fact that they were not was a consequence of sin; it was the duty of Christian warriors to set aside internecine conflicts and direct their efforts to attaining their recovery.[25] Celestine was concerned that there were many who had vowed to go on crusade but who had failed to do so; these people should be made to go, and if prevented by ill health they should pay someone to go in their stead.[26] Clearly the pope was not yet prepared to allow people to redeem their vows. On the other hand, neither was he prepared to allow the crusade to be used as a pretext for

---

23 The fullest account of the crusade is given by Naumann, *Der Kreuzzug*. On the effect on the succession, see Hiestand, 'Kingship and Crusade', 260, 264–5.

24 Hiestand, *Vorarbeiten*, iii, no. 173; *The Cartulary of the Cathedral of Holy Wisdom of Nicosia*, ed. N. Coureas and C. Schabel (Nicosia, 1997), no. 2. More generally on Henry and Byzantium, see C. Brand, *Byzantium Confronts the West, 1180–1204* (Cambridge, Mass., 1968), 191–4, 223–4.

25 The fullest exposition of his views on the crusade are in his letters to the English clergy of January 1193 and July 1195. Howden, *Chronica*, iii 200–202; Diceto, ii, 132–5.

26 Howden, *Chronica*, iii, 317; cf. *Reg. Inn.*, ii, no. 23.

making excessive demands on individual churches. That at least is the conclusion to be drawn from a letter of 1193 to the abbot of St Albans and his community in which Celestine praised the abbey's contribution of a tithe of its entire income for the crusade and agreed to the abbot's request that this payment should not be cited as precedent for demands in the future.[27]

In one respect, however, Celestine did anticipate the action of his successor in broadening the scope of the crusade. The mid-1190s were a period of sustained Almohad attack on the Christian kingdoms in Spain at a time when Alfonso IX of León and Sancho VII of Navarre were in conflict with King Alfonso VIII of Castile. In July 1195 Celestine wrote warning the Spanish kings against fighting among themselves at a time of Muslim advance.[28] It then transpired that Alfonso IX of León was actually allied with the Almohads, and so on 31 October 1196 the pope ordered the archbishop of Toledo to declare the king of León excommunicate and announce that those who should take arms against him were to have 'the same remission (of their sins) as we give those who take up arms against the Saracens (*illam remisionem quam illis qui contra sarracenos arma suscipiunt*)'.[29] Alfonso IX ended his Muslim alliance and came to terms with his cousin and namesake in Castile within a year of Celestine's order, although his disputes with the papacy were to rumble on for several more years.[30] Celestine had thus shown himself prepared to grant crusading indulgences to those who would oppose a Christian ruler who was allied with Muslims against his fellow Christians. Something similar had happened as far back as 1135 when the Council of Pisa had held out the offer of 'the same remission … which Pope Urban decreed at the Council of Clermont for all who set out to Jerusalem to free the Christians' to those who would take up arms against Roger II of Sicily, the mainstay of the antipope Anacletus II. However, after 1135 there does not seem to have been any repetition of this course of action until 1196.[31] Celestine's mandate therefore predates Innocent III's more famous crusade of 1199 against Markward of Anweiler when the pope announced that he was granting 'the pardon of sins that we allow those who cross over in defence of the eastern land (*veniam peccatorum, quam in defensionem terre orientalis transfretantibus indulgemus*)'.[32] Markward had Muslim troops in his service and was using them to secure power in the face of papal opposition. The much-repeated view that Innocent's crusade against him was the first 'political crusade' surely needs to be revised.

---

27 W. Dugdale, *Monasticon Anglicanum*, 6 vols (London, 1846), ii, 232.

28 JL 17265.

29 See Smith, above, Ch. 3, at n. 195.

30 The bull of October 1196 is edited by R. Riu in *Boletín de la Real Academia de la Historia*, 11 (1887), 457–8. For discussion with further references, see J. O'Callaghan, 'Innocent III and the Kingdom of Castile and León', in *Pope Innocent III and his World*, ed. J.C. Moore (Aldershot, 1999), 319–25; idem, *Reconquest and Crusade in Medieval Spain* (Philadelphia, 2003), 62–3.

31 N. Housley, 'Crusades against Christians: their origins and early development, *c.* 1000–1216', in *Crusade and Settlement: Papers read at the First Conference of the Society for the Study of the Crusades and the Latin East and presented to R.C. Smail*, ed. P.W. Edbury (Cardiff, 1985), 23, 27.

32 *Reg. Inn.*, ii, 414 no. 212.

136

Quite apart from his promotion of the crusade and his desire to see Jerusalem restored to Christian rule, Celestine had to attend to the requirements of the Military Orders and the Latin East. So far as is known, he did not intervene directly in the dynastic politics of Frankish Syria. In 1190, a few months before his election, Isabella, the heiress to the throne of Jerusalem, and her husband, Humphrey of Toron, had divorced so that Isabella could marry the leading political figure in the East, Conrad of Montferrat. The senior clergy from the West who were present as participants on the Third Crusade had sanctioned the divorce, although there had been dissentient voices, not least Archbishop Baldwin of Canterbury, and, when many years later Innocent III commissioned an enquiry into the circumstances, witnesses were readily found who believed that what had happened on that occasion had been distinctly irregular. It was also claimed that Conrad already had no less than two wives, one in the West and one in Constantinople.[33] Isabella subsequently married Henry of Champagne (1192) and Aimery of Lusignan (1197) while her first husband was still alive. As Rudolf Hiestand has pointed out, the scandal of these consecutive bigamous marriages did not provoke papal intervention. Had Celestine condemned Isabella's marriages, it would have been tantamount to declaring the next heir to the throne of Jerusalem illegitimate, which, given the fragile state of the Christian possessions in the East, would have been too high a price to pay.[34] One wonders whether Innocent III would have been so complaisant.

Like his immediate predecessor, Clement III, Celestine was strongly supportive of the Military Orders. No doubt he was well aware of the importance of their role in the Third Crusade, and, though he wrote telling the Hospitallers not to abuse their papal privileges in matters such as opening their churches in time of interdict, he threatened stern measures against those who brought trivial accusations against them. More specifically, he showed himself willing to encourage donations to both the Templars and Hospitallers in view of the heavy expenses they had incurred in warfare in the East.[35] Celestine seems to have been the first pope to issue a bull endorsing the legendary history of the origins of the Hospitallers. As far back as 1141 his namesake, Celestine II, had accepted the Templar claim that their order had been founded by Judas Maccabeus. Now Celestine III lent credence to the story that the Hospital in Jerusalem had been sanctified by the presence of Christ himself and that the Blessed Virgin had lived there for three and a half years after the Ascension.[36]

33 *PL*, ccvi, 980–81; Ambroise, i, 66–7 (text), ii, 88–9 (translation). See P.W. Edbury, *John of Ibelin and the Kingdom of Jerusalem* (Woodbridge, 1997), 20–22.

34 Hiestand, 'Some Reflections', 11–12.

35 J. Bronstein, *The Hospitallers and the Holy Land: Financing the Latin East, 1187–1274* (Woodbridge, 2005),105–6. For Celestine's grants of privileges to the Hospitallers, see JL 16935–6, 16981, 17276; R. Hiestand, *Vorarbeiten zum Oriens Pontificius* ii: *Papsturkunden für Templer und Johanniter* (Göttingen, 1984), nos. 19, 21, 107–20. For grants to the Templars: JL 16722, 16743, 16769, 16841 (spurious?), 16911, 17107α; Hiestand, *Vorarbeiten*, ii, nos. 16–18, 20.

36 *Cartulaire général de l'ordre des Hospitaliers de S. Jean de Jérusalem*, ed. J. Delaville le Roulx, 4 vols (Paris, 1894–1905), no. 911; A. Calvet, *Les Légendes de l'Hospital de Saint-Jean de Jérusalem* (Paris, 2000), 27–30.

Celestine also issued at least one privilege to the Order of Saint Lazarus,[37] and he was supportive of the nascent Teutonic Order, confirming their possessions in a bull of December 1196 that went a long way towards sanctioning the establishment of the order as a community dedicated to both the defence of Christendom and works of charity on the same privileged footing as the Templars and Hospitallers.[38]

But there were limits to the pope's endorsement. When the canons of the Holy Sepulchre complained that the Templars had broken their tithe agreements, he censured the order.[39] More complex was the situation relating to the bishopric of Valenia which was situated in the south of the principality of Antioch. Most of the diocese lay within the Hospitaller lordship of Marqab, and, since Saladin's conquests in this region in 1188, it would seem that the bishop customarily resided within the castle. At some point in the mid 1190s the new bishop was persuaded to enter the order and take an oath of obedience to it in return for permission to remain resident. In 1197 Celestine wrote approving the present arrangements, but made it clear that they should not become permanent or be cited as precedent. The pope did not want the see to become the preserve of the Hospitallers, but his efforts seem to have been largely in vain; in the mid 1210s it was agreed that the Hospitaller master should have the same rights of confirmation and presentation to the bishopric as did the prince of Antioch or the king of Jerusalem in their respective realms.[40]

These two examples show that, for all his support, Celestine was not prepared to give the orders free rein when it came to relations with the secular Church.[41] The pope must have been conscious that the clock could not be turned back to the situation that had prevailed before 1187. The Third Crusade had been only a partial success, and, by the truce agreed in 1192, Jerusalem and much else besides remained in Muslim hands. The territories that the Christians had managed to salvage needed to be organized. How the Church in the East and the various other political interests there would adjust to the new circumstances were not things that a conservatively minded pope could control. Celestine seems to have been largely reactive rather than proactive in formulating his policies, depending, like any other pope, on the reports and allegations of his petitioners. We can get some idea of the extent of his involvement from his *acta*, although it has to be remembered that their survival is, to say the least, uneven.

---

37 Hiestand, *Vorarbeiten*, iii, no. 168.

38 *Tabulae Ordinis Theutonici*, ed. E. Strehlke (Berlin, 1869), no. 296; Hiestand, *Vorarbeiten*, iii, no. 177; M.-L. Favreau, *Studien zur Frühgeschichte des Deutschen Ordens* (Stuttgart, 1974), 38–9, 41, 60, 75, 144–51; A. Demurger, *Chevaliers du Christ: Les ordres religieux-militaires au Moyen Age, xiᵉ–xviᵉ siècle* (Paris, 2002), 91, 304–5; cf. Hiestand, *Vorarbeiten*, iii, no. 185.

39 *Cartulaire du Chapitre du Saint Sépulchre de Jérusalem*, ed. G. Bresc-Bautier (Paris, 1984), no. 171; Hiestand, *Vorarbeiten*, iii, no. 174.

40 *Cartulaire général de l'ordre des Hospitaliers*, no. 999; Hiestand, *Vorarbeiten*, ii, no. 106; J. Riley-Smith, *The Knights of St John in Jerusalem and Cyprus, 1050–1310* (London, 1967), 411–13; B. Hamilton, *The Latin Church in the Crusader States* (London, 1980), 215, 223.

41 Celestine also appointed judges delegate to determine a dispute over the church at Nephin between the bishopric of Tripoli and Hospitallers. *Reg. Inn.*, ii, no. 261.

138

We know, for example, that representatives of the three great Italian trading cities, Genoa, Venice and Pisa, all approached Celestine with the intention of gaining his support for their interests in the Latin East. In the case of the Venetians the issue was the long-running dispute with the archbishop of Tyre over the parochial rights of the church of Saint Mark in the Venetian sector of Tyre. In 1196, following representations from the *plebanus* of the church, Celestine instructed the archbishop of Nazareth and the bishop of Bethlehem to see to it that an earlier ruling was obeyed. Disagreements, however, were to continue late into the thirteenth century.[42]

Well aware that such disputes could easily arise, the Genoese approached the pope requesting confirmation of Archbishop Joscius of Tyre's grant permitting them to establish a chapel in Tyre. Joscius's original grant is dated 14 April 1190 and had come about following a request from the ruler of Tyre, Conrad of Montferrat.[43] It is doubtless significant that three days earlier, on 11 April, Conrad himself had issued a charter to the Genoese enlarging or re-defining their commercial privileges. The recent arrival of a large Genoese fleet meant that Conrad needed to ensure their support, even if the terms of his grant were sufficiently restrictive to imply that he was not in a particularly weak bargaining position.[44] The danger facing the Genoese, and, as we shall see in a moment, the Pisans, was that concessions granted at times of political crisis – and the entire period from the battle of Hattin in July 1187 to the arrival of the Kings of France and England in the summer of 1191 was a time of crisis – might be revoked when something resembling normality returned. Celestine's confirmation of Joscius's grant was issued in February 1192, and so it would seem that the Genoese had wasted little time in making their approach.[45]

On 8 April 1193 Pope Celestine addressed a bull to the citizens of Pisa confirming the privileges granted them by Guy, the former (*quondam*) king of Jerusalem, and Sybilla his wife, the late Conrad Marquis of Montferrat and King Richard of England.[46] Like the Genoese, the Pisans had been able to take advantage of the crisis in the Latin East to enlarge their properties and trading rights in the Latin Kingdom. In 1187 they had received major grants from the surviving barons who had escaped to Tyre and then from Conrad of Montferrat. In 1189 they transferred their support from Conrad to his great rival, King Guy, who, together with his wife, gave them a privilege in November that year; but in the autumn of 1190 they were again siding with Conrad, only to switch sides once more in the summer of 1191 when Richard

---

42 Hiestand, *Vorarbeiten*, iii, no. 175; cf. M. L. Favreau-Lilie, 'Die italienischen Kirchen im Heiligen Lande 1098–1291', *Studi Veneziani*, n.s. 13 (1987), 15–101.

43 *Codice diplomatico della repubblica di Genova dal MCLXIII al MCLXXXX*, ed. C. Imperiale di Sant'Angelo, 3 vols (Rome, 1936–42), ii, no. 195. See Favreau-Lilie, 'Die italienischen Kirchen', 22–6.

44 *Codice diplomatico*, ii, no. 194. See D. Jacoby, 'Conrad, Marquis of Montferrat, and the Kingdom of Jerusalem (1187–1192)', in *Dai feudi monferrini e dal Piemonte ai nuovi mondi oltre gli Oceani*, ed. L. Balletto, Biblioteca della Società di Storia Arte et Archeologia per le Province di Alessandria e Asti, 27 (Alessandria, 1993), 187–238, at 207–9.

45 Hiestand, *Vorarbeiten*, iii, no. 164. In April 1193 the pope confirmed the possessions of the cathedral of Genoa including property in the Latin East: *PL* ccvi, 991–5; cf. Hiestand, *Vorarbeiten*, iii, no 167.

46 Hiestand, *Vorarbeiten*, iii, no. 203.

arrived in the East. In October 1191 Richard issued a charter confirming Guy's grant of November 1189.[47]

While it is clear that the Pisans did play a major part in the military and naval activities in the East in these years and gave Richard significant backing as late as February 1192, it would seem that they had overplayed their hand. Directly after the murder of Conrad of Montferrat on 28 April 1192, Henry of Champagne took over as the ruler of those parts of the kingdom of Jerusalem that had been restored to Christian control. Immediately, in May 1192, he issued a privilege for the Pisans, pointedly confirming only such rights as they had held in the time of King Amalric and his son, Baldwin IV and limiting the number of Pisans who could remain resident in Tyre for more than a year.[48] In other words, the new regime was not prepared to honour the concessions made since the battle of Hattin. Needless to say, the Pisans refused to give way easily, and their approach to the pope was part of their campaign to regain what Henry was determined to withhold. They also attempted to destabilize Henry's rule by attempting to restore the ousted Guy of Lusignan, and that in its turn led to their expulsion from the kingdom in the spring of 1193. In January 1195 Henry and the Pisans came to terms, and the latter had to settle for far less than they would have hoped.[49] The papal confirmation of April 1193 had availed them nothing. Indeed, we might wonder whether Celestine paused to consider the implications of agreeing to the Pisan request: had Henry backed down and allowed the concessions granted between 1187 and 1191 to stand, that in itself would have severely undermined his credibility and, by the very nature of the concessions he had revoked, hurt him financially.

Various other minor matters concerning the Church in the East required papal attention. In February 1196 Celestine confirmed the properties of the Holy Sepulchre; quite possibly the petition requesting this confirmation was prompted by the hope that Henry VI's impending crusade would restore Jerusalem and the surrounding region to Christian control.[50] At the same time the canons complained to the pope about the tithe dispute with the Templars mentioned earlier. Celestine also confirmed some German possessions of the Jerusalem abbey of St Mary of the Latins,[51] and, in a letter which was then preserved as a decretal, ruled on the decision of the pluralist

---

47 Jacoby, 'Conrad, Marquis of Montferrat', 194–202.

48 *Documenti sulle relazioni delle città toscane coll'Oriente cristiano e coi Turchi fino all'anno 1531*, ed. G. Müller, Documenti degli archivi toscani (Florence, 1879), no. 37. For the date, see M. L. Favreau-Lilie, *Die Italiener im Heiligen Land vom erstern Kreuzzug bis zum Tode Heinrichs von Champagne (1098–1197)* (Amsterdam, 1989), 300 n. 218; H. E. Mayer, *Die Kanzlei der lateinischen Könige von Jerusalem*, 2 vols (Hanover, 1996), ii, 558–65.

49 For exhaustive treatment, see M. L. Favreau, 'Graf Heinrich von Champagne und die Pisaner im Königreich Jerusalem', *Bollettino Storico Pisano*, 47 (1978), 97–120; Favreau-Lilie, *Die Italiener*, 299–322.

50 *Cartulaire du Chapitre du Saint Sépulchre*, no. 170; Hiestand, *Vorarbeiten*, iii, no. 172. For the perhaps unthinking replication of phraseology from earlier confirmations in this bull, see D. Pringle, *The Churches of the Crusader Kingdom of Jerusalem: a Corpus*, 3 vols so far (Cambridge, 1993, 1998, 2007), ii, 102–3.

51 Hiestand, *Vorarbeiten*, iii, no. 184.

XXIV

140

dean of Acre cathedral and archdeacon of Le Mans to reside in France.[52] Another series of rulings recorded as a decretal concerned some perhaps hypothetical questions relating to Muslim conversion put to him by Bishop Theobald of Acre: may a Muslim captive who killed his Christian captor with the wife's connivance and then converted to Christianity legally marry the captor's widow? (No); may a Muslim who killed a Christian in battle and then converted to Christianity marry the dead man's widow, and may a Christian marry the converted widow of a Muslim he slew? (Yes); and suppose a man abandons his Christian faith, leaves his wife and takes a 'pagan' (i.e. Muslim) woman who bears him sons – can he, after the death of his Christian wife, return to Christianity and marry his 'pagan' wife who now converts to Christianity? (Yes, and the children will be considered legitimate).[53]

Of far greater importance was Celestine's decretal *Cum terra*, addressed to all the clergy of the Eastern Church, which condemned the practice of dual postulation in conventual and episcopal elections. Evidently electors had been in the habit of putting forward two names to the king or patriarch of Jerusalem who would then choose whichever candidate he preferred. From the survival of the full text in the *Collectio Seguntina*, which derived much of its material from papal registers, it can reasonably confidently be assigned to April–Oct. 1191 (*Rome apud s. P. eodem anno*), despite Hiestand's hesitations.[54] Although there is no known *cause célèbre* in the years immediately before 1191 that would have given rise to this ruling, one admittedly late version of the Old French Continuation of William of Tyre would link it to the election of Monachus, the archbishop of Caesarea, as patriarch in Jerusalem in 1194 or 1195. Patriarch Eraclius had died at the siege of Acre, most likely in the late autumn of 1190, and after his death it would appear that, although various individuals were nominated to succeed him, no one was confirmed or installed.[55] Eventually Monachus, who by then was one of only two bishops in the Kingdom of Jerusalem to have been in office since before Hattin, was chosen. According to the anonymous author of the French Continuation, Henry of Champagne reacted violently to the election as the canons had omitted to secure his confirmation of their choice. Eventually things were smoothed over, but, according to the Continuation, not before Pope Celestine had issued a decretal which in the French text opened with the words, 'Com la terre qui est commeue et apelee l'eritage et la partie de Deu', condemning the practice of dual postulation.[56] It is most unusual to find a direct reference to a decretal in a medieval narrative source, especially one written in a vernacular language, but in any case it looks as if the author of this passage was confused. Quite apart from the evidence that would date the decretal to 1191,

52 Hiestand, *Vorarbeiten*, iii, no. 186.
53 B. Z. Kedar, *Crusade and Mission: European approaches toward the Muslims* (Princeton, 1984), 80–81; see Duggan, below, Ch. 9, at nn. 44–9 and Appendix, no. 2.
54 Hiestand, *Vorarbeiten*, iii, no. 171; cf. *Seg.* 38; *X* 1. 6. 14. For *Seguntina*, see Duggan, below, Ch. 9, at n. 19.
55 K.-P. Kirstein, *Die lateinischen Patriarchen von Jerusalem: Von der Eroberung der Heiligen Stadt durch die Kreuzfahrer 1099 bis zum Ende der Kreuzfahrerestaaten 1291* (Berlin, 2002), 358–62.
56 *La Continuation de Guillaume de Tyr*, 161, 163. The Latin text begins: 'Cum terra, que funiculus hereditatis domini censebatur …'

the story the continuator tells is not of a dual postulation but of the electors' failure to seek the ruler's confirmation. In *Cum terra* the pope had been careful to allow the right of the king or the patriarch to signify his assent to choice of bishop-elect. But then Henry of Champagne was never a crowned monarch. It is therefore quite possible that the decretal had nothing to do with the election of the new patriarch.[57] Moreover, the general address of the letter, and its prescription of canonical election *in omnibus conventualibus ecclesiis*, suggests that it was not directed to a specific but to a general problem.

So was dual postulation an established custom in the Latin East? That was the view of the continuator, but the only known instance before the 1190s in which it is claimed that that procedure had been followed occurred in 1180 with the election of Eraclius to the patriarchate of Jerusalem. Here too we are dependent on the French Continuations of William of Tyre and the associated *Chronique d'Ernoul* for our information, perhaps not the most dependable group of sources.[58] All that can be said for certain is that the pope, the author (or authors) of the Continuation, and also King Hugh I of Cyprus in the early 1210s, all believed it to have been established custom. Celestine's decretal, however, was not quite the last word on the subject. In 1213 Pope Innocent III intervened to back up the decision taken by the then patriarch of Jerusalem and *legatus natus* in the East, Albert of Vercelli, in quashing the election of the new archbishop of Nicosia. King Hugh had insisted that the canons of Nicosia postulate two candidates so that he himself could choose one of them and had then told the patriarch that the election had been *secundum antiquam consuetudinem celebrata*. Innocent, however, would have none of it and overrruled Hugh's defence with the words: *diuturnitas temporis non minuit peccatum, sed auget*.[59]

Celestine's pontificate and the reign of Emperor Henry VI coincided with the elevation of both Cilician Armenia and the island of Cyprus to the status of kingdoms. In 1194 Leo II, the prince of Cilician Armenia, sent envoys to both the pope and the western emperor requesting a crown. It was significant that he turned to the West rather than to the Byzantines, and when the Byzantine emperor, Alexios III, tried to pre-empt these negotiations by offering Leo a crown, Leo is said to have made demands that he knew would be unacceptable in Constantinople. Presumably he was not prepared to expose himself and his people to the traditional Byzantine ambitions of political and ecclesiastical dominance, preferring to accept the role of a western imperial client king and allow the Armenian Church to come into union with the Roman Church. Leo's overtures were favourably received, and towards the end of 1197 a party of western prelates arrived in Cilicia, led by Bishop Conrad of Hildesheim, the imperial chancellor and leader of the vanguard of Henry's crusading

---

57 For further discussion see, P. W. Edbury and J. G. Rowe, 'William of Tyre and the Patriarchal Election of 1180', *English Historical Review*, 93 (1978), 12–13, 15–18; Kirstein, *Die lateinischen Patriarchen*, 371, 376–7.

58 'L'Estoire d'Eracles empereur et la conqueste de la Terre d'Outremer', *Recueil des historiens des croisades. Historiens occidentaux*, ii, 59; *La Continuation de Guillaume de Tyr*, 49–50; *La Chronique d'Ernoul et de Bernard le Trésorier*, ed. L. de Mas Latrie (Paris, 1871), 82–4.

59 *PL*, ccxvi, 733; Edbury and Rowe, 'William of Tyre and the Patriarchal Election', 13–14.

army, who brought a crown, and the papal legate on the crusade, Archbishop Conrad of Mainz. The pope had instructed Conrad of Mainz (who was also the cardinal bishop of Sabina) not to allow the coronation to go ahead until after the union of the churches had been proclaimed. The Armenian Church was required to acknowledge papal primacy and institute various liturgical reforms including bringing its calendar into line with that of the western Church so that, for example, Christmas would be celebrated on the same day. The Armenian catholicus and 11 other Armenian bishops swore to implement these conditions; the catholicus was then invested with a pallium, thereby signifying that unity had been achieved, and at Epiphany 1198 Leo was crowned by Conrad of Hildesheim in his capital at Sis.[60] It soon became apparent that the Armenians were not going to implement the reforms that the legate, Conrad of Mainz, had stipulated, but well into the thirteenth century the papacy tried to maintain friendly relations with the Armenian Church. It was a relationship based largely on mutual self-interest.[61]

Undoubtedly Celestine's most enduring legacy in the Latin East was the institution of the Latin ecclesiastical hierarchy in Cyprus. King Richard had seized the island from a Byzantine usurper in 1191 and the following year had installed the dispossessed king of Jerusalem, Guy of Lusignan, as its ruler. On Guy's death, which seems to have occurred towards the end of 1194, his brother Aimery had taken control and started negotiations to elevate Cyprus to the status of a kingdom with himself as the first king. He accepted that the crown was in the gift of the western emperor, and he was happy to accept the imperial suzerainty that that entailed. He probably believed that the Byzantines would try to regain his island and reckoned that any limitations on his own position that Henry's overlordship might bring were more than outweighed by the support he could offer.

Before Cyprus could be numbered among the kingdoms of the West, however, it needed a Catholic hierarchy. It would seem that Aimery made his initial move in 1195, dispatching the archdeacon of Latakia to the papal Curia. Writing in February 1196 Celestine responded positively, praising the intention of bringing Cyprus back into unity with the Church – the island, with its 14 Greek dioceses, was part of the Orthodox world – and commissioned Aimery's envoy, together with Alan, archdeacon of Lydda, who was Aimery's chancellor, to sort out arrangements for tithes and endowments.[62] It is impossible to know how far the pope was content to let the local clergy draw up the blueprint for the diocesan structure that now emerged and how far he and the Curia took the lead. Four further bulls issued by Celestine and dating from December 1196 and January 1197 survive in the cartulary of Nicosia cathedral.[63] By then, acting on Celestine's instructions in a letter that does not survive, the archbishop of Nazareth and the bishops of Acre and Bethlehem had consecrated Alan as the new archbishop of Nicosia; his colleague, the archdeacon of Latakia,

---

60 Hamilton, *Latin Church*, 335–6; Naumann, *Der Kreuzzug*, 39–42.

61 Hamilton, *Latin Church*, 336–47.

62 Hiestand, *Vorarbeiten*, iii, no. 173; *Cartulary of Nicosia*, no. 2. For Alan, see Mayer, *Die Kanzlei*, ii, 284–9.

63 Hiestand, *Vorarbeiten*, iii, nos. 176, 181–3; *Cartulary of Nicosia*, nos 8, 1, 4, 3 respectively.

was now bishop of Paphos. Accordingly the pope now sent Alan the pallium, and confirmed the establishment of the province comprising the archbishopric and three suffragan sees at Paphos, Limassol and Famagusta. In addition to the extant bulls, the pope evidently addressed separate letters to the suffragan bishops confirming among other things their rights to tithes and defining diocesan boundaries.[64] Aimery's coronation as king of Cyprus followed in September 1197.

For all the papal rhetoric about 'recalling the island of Cyprus to the bosom of the Roman Church', the Greeks, who made up the overwhelming majority of the population, remained resistant to assertions of papal supremacy for many decades to come, and the Latin clergy had a long struggle before the Frankish nobles accepted that they should all pay tithes.[65] Even so the structures put in place under Celestine's aegis in the 1190s provided a coherent, workable, and in the long term, successful solution which survived until the Ottoman conquest of Cyprus in 1570–71.

---

64 For evidence that Celestine wrote guaranteeing the right of the bishop of Paphos to tithes throughout his diocese, see Hiestand, *Vorarbeiten*, iii, nos. 178 (a reference from a letter of Gregory IX of 1238), 187 (from a letter of Innocent III of 1200). For evidence that he specified the diocesan boundaries of Famagusta, see Hiestand, *Vorarbeiten*, iii, no. 179 (from a letter of Honorius III of 1222).

65 For the history of the Latin Church in Cyprus, see N. Coureas, *The Latin Church in Cyprus, 1195–1312* (Aldershot, 1997); C. Schabel, 'Religion' in *Cyprus: Society and Culture 1191–1374*, ed. A. Nicolaou-Konnari and C. Schabel (Leiden, 2005), 157–218.

ADDENDA AND CORRIGENDA

II   Fiefs and vassals in the kingdom of Jerusalem: from the twelfth century to the thirteenth

p. 55 – It is now thought that the 'Comes Bertot' or 'Bertoldus' of *RRH* nos. 812, 818, 819, 821 was more likely to have been Berthold of Neuenburg than Berthold of Katzenellenbogen. See B. Hamilton, 'King Consorts of Jerusalem and their entourages from the West from 1186 to 1250' in H.E. Mayer (ed.), *Die Kreuzfahrerstaaten als multikulturelle Gesellschaft* (Munich, 1997), p. 19 n. 38.

III   Philip of Novara and the *Livre de Forme de Plait*

p. 556 n. 7 – There is a single ref to *cour, coins et justise*. See Philip of Novara, *Le Livre de Forme de Plait*, ed. P.W. Edbury (Nicosia, 2009), pp. 139, 272 and n. 217.

p. 557 n. 10 – This chapter is now edited: John of Ibelin, *Le Livre des Assises*, ed. P.W. Edbury (Leiden, 2003), pp. 620–22.

p.557 – For arguments for dating the composition to 1250–53, see Philip of Novara, pp. 20–22.

p. 557 – This essay was written in 1996. When about ten years later I came to prepare my edition I realised that, although the Munich manuscript would appear to preserve authentic elements not found in the other manuscripts, trying to use it as the base for that edition was not feasible. See Philip of Novara, pp. 27–9.

VIII   The French translation of William of Tyre's *Historia*: the manuscript tradition

p. 69 – Philip Handyside has now dated the translation to the early 1220s, the closing years of the reign of Philip Augustus. Handyside's forthcoming monograph, *The Old French William of Tyre*, develops many of the points made in this paper.

XI   The Lyon *Eracles* and the Old French Continuations of William of Tyre

p. 140 – The Colbert-Fontainebleau Continuation and Lyon Continuation were both composed in the Latin East, but the *Chronique d'Ernoul*, while incorporating material originating in the East, was composed in the West. It is likely that the form of the Continuation that largely replicates the *Chronique d'Ernoul* was also originally made in the West.

p. 141 – I now believe that the Colbert-Fontainebleau version is no earlier than the late 1240s and that the Lyon *Eracles* is later still.

p. 152 – Having familiarized myself with the manuscripts since writing this paper, I am now convinced that there was no putative 'O' text. The *Chronique d'Ernoul*, more or less in the form in which it was edited by de Mas Latrie, was grafted on to the end of the Old French translation of William of Tyre (see essays XII and XIII in this volume) and it was that text that was then adapted to form the Colbert-Fontainebleau (*a–b*) version.

XII   New perspectives on the Old French Continuations of William of Tyre

p. 109 – I now believe that Ernoul's original narrative ended with the evacuation of Jerusalem and not with the defence of Tyre.

p. 111 – The statement concerning Philip of Novara is wrong. Philip did not use the Continuation; what happened was that a later redactor interpolated passages adapted from it into the surviving version of Philip's narrative.

XV   Redating the death of King Henry I of Cyprus?

A central suggestion in this paper, that Henry I died on 18 January 1254, has been challenged by C. Schabel, 'The Greek bishops of Cyprus, 1260–1340 and the *Synodikon Kyprion*', Κυπριακαί Σπουδαί, 64/65 (2000/2001), p. 220 n.10. Schabel adduces evidence not employed in this paper to argue that Henry died on 18 October 1253, and I am happy to accept his arguments. Professor H.E. Mayer, however, remains unpersuaded by Schabel's conclusion: *Die Urkunden der lateinischen Könige von Jerusalem*, 4 vols (Hannover, 2010), vol. 3, pp. 1396–9.

p. 339 – It is more accurate to say that the language of the *Chronique d'Amadi* is Venetian-influenced, rather than that is written 'in a Venetian dialect'.

XVIII Latins and Greeks on crusader Cyprus

p. 134 – There is now a modern published corpus of the engraved tomb slabs from Cyprus: B. Imhaus, *Lacrime Cypriae: Les larmes de Chypre*, 2 vols (Nicosia, 2004).

XIX The Templars in Cyprus

p. 190 – My views on the Old French Continuations have changed radically. What I then called the 'later versions' (note 4), I now believe to be the earliest; what I then thought was the 'version closest to the events', I would now argue is the most distant.

XX The 'Cartulaire de Manosque': a grant to the Templars in Latin Syria and a charter of King Hugh I of Cyprus

p. 176 – From his position in the list of names in the *Itinerarium peregrinorum*, 'comes Iocelinus' would appear to be the 'Jocellinus comes de Apulia' in the similar list given by Roger of Howden (*Chronica, ed. W. Stubbs, Rolls Series (London, 1868-71), vol. 3, p.* 88). My thanks are due to Professor Graham Loud who informs me that this is Count Joscelin of Loreto (in the Abruzzi).

INDEX

Key: abp – archbishop of   pat. – patriarch of
          bp – bishop of   pr. – prince of
          Byz. – Byzantine   q. – queen of
          H. – Hospitaller   T. – Templar
          k. – king of

Abbasid caliph: XXI 192
Abergavenny: XXIII 227
Abrégé du livre des assises de la cour des bourgeois: IV 173
Acharie, seneschal of Antioch: XIV 151
Acre: I 145–6; II 49, 56–7; III 560; IV 169, 171–2; VI 230n; VIII 70, 77, 79–86, 88–90, 93–4; IX 158–9, 162; X 32–4; XI 139, 144, 146–7; XII 108, 110–13; XIII 47, 49; XIV 145–6, 148, 150–54, 156–61; XV 340, 342–3, 345; XVI 3–5, 7; XIX 192–3; XX 177, 180
    bp: XXIV 142, and see Florence, Theobald, Walter
    cathedral of the Holy Cross: XIV 151
        dean: XXIV 140
    cour des bourgeois: XV 341
    Montmusard: XIV 153
    siege 1189–91: II 54–5; XI 139, 145, 149n; XIII 45; XIV 150; XIX 189; XX 176–8; XXIII 232–3; XXIV 129–30, 140
    St Nicholas: XIV 146, 157
Adalia: XIV 151
Adelbert, abp Salzburg: XXIV 132
al-ʿAdil Sayf al-Din, sultan of Egypt: XI 141, 149; XIV 150
Adolf of Schauenburg, count of Holstein: XXIV 131
Adrian V, pope: XIV 161
adultery: V 289
al-Afdal, son of Saladin: XIII 50, 55–7
Agnes of Courtenay: XX 178
Agnes, mother of John of La Baume: XX 175, 179
Aimery Barlais: XI 141; XIV 153
Aimery of Lusignan, k. Cyprus and Jerusalem: II 54–9; VI 233; XI 151;

XIV 150–51; XX 175, 180–81; XXIV 136, 142–3
Aimery of Lusignan, constable of Cyprus: XVII 253, 256
Aimery of Rivet, seneschal of Cyprus: XX 175, 180
Aimery, pat. Antioch: XIV 150
Akoursos: XIX 191n
Alan, archdeacon of Lydda, abp Nicosia: XXIV 142–3
Albert of Vercelli, pat. Jerusalem: XIV 151; XXIV 141
Albert Rezatto, pat. Antioch: XIV 153–4
Albigensian Crusades: XI 142, 144; XXI 184, 187
Aleppo: I 148; II 51; XIV 149, 157; XV 344; XXI 181, 192
Alexander III, pope: X 26, 29
Alexander IV, pope: XIV 156–7
Alexander, archdeacon of Bangor: XXIII 224
Alexandria: XIV 149; XVIII 133
Alexius I Comnenus, Byz. emperor: XXI 182
Alexius III Angelus, Byz. emperor: XXIV 141
Alexius IV Angelus, Byz. emperor: XIV 151
Alexius V Murtzuphlus, Byz. emperor: XIV 151
Alfonso VIII, k. Castile: XXIV 135
Alfonso IX, k. Léon: XXIV 135
Algeria: XXI 190
Alice of Champagne, q. Cyprus: XIV 151–4, 158; XVI 3
Alice of Montferrat, q. Cyprus: XIV 152
Alishan, Léonce: VII 241n
allods: I 147
Almeria: XXII 165
Almohads: XXIV 135
Alphonse, count of Poitiers: XIV 155
Amanus Mountains: VII 242

Amaury, k. Jerusalem: II 51, 56, 58–60;
    X 25–6, 29–33; XIV 149–50;
    XXIV 139
Amaury of Bethsan: XIV 153
Amaury of Lusignan, lord of Tyre: XV 340;
    XVI 5; XVII 250–58; XIX 194–5
Amaury, count of Montfort: XIV 153;
    XVI 2, 8
Amaury of Montfort, son of Humphrey:
    XVI 2
Amé of Montfaucon, count of Montbéliard:
    XX 180
Anacletus II, anti-pope: XXIV 135
Anales de Tierra Santa: XV 339
Anatolia: XVIII 133; XXI 185; XXIV 129
Andrea Tartaro, canon of Limassol: XVII 253
Andrew II, k. Hungary: XIV 152
Anglesey: XXIII 223–5
Annales de Terre Sainte: VIII 86, 94; XII 111;
    XIV *passim*; XV 339, 342–3, 345;
    XVII 249
Annunciation of the Blessed Virgin Mary,
    Feast of: XV 339, 341, 344
Anoyira: XIX 191n
Antioch, city: I 148; II 51; VII 241–2, 244–5;
    VIII 74–5, 77, 81, 92–3; IX 158;
    X 33; XI 139, 148; XIV 148–52,
    157, 159; XXI 181–2
    commune: XIV 151
    patriarch: XV 346; XVIII 141, and see
        Aimery, Albert Rezatto, Opizo
        Fieschi, Peter of Angoulême
    princes: VII 242–3; XIV 147, and see
        Bohemond, Raymond of Poitiers,
        Raymond-Rupen, Roger of Salerno,
        Tancred
    princess, see Lucia
    principality: VII 241–3, 247–8; XVI 3;
        XXIV 137
Apsiou: XIX 191n
Apulia: VII 241; XIV 150, 152, 156, 158
    T. commander: XVII 255; XIX 193
Arabs: XXI 181
archontes: III 559, 565; XVIII 138
al-Arish: XIV 149
Aristotle: IV 175
Arles: XIV 161
Armenia, Cilician kingdom/Armenians:
    I 142; III 558–9; IV 169; VI 231;
    VII 242–5; XI 139; XIV 150, 159,
    161; XV 344; XVI 3; XVII 252, 256;
    XVIII 133; XXII 164, 167;
    XXIV 141
    Church: XXIV 141–2
    kings, see Hetum I, Leo I

Arqa: XIV 149, 151
Arsur: II 55n; XIV 150, 153, 157–8; XV 345
    battle: XI 145
    lord, see Balian of Ibelin, John of Ibelin
Arthur of Brittany: VII 243
Ascalon: I 144, 145n; X 25; XI 142n;
    XIV 148, 149n, 150, 153–4;
    XXII 167
al-Ashraf Musa, sultan of Damascus (*Sseiraf*):
    XIV 153
Asia Minor: XXII 166
Assassins: X 25–7, 29–30; XI 151; XIV 150,
    154, 160; XVI 5
assault: V 290–91; VI 233
assise de cop aparant of King Baldwin:
    V 291; VI 233
assise de vente: V 288
assise sur la ligece: II 56
Assises d'Antioche: VII *passim*
'Athlit: II 55; XIV 152; XIX 195
Audeth family: XVIII 139
Audita tremendi severitate: XXIV 129, 131
Austria: XIV 150; XXIV 130
avantparlier: V 290
Avignon: XV 341
Ayer, A.J: XXI 180, 194
Aygue of Bethsan: XIX 195
Ayios Konstantinos: XIX 191n
Ayios Seryios: XX 179n
Aymon d'Oiselay, T. marshal: XVII 252–6
    258n
Ayyubid dynasty: II 58

Ba'rin (*Monferrand*): XIV 153
Babin family: I 142
Baghdad: XXI 157; XXI 192
Baghras: VII 242–3; XI 141, 148
Bahr as-Seghir river: XV 344
Bailliage pleading (1260s): IV 176, 179
Baldwin, abp Canterbury: XXIII *passim*;
    XXIV 136
Baldwin IX, count of Flanders, Byz. emperor:
    XI 141n, XIV 151
Baldwin of Ibelin, lord of Ramla: I 143; II 53;
    XI 149, XIII 45; XIV 149
Baldwin of Ibelin, seneschal of Cyprus:
    XV 343; XVI 1
Baldwin of Ibelin, constable of Cyprus:
    XV 340
Baldwin of Ibelin (fl. 1300s): XIX 194
Baldwin I, k. Jerusalem: XIV 148, 149
Baldwin II, k. Jerusalem: VIII 92, 94; IX 154;
    XIV 149
Baldwin III, k. Jerusalem: I 146n; X 27;
    XIV 149; XXII 167

Baldwin IV, k. Jerusalem: I 146–7; II 51,
58–9, 61; VIII 70, 79; IX 152; X 27,
29n, 30n; XI 142, 146–7; XIV 149;
XX 178; XXIV 139
Baldwin V, k. Jerusalem. II 50, 59;
XIV 149–50
Baldwin, canon of Nicosia: XVII 253
Balian of Ibelin (fl 1170s–80s): II 54; XI 143,
148; XII 109; XIII 45–7, 49, 51–3,
57–8
Balian of Ibelin, lord of Arsur: XIV 146, 155,
157, 161
Balian of Ibelin, lord of Beirut: III 556;
XIV 154; XVI 1, 4
Balian of Ibelin, pr. Galilee: XVII 252–3
Balian, lord of Sidon: XI 141; XIV 152–3;
XVI 1–2
Baltic lands: XXI 184
Bangor: XXIII 223, 226, 228
archdeacon, see Alexander
bp: XXIII 226, 228
Banyas: I 145; II 58n; XIV 149
Barber, Malcolm: IX 151; XIII 45
Barisan, lord of Ibelin: XVII 258
Barons' Crusade: VI 235; XII 112; XVI 1
Barons' War, England: XVI 7–11
Bartholomew of Gordo, T. turcopolier:
XVII 253, 255
bastards: V 289; VI 231
La Baume family: XX 179
Baybars, sultan of Egypt: XIV 157–61;
XV 344–5; XVI 5
Beaufort (Qal'at al-Shaqif): I 144; XI 149;
XIV 153, 159
Bedouin: I 143; XI 146
Beirut: III 555; XI 143, 148; XIV 148, 151,
153; XVI 5–6; XXIV 134
Bellapaïs: XVII 252
Benedict XII, pope: XVI 6
Benedictine monasteries: IX 152
Benevento: XIV 158
battle: XV 345
Bernard of Clairvaux: IX 154, 160; XXII 164,
168; XXIII 224
Bernard, treasurer of Corbie: XII 108–9
Bernard of the Temple: XI 151n
Berthold of Katzenellenbogen: II 55 and
Corrigenda
Berthold of Neuenburg: Corrigenda
Bertrand le Mazoir: VII 242
Bertrand son of Raymond of Toulouse:
XIV 148
Bethlehem, bp: XXIV 138, 142, and see
Ralph, Thomas of Lentino
Bethsan, I 144–5; II 51n; XIV 154

Beugnot, Count A: III 557–8, 560–61, 566;
IV 170–71, 175, 178–9
Bilbais: XIV 149
Blanche, q. France: XIV 155
Blanchegarde, lordship: I 145n
Bohemond I, pr. Antioch: VII 241
Bohemond II, pr. Antioch: VII 241
Bohemond III, pr. Antioch: II 60–61;
VII 243–4; XIV 149–51
Bohemond IV, pr. Antioch: VII 243–5;
XIV 151–3
Bohemond V, pr. Antioch: XIV 152–3, 155;
XV 345
Bohemond VI, pr. Antioch: XIV 155–6, 161;
XV 345
Boniface VIII, pope: XIX 195
Botron, lord: XIV 154
Bourges, archbishopric: XXII 164
Bouvines, battle: XIV 151
Brand, Charles: XXIV 134
Brecon: XXIII 222
Bremen, abp: XXIV 131
Brie: I 142
Brienne, counts: XVI 3, and see Hugh, Walter
claim to Cyprus: XVII 257
Buchthal, Hugo: VIII 70
burgesses: III 562; VI 233; VII 245
Burgtorf, Jochen: XIII 49
Burgundia of Lusignan: XX 180–81
Burgundy: XVII 256n
Bush, George W: XXI 181
Byzantine empire: III 565; XVIII 136, 138,
141–2; XXI 181, 185; XXII 164 5;
XXIV 134, 141–2
emperors, see Alexius, Baldwin,
Heraclius, Isaac II Angelus, John
II Comnenus, Manuel I Comnenus,
Michael VIII, Paleologus

Cabor: XX 174, 176–8
Caesarea: II 55; X 34; XIV 148, 150, 152,
155, 157–8; XV 345
lordship: I 144–5; II 51n; XX 180, and
see John, John l'Aleman, Nicholas,
Walter
abps, see Lociaumes, Monachus, Peter
Caesarius of Heisterbach: XXIII 226n
Cahen, Claude: VII 245
Cairo: XXI 181
Calabria: XIV 150
Candeira, Alfonso Sáchez: XIV 145
Canterbury, province: XXIII 228–9
abp, see Baldwin, Hubert Walter, Thomas
Becket
Caracois: XI 145

Cardigan: XXIII 222, 225–6
Carpentras, Bibliothèque Inguimbertine:
      XX 174
Casal Robert: XIV 150
Castile: XIV 158
Catalans: XVIII 140
Celestine II, pope: XXIV 136
Celestine III, pope: II 58; XI 149; XIV 150;
      XXIV passim
chamberlain, fief of: I 146
Chamberlayne, Tankerville J: XVIII 134
Champagne: IX 160; XIV 153; XVI 3
      counts, see Henry II, Theobald IV,
      Theobald V
champions: V 289–90; VI 231
Charles I, count of Anjou, k. Sicily: XIV 155,
      157–61; XVI 1n, 5; XIX 189, 192, 195
Charlotte, q. Cyprus: III 559
Château Pèlerin, see 'Athlit
Château-Gaillard: XXIV 131
Chester: XXIII 223
children: V 291
Chronique d'Amadi: V 290; XIV 145;
      XV 339–40, 342–3, 346–7 and
      Corrigenda; XVII 249–52, 253n,
      254–7
Chronique d'Ernoul et de Bernard le
      Trésorier: II 54; VIII 72–4, 79, 94–5;
      IX 161n; X 35n; XI 139–40, 142–3,
      152–3 and Corrigenda; XII 107–11;
      XIII 45–50; XXII 166, 169n;
      XXIV 141
Church courts: V 289
Cicero: IV 175
Cilicia: VII 245, and see Armenia
      plain: VII 242–3
Cistercians: IX 152; XXIII 224
Clement III, pope: XXIII 227; XXIV 136
Clement IV, pope: XIV 158, 159
Clement V, pope: XVII 251–3, 256–7
Clement VI, pope: XVI 6
clergy: V 291; VI 231
Clerkenwell: XXIII 229
Clermont, council: XIV 148; XXI 181, 188;
      XXIV 135
Columbus, Christopher: XXI 189
Conrad III, k. Germany: XIV 149; XXII 165,
      167–8
Conrad, bp Hildesheim, imperial chancellor:
      XXIV 141
Conrad of Hohenstaufen, k. Jerusalem
      (Conrad IV): XIV 156; XVI 3
Conrad V (Conradin): XIV 159; XVI 4
Conrad of Montferrat: II 59; XI 139, 143,
      145, 147–50; XII 109; XIV 150;

XIX 190; XX 177–9; XXIV 136,
      138–9
Conrad von Wittelsbach, abp Mainz:
      XXIV 133, 142
Constable, Giles: XXII 163
Constantine of Lampron: XIV 152
Constantinople: VII 243; XII 108–9;
      XIV 149, 151;XVIII 141; XXI 182,
      192; XXII 165; XXIV 129, 134,
      136, 141
cour des bourgeois: II 61; VI 230, 236
cour, coins et justice: I 149; II 61; III 556n
      and Corrigenda; V 291; XX 179n
Crac des Chevaliers: XIV 160; XV 344–5
Le Cresson, battle: XI 142–3; XIII 45–6,
      48–9, 51, 56; XXIV 129
Crete: XVIII 140; XXI 185
Crionero: XX 175, 179
Croce, Benedetto: XXI 180
Cruker: XXIII 226
Crusade
      First: I 147, 149; VII 241; XII 107, 112;
            XVII 249; XXI 179, 181, 183–6,
            190; XXII 164; XXIII 226–7
      Second: XXII passim; XXIII 224, 226
      Third: I 150; II 49, 54–5, 57; VII 242;
            VIII 69; IX 152; X 27; XI 142;
            XII 111; XVIII 133; XXII 163–4,
            167–8; XXIII 221, 227, 231;
            XXIV 129–32,136–7
      Fourth: II 55; VII 243; IX 152; XI 142,
            146; XII 111; XIV 151; XVI 1;
            XX 180; XXIV 129
      Fifth: II 55; XI 141, 146, 152; XIV 152;
            XXIII 226n
curtesy of England: VII 248
Cyprus: II 59–60; III 555–6, 562, 569;
            IV 169–70, 172–3, 175, 177, 179;
            V 287, 289; VII 246; XI 139, 148,
            150–51; XIV 150–54, 157–9;
            XV 340, 343, 346–7; XVI 6–8;
            XVII 249–52, 254–8; XVIII passim;
            XIX passim; XX 179; XXI 185, 187
      chancery: XV 340
      ecclesiastical province: XXIV 142
      High Court: III 555–6, 561–3; IV 170,
            176; VI 229–32, 236; XVIII 136, 141
      kingdom: I 142; III 556; V 289; VI 229;
            VII 246–8; XV 339; XVI 6;
            XXIV 141–2
      knights: IV 173
      lords: III 563–4, 566
      Lusignan dynasty: III 555, 562; IV 169;
            VII 246; VIII 94; XVI 2; XVII 257;
            XVIII 133–4

regent: IV 169
secrète: XVIII 139

Dafydd ab Owain of Gwynedd:
    XXIII 222–3
Damascus: I 145; XIII 55; XIV 149–50,
    152–3, 155, 157, 161; XV 342;
    XXI 181, 192; XXII 165, 167
    sultan: II 58, and see al-Nasir Dawud,
    al-Nasir Yusuf
Damietta: XI 141; XIV 149, 151–2, 154–5
Dar al-Islam: XXI 181, 192
Darbsak (*Trepessac*): XIV 153
Daron: XI 146
Deheubarth: XXIII 222, 224
Delaville le Roulx, J: XV 341; XX 174
divorce: V 289
Doc: XIV 155; XV 342
Dominicans: XVII 254
Douai: I 142
dower: V 285, 288, 292; VII 246–7
Du Cange, C. du Fresne: XX 176
Durand, Ursin: XII 110
Dyfi river: XXIII 223

Eco, Umberto: II 52
Edessa: XXII 164, 167
Edmund Crouchback, earl of Lancaster:
    XIV 160
Edward I, k. England: XIV 158, 160–61;
    XVI 7–11; XXI 193
Edward II, k. England: XXI 193
Edward III, k. England: VII 244
Egypt: XI 141; XII 112; XIV 149, 151, 155;
    XV 342; XVI 4, 8; XVIII 133, 140;
    XIX 194; XXI 181, 187, 189, 192
    Babiloine: I 146n; II 51; XIV 148–50
    153, 155, 157, 159
Einion son of Einion Clud: XXIII 226
Eleanor of Aquitaine, q. England: XXII 167;
    XXIV 131
Eleanor of Auxerre, wife of Philip of
    Montfort: XVI 2
England/English: VII 246–7; IX 152–3;
    XI 142; XIV 151, 159; XVI 7–9;
    XVIII 141; XXI 185; XXII 165,
    167–8; XXIII 223n, 224, 227,
    229–32; XXIV 129–30
    feudal incidents in: II 59–60
Enlightenment: XXI 188–9, 193
Enrico Dandolo, doge of Venice: XIV 151
Episkopi: XIX 191, 194
Eracles, see William of Tyre
Eraclius, pat. Jerusalem: XI 148; XII 110;
    XXIII 229, 233; XXIV 140

Erard of Nantueill: XIV 158
Erard of Valery: XIV 158
Ernoul: XI 143–4 and Corrigenda; XII 108–9,
    111; XIII 45, 47, 49, 52, and see
    Chronique d'Ernoul
Eschiva of Ibelin, lady of Beirut: XVI 2, 5–6
Eschiva of Montfort, wife of Peter I:
    XVI 2, 6
*Estoires d'Outremer et de la Naissance
    Saladin*: VIII 95; X 35n; IX 161n
Eugenius III, pope: IX 154
Eustace Grenier: I 145
Eustorgue, abp Nicosia: XV 340, 343
Evesham, battle: XVI 7, 10–11
De Excidio Urbis Acconis: VIII 91

fakirs: XI 148
Falaise: I 142
Famagusta: XVII 253n, 254–5; XIX 191n,
    192, 194; XX 179n
    bishopric: XXIV 143
    St George of the Greeks: XVIII 141
Farama: XIV 149
Fatimid caliphate: XXI 181, 192
fiefs: I 142–3, 146–9; II 49–54, 56, 59;
    III 563, 565; V 285–8, 290; VI 230,
    233, 236; VII 246
Florence, bp Acre: XIV 156
Florio Bustron: XV 339; XVII 251, 252n
La Forbie, battle: XIV 154
Folda, Jaroslav III 560; IV 172; VIII 69n, 70,
    72–4, 77, 79–80, 82, 85, 92, 95;
    IX 152, 161; X 28, 35; XIV 145–6
force de Turs ne tolt seisin II 57–9; V 292
Ford Abbey: XXIII 224
Forey, Alan: XVII 256
France/French: I 142–3, 149; II 53; IV 177;
    VII 244, 248; VIII 77, 93, 95n;
    IX 152, 154; X 32, 35; XII 112–13;
    XIV 150, 154, 159; XVI 1;
    XVII 252, 256; XVIII 135n, 140;
    XIX 193; XXI 181, 190–92;
    XXII 167; XXIII 227, 230–32;
    XXIV 129, 131, 140
    customary law: II 57; IV 174
Francesco Amadi, see *Chronique d'Amadi*
Francesco Attar: IV 172
Francesco Pipino: XII 110
Franciscans: XVII 254
Franks: III 563–5; VI 230–31, 233–6;
    VII 243, 245; XI 145; XVIII 135–7,
    139–42; XXI 182, 191
Frederick I Barbarossa, emperor: XI 139,
    145–6; XIV 150; XXII 167;
    XXIV 129, 131, 133

Frederick II, emperor: III 555–6; IV 169;
　VI 230, 235; XI 141; XII 108–9,
　111–12; XIV 152–5; XVI 2–3;
　XVII 249; XIX 192; XXI 187
al-Fula (*le Feve*): XIII 46, 50–52, 56, 58
Fulk, k. Jerusalem: XIV 149
Fulk of Neuilly: XIV 150; XXIII 230
Fuller, Thomas, *History of the Holy Warre*:
　XXI 187

Galilee, prince/principality: I 144; II 51,
　and see Balian of Ibelin, Hugh of
　Lusignan
Garin of Montaigu, H. master: XIV 152;
　XX 175
Gastria: XIX 191n, 192
Gautier del Mesnil, see Walter of Mesnil
Gaza: XIV 153; XXII 167
Geddington: XXIII 229–31
Genoese: IV 169; VI 232; XI 141; XIV 148,
　153–5, 156, 159; XV 341; XVI 4;
　XVII 255; XVIII 140; XXIV 138
Geoffrey, count of Anjou: XXII 167
Geoffrey of Lusignan: XI 151
Geoffrey of Sergines: XIV 153–4, 157–9
Geoffrey of St Omer: IX 154, 157
Geoffrey le Tor, treatises: III 558, 562;
　IV 170, 173, 175–6, 178
Gerald, pat. Jerusalem: XI 141; XIV 152–3
Gerald of Wales: XXII 164, 167; XXIII
　passim
Gerard of Montaigu: XIV 153
Gerard of Ridefort, T. master: XIII 45–53,
　56–8; XX 178
Germany/Germans: XI 150; XIV 151–2, 159;
　XXI 190; XXII 164–5; XXIII 224,
　226n
Gervase of Canterbury: XXII 165–6
Gestes des Chiprois: XIV 145; XV 339–41,
　345; XVI 7; XVII 250n
Gibbon, Edward: XXI 189
Gibelacar: XIV 151, 160
Gideon: XXI 182
Gilles, bp Damietta, later abp Tyre: XIV 155,
　159; XV 342–4
Gillingham, John: II 52; XII 109
Gioan Cercasso: XX 179n
Gisors: XXIII 230
Gloucester, earls: XVI 7–8
Godechauz de Torhout: X 29
Godfrey of Bouillon: IV 172n; XIV 148
Gormond of Piquigny, pat. Jerusalem: IX 154
Graboïs, Aryeh: XXII 164
Grandclaude, Maurice: III 557, 562, 566;
　IV 170

Greece, Frankish: VIII 73
Greeks: III 563–4; VI 231, 234–5; XIV 149;
　XVIII 134–42; XIX 194; XXI 181;
　XXII 166
Gregory VIII, pope: XXIV 129, 131
Gregory IX, pope: XII 108, 112; XIV 153;
　XXIV 143n
Gregory X, pope (Tedaldo Visconti):
　XIV 160–61
Greilsammer, Myriam: II 56
Gremont, lord of Bethsan: XX 180
Grenada: XIV 158
Grenier family, lords of Caesarea: I 144
Grivaud, Gilles: III 565n; XVII 251n;
　XVIII 140–41
Guillaume de Nangis: VIII 79; XII 111
Guillielmo de S. Stephano: VIII 83n
Guizot, François: XII 110
Gutenberg, Johannes: XXI 188
Guy of Bazoches: X 26
Guy of Ibelin, constable of Cyprus: XVI 1;
　XVIII 135
Guy of Ibelin, count of Jaffa: XIX 194
Guy of Lusignan, k. Jerusalem: I 144, 147,
　149; II 51–4, 56, 59; XI 139, 142,
　145–7, 149, 151; XIII 45–6, 48,
　51–3, 56–9; XIV 150; XIX 190–91;
　XX 176–9; XXIV 129, 138–9, 142
Guy of Lusignan, son of Hugh III: XVI 2, 6
Guy of Lusignan, son of Hugh IV: XVI 6
Guy of Mimars, bp Paphos: XIV 155;
　XV 342–3
Guy of Montfort, brother of Simon the Elder:
　II 55; XVI 1–2
Guy of Montfort, son of Simon earl of
　Leicester: XVI 11
Guy, abp Nazareth: XIV 146, 159
Gwynedd: XXIII 222–3

hadjis: XI 148
Haifa: XIV 150
Haimo l'Estrange: XIV 161
Hama: XIV 157
Hamilton, Bernard: II 54; VIII 70–71; IX 152
Harim: XIV 149
Hattin, battle: I 141–2; II 54, 62; XI 139, 142,
　144, 147; XII 108, 111; XIII 45, 47;
　XIV 150; XX 177; XXIV 129, 139–40
Haverfordwest: XXII 164; XXIII 222–5, 232
Hay-on-Wye: XXIII 226
Hector Podocataro: XVII 251n
heiresses: I 142; II 59, 61; V 285–9, 292;
　VII 247
Helvis of Ibelin, wife of Guy of Montfort:
　XVI 1–2

Henry of Almain: XVI 8, 11
Henry of Antioch, son of Bohemond V: XIV 158, 161
Henry count of Le Bar-Duc: XIV 153
Henry le Bufle: II 61; III 559n; V 286
Henry II, count of Champagne: II 55, 58–9; XI 139, 141, 144, 148, 151–2; XIV 150; XXIV 136, 139–41
Henry I, k. Cyprus: III 555; IV 169; V 287; XIV 152, 154–5; XV 339–44, 346–7 and Corrigenda; XVI 4; XVII 254; XX 175
Henry II, k. Cyprus: XV 340; XVI 5; XVII 250, 252, 254–5, 258n; XIX 193–5
Henry I, k. England: XXIII 222
Henry II, k. England II 62; XXI 193; XXII 167; XXIII 222, 225–6, 229–33
Henry III, k. England: XIV 158; XVI 2, 7–10
Henry VI, emperor: VII 243; XI 139, 151; XIV 150–51; XXIV 131–4, 139, 141–2
Henry of Huntingdon: XXII 163–6
Henry IV, duke of Limburg: XIV 152
Henry, abp Nazareth: XIV 159
Henry Sanglier, abp Sens: IX 154
Heraclius, Byz. emperor: VIII 69; XI 139
Hereford: XXIII 222–3
Hetum I, k. Armenia: VII 245; XIV 155, 157; XV 342–4; XVI 3
Hetum of Gorhigos: XVII 252, 256–7
Hiestand, Rudolf: XXIV 136, 140
highway robbery: V 290
Hill, George: XV 346
Hims: XIV 157
Histoire Universelle: VIII 80
Historia Tripartita: XXII 164
Hohenstaufen dynasty: XXI 193; XXIV 133–4 supporters in the East: III 555
Holy War: XXI 182–3
Honorius II, pope: IX 154, 159–60
Honorius III, pope: XIV 152; XXIV 143n
'Hospitaller Master', see 'Paris-Acre Master'
Hospitallers: II 55–6; VII 242–3; IX 159, 161, 164; X 26; XI 141; XIII 46, 51, 56; XIV 153–4, 156–60; XV 341, 344; XVII 250, 256; XIX 191–2, 194; XX 174–5, 178–80; XXIV 136–7 masters, see Garin of Montaigu, Rogers des Moulins; William of Château Neuf prior: XVII 254
Hubert Walter, abp Canterbury: XXIV 131, 133
Hugh of Brienne: III 555
Hugh III, duke of Burgundy: XI 150

Hugh IV, duke of Burgundy: XIV 153
Hugh, heir to Caesarea: XIV 158
Hugh I, k. Cyprus: VII 243; XI 141n; XIV 151–2, 158; XIX 192; XX 174–5, 179–80; XXIV 141
Hugh II, k. Cyprus: III 555; XIV 156, 159; XV 339, 343, 345, 347
Hugh III, k. Cyprus and Jerusalem: III 558; IV 173; XIV 157–61; XV 339; XVI 4–6; XIX 189, 192
Hugh IV, k. Cyprus: IV 176, 179; VII 244; XV 341; XVI 2, 6; XVII 250
Hugh of Fagiano ('the Pisan'), abp Nicosia: XV 343, 346–7
Hugh of Jubail: XIV 153
Hugh of Lusignan, son of Amaury of Tyre: XVII 256
Hugh of Lusignan, pr. Galilee: XVIII 133
Hugh, abp Nazareth: XIV 153
Hugh of Paiens, T. master: IX 154, 157
Hugh of St Omer: XIV 148
Hugh of Tiberias: II 54; VIII 80
Humphrey of Montfort, lord of Tyre: XV 345; XVI 2, 5–6
Humphrey of Montfort the younger, lord of Beirut: XVI 2, 5–6
Humphrey IV of Toron: II 54; XI 149; XIV 150; XXIV 136
Hundred Years' War: XII 113
Hungary/Hungarians: XIV 152; XXI 187 king, see Andrew II
Huygens, R.B.C.: II 52; VIII 69, 98; IX 151; X 27

Ibelin: XVII 258 family: III 555; IV 169; XIII 49; XVI 3; XVII 249, 258; XIX 192 lordship: I 143; II 51n; V 292
Iconium, sultan: XIV 151
Innocent III, pope: VII 243; XIV 150–52; XXIII 223n, 227; XXIV 129, 135–6, 141, 143n
Innocent IV, pope: XIV 154–6; XV 346–7
Innocent V: XIV 147
Innocent VI, pope: XVIII 133
Iraq: XXI 181, 191
Isaac II Angelus, Byz emperor: XI 146; XIV 151
Isaac Ducas Comnenus, ruler of Cyprus: XIV 150; XVIII 135; XXIV 142
Isabella I, q. Jerusalem: II 54; XIV 150; XXIV 136
Isabella II, q. Jerusalem: XIV 152
Isabella of Lusignan, sister of Henry I: XIV 158

Isabella of Ibelin, lady of Beirut: XVI 5
Islam: X 26, 31; XI 148; XXI 185, 191
Israel: XXI 191, 193
Italy/Italians: II 55–6; III 555; VII 241–2;
    XII 108; XVIII 140; XX 181;
    XXI 185; XXIV 132–4
Itinerarium Kambriae: XXIII *passim*
Itinerarium peregrinorum: XI 147; XIX 190;
    XX 176 and Corrigenda

Jabala: XIV 149
Jacobites: VI 231
Jacques de Mailli, T. marshal: XIII 48–9,
    56–7; XIV 150
Jacques de Molay, T. master: XVII 251–2;
    XIX 194–5
Jaffa: I 144; II 55–6; III 557; IV 170; XI 141;
    XIV 150, 152–6, 159; XV 342–4;
    XVII 258
    treaty (1229): XI 141
Jaffa and Ascalon, count/county: I 143–5;
    II 51n; IV 169, and see Guy of
    Ibelin, John of Ibelin
    countess: I 143
James of Avesnes: XI 145, 151
James II, k. Cyprus: XX 179n
James of Doumanin, acting T. commander of
    Cyprus: XVII 253n, 254–5
James of Ibelin: IV 174
    treatise: IV 170, 173, 175–6, 179
James Panteleon, pat. Jerusalem, later Pope
    Urban IV: XIV 157
James of Vitry: X 26
Janus, k. Cyprus: XVIII 140
Jean de Comminges, cardinal: XVI 6
Jean de Joinville: XVIII 135
Jericho: XIV 154
Jerusalem
    city: I 141; IV 172n; IX 151, 152; X 27;
    XI 139, 146–9; XII 110; XIV 148–50
    152, 154; XVII 258; XIX 194;
    XXI 179, 181–2, 184, 186, 188, 191;
    XXII 164, 167; XXIII 221, 224;
    XXIV 129–30, 132–7
    Dome of the Rock/*Templum Domini*:
    IX 154, 157, 160; XI 148; XIV 154
    Holy Sepulchre: II 58; XI 148;
    XIV; XX 180; XXIV 130, 137, 139
    Hospital: XXIV 136
    kingdom: I 141–3, 145, 147–50;
    II 49–50, 54–61; III 555–6, 558;
    IV 169–70, 173; V 289; VI 229, 233,
    235; VII 241–2, 245–8; VIII 73;
    X 26, 33; XI 139, 149; XIII 57;
    XIV 149, 154, 156–8; XIV 148,

    150–51, 153; XVI 1, 3–6;
    XVIII 133; XIX 190, 192, 195;
    XX 179; XXI 191; XXIV 129–30,
    132, 136, 139–40
    constable: XX 181
    customary law: II 57
    High Court: I 141; II 62; III 556,
    561; IV 170, 175; V 285, 289,
    291–2; VI 229–2, 236; XV 341
    kings: I 141, 143–5; II 60–62;
    IV 169; VIII 94; XV 340;
    XVI 2–5; XVII 253, 257;
    XIX 189; XXIV 137, and
    see Aimery of Lusignan,
    Amaury, Baldwin, Conrad of
    Hohenstaufen, Fulk, Guy of
    Lusignan, Hugh III of Cyprus,
    John of Brienne
    knights: I 141, 143–9; II 49–50 52–3,
    56, 60
    lords: I 141, 143, 145, 147–50;
    II 49–50, 52–3, 56, 60–61
    lordships: I 147–50; II 50, 52–3, 61,
    V 291
    queens, see Isabella I, Isabella II,
    Maria Comnena, Maria of
    Montferrat, Sibylla
    royal domain: I 141; II 50
    seneschal, see Ralph of Tiberias
    sergeants: I 141
    patriarch: IX 151, 154–5, 157–8, 160;
    X 26, and see Albert of Vercelli,
    Eraclius, Gerald, Gormond of
    Picquigny, Monachus, Ralph of
    Merencourt, James Panteleon,
    Robert, Stephen, Thomas Agni,
    William
    St Mary of the Latins, abbey: XXIV 139
Jews III: 563n; VI 235; VII 245; XXI 184
Joan, widow of William II of Sicily: XI 142
John l'Aleman, lord of Caesarea: XIV 157
John of La Baume: XX 175, 179
John of Brienne, k. Jerusalem: XII 108–9;
    XIV 151–2; XX 180
John II duke of Brittany: XIV 160
John, lord of Caesarea: XIV 153; XVI 2
John II Comnenus, Byz. emperor: I 148;
    II 51
John, k. England: VII 243–4 247; XIV 151;
    XXIII 232
John Foinon: XIV 154
John Gale: XI 148–9
John of Gaunt: VII 244
John of Ibelin, lord of Arsur: XIV 153–7;
    XV 345; XVI 1

John I of Ibelin, lord of Beirut: III 556;
IV 169, 174, 176; XIV 153; XVI 1;
XVIII 135; XX 181
John II of Ibelin, lord of Beirut: III 556;
XIV 157–8
John of Ibelin, count of Jaffa: I 141;
III 556–7; IV 169; V 285; VII 245;
XIV 156, 158–9; XV 340–41;
XVI 2; XIX 191
legal treatise: I 141, 143, 150; II 50–51
54n 57–9 61–2; III 556–7, 559–62,
563n, 569; IV passim; V passim;
VI 229, 231, 233–36; VII 246, 248;
XVIII 141; XX 176
John, count of Montfort: XVI 2, 8
John of Montfort, lord of Tyre: XVI 2, 4–5
John the rays (raïs): XX 175
John of Salisbury: XXII 165, 167
John Tristan, son of Louis IX: XIV 160
John of Vilaers, T. draper: XVII 254n
Joiette, owner of Cabor: XX 178
Joinville, lords: XVI 3
Jordan river: I 144; II 58
Joinville, John of: XV 343
Joscelin II, count of Edessa: XXII 164–5,
167
Joscelin III, count of Edessa: I 146; II 61;
XI 147; XX 174, 176–8
lordship: I 145–6; II 50
Joscelin Pisellus: I 146n; II 51
Joscius, abp Tyre: II 54; XIII 46–7, 50, 53, 56,
58; XX 174–6, 178–9; XXIV 138
Jubail: XI 148; XIV 148, 150–51; XXIV 134
Judas Maccabeus: XXIV 136
Julian, lord of Sidon: III 558; XIV 155, 157,
161; XV 341
Julius Caesar: VIII 79, 80
Just War: XXI 182–3

al-Kamil, sultan of Egypt: XII 109; XIV 152–3
Kato Deftera: XIX 191n
Kedar, Benjamin: II 49n; XIV 145
Keen, Maurice: XVIII 135
Kellaki: XIX 191n
Kerak: XI 149; XIII 57; XIV 157
Kerynia: XIV 153; XVII 252, 256
Khirokitia: XVII 255–6; XIX 191n, 192
Khwaresmians: XIV 154
Kibbutz Somrat: VI 232
Kitchener, Lord: XX 179
Knights of St John, see Hospitallers
Kolossi: XIX 191n
Kurds: XXI 192

al-Lajjun: XV 344

Lamberto di Sambuceto: XIX 194
Lampeter: XXIII 224
Lapithos: III 556; XVI 6; XVII 258n
Latakia: XIV 149
archdeacon: XXIV 142
Lateran Council, Third: X 25–6
Lateran Council, Fourth: XIV 151
'Law of Rome': VI 231 234 235; XVIII 136
Lawrence of Morphou: XX 175, 180
League of Nations: XXI 191
Lebanon: XXI 191
Lefcomiati: XX 179
Lefkara: XVII 255
Leo I, k. Armenia (Leo the Roupenid):
VII 243–4; XIV 150–52; XXIV 141
Leo, son of Hetum of Armenia: XIV 159
Leontios Makhairas: XV 341; XVII 250–51;
XVIII 133, 139, 141–2
Leopold V, duke of Austria: XXIV 130–32
Leopold VI, duke of Austria: XIV 152
Letres dou Sepulcre: II 57; III 562; IV 173,
178
Lewes, battle: XVI 7
Libellus de Expugnatione Terrae Sanctae:
XIII 49
Libri Feudorum: I 143
Lignages d'Outremer: IV 173, 175–6, 179;
XVII 258
Limassol: XI 150; XIV 160; XVII 252–6;
XVIII 134; XIX 191n, 192–3
bishopric: XXIV 143
Lisbon: XXII 165
Livre au Roi: II 54, 56–7, 60; III 558;
IV 175–6, 179; VII 241
Livre des assises de la cour des bourgeois:
IV 175, 178–9
Llandaff: XXIII 224
Lociaumes, abp Caesarea: XIV 159
Logical Positivism: XXI 180, 194
Lombardy: I 143; VIII 83
London: XXI 190; XXIV 133
Longobards: XIV 153
Lorenzo Tiepolo: XIV 156
Louis VII, k. France: XIV 149; XXII 164–5,
167–8, 169n
Louis VIII, k. France: XIV 151–2
Louis IX, k. France: VIII 74; XII 112–13;
XIV 154–7, 159–60; XV 340, 342–5;
XVI 4, 8; XXI 187
Louis Philippe, k. France: XXI 190
Louvaras: XIX 191n
Lower, Michael: XII 113
Lucia, princess of Antioch (wife of Bohemond
V): XIV 155
Lusignan: XVII 257

10 INDEX

Lusignan family: XVI 6–7; XVIII 138, 140;
XIX 192–3, 195
Luther, Martin: XXI 187–8
Lydda: I 145; XIV 152
Lyon: XIV 155
Second Council: XIV 161

Magaza, estate in Cyprus: III 556n
Magna Carta: II 60; VII 248
Mainz: XXI 188
abp: XIV 150
Malembec family: I 142
Mamluks: VII 245; XXI 189; XV 342;
XVIII 133–4, 140
Manfred, son of Frederick II: XIV 158
Manosque, H. commandery: XX 176
Le Mans: XXIII 230; XXIV 140
Mansurah: XIV 154–5; XV 344
Manuel I Comnenus, Byz. emperor:
XXII 165–6
Margaret of Antioch-Lusignan, sister of Hugh
III: XVI 2, 4, 7
Margaret of Ibelin, lady of Caesarea: V 292
Margaret, lady of Sidon: XIV 156
Margat, see al-Marqab
Maria of Armenia, heiress to Toron: XVI 2–3
Maria Comnena, q. Jerusalem: II 54;
XIII 52, 58
Maria of Montferrat, q. Jerusalem: XIV 151
Marino Sanudo: XIV 145; XV 339, 345
Marinus of Bombel: XX 175, 180
Marj Ayun: X 25; XIV 149
Marj as-Suffar: XIV 149
Markward of Anweiler: XXIV 135
Marochetti, Carlo: XXI 190
al-Marqab (Margat): VII 242; XIV 160;
XXIV 137
marriage: V 285–8
Marseilles: XIV 157
Marsilio Zorzi: VIII 86, 93
Martène, Edmond: XII 110
Martin IV, pope: XIX 193
Mas Latrie, Louis de: VIII 72, 95;
XII 109–10; XV 346
Mathikoloni: XIX 191n
Matthew, cardinal bp Albano: IX 154
Matthew Paris: X 27
Maurists: VIII 95; XII 110
Mayer, Hans E: I 144; XV 341, 346 and
Corrigenda
Mechelen: I 142
Michael the Syrian: XXII 165
Michael VIII Paleologus, Byz. emperor:
XIV 157
Midianites: XXI 182

Military Orders: I 141; II 56; VII 242; X 25;
XXI 191; XXIV 136
Milo *Brebenz*: II 55
Milo of Colovardino: II 54n
Mimars family: I 142
Monachus, abp Caesarea, pat. Jerusalem:
II 54, 58–9; XI 148, 151;
XXIV 140–41
Monagroulli: XIX 191n
Mongols: XIV 146, 155, 157, 159, 161;
XV 342–3; XIX 194; XXI 187
Mont St Michel: XXII 163
Montbéliard family: XVI 3
Montfort: II 55; XIV 152, 160
de Montfort family: XVI *passim*
Montgisard: XIV 149
Montgisard family: I 142
Montreal: XI 149; XIV 148
Mora: XIX 191n; XX 175, 179
Morgan, Margaret Ruth: VIII 69–70;
XI 139–40, 142–4, 146, 148, 150,
152; XIII 46
Mount Tabor: XIV 152, 156
Muslims I: 145 149–50; II 55, 57–8, 60;
III 558, 563–4; IV 170; V 292;
VI 231, 234–6; VII 242–3, 245;
VIII 79, 89; X 26–7; XI 143–5, 151;
XII 108; XIII 46–51, 53, 56–9;
XIV 146, 148–52, 154–5, 157–8,
160; XV 343; XVI 4–6; XVII 253;
XVIII 133–4, 136–7, 142; XX 177;
XXI 181, 184–6, 192; XXII 164–6,
168; XXIII 224; XXIV 130, 132,
134–5, 140

Nablus: XIII 51–2, 57–8; XIV 154
Napoleon: XXI 189–90
al-Nasir Dawud, sultan of Damascus
(*Coreidin*): XIV 152
al-Nasir Yusuf, sultan of Aleppo and
Damascus: XIV 155–6; XV 342, 344
Nazareth: I 145; XIII 46–7, 49–53, 56–8;
XIV 152, 160
abp: XXIV 138, 142, and see Guy, Hugh,
Henry
Nephin: XI 141n; XIV 151; XXIV 137n
Nicaea: XIV 148; XXI 182
Nicetas Choniates: XXIV 134
Nicholas Larcar, abp Tyre: XIV 155;
XV 342–4
Nicholas V (wrongly 'Clement'), pope:
XIV 161
Nicholas, lord of Caesarea: XIV 161
Nicholson, Helen: IX 151n, 161, 164;
XI 147n; XVII 257

Nicosia: XV 343; XVI 8; XVII 253, 255; XIX 190. 191n, 193; XX 175, 179; XXI 188
  archbishopric: XVII 252
  abp: XIX 191; XXIV 141, and see Alan, Eustorgue, Hugh Fagiano
  canons: XXIV 141, and see Baldwin
  cartulary: XXIV 142
  diocese: XV 346; XIX 192
  Franciscan church: XVII 255
  Templar church: XV 339, 343; XVII 254–5
  viscount: XVII 254
Nissou: XVII 253, 254
Normandy/Normans: VII 242 244 248; XXII 168; XXIII 222, 232; XXIV 131
North Africa: XVIII 133
Novara: III 555, and see Philip
Nur al-Din: XXI 192; XXII 165

Odo of Burgundy, count of Nevers: XIV 158–9
Odo of Châtearoux, bp Tusculum: XIV 156; XV 340
Odo of St Amand, T. master: X 25–6, 29, 34; XIV 149
Oliver of Termes: XIV 158–61
Opizo Fieschi, pat. Antioch: XIV 156
Ordene de la Chevalrie: VIII 80
Orontes river: VII 242
orphans: V 288
Oswestry: XXIII 223
Otranto: XIV 156
Otto of Brunswisk, emperor: XIV 151
Otto, bp Freising: XXII 168
Ottomans: XVIII 141; XXI 189
out-of-court settlements: V 290; VI 230
Outrejourdain, lordship: I 146; II 50; X 29n; XI 149; XVI 3
Owain Cyfeiliog of Powys: XXIII 223
Owain Gwynedd: XXIII 228
Oxford: XXIII 222

Pactum Warmundi: II 52
Palekhori: XIX 191n
Palestine: XV 345; XVIII 133; XIX 189; XXI 179, 181, 191, 193; XXIV 129
Paolo di Segni: XIV 153
Paphos: XIV 152; XVII 254
  bp: XXIV 143, and see Guy of Mimars
Paramytha: XIX 191n
Paris: VIII 72, 74, 79–80, 93–4; IX 152; X 28, 34
  Peace of (1229): XI 142
'Paris-Acre Master' (or 'Hospitaller Master'): IV 172; VIII 83, 87, XII 108, 112
Paris, Paulin: VIII 69–70, 72–4, 98; IX 153

paroikoi/vilains: III 564–6, and see serfs
Partner, Nancy: XXII 166
Pastoralis praeeminentiae: XVII 251, 254n
Pedhieos river: XX 175, 179
Peiresc, Nicolas-Claude Fabri de: IV 177; XX 174, 176
Pelagius, bp Albano: XIV 152
Pembroke: XXIII 222, 232
Peristerona: XIX 191
Persia: XIV 157
Peter of Angoulême, pat. Antioch: XIV 150–51
Peter of Blois: XXIII 229; XXIV 132
Peter Brice: XI 147
Peter Cadelli, T: XVII 254n
Peter, abp Caesarea: XIV 153
Peter Chappe: XX 175, 180
Peter I, k. Cyprus: IV 176–7; VII 244; XV 340–41; XVI 2, 6; XVIII 133
Peter II, k. Cyprus: XVIII 142
Peter of Dreux, count of Britanny: XIV 153
Peter l'Ermin: I 142
Peter the Hermit: XIV 148; XXIII 230
Peter des Roches, bp Winchester: XIV 152
Peter, bp Rodez, papal legate: XVII 256
Peter, bp St Davids: XXIII 225
Peter, abp Tyre: XIV 154
Phasouri: XIX 191n
Philip of Antioch, son of Bohemond IV: XIV 152
Philip II Augustus, k. France: II 62; XI 139, 144; XIV 149–52; XXII 167; XXIII 230; XXIV 129, 131, 133
Philip IV, k. France: XVII 251, 254, 257
Philip of Ibelin, regent: IV 169; XIV 152
Philip of Ibelin, seneschal of Cyprus: XIX 194
Philip of Montfort, lord of Tyre and Toron: XIV 158, 160; XVI 1–7
Philip of Montfort, son of Philip: XVI 1n
Philip of Nablus, lord of Outrejourdain: I 146
Philip of Novara: *Le Livre de forme de plait*: II 57, 59, 61; III *passim*; IV *passim*; V 286–7; VI *passim*; VII 246, 248; XVIII 136–9, 141; XX 179n
  Les quatre âges de l'homme III 555; XVIII 135
  Wars of Frederick II against the Ibelins: XII 111 and Corrigenda; XVII 249–50; XVIII 136
Philip of Swabia: XIV 151
Philippe le Roux: I 146
Phinikas: XIX 191n
Picquigny: I 142
Pierre de Ravendel: VII 244–5

Pisa/Pisans: XI 141, 151; XIV 150, 154, 156, 159; XX 177–8; XXIV 138–9
council (1135): XXIV 135
Plaisance of Antioch, q. Cyprus: IV 169; XIV 155–7; XV 345
Plataniskia: XIX 191n
Poitou/Poitevins: XI 147; XIV 151; XVII 257
Pol Castressio: III 559
Poland: XXI 187
Pontigny: VIII 75n; IX 154n
Portugal: XXII 165
poulains: XI 147
Powys: XXIII 223
Prawer, Joshua: I 143 149–50; II 53, 60
property litigation: V 290
Protestants: XXI 185, 187, 193
Pryor, John: VIII 70
Psimolophou: XIX 191n

Qaqun (*Caco*): XIII 50, 56; XIV 160
Qaraqorum: XV 344
Quantum Predecessores: XXII 164
Qutuz, sultan of Egypt: XIV 157

rabbinical courts: VI 230n
Radnor: XXIII 225
Raimbaud de Caromb, T. commander of Cyprus: XVII 253n
Ralph, bp Bethlehem and royal chancellor: X 30, 33
Ralph of Coggeshall: XXII 165
Ralph of Cossi: XIV 155
Ralph of Diceto: XXII 163–4; XXIV 133
Ralph, bp Lydda: XIV 154
Ralph of Merencourt, pat. Jerusalem: XIV 151–2
Ralph Niger: XXII 168
Ralph of Soissons: XIV 153
Ralph of Tiberias, seneschal of Jerusalem: II 54 57; VI 233; XX 176
Ramla: II 55n; XIV 148, 156
Ramla and Mirabel, lordship: I 143–4; II 51n
rape: V 289–90; VI 233
Raymond Antiaume VI 233
Raymond of Antioch, son of Bohemond III: VII 243; XIV 150
Raymond Babin: XVIII 133–4
Raymond of Jubail: XI 149
Raymond of Poitiers, pr. Antioch: I 148; II 51; VII 241–2; XXII 167
Raymond IV, count of Toulouse: XIV 148
Raymond VI of Toulouse: XI 142
Raymond VII of Toulouse: XI 142, 144
Raymond II, count of Tripoli: X 27

Raymond III, count of Tripoli VII 243; VIII 73; XI 142, 149n; XIII 46–7, 50–51, 53, 55–9; XIV 149
Raymond Viscount: XVII 253
Raymond-Rupen, pr. Antioch: VII 243–5; XI 141n; XIV 150–52
Raynaud, Gaston: XIV 145–6
rays (*raïs*): XX 175, 179
Recordane: XIV 155; XV 342
Recueil des historiens de croisades (*RHC*)
    Historiens occidentaux: VIII 69, 72, 74, 98; XI 139–40, 146; XII 110–11; XIII 46–7
    Lois: IV 170 178
Reginald of Vichiers, T. master: XIV 156
Reiner, bp St Asaph: XXIII 230
Renier of Jubail: XI 151
Rey, E-G: XX 176
Reynald of Châtillon, lord of Outrejourdain: I 149; II 53; XIII 48–9, 55, 57
Reynald II, abp Reims: IX 154
Reynald, lord of Sidon: II 54; XIII 46, 53, 58; XVI 1–2
Reynald of Soissons, marshal of Cyprus: II 54n; XX 175, 180
Reynolds, Susan I 142–3, 145, 148; II 49–50, 52, 59
Rhodes: XVII 250
Rhodri ab Owain: XXIII 225
Rhuddlan: XXIII 223
Rhys ap Gruffydd of Deheubarth: XXIII 222, 225–6, 229, 232
Riant, Paul: VIII 72, 95; IX 161; X 35
Richard earl of Cornwall, k. Germany: XIV 153, 158; XVI 9, 11
Richard of Devizes: XXII 167; XXIII 229
Richard I, k. England: XI 139, 142, 144–5, 150–51; XIV 150; XVIII 133, 135, 139; XIX 189–90; XXI 190, 193; XXII 167; XXIII 232; XXIV 129–33, 138–9, 142
Richard II, k. England: VII 244
Richard, Jean: I 141; XV 340–41
Riley-Smith, Jonathan: II 59
Robert, count of Artois: XIV 154
Robert de Boron: XVIII 135
Robert of Crésèques: XIV 159–60
Robert Guiscard, duke of Apulia: VII 241
Robert, pat. Jerusalem: XIV 154, 156
Robert of Torigni: XXII 163–5
La Roche Guillaume: XI 148, 149n
Roger of Howden: XXII 163, 168, 169n; XXIII 230; XXIV 131–2
Roger des Moulin, H. master: XIII 46, 48–52, 56–8; XIV 150; XXIV 129

INDEX

INDEX 13

Roger of Salerno, pr. Antioch: VII 241
Roger of S. Severino: XIV 161
Roger II, k. Sicily: XXII 169n; XXIV 135
Rohard, owner of Cabor: XX 178
Röhricht, Reinhold: XIV 145–6
Rome: VIII 83; X 29; XII 110; XIII 49;
    XIV 152–3, 158; XVI 11
Roman Law: II 57
Rosso Aldobrandini: XVI 11
Round Table, romances: XVIII 135
Ruad: XIX 189, 193–4
Rupen of Montfort, lord of Beirut: XVI 2, 5;
    XVII 258n; XIX 194–5

Saddam Hussein: XXI 181, 191
Safed: XIV 153, 157–60; XVII 253
Safita: XIV 160
Sahyūn (Qal'at Salāh al-Dīn): VII 242; XI 148
St Albans, abbot: XXIV 135
St Augustine: XXI 182
St Bertin: I 142
St Davids: XXIII 222, 224, 228
St Denis: I 142
St Francis: XII 109
St George of Labana: III 559n
St George: XIV 160
St Gilles, H. priory: XX 176
St Lazarus of Bethany: XIV 157
St Lazarus, Order: XXIV 137
St Sabas, War: IV 169; XIV 156; XV 345;
    XVI 4
St Sergius (Cyprus): XX 175, 179
Saladin: I 141, 149; II 49; VII 242; VIII 80;
    IX 152; X 27; XI 139, 142n, 145,
    147–9, 151; XIII 46, 48, 50, 55–6;
    XIV 149–50; XX 178; XXI 191–2;
    XXIV 129, 132, 137
Saladin Tithe: XXIII 230–31
Salef river: XIV 150
al-Salih Ayyub, sultan of Egypt: XIV 154
al-Salih Ismail, sultan of Damascus:
    XIV 153–4
Salisbury: XVI 7, 11
Sancho VII, k. Navarre: XXIV 135
Sanidha: XIX 191n
Scotland: XXIII 230
Scott, Sir Walter: XXI 190
Sebastea: XIII 51, 52, 57–8
Seher de Mamedunc: X 29
Sempad (Smbat), constable of Armenia:
    VII 245
serfs: III 563–4; IV 174; V 291; VI 231,
    233–4
servise de cors: V 286–9, 291
servise de mariage: IV 174; V 286–9

Shaizar: I 148; II 51
Shia Islam: XXI 181, 192
Shrewsbury: XXIII 223–4
Sibylla of Armenia, wife of Bohemond VI:
    XIV 156
Sibylla, q. Jerusalem: II 52; XIV 149–50;
    XX 178; XXIV 138
Sicily: VII 241; XI 142, 144, 151; XIV 158;
    XIX 194; XXI 185, 192; XXIV 132
Sidon: II 55; X 26, 29, 34; XI 148; XIV 148,
    152, 155, 157; XV 342–4; XIX 195
    lady, see Margaret
    lord: I 144, and see Balian, Julian,
       Reynald
    lordship: I 144–5; II 51n
    bp: XIX 193
Simon, constable of Antioch: VII 245
Simon l'Ermin: I 142
Simon de Montfort the Elder: II 55; XVI 1–2
Simon de Montfort, earl of Leicester:
    XIV 158; XVI 2–3, 6–11
Simon of Paphos: XX 175, 180
Simon, abp Tyre: XIV 152
Sis: XXIV 142
Society of Jesus: XX 174
Soissons: I 142
Solomon, king: XXI 186
Southern, Richard: XXI 188
Spain: XIV 159; XXI 184–5, 189, 192;
    XXII 165; XXIV 135
    Spanish Armada: XXI 185
Stephen Harding, abbot of Cîteaux: IX 154,
    160
Stephen, pat. Jerusalem: IX 154, 157
Stephen, count of Sancerre: III 559n; V 286
Strassbourg: XXIV 129
Strata Florida, abbot: XXIII 224
Sunni Islam: XXI 181
Swansea: XXIII 227
Sydney Sussex College, Cambridge: XXI 187
Syria: I 142 147; III 556 558–9; X 29–30,
    32, 34; XI 141; XIV 148–9, 151–2,
    154–6, 159–60; XV 340; XVI 6;
    XVIII 133, 137–8; XIX 190, 192–5;
    XXI 179, 181, 191, 193; XXII 167;
    XXIV 136
Syrian Christians: III 564; VII 242; VI 230n,
    231, 234–6; XIV 154; XVIII 137–8
Syrianokhori: XIX 191n

Tagliacozzo: XVI 4
Tancred, pr. Antioch: VII 241
Tancred de Hauteville: VII 241
Taticius (*Tatinus*): VIII 86
Tekrit: XXI 191

Temblos: XIX 191n
'Templar of Tyre': XVI 7; XVII 250, 252
Templars: II 52; VII 242; VIII 92; IX 151,
  154–5, 157–61; X *passim*; XI 141,
  145, 148; XIII 45–6, 49, 51–2, 56–8;
  XIV 152–5, 157–9; XV 344;
  XVI 7; XVII 249–58; XVIII 139;
  XIX *passim*; XX 174–9;
  XXII 165–7; XXIV 136–7, 139
  marshal, see Aymon d'Oiselay, Jacques
    de Mailli
  master, see Gerard of Ridefort, Hugh of
    Paiens, Jacques de Molay, Reginals
    of Vichiers, Thomas Bérard, William
    of Beaujeu
  turcopolier, Bartholomew of Gordo
Teodorico, abp Ravenna: XIV 153
Teutonic Order: I 146; II 50–51, 55; VII 243;
  XI 141; XIV 150, 152, 159–60;
  XXIV 137
Thaumas de la Thaumarière, G: IV 170, 175n,
  179
theft: VI 233
Theobald, bp Acre: XXIV 140
Theobald V, count of Blois: III 559n
Theobald IV, count of Champagne, k.
    Navarre: XI 141, 146, 149; XIV 153;
    XVI 23
Theobald V, count of Champagne, k. Navarre:
    XIV 159–60
Theodore Lascaris, emperor of Nicaea:
    XIV 151
Thibault Belfarage: XVIII 139, 142
Thierry of Dendermonde: II 55
Thierry of *Orca*: II 55
Thomas of Acerra: XIV 152
Thomas Agni, pat. Jerusalem: XIV 161
Thomas Barech: XVIII 139
Thomas Becket, abp Canterbury: XXIII 228n
Thomas Bérard, T. master: XIV 156
Thomas of Clare: XIV 160
Thomas of Lentino O.P., bp Bethlehem:
    XIV 157–8
Thomas the Marshal: VII 244–5
Tiberias: XIII 45–7, 50–53, 55–8; XIV 148–9,
  154, 157, 159
Tirel family: VII 244
Toledo, abp: XXIV 135
Toron and Maron/Château Neuf, lord/
    lordship: I 145–6; II 50
  Toron: XI 151; XIV 148, 151, 157;
    XVI 3–4, 6; XXIV 134
Tortosa: X 25; XI 149; XIX 195
  archdeacon: XIX 193
Trakhoni: XIX 191n

Trapani: XIV 160
Très Ancien Coutumier: VII 241
Tripi: XIX 191n
Tripoli: X 29; XIV 148–9, 160; XX 180
  bishopric: XXIV 137n
  county: VII 243–4
  hospital of St John: XIV 152
Troodos: XIX 191n
Troyes: IX 154, 157
  council: VIII 92; IX 151, 160
Tunis: XIV 160
Turcomen: XIV 154, 157, 160
turcopoles: I 141
Turkey/Turks: XIV 148, 154–5, 159;
    XVIII 133; XXI 181; XXII 164
Tuscany: XVI 11
Tyre: VIII 86; X 26, 29; XI 139, 143, 145,
    147–9, 151; XII 109; XIV 148–52,
    158–60; XVI 3–6; XX 177–8;
    XXIV 138–9
  abp: XXIV 138, and see Gilles, Joscius,
    Nicholas Larcar, Peter, Simon,
    William
  church of St Mark: XXIV 138

Urban II, pope: XIV 148; XXI 181, 183;
    XXIII 227; XXIV 135
Urban III, pope: XXIV 129
Urban IV, pope: IV 169; XIV 157–8
Usama Ibn Munqidh: VI 229
Usk: XXIII 224
  river: XXIII 222

Valenia: XIV 149; XXIV 137
Valens, Roman emperor: XXII 164
vassals: I 142–3, 147–50; II 51–5; III 555,
    562, 565; V 287, 289; VI 230, 233–4,
    236; VII 242, 244–5, 247
vavassors: VI 230
Venice/Venetians: IV 169–70, 172, 176;
    XIV 156–59; XV 341; XVI 3–4;
    XVIII 140–41; XIX 193;
    XXIV: 130, 138
  Marciana Library: XVII 249
Versailles: XXI 190
Villein of *Alneto*: II 55
Virgin Mary: XXIV 136
Viterbo: XVI 11
Voltaire: XXI 189

wager of battle: V 289, 291; VI 230–31,
    233–4
Wales/Welshmen: XXII 164; XXIII *passim*
Walter, bp Acre: XIV 155; XV 342–3
Walter le Bel: II 54n; XX 175, 180

Walter of Bethsan: XX 175, 180
Walter III, count of Brienne: XX 181
Walter IV, count of Brienne: XIV 154
Walter the Chancellor: VII 242
Walter of Caesarea, constable of Cyprus:
 XIV 153; XX 175, 180
Walter Juvenis: XX 180n
Walter Map: X 26; XXII 164, 166–7
Walter of Mesnil, T: X 29–30, 33–4
Walter of Montbéliard: II 55; XIV 151;
 XIX 192; XX 180–81
Walter, abp Rouen: XXIV 131–2
Walter of St Bertin: XX 180n
Waverley Abbey: XXII 163
Whitland, abbot: XXIII 224, 226
Widows/widowhood I 142; II 56; V 285,
 288–9, 292
Wilbrand of Oldenburg: II 54
William abp Tyre VII 242; VIII 69–70, 75n,
 79; IX 151–2, 157–8; X 25–7, 31–32,
 34; XXI 189; XXII 165–6
 Historia: I 146–8; II 50–54; VIII 69–70,
  72–5, 80–81, 90, 92, 98, 104;
  IX 151–3, 157; X 27–8, 32, 34;
  XI 139, 146, 147; XII 107–8
 French translation/*Estoire de Eracles*:
  VIII *passim*; XI 139, 146, 153;
  XII 107–9; XIII 45; XIV 145;
  XV 339, 345; XVII 249, 258
 Continuations: II 54, 57; IX *passim*;
  X *passim*; XI 139–40; XII 107–10;
  XIII 46–9; XIV 146; XVIII 135;
  XIX 190 and Corrigenda;
  XXIV 140
 Acre or Noailles Continuation:
  VIII 73, 77, 81, 83, 94, 97;
  IX 161; X 35, XII 108
 Colbert-Fontainebleau Continuation
  (*a-b*): VIII 82; XI *passim* and
  Corrigenda; XII 110–12;
  XIII 46–7; XVII 249

Florence *Eracles*: XI 140–42, 143n,
 144
Lyon *Eracles*: VIII 86; XI *passim*
 and Corrigenda; XII 112;
 XIII 46–9
Rothelin Continuation': VIII 73, 75,
 91, 94, 96; IX 161; X 35
William IX, duke of Aquitaine: VII 242
William of Beaujeu, T. master: XVI 7;
 XIX 192–3
William Briwere, bp Exeter: XIV 152
William of Château Neuf, H. master:
 XIV 154–5
William Farabel: XIV 152
William, count of Flanders: XIV 155
William V of Montferrat: XI 147–8
William of Montferrat 'Longsword': XIV 149
William of Newburgh: XXII 164–7;
 XXIV 131
William of Orange, romances: XVIII 135
William of Rousssillon: XIV 161
William II 'Longsword', earl of Salibury:
 XIV 155
William of Valdreys, T: XVII 256n
William of Valence (brother of Guy of
 Lusignan): XX 177
William of Valence, earl of Pembroke:
 XIV 160
William, pat. Jerusalem: XIV 158–60
Wittenberg: XXI 187, 188
Wittgenstein, Ludwig: XXI 180
wives: V 289, 292
women litigants: V 285 289–90
Wurzburg Annalist: XXII 165

Xerxes: VIII 81, 90

Yerasa: XIX 191n
Yermasoyia: XVII 255; XIX 191n, 192

Zara: XVI 1; XXIV 129